THE JOHNSON COUNTY WAR

BILL O'NEAL

EAKIN PRESS ◆ Fort Worth, Texas

For my oldest daughter and
fellow history teacher,
Lynn O'Neal Martinez.

Copyright © 2004
By Bill O'Neal
Published By Eakin Press
An Imprint of Wild Horse Media Group
P.O. Box 331779
Fort Worth, Texas 76163
1-817-344-7036
www.EakinPress.com
ALL RIGHTS RESERVED
1 2 3 4 5 6 7 8 9
Paperback ISBN 978-1-57168-876-7
Hardback ISBN 978-1-68179-277-4
eBook ISBN 978-1-68179-232-3

Contents

Acknowledgments

This book would not have been written without the encouragement and assistance of Col. Bob Edwards of Buffalo, Wyoming. Retired from the U.S. Army Reserve, Bob researches regional history with passionate interest, and he is an antique firearms expert. I met Bob while we both participated in summer conferences at Buffalo's Jim Gatchell Museum and at the historic TA Ranch. Bob urged me to write an updated version of the Johnson County War, suggesting numerous new directions for the project and offering to open his extensive files to me. When I traveled to Wyoming to research this subject, Bob generously provided a vast amount of information, and he has been a constant source of ideas.

Gary "Andy" Anderson, curator of the Johnson County Jim Gatchell Memorial Museum, granted me complete access to the museum's remarkable collection of artifacts and information about the Johnson County War. During one memorable afternoon, Andy, assisted by his charming wife, Bonnie, brought guns and various other valuable items from their display cases to the museum basement, so that my wife and I could photograph them. As the resulting images in this book suggest, Andy has built the Jim Gatchell Museum into a premier repository of western history. The museum's registrar, Linda Newell, meticulously copied for my use numerous archival photographs.

At the Johnson County Library in Buffalo, genial Nancy L. Jennings presides with encyclopedic mastery over a vast array of materials about the famous range war. For two days Nancy anticipated my research needs, unearthing one invaluable file after another.

Also in Buffalo I was aided by Bob Ferris, museum curator of the storied Occidental Hotel.

One Sunday afternoon in Buffalo, I was guided through the Willow Grove Cemetery by Jim Browning. Now deceased, Jim spent every summer for decades traveling to the most isolated corners of the West. Specializing in gravesites of famous and infamous westerners, Jim pointed out to me the burial locations of numerous participants of the Johnson County War. I am indebted to Jim for his help with numerous projects, as well as for his friendship.

Barb and Earl Madsen have performed a superb historic service with their loving restoration of the TA Ranch. They are generous hosts to overnight guests, tourists, and conference participants. It has been my good fortune to present programs at the TA and to take tour groups there. My wife and I have spent nights at the old log ranch house, we have climbed into the bullet-riddled loft of the barn, and we were the first persons to stay in the Frank Canton ranch cabin after it was moved by Barb and Earl to the TA.

My visits to the TA, along with the gracious hospitality of the Madsens, were instrumental in inspiring me to tell the story of the Johnson County War.

At the Hoofprints of the Past Museum in Kaycee, rancher Brock Hanson showed me artifacts that he had helped to excavate from the site of the burned KC Ranch cabin. During a time of heightened security measures, Lt. Rachel Van Tine made possible a visit to F. E. Warren Air Force Base, formerly Fort D. A. Russell. Staff members at the Sheridan County Fulmer Public Library in Sheridan and at the Wyoming State Archives in Cheyenne provided me with numerous files from their rich depositories. Important files also were made available to me by Kim Winters, reference librarian of the American Heritage Center at the University of Wyoming in Laramie. More fascinating information in Laramie was provided by Brian Fox, costumed tour guide at the Wyoming Territorial Prison. Kristine L. Southwell, manuscripts librarian of the Western History Collections of the University of Oklahoma, and graduate assistant Josh Clough located and copied for me the invaluable typescript of George Tucker.

A widely respected researcher and author of outlaw-lawman history, Nancy Samuelson of Sacramento, graciously provided detailed information from her files about the hired gunmen of Texas. Many of these gunmen wore a badge at one time or another in Oklahoma, and a preeminent expert on Oklahoma lawmen, Dee Cordry of Piedmont, vigorously shared information and well-considered opinions with me.

When I first began to collect literature for this project, I called on an old friend, book dealer Jim Dullenty of Rocky Mountain House in Hamilton, Montana. Resourcefully Jim located many books that I needed, including several collectible volumes at prices I could afford. Another valued friend, Robert K. DeArment of Toledo, Ohio, offered encouragement and advice at a crucial point. A distinguished western historian who researched this period in his biography of Frank Canton, Bob was a welcome source of wisdom.

I appreciate the efforts of Bonnie Brooks, of the Taylor, Texas, Public Library, in trying to find information about Tom Smith. Smith's grave was located for me by Gilbert Baran, of the Taylor City Cemetery. Daisy Harvill, director of the Aiken Regional Archives of Paris Junior College, expertly located images of Paris, Texas, during the late nineteenth century. Also in Paris, I was fortunate enough to encounter Mrs. Kay Brown Black, a researcher from Antlers, Oklahoma, who generously provided information about Kinzie Pickard and his wife. James F. Barling of New Boston, Texas, graciously offered materials about his grandfather, Bob Barling, and Bob's brothers, Jerry and Frank.

At Eakin Press I am deeply grateful to Virginia and Tom Messer for their support of this project. My longtime editor, Melissa Locke Roberts, improved my manuscript with her customary expertise and eye for detail.

At Panola College in Carthage, Texas, where I teach history, librarian Christie Ferguson resourcefully provided scarce volumes for me through interlibrary loan services. Another member of our library staff, Pansy Tinkle, and Dazell Hicks, secretary to our academic dean, expertly produced needed images through technology that is beyond my feeble skills. John Hughes and Becky McNeely, student workers at Panola, assisted in preparing the manuscript. I am deeply grateful to each of these able colleagues.

Three of my daughters and a son-in-law—Dr. Shellie O'Neal, Dr. Berri O'Neal, and Causby and Dusty Henderson—were working on various college degrees while this project was in progress. At different times I called on them to utilize on my behalf the research facilities to which they had access. Shellie, Berri, Causby, and Dusty made individual contributions for which I have a special gratitude.

My wife Karon accompanied me on each trip to Wyoming, along with research forays to Oklahoma and to Paris and Taylor, Texas. In various libraries, while I pursued sources, Karon located other sources and toiled at the photocopiers, producing hundreds of copies. She photographed numerous sites and museum artifacts, and she developed hardcopy and disk manuscripts from my pad and pencil pages. Karon has assisted me in these ways with many previous projects, but she was especially involved in the development of this book. Therefore I relied upon her even more than usual for suggestions and as a sounding board, and I owe her a special expression of gratitude.

Owen Wister, a Philadelphian educated at Harvard and in Europe, visited Wyoming for his health in 1885. Returning regularly in ensuing years, he met many of the men who led the Johnson County War, which he would chronicle in landmark fiction. (Author's collection)

Chapter 1

A Visitor to Wyoming

"Everything is immense ..."
OWEN WISTER

Owen Wister arrived at Wyoming's VR Ranch early on Sunday afternoon, July 5, 1885. Wister, an artistic, cultivated Easterner, had been told to go west for his health. Although well-traveled in Europe and the East, Wister had never been closer to the frontier than a few miles west of Philadelphia. By the time his train rumbled across Nebraska, he was awestruck by the vastness of the plains and the spirit of the Westerners. "I don't wonder a man never comes back after he has once been here a few years," he confided to his journal. When the train penetrated Wyoming, he witnessed a stunning change of scenery: "I can't possibly say how extraordinary and beautiful the valleys we've been going through are." Wister was again overwhelmed after reaching the ranch: "Everything is immense, including my sunburn." [1]

These observations were penned by an educated man who, like many other Americans of his generation, was captivated by the West, big cattle ranching, and cowboy culture. Indeed, Theodore Roosevelt, a friend of Wister's from Harvard, had purchased two ranches in Dakota Territory, and by 1885 T. R. had immersed himself in ranching life after his wife and mother died on the same day. Three other Harvard classmates of Wister's—Hubert Teschemaker, Frederic deBillier, and Richard Trimble—were engaged in ranching in Wyoming. Through one of his Eastern connections, Wister was scheduled to visit the Wyoming ranch of another Easterner, Maj. Frank Wolcott. Wolcott, Teschemaker, and deBillier would be key figures in the Johnson County War of 1892, and Wister would chronicle their activities in landmark western fiction.

An only child, Wister had been educated at boarding schools in England and Switzerland and at Harvard. His father was a Philadelphia physician, and his great-great-grandfather had signed the U.S. Constitution. Wister's maternal grandmother was a noted actress, Fanny Kimble, while his mother frequently entertained novelists and painters. Wister majored in music at Harvard, where he was elected to Phi Beta Kappa

1

and to prestigious social clubs. After obtaining a music degree in 1882, he returned to Europe in hopes of launching a career as a pianist-composer. However, he was summoned back to Philadelphia by his father, who insisted that he accept a business position.

Maintaining a circle of literary and musical acquaintances, Wister was increasingly frustrated by his professional chores. Stress led to physical problems, and Dr. Weir Mitchell, who had delivered Wister, prescribed a lengthy trip to the West. Wister's mother arranged for him to be accompanied by two of her spinster friends.[2]

They boarded a train in Philadelphia on Tuesday, June 30. Richard Trimble joined the train at Omaha on the night of July 2, and the following evening, during a stopover in Cheyenne, he treated Wister to a drink at the famous cattlemen's retreat, the luxurious Cheyenne Club. "It's the pearl of the prairies," remarked Wister.[3]

The train proceeded on that night, before Wister and his companions debarked to catch a dawn stagecoach. The fifty-mile stagecoach ride took the entire day of July 4 and, after a night at a remote station, half of the following day.

When Wister finally reached the VR Ranch headquarters, he was enchanted by his surroundings and his hosts. Even today, although there is a new generation of ranch buildings, the setting is idyllic. Despite an elevation of 6,640 feet, the site is topped by nearby mountains. The clear water of Deer Creek ripples over a rocky stream bed a short distance from the ranch structures. When noted rancher John Clay first saw the VR in June 1885, he reminisced that "a scene of supreme beauty met [his] eyes." The stone ranch house featured a vast hearth, Persian rugs, and a fine piano. "As you stepped out of the house there was a pleasant garden, little rills of water bubbling, singing, spreading themselves about the plots of vegetables, and over the lawn. Then away southwards were towering mountains, a deep rift in their side where Deer Creek rush-

Maj. Frank Wolcott's VR Ranch is largely intact today, owned by the True Oil Company. Ranch headquarters remains in the same striking location that captivated Owen Wister in 1885. (Photo by Karon O'Neal)

ing down a cañon reached the vale and wandered carelessly amid cottonwoods, willows, and box elders. It was a beautiful stream surrounded by a lovely landscape."[4]

A few weeks after Clay's visit, Wister arrived and was similarly impressed, writing that the "house is a sort of miracle for these parts—so clean—comfortable—pretty." There he was graciously received by the Wolcotts: "Major and Mrs. Wolcott are delightful hosts. . . ."[5]

In referring to Frank Wolcott as "delightful," Wister was not adhering to consensus opinion. "He is known as the meanest man alive in this world," wrote one detractor, who also flatly declared, "Wolcott is a thief." When Wolcott was removed as U.S. marshal of Wyoming Territory, Governor John M. Thayer declared that he had become "offensive to almost the whole people." John Clay generally admired his fellow rancher: "He was a fire-eater, honest, clean, a rabid Republican with *a complete absence of tact* [author's italics], very well educated and when you knew him a most delightful companion." But Clay recognized Wolcott's effect on others. "Most people hated him, many feared him, a few loved him,"[6] he wrote.

Francis Edwin Wolcott, destined to be a principal leader of the Johnson County invasion, was born in New York State on December 13, 1840. Twenty years old when the Civil War broke out in April 1861, Frank Wolcott enlisted immediately as an infantry private. Aggressive and better educated than most enlisted men, Wolcott was commissioned in 1862. He was mustered out of the Union Army in 1866 as a major and judge advocate of U.S. Volunteers. Major Wolcott—he always relished his military title—moved to Cheyenne in 1870 as receiver of the U.S. Land Office. By 1872, when fellow Republican Ulysses S. Grant was reelected president, the former army officer secured appointment as U.S. marshal for Wyoming Territory. But Major Wolcott's tenure was controversial, and he was removed from office in 1875.

By this time Wolcott was interested in cattle ranching. Using his own savings and working with a Scottish syndicate, the Tolland Company, Wolcott established the VR ("Valley Ranch") in its magnificent location. Major Wolcott became one of Wyoming's pioneer cattlemen, helping to create the colorful industry that would provide the lasting image of the "Cowboy State." One November afternoon, beside the creek a mile from his house, Wolcott shot twenty bull elk, providing winter meat for his ranch.

As the VR thrived, Wolcott married in 1880. When Owen Wister arrived at the VR five years later, the Wolcotts

Maj. Frank Wolcott was a Union officer during the Civil War, a territorial U.S. marshal, and a pioneer Wyoming cattleman. (Author's collection)

3

Gold watch and 1873 Winchester belonging to Maj. Frank Wolcott. (Photo by Karon O'Neal from Jim Gatchell Museum collection)

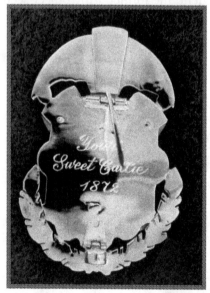

Major Wolcott wore this handsome badge while serving as U.S. marshal of Wyoming Territory, 1872-75. Engraved on the back was "Your Sweet Callie, 1872." (Courtesy L. F. Blake, Amarillo)

had a little girl. Wister was extended traditional western hospitality by the confident rancher and his charming wife.

For two months Wister rode horseback and hunted and camped and bathed in mountain streams. He visited roundups and watched as a clash developed between "squatters" and Major Wolcott. On July 14 he turned twenty-five. Wister reveled in the summer experience: "This living among such scenery and breathing such air satisfies me perfectly."[7]

Wister would return to the West year after year. His sixth trip was in 1892, the year of the Johnson County War, and he visited Buffalo and area cattle ranches. With every trip Wister absorbed more experiences and atmosphere—all of which were recorded in his journals, and which he increasingly would feel compelled to distill into short stories and novels.

Of course, conflict is a key element of drama, and conflict soon would explode across Wyoming. That conflict would result in the West's only lynching of a woman, murderous ambushes, a well-financed invasion of Johnson County, a courageous last stand, a large-scale gun battle, and controversial courtroom maneuvers, all generating national attention. Participants included cattle barons, cattle thieves, hired gunmen, stock detectives, assassins, U.S. cavalrymen, and prominent public officials. The Johnson County War would prove to be so extraordinary that Owen Wister would be joined by later novelists and historians in writing about it, and filmmakers also would be attracted to these men and events. Even today the Johnson County War can be a touchy subject among descendants of the participants.

Chapter 2

The Ranching World Changes

"It was not until the spring roundups that the real truth was discovered and then it was only mentioned in a whisper."

RANCH MANAGER JOHN CLAY

The world of Wyoming cattlemen that was visited by Owen Wister in 1885 changed drastically the following year. For several years big ranchers had provided most of the economic base of frontier Wyoming, and accordingly they enjoyed unchallenged political power and social status. But a winter calamity accelerated forces that would challenge the dominance of the cattlemen. Cattle barons would try with ruthless and sometimes deadly determination to maintain their position in Wyoming, and their efforts would result in the Johnson County War.

Although cattlemen achieved rapid success and prominence in Wyoming Territory, they were not the first Anglos to penetrate the region. The Anglo pioneers who initially explored the vast plains and soaring mountains of Wyoming were adventure-seeking fur trappers. John Colter, among those who penetrated the magnificent Yellowstone country, was astounded at the steaming geysers that would be nicknamed "Colter's Hell." Beginning in 1824, fur trappers and traders began to hold a raucous "Rendezvous" each year at various locations in western Wyoming. During the 1840s, a parade of wagon trains transported settlers northwestward across Wyoming along the Oregon Trail. Another emigrant route, the Bozeman Trail, was opened in the 1860s, angling northwest across Wyoming and future Johnson County toward the gold fields of Montana. This passage was challenged by horseback warriors of the Sioux and Cheyenne tribes, and the battle was joined by soldiers from forts built along the trail.

During these hostilities, Nelson Story and a large crew of heavily armed cowboys drove a herd of Texas Longhorns through Wyoming along the Bozeman Trail to a rich market in Montana. The year of Story's drive, 1866, marked the beginning of the great cattle drives north out of Texas. A successful, timely drive could bring enormous profits. Ranches were organized across the open range of Texas, many of them financed by Eastern or British investors. The American public became captivated by hard-riding cowboys in their colorful garb, by the adventure of the long, dangerous drives, and by great ranching empires.

As cattle ranching spread to ranges throughout the West, Wyoming's vacant grasslands beckoned. There were so few people in Wyoming (only 9,118 in the Census of 1870, and 20,789 in 1880) that little acreage was privately owned. The federal government therefore held title to almost all land in Wyoming, but it would be years before these lands would even be surveyed, much less parceled out for sale or lease. Most of Wyoming was arid and unpromising for farmers, but enterprising ranchers could drive cattle onto great expanses of empty land. A prospective rancher could homestead 160 acres, a quarter-section which would include a stream, then build a cabin, barn, and corrals as headquarters for his spread. His capital would go into the purchase of cattle, along with wages for cowboys, who worked seasonally. It took thirty or fifty or one hundred or more acres of grasslands in various Wyoming locations to support a single cow, so ranchers simply followed the western practice of turning livestock onto open ranges.

Longhorn cattle were bought in Texas, driven to Wyoming, then left free to graze on public lands in the vicinity of ranch headquarters. Untended during the winters—like buffalo before them, and Longhorns in Texas and elsewhere—the cattle were rounded up by cowboy crews in May and June, after calves were born in the spring. The animals were branded and earmarked, and most of the young bulls were castrated. Nearby markets included garrisons at Wyoming forts, reservation Indians, and Colorado miners. Pioneer ranchers began to improve their Longhorn herds by importing Herefords and Shorthorns, and the natural increase of their unsupervised herds encouraged cattlemen to feel that their capital was multiplying. The numerical totals of open-range herds always were vague. In 1870, 8,143 cattle were listed in Wyoming, a total which more than doubled to 19,687 the next year. But Wyoming's leading historian, Dr. T. A. Larson, regarded these figures as incomplete: "Probably less than half were reported to the assessors."[1] Open-range ranchers never knew precisely how many animals they owned. Wyoming ranchers quickly adopted the Texas practice of "mavericking," a term sparked when early-day Texan Sam Maverick, ranching along the San Antonio River, neglected his branding and soon found that most of his open-range calves had been branded by other men. An unbranded calf soon became known as a "maverick," which suggested a threat of loss, just as Sam Maverick had lost his young livestock to opportunistic riders with long ropes and branding irons. But in cow country an unbranded calf was generally considered public property, and few ranchers—or ambitious cowboys who aspired to become ranchers—felt any reluctance about lassoing a maverick.

So Longhorns and cowboys came to Wyoming, and so did roundups and mavericking, along with other practices and attitudes of the cattle culture. The seemingly endless expanses of Wyoming rangeland exerted a powerful call upon cattlemen and cowboys. For strong men Wyoming offered the chance of building cattle kingdoms in a setting of barbaric grandeur. At first there was the danger of hostile warriors, along with utter isolation and the annual threat of disastrous winters. But for a certain breed of men these conditions meant exhilarating freedom and challenging opportunity. Such men produced a ranching boom in Wyoming. The large ranchers comprised the territory's principal economic and political force, and Wyoming was on its way to becoming known as "The Cowboy State."

But before Wyoming became a state, it was a territory; and before it was a territory, it was a remote frontier. And before there was cattle ranching in Wyoming, there was the Union Pacific Railroad—America's biggest employer. The development of this remote frontier was profoundly impacted by the routing of the nation's first transcontinental railroad across southern Wyoming. Construction began in 1864 on the Central Pacific Railroad, building eastward from California, and the Union Pacific, heading westward from Omaha. (These two lines would meet in 1869 in Utah.) The chief engineer of the Union Pacific, Grenville M. Dodge, determined the future location of Cheyenne in the summer of 1867. (The Union Pacific, along with other western railroads that were granted large tracts of government land, realized great profits through the sale of town lots along its right-of-way.) The newly formed city council of Cheyenne approved Dodge's townsite plan on February 1, 1868. Measuring two miles on each side, the town-site was laid out on a regular grid, featuring streets that were eighty feet wide.[2]

The railroad's land agent began selling lots in July 1868. Although the approaching tracks were more than twenty miles to the east, the town boomed with growth. Various commercial structures were erected, and, when the tracks reached Cheyenne, a large number of houses arrived by rail, built to order in Chicago. The population rapidly soared to 6,000.

Woodcut of Cheyenne's Union Pacific Hotel in 1869. (Author's collection)

In the summer of 1868 the Denver and Pacific Railroad reached Cheyenne, establishing a connection with Denver, one hundred miles to the south. When the Union Pacific decided to construct shops, a roundhouse, and a railroad hotel, Cheyenne was guaranteed a permanence that was not enjoyed by many railroad boomtowns. Indeed, most of the gamblers, prostitutes, and other end-of-track riffraff soon ventured farther west to newer railroad towns, partially because of the lethal encouragement of a large vigilante group. Even though there remained plenty of saloons and gambling halls in Cheyenne, there also were five churches and a school. When the territory of Wyoming was organized in 1869, Cheyenne was designated the territorial capital.[3]

Steady growth continued. The business section soon boasted handsome brick buildings, and cattlemen began to build impressive Victorian homes on Seventeenth Street, which also boasted the Cheyenne Club. When attorney Willis Van Devanter arrived in 1884, he found Cheyenne "a lively, busy and substantial" frontier community.[4] As a capital since its first year, Cheyenne was well policed and never became the scene of frequent gunplay, despite the fact that the Wild West was in its heyday. For example, Tascosa, the "Cowboy Capital of the Panhandle" of Texas, was the site of ten gunfights and a cowboy strike during the 1880s. Dodge City, despite the pressure of such noted frontier peace officers as Wyatt Earp, Bat Masterson and Bill Tilghman, was wild enough to be called the "Bibulous Babylon of the Plains." In the 1880s Earp and other western gunmen gravitated to Tombstone, a murderous Arizona boomtown dubbed "The Town Too Tough to Die." Texas drovers shoved herds of Longhorns north through Waco, known as "Six-Shooter Depot," and through Fort Worth, a gunfighter haven with a red-light district accurately called "Hell's Half-Acre." But Cheyenne did not experience wild street fights like Dodge and Tombstone and Tascosa did. Cheyenne was safe for cattle buyers and for cattlemen

The Cheyenne Club, organized in 1880 as a social center for cattlemen. A glass-enclosed observatory is visible at the middle of the roof. (Courtesy Wyoming State Archives, Cheyenne)

The Cheyenne Club

Englishmen and Easterners who ventured west to engage in cattle ranching brought with them an aura of sophistication which appealed to successful Westerners desirous of displaying the affluence they had earned on the frontier. Western ranchers who had carved cattle empires from a primitive land wanted to prove that they could be gentlemen, like Englishmen and Easterners. Soon gentlemen's clubs, which abounded in England and in the East, began to be organized across the West. Among the better clubs were the Denver Club and the Montana Club, in Helena. Most notable of all, however, was the Cheyenne Club, chartered in 1880. Dick Frewen was one of the twelve founders, and his brother, Moreton, became an early member.

The club originally admitted fifty members, but demand for entry to this fashionable establishment quickly raised the membership level to two hundred, with an initiation fee of $100. Applicants had to be sponsored by a club member, and even after a careful background check an aspiring applicant might be blackballed. Intoxication and fighting were forbidden, and so were profanity and cheating at cards. When one of the founders, C. M. Oelrichs, drunkenly struck a Cheyenne Club bartender, his membership was rescinded.

This exclusive group was housed in a three-story frame and brick building with a mansard roof and sweeping veranda. There was a library which boasted the leading newspapers and magazines, a billiard room, two wine vaults, and a dumbwaiter which sent gourmet meals from the basement kitchen up to the wood-paneled dining room. Members played chess on the veranda and tennis on the Cheyenne Club court, and staged harness races and polo matches. "No wonder they like the club at Cheyenne," approved the cultivated and widely traveled Owen Wister, who belonged to a club in Philadelphia. "It's the pearl of the prairies."

In August 1883 the British members of the club hosted a dinner for the American members who were in town. The forty-one men who participated in the event consumed twenty bottles of red wine and sixty-six bottles of champagne. Such occasions at the Cheyenne Club demanded black evening wear with stiff white shirt fronts—attire which the ranchers nicknamed "Herefords."

The dining room of the Cheyenne Club could be reserved by members for two dollars per evening. (Courtesy Wyoming State Archives, Cheyenne)

and their families. In Cheyenne they built homes, as well as the West's most famous gentleman's club, and their town headquartered the Wyoming Stock Growers Association. Cheyenne was branded "The Holy City of the Cow."

Many of the first cattle brought to Wyoming were turned out to graze on the hills around Cheyenne. By the mid-1870s several Wyoming ranches boasted 1,000 or more head of cattle, and soon truly great ranching empires began to emerge. In Wyoming, as well as in Texas and elsewhere in the West, many large ranches were financed and sometimes managed by Easterners and Englishmen. A visionary Englishman, twenty-five-year-old Moreton Frewen, went to Wyoming in 1878, following a visit to the JA Ranch in Texas. The JAs was owned by a friend and fellow Englishman, John Adair, and by legendary cattleman Charles Goodnight, who fired Frewen's imagination with the possibilities of building a great ranch. Enthralled by the prospect of immense profits available through open-range ranching, Frewen determined that he would find his own unclaimed rangelands in Wyoming. Riding north from the Union Pacific Railroad in December 1878, Frewen, his older brother Dick, and their guides forced their mounts into a path broken through deep snow by a buffalo herd. At the Powder River Valley, Moreton Frewen determined to build a cattle empire in the magnificent but isolated region that soon would become Johnson County.

Moreton had $39,000 from an inheritance, which he pooled with Dick's larger investment, and he intended to raise far more capital through English investors. Partially to impress prospective investors, Moreton built a two-story log ranch house, sixty feet on a side, modeled after British hunting lodges. Erected in 1879, "Frewen's Castle," as

Wyoming frontiersmen called it, stood a hundred yards back from the Powder River, just below the junction of the North and Middle Forks.

Frewen's big log structure was two hundred miles north of the nearest railroad connection, at Rock Creek Station, about forty miles northwest of Laramie. But he imported fine hardwoods from England for the interior, and furnishings, windows, doors, and shingles from Chicago were hauled by ox-teams from the railroad. The main room was forty feet square, with two big fireplaces and a wide walnut stairway leading up to a mezzanine balcony, where an orchestra would play for dinner guests and dancers. Also on the first floor were sitting rooms, an office, library, kitchen, and pantry; bedrooms were on the second floor. Stables, corrals, bunkhouses, and other outbuildings were built near Frewen's lodge.[5]

Frewen bought 2,000 head of Shorthorns bearing a "76" brand, which would label his great ranch. Newspapers reported that also in 1879 he purchased 10,000 cattle from Texas. Fred G. S. Hesse, a young, capable Englishman, brought a herd from Texas and was hired as foreman of the 76. Born in Essex in 1853, Hesse migrated to the United States. Educated to be a law clerk, he was one of thousands of young men who were captivated by the notion of cowboying in the West. Forsaking the drabness of a law clerk's desk, Hesse traveled to Texas to experience life astride a cow pony. His intelligence and leadership skills soon made it obvious that he had a future in the cattle business, a future he would pursue in Johnson County.

Moreton Frewen tirelessly promoted the cattle business in Wyoming. He wrote countless letters to wealthy Englishmen, asking them to come to his ranch to hunt and play polo and consider investment prospects. Guests were escorted from Rock Creek Station in carriages, and were met at the 76 by butlers, maids, valets, and chefs. They rode quality mounts into the Big Horn Mountains for hunting, with wagons hauling camp supplies, tents, beds, and portable bathtubs.

In 1879 cattleman and promoter Moreton Frewen built a frontier lodge that became known as "Frewen's Castle." (Courtesy Johnson County Jim Gatchell Memorial Museum)

Moreton Frewen

"I begin to believe that being a gentleman is much against one here, as in the colonies generally."

Moreton Frewen was an English gentleman to the core, but he brought the spirit and creative energy of a true visionary to the "colony" of Wyoming. Cowboys inevitably made this proper Englishman the butt of their humor. Their favorite story—later proven untrue—was that he bought his first herd twice, after they cleverly drove the cattle around a hill to be tallied a second time by the greenhorn foreigner. Frewen confided to his wife that "these western men, at least some of them, are the most impracticable, aggressively independent people possible, and I often long to thrash one or two but for the want of dignity in such a proceeding."

Frewen certainly was big enough to deliver a thrashing. He was six-foot-three, blond, mustachioed, and handsome. With utter confidence he asserted that every woman he had ever slept with had been "completely paralyzed by the vigor" of his physical charms. While in New York in early 1881, Frewen met thirty-one-year-old Clara Jerome, the eldest of three daughters of millionaire Leonard Jerome, and they married in April 1881. (All three Jerome daughters married Britishers; Jennie Jerome became the mother of Winston Churchill.) In Wyoming, despite a guest list that bristled with English nobility and U.S. Army officers and their wives, Frewen's bride was daunted by the isolation of the ranch. After suffering a miscarriage she moved back to the more civilized environs of New York.

Moreton visited New York as much as possible. But he invested his entire personal fortune in the West, and this true English dude displayed many of the finest qualities of frontiersmen, including courage, stamina, and boundless optimism.

The enthusiastic Frewen persuaded a number of his well-heeled visitors to help him form the Powder River Cattle Company. Frewen agreed to serve as manager for no salary, although he would enjoy a large portion of any profits. By 1883 almost 10,000 calves were branded in the spring roundup. During that year Frewen purchased 50,000 head of cattle from Nebraska and Oregon, and he imported fifty purebred Sussex bulls.

Soon it was estimated that 70,000 cattle grazed Frewen's range, which extended about eighty miles north to south and fifty miles east to west. At the height of Frewen's operations, seventy-five cowboys were employed to ride this vast range. The heart of the ranch stretched across southern Johnson County.

Other ranchers were attracted to this sprawling new county. The promotions of open-range ranching by Moreton Frewen were supplemented by a captivating book published in 1881, *The Beef Bonanza; or, How to Get Rich on the Plains.* The author, Maj. James S. Brisbin of the Second Cavalry, had been stationed in the West since 1868, including several years at posts in Wyoming. *The Beef Bonanza* featured Brisbin's personal observations as well as testimonials from numerous ranchers. Brisbin also included a great many tables and statistics indicating that enormous profits could be gained with minimal investments in western ranching. Chapter titles such as "Estimated Fortunes," "The Money to Be Made," and "Millions in Beef" underlined his passionate belief in the opportunities that abounded in "The West! The mighty West!"[6]

The "mighty West" attracted opportunistic men who hoped to make fortunes by raising livestock in unoccupied grazing lands. Like the Frewen brothers, many of these men were British. John Clay, for example, was a university-educated Scotsman who visited the United States and Canada in 1874 to investigate cattle-raising. Launching a career as an efficient manager of ranching operations, Clay also organized a profitable livestock commission firm, headquartered in Chicago, and he founded a network of banks in the West. He was employed in 1883 to run Wyoming's largest ranching operation, the Swan Land and Cattle Company. This company was organized in 1883 by veteran Wyoming cattleman Alexander Hamilton Swan, who, like Moreton Frewen, aggressively enlisted investors. "In our business," admitted Swan, "we are often compelled to do certain things, which, to the inexperienced, seem a little crooked."[7]

CLAY & FORREST,
"THE ROOKERY"
CHICAGO.

Cable Address
"Kelso" Chicago.

The letterhead of John Clay's Chicago firm, probably the country's most successful livestock commission company. (Author's collection)

Rapid expansion led to the occupation of 1.5 million acres of land. Two hundred Swan cowboys tended herds that totaled a reported 113,000 head of cattle. Corporate offices were located in Edinburgh, Scotland, while the ranching headquarters was the Two Bar Ranch at Chugwater, with a set of substantial buildings that still stand. With millions of dollars in investment and a large number of employees, the Swan was an important economic force in Wyoming. The manager of the Swan, John Clay, became president of the highly influential Wyoming Stock Growers Association, serving from 1890 through 1896. Clay, then, was president of the WSGA during the Johnson County War of 1892.

Clay was succeeded as WSGA president by William C. "Billy" Irvine, who served from 1896 through 1911, and who already was a longtime member of the board of trustees and the executive committee. Born in 1852 in Pennsylvania (he always would use a Keystone brand in honor of the "Keystone State"), Billy Irvine found work in 1872 on a large Nebraska ranch and soon became foreman. Striking out on his own in 1876, he bought 4,000 Texas Longhorns and drove them north to Wyoming. Locating a ranch on the North Platte River near Fort Fetterman, Irvine doubled the size of his herd within two years. In 1881, the year *The Beef Bonanza* was published, Irvine and a group of investors organized the Converse Cattle Company. Irvine managed this company, then later agreed to manage another big outfit, the Ogallala Land and Cattle Company. Irvine's Ogallala headquarters was on the old Bozeman Trail, about forty miles north of Fort Fetterman, and not far southeast of Johnson County. Billy Irvine, a gifted leader and a formidable figure within the WSGA, would play a commanding role in the invasion of nearby Johnson County.[9]

Wyoming cattlemen such as Billy Irvine, John Clay, Moreton Frewen, and Frank Wolcott enjoyed a heady existence. Like medieval nobles they controlled vast domains, and like medieval nobles they rode horseback, booted and spurred, across their land. Other mounted men, the proud and picturesque cowboys, rode for them and tended their great herds. Masters of men and cattle and land, the big ranchers also were pioneers in an enormous, harsh, and nearly empty country. The cattle barons brought capital to Wyoming and provided economic, political, and social leadership. As Wyoming Territory developed economically, the big cattlemen provided a great majority of that development, more than the Union Pacific, the federal government (principally through military installations), and coal mining combined.

Hen Wranglers and Fodder Forkers

Cattle barons and their cowboy employees usually were contemptuous of farmers and homesteaders, and their disdain was reflected in slang references to "squatters," "nesters," "sodbusters," and "plow chasers." A "sky farmer" was a settler who had not irrigated his farm and who therefore depended on unreliable western skies for water. But in Johnson County there were many "dry-landers" who dug irrigation ditches. A "hen wrangler" chased chickens instead of Longhorns, while a "flat-heeled puncher" wore work shoes instead of high-heeled cowboy boots.

Big ranchers let their cattle fend for themselves during winters on the open range. But homesteaders cut and fed hay to their few animals, and therefore were called "hay shakers," "hay shovelers," and "fodder forkers." Other activities beneath the dignity of cowboys earned homesteaders such nicknames as "churn twisters," "pea pickers," and "pumpkin pilers." Farmers also were dubbed "stubble jumpers" and "stump ranchers." Settlers who belonged to the national farm organization, the Grange, were dismissed as "grangers"—by men who banded together in stock growers' associations.

High cattle prices in the early 1880s stimulated boom conditions in Wyoming. By 1880 there were already 300,000 head of cattle on Wyoming's grasslands. Just five years later, when Owen Wister reached Wyoming, there were two *million* cattle, mostly on large ranches. With large herds in virtually every valley, the seemingly inexhaustible Wyoming ranges became overgrazed. The quality of grazing land can change with alarming rapidity. The grasses of arid Wyoming, while nutritious, are comparatively short and sparse. Those grasses once had supported bison herds, but cattle crop grass closer than buffalo. Furthermore, the high prices of 1882, 1883, and 1884 dropped severely in 1885 and 1886. "During the years 1885 and 1886 everyone seemed to be hard up in Wyoming," recalled John Clay. "The flow of money from abroad and the East had stopped."[10]

Clay and other prudent ranchers became concerned about the careless overstocking of the range which had taken place. To make matters worse, the damaged grasslands were finished by drought in the summer of 1886. "The summer was very dry—no rain of any moment in May, June, and July, the growing months for grass on the range," Clay explained. A trip in July revealed disastrous conditions. "There was scarce a spear of grass by the wayside," continued Clay. "We rode many miles over the range. Cattle were thin and green grass was an unknown quantity. . . . It was a painful sort of trip." Cattle became further weakened by lack of water. "By August it was hot, dry, dusty and grass closely cropped. Every day made it apparent that even with the best of winters cattle would have a hard time."[11]

There had not been a truly severe winter in Wyoming since 1871-72, when no more than 50,000 cattle were in the territory. But the winter of 1886-87 was calamitous. Temperatures plummeted to polar levels—more than forty degrees below zero in January 1887. The first blizzard struck in November 1886, and weakened cattle began to die by December. Deep snow froze so solidly that cattle could not paw through or melt through with their breath to any grass which might remain. "Winter came early and it stayed long," John Clay remarked grimly. Chilled to the bone, emaciated cattle "were compelled to keep moving in order to keep from freezing," wrote Johnson County rancher O. H. Flagg, "and their feet were cut by the frozen snow until their trail could be followed by the blood which flowed from them."[12]

"Three great streams of ill-luck, mismanagement, greed met together," explained Clay, whose foresight and prompt action avoided calamity for his company. But many others suffered disaster: "It was not until the spring roundups that the real truth was discovered and then it was only mentioned in a whisper." One outfit recovered just 100 out of 5,500 three-year-olds, and another suffered ninety-eight percent losses. "The roundup that spring was a small affair," reported Flagg; "from 27 wagons in the spring of 1883, the number had been reduced until only four were present in 1887." Frank Wolcott lost two-thirds of his cattle and "practically went to the wall," while many other cattlemen went "flat broke," according to Clay. "They had not the heart to face another debacle such as they had gone through and consequently they disappeared from the scene. Most of the eastern men and the Britishers said 'enough' and went away."[13]

In addition to the staggering losses suffered by cattle ranchers in Wyoming—and elsewhere—their surviving animals were so poor that many could not be marketed.

Cattle prices had been dropping for years, and with everyone trying to sell in 1887, prices plunged so low that many ranchers could not recover their shipping costs. Furthermore, drought conditions continued into the summer of 1888. The reckless expansion of earlier years, combined with vicious weather conditions, wiped out so many ranchers that membership in the WSGA plummeted. "It was a pathetic experience to attend the fall meetings of 1887," reflected John Clay. "Worse than pathetic to wander among the ruins of past glories in the spring of 1888."[14]

Hardest hit were absentee owners of vast open-range outfits, because it was virtually impossible for such an operation to respond effectively during a catastrophic winter. "Small operations withstood the troubles of 1886-1887 more successfully than the big operators," concluded T. A. Larson, "perhaps because they were closer to their cattle, knew what was going on, and reacted quickly."[15] Small ranchers found more opportunities than ever to round up mavericks and other strays, a practice which deeply antagonized the big operators who were struggling to stay in business. It was understandable that big ranchers would want to maintain their cattle kingdoms, and a key to survival would be the WSGA, still the most influential institution in Wyoming.

Chapter 3

The Wyoming Stock Growers Association

"The Americans ... are certainly of all people in the world the most prompt to organize and combine to carry out a common object."
SCOTSMAN J. D. BORTHWICK AFTER THREE YEARS IN CALIFORNIA'S GOLD FIELDS

Wherever ranching was practiced in the West, livestock associations were organized. Some were small, open only to ranchers of a single county. Others were statewide organizations. The Wyoming Stock Growers Association had its origins as a countywide organization but grew to become the most powerful stockman's association in the West.

Ranchers met in Laramie in April 1871 to form the Wyoming Stock and Wool Growers Association. Governor John A. Campbell attended the organizational meeting and was elected president. The men selected as secretary and treasurer were officials of the Union Pacific Railroad. Maj. Frank Wolcott, who had moved to Cheyenne in 1870 as receiver of the U.S. Land Office, also attended the charter meeting. At the next meeting, in October 1871 in Cheyenne, members formulated proposed legislation and adopted a new name, the Wyoming Stock Growers Association. But soon after this meeting, vicious blizzards initiated a destructive winter across Wyoming. Indeed, the winter of 1871-72 would rival the notorious winter of 1886-87. Although there were far fewer Wyoming ranchers in 1871-72 than in 1886-87, many stockmen were driven out of business, and the Wyoming Stock Growers Association became defunct.

But stockmen hoped that the winter of 1871-72 was an aberration. New ranches continued to be organized, particularly in the vicinity of Cheyenne. Meeting in Cheyenne on November 29, 1873, ten ranchers organized the Laramie County Stock Growers Association. The next year the association introduced the practice of cooperative roundups, dividing the range into districts. Member ranches would work together, providing crews and chuckwagons for spring and fall roundups in each district. Each spring the calves would be branded according to the brand of the mother cow that was followed. During fall roundups marketable cattle were sorted out for disposal by the various owners. As ranching boomed in Wyoming, these roundups grew along with the association (there were six roundup districts in 1880—and thirty-one just four years later). In 1879 the expanding organization renamed itself the Wyoming Stock Growers Association.[1]

Membership grew rapidly, by 1885 swelling to 363 paid members, including out-of-state ranchers who did business in Wyoming.[2] John Clay joined the WSGA in 1883 and found his fellow members to be "generally an exceedingly bright set of men. They were young, courageous, possibly wanting in conservativism. In their idle hours they drank too much and did other naughty things, but the western folks forgave them for their hearts were true and leal [loyal]. In adversity they showed up better than in success and this feature is to their eternal credit." In time "the western folks" would become rather unforgiving of WSGA members, but Clay found a great deal to admire about "the old timers."[3]

In the early years of the association, new members were assessed an "entrance fee" of five dollars, plus monthly dues of fifty cents. But these fees did not produce sufficient revenue for the association to offer members much protection. Only a single inspector could be hired, in 1875, and there was not enough money to retain a lawyer.

So there was an increase in dues in 1879, and the next year association members were assessed "one cent per head on all horses, cattle and mules." Soon the WSGA employed "five of the ablest [lawyers] in Wyoming," according to John Clay,[4] and more than a score of brand inspectors.

The inspectors were stationed at various locations around the territory and at shipping points outside Wyoming, regularly intercepting livestock stolen from WSGA members, often with altered brands. In 1882 Thomas Sturgis, the enormously influential secretary of the WSGA (1876-87), pushed a bill through Legislative Assembly establishing a territorial veterinarian. Aided by WSGA inspectors, the veterinarian would try to keep infected cattle from entering Wyoming. In 1883 a hospital for cowboys and other range workers was opened in the old post hospital at Fort Fetterman. Supported by prominent WSGA members, the hospital in 1885 fell under the leadership of Dr. A. W. Barber, who would be governor of Wyoming during the Johnson County War.[5]

During the early 1880s the WSGA operated a stock exchange in Cheyenne, providing market repots and other financial information from June 1 to November 15 each year to eastern capitalists who ventured west to visit their ranches. These men, of course, enjoyed the amenities of the famous Cheyenne Club, and all members were required to belong to the WSGA. WSGA members exercised great influence in Wyoming, because they provided most of the capital invested in the territory. Association members were elected to the legislature and to county and local offices. Members of the WSGA served Wyoming as judges, congressmen, and governors. When cattlemen needed legislation or official action, more often than not they got it. WSGA members dominated the economy and, consequently, the politics of Wyoming. In 1884 a WSGA committee traveled to Washington, D.C. to lobby for changes in the Animal Industry Act. The rulers of Wyoming's cattle kingdoms were comfortable with the exercise of power, even in the nation's capital.[6]

Cattlemen's Associations

During the years following the Civil War, the beneficial possibilities of collective action were sought by groups such as industrial workers, through labor unions, and farmers, through the Grange and the Farmers Alliance of the South. Stockmen quickly recognized the need to organize themselves against cattle thieves and to coordinate roundups and other ranching practices.

Founded in 1865, the Cattle Theft Association was the first of several New Mexico associations organized to battle rustlers. In Silver City the Southwestern Stockman's Association was established in 1881. At the 1884 meeting of the Northern New Mexico Stock Growers Association, there were 125 ranchers in attendance. That same year the Central New Mexico Cattlegrowers Association was founded in Albuquerque. In 1886 in Hillsboro, the Sierra County Cattle and Horse Protection Association was established, one of several county associations formed in New Mexico.

In Colorado the Stock Growers Association employed stock detectives to deal with thievery, supervised branding, and sought to protect ranges from Texas cattle. Founded in 1867, the organization's name was changed to the Colorado Cattle Growers Association. In northeastern Colorado the Williams River Cattle and Horse Growers Association surely had an easier task than its northwestern Colorado counterpart, the Brown's Park Cattle Association, which operated in one of the most popular outlaw hideout regions in the West.

The Montana Stock Growers Association was established in 1884. One of its members was Dakota rancher Theodore Roosevelt, whose cattle regularly crossed into Montana to graze. Roosevelt founded and served as president of the Little Missouri Stockmen's Association. During the 1890s, Idaho cattlemen, irked with the encroachment of sheep, boldly organized the Izee Sheep Shooters, which unapologetically lived up to its name.

Forty Texas ranchers, increasingly alarmed at cattle thievery, met in Graham in 1877 to establish the Stock-Raisers Association of Northwest Texas. (Scornful of the relatively mild term "rustlers," association members long have preferred "damn cattle thieves.") As the organization grew in effectiveness and membership, the name was changed to the Cattle Raisers Association of Texas, then to the Texas and Southwestern Cattle Raisers Association.

A roundup crew during the big 1884 roundup. (Courtesy Johnson County Jim Gatchell Memorial Museum)

A WSGA spring roundup crew in Johnson County, branding in a corral. (Courtesy Johnson County Jim Gatchell Memorial Museum)

WSGA Roundups

The spring and fall roundups organized annually by the WSGA became major events in Wyoming. Planned by association committees, the roundup plans were posted on large diagrams at the April meeting of the WSGA. Detailed printed plans were distributed among members and published for the public.

Soon afterward, as soon as grass permitted, spring roundups were conducted in each district. Districts were defined by natural boundaries, which generally followed rivers and streams. The assigned foreman, who was paid eight dollars per day, held complete authority over anyone who worked in the district. Each cowboy was given a string of horses—as many as ten for a top hand. During a period of four or five weeks, the district was searched in a pre-determined design, and calves were branded, earmarked, and castrated. In one large district in 1884, twenty different ranches provided 200 cowboys and 2,000 horses, and during a six-week roundup 400,000 cattle were worked.

The beef roundup in the fall gathered steers for sale. Herds were formed and trailed to shipping points. During the "Cattlemen's Commonwealth" heyday of the 1880s, 120,000 to 180,000 head were sent to market each year. "This was when students of cowcraft passed their finals," explained Maurice Frink, historian of the WSGA. "It was semi-annual inventory and payoff, the twice-a-year climax in the process of growing cattle, when every cow on the ranges had to be tallied and accounted for."

The two most influential rancher-politicians in Wyoming formed a powerful team during the era of the Johnson County War. Joseph M. Carey and Francis E. Warren built impressive livestock operations, and both provided long service to the WSGA and to Wyoming in a variety of positions, including governor and United States senator. Both men were born in the East within seven months of each other, and they moved to Cheyenne within a year of each other.

Joseph Maul Carey was born in Delaware in 1845. Educated at Union College and the University of Pennsylvania law school, he began practicing in Pennsylvania. After campaigning for Republican candidates in the election of 1868, he was appointed by President Grant as the first United States attorney for

Joseph M. Carey, pioneer cattleman, U.S. senator, governor, and WSGA president (1883-88). (Author's collection)

Joseph M. Carey's CY Ranch. (Author's collection)

newly created Wyoming Territory. Settling in Cheyenne in 1869, Carey immediately began to exercise his energetic leadership abilities. In 1872 he moved to the territorial Supreme Court, serving for four years. Judge Carey also was twice elected mayor of Cheyenne, and he won election in 1884, 1886, and 1888 as Wyoming's territorial delegate to Congress. In 1890 he introduced the bill to admit Wyoming as a state (he was dubbed the "Father of Wyoming Statehood"), and he successfully defended the provision of the new constitution which provided for women's suffrage. Along with his friend, Francis E. Warren, Carey was appointed to the U.S. Senate in 1890. After serving one term in the Senate, Carey withdrew from politics until his election as governor in 1910.[7]

In the early 1870s, Carey became active in ranching and in real estate. He was the first rancher to place cattle above the North Platte River, building a stone residence for his CY Ranch in the vicinity of Casper. (His permanent home was in Cheyenne, where he married a local girl; the oldest of their two sons, Robert, was elected governor in 1918.) An early member of the WSGA, Judge Carey provided the association with invaluable legal expertise, and he served as president from 1883 to 1887.

Francis E. Warren was born in 1844 in Hinsdale, Massachusetts, where he attended Hinsdale Academy. At the early age of eighteen he enlisted in the 49th Massachusetts Infantry, earning the Congressional Medal of Honor in 1863 for daring exploits near Port Hudson, Louisiana. Heading west after the war, the vigorous and personable young man settled in Cheyenne in 1868. While actively engaging in business and ranching, Warren immersed himself in public affairs. He was elected to Cheyenne's town council, then to the mayor's office. After serving as a territorial senator and as territorial treasurer, he was appointed territorial governor by outgoing Republican President Chester A. Arthur. The following year a Democratic president, Grover Cleveland, appointed a new governor, but in 1889 Republican president Benjamin Harrison reappointed Warren. A year later Warren was elected first governor of the new state of Wyoming. But Governor Warren resigned within days to accept an appointment to the U.S. Senate, where he would serve—with a two-year absence due to the Johnson County War—until his death in 1929.[8]

At the same time that Warren built his distinguished political career, he developed a vast ranching empire. He joined the WSGA in 1879, and in 1883 he organized the Warren Live Stock Company, one of Wyoming's first corporations. In addition to cattle, Warren began raising sheep. Soon becoming known as "the greatest shepherd since Abraham," Warren owned 93,000 sheep by 1893, and from 1901 until 1907 he served as president of the National Wool Growers' Association. Warren also operated a successful mercantile enterprise. As a rancher-businessman, Warren quickly realized that government assistance was essential for the economic development of an arid frontier state. His political efforts always were focused on improving Wyoming's economy. Possessing a gifted capacity for friendship, he developed a network of political allies, including Joseph Carey. Warren married a Massachusetts girl in 1876; their son eventually would serve as president of the WSGA, while their daughter would marry an ambitious cavalry officer, John J. Pershing.

A powerful array of political and legal and business connections gave the WSGA enormous influence in Wyoming. But association members seemed uncharacteristically helpless in battling rustlers. Of course, vast open-range ranching operations offered optimal conditions for stock thieves. The problem was so great that the WSGA decided to supplement their stock inspectors with Pinkertons and other professional detectives. When these agencies proved unsatisfactory, the WSGA determined to employ full-time range detectives, supplemented by well-funded legal teams.

The WSGA called a special meeting in July 1883 to organize the association's own detective bureau. N. K. Boswell of Laramie, a former sheriff, superintendent

Francis E. Warren, who won the Medal of Honor during the Civil War. A pioneer citizen of Cheyenne, he built a business and ranching empire, while serving Wyoming for nearly four decades as a U.S. senator. (Courtesy Wyoming State Museum)

of the territorial prison, and "famous sleuth," was named as chief of detectives, while Judge Charles W. Wright was retained as legal counsel. Boswell was empowered to hire detectives, and their salaries and expenses would be paid by the association and by the counties where they worked. Ranchers were expected to write to the WSGA office in Cheyenne asking for detective help, and these requests were forwarded to Boswell. The bureau was under the supervision of the WSGA Executive Committee, but Boswell and his detectives were given a free hand. The detectives were not asked to submit written reports—they were expected to stay in the field.[9]

Elwood P. Mead in Wyoming

State Engineer Elwood P. Mead, one of the world's foremost irrigation experts, worked for years in Wyoming to reform western water policy. Educated at Purdue University and Iowa State College, Mead served on the faculty of Colorado State Agricultural College in Fort Collins, learning firsthand that eastern water policies were totally inadequate in the arid West.

In 1888 Mead was appointed territorial engineer of Wyoming, largely through the influence of Francis E. Warren. Progressive and farsighted, Warren was seeking ways to improve the chaotic methods of measuring and allocating water rights then in practice. By the late 1880s big cattlemen were increasingly pressured by homesteaders and small ranchers for the water access that was absolutely crucial to sustaining large herds. Water disputes usually were referred to the courts, where litigation proved time-consuming and expensive, and where Wyoming judges had scant understanding of irrigation technicalities. In Elwood Mead, Warren found a man who had unmatched expertise in water matters and innovative ideas about restructuring allocation.

Soon after Mead was brought to Wyoming, Warren was appointed governor, with the primary duty of preparing Wyoming for statehood. Governor Warren assigned Mead to write the implementing legislation for what became Article VIII of the Wyoming State Constitution. In Article VIII Mead established a system in which water was "hereby declared to be the property of the state," and in which "the public interest" would be a principal determinant in allocation. Water policy would be administered by a state engineer, a board of control, and four administrative water divisions. Wyoming's big cattlemen were elated that water disputes now were removed from the courts and were controlled by appointed officials who would fall under their influence.

Mead served as state engineer for a decade, successfully implementing his new system and redistributing water rights with admirable fairness. Wyoming water reforms began to spread to other western states, as well as to Canada, Australia, New Zealand, and South Africa. Mead left Wyoming in 1899, working with distinction for the U.S. Department of Agriculture, the state of Victoria in Australia, the University of California, and the Bureau of Reclamation. As head of the Reclamation Bureau, one of his projects was the great Hoover Dam, and the huge storage reservoir behind it was named Lake Mead.

(NOTE: These ideas were suggested to the author by Law Professor Andrew Morriss of Case Western University. Professor Morriss detailed this story in Chapter 20 of Bakken, ed., *Law in the Western United States.*)

Boswell and his men hounded stock thieves, securing indictments and having arrest papers served as far away as Arkansas and Texas. At the annual meeting of the WSGA in April 1884, the detectives were enthusiastically praised: "The expenditure has been large but results fully justify it." It was suggested that some of the detective efforts were extralegal: "Much of their work is of such a nature as cannot be properly discussed in detail." But WSGA members were assured that "the work of the bureau ... need only be continued with equal energy for a reasonable time to free the country of the men who make a profession of cattle stealing." [10]

Concurrently the WSGA secured key legislation in battling stock thieves. In 1884 the Wyoming Legislative Assembly recognized WSGA by-laws and rules, and endorsed association control of roundups. This legislation defined the "maverick" and authorized foremen of roundup districts to collect mavericks, apply an "M" brand, and sell them to the highest bidder—as long as the bidder was a WSGA member with at least $500 on deposit in a Wyoming bank. Maverick sale proceeds would be deposited in the WSGA treasury. Part of this "Maverick Law" was a resolution adopted by the WSGA in November 1883: "all rustlers' brands and stray brands for which there are no known owners [will] be treated as maverick cattle." [11] To further discourage mavericking, cowboys who owned a few head of cattle were prohibited from working roundups, and ranchers who employed these blacklisted cowboy-owners would lose their WSGA membership and, therefore, the privilege of participating in roundups.

The blacklist angered cowboys who were trying to build little herds of their own, as well as some WSGA members who disliked being told which men they could not hire. And the Maverick Law aroused bitter resentment among small ranchers whose brands were not recognized and whose strays often were rounded up and sold by the WSGA, as well as among cowboys who did not appreciate this longtime range practice being categorized as a criminal activity. Mavericking was widely practiced in Texas, providing the founding nucleus for numerous ranches. During the 1870s and 1880s, vast herds of Texas Longhorns were trailed into Wyoming and Montana, and many of the cowboys stayed in the north to work on new ranches. These Texas cowboys brought with them "the idea that a horse or a cow was a sort of public property," according to John Clay. The Texans were characterized by Clay as "expert cowmen, handy with their rope, light-fingered in ranch and camp, exceedingly fond of card-playing, a bit brutal to their horses, quiet at their work, but noisy and treacherous under the influence of liquor." [12]

According to Clay, these rowdy Texans exerted a negative influence on Easterners and other admirers who came to Wyoming to be cowboys. In addition to passing on their cowboying skills, some of the Texans also demonstrated the techniques of mavericking. Certainly Wyoming's enormous open ranges provided a perfect setting for mavericking. Since cattle were expected to fend for themselves during the winter months, most cowboys were unemployed until spring roundups began. Many cowboys wintered in ranch country, often "riding the grub line." A "grub-liner" visited from ranch to ranch throughout the winter, providing welcome company and news from the outside, in return for a bunk and a few meals. Riding the grub line was a common practice on the open range, especially where absentee owners spent the winters in Cheyenne or back East or in England, leaving foremen in charge of lonely ranch headquarters. "They led idle lives," said Clay, referring not to the absentee owners but to the unemployed cowboys, "and as they had a good horse or two they began mavericking, and it was only a step from this to stealing outright."[13]

Firearms "Discountenanced"

When the WSGA published the 1882 roundup information, the association also included several resolutions. The final resolution is ironic, considering the events of a decade later:

> "*Resolved*, That whereas the custom of carrying firearms by those engaged in the round-up and in working the cattle ranges is productive of great evil and frequently results in the damage of persons and property. Be it therefore
> "*Resolved*, That the custom of carrying fire-arms, except in the immediate vicinity of Indian reservation, should be discountenanced, and it is hereby made the duty of the members of this association, foremen of round-ups and foremen of ranges to use every effort in their power to prevent the carrying of fire-arms by cattlemen at all times and places, except when absolutely necessary. The members of the association hereby pledge themselves so far as in their power to carry out the spirit of this resolution."

The "spirit of this resolution" seems to have been forgotten by 1892.

When such cowboys spotted a maverick, "they would brand the calf if it was old enough to wean, separate it from its mother and turn it loose," reported Frank Canton, longtime WSGA detective and sheriff of Johnson County. "At other times they would brand the calf, then run the cow off in some canyon, shoot her down, and leave the meat for the gray wolves and coyotes."[14]

Mavericking often led to other forms of cattle theft. Rustlers carried a "running iron," an iron rod without a brand face which could be used to alter an existing brand. The only way to determine the owner's brand was to kill and skin the animal in question, then "look at the inside of the hide which would show a white welt, or scar, so plainly that you could easily tell what the original brand was," said Frank Canton, who collected evidence with this technique.[15] Because cattle with altered brands often were sold to a butcher for slaughter, a Wyoming law required that the hide of such beeves be shown to an officer so that the brand could be checked from the inside. But a rustler would skin one beef bearing his brand, then produce this hide repeatedly to represent stolen cattle that were slaughtered. Like most thieves, cattle rustlers employed myriad ingenious methods.

Although Canton, Boswell, and the other detectives managed to secure evidence against numerous rustlers, there was little satisfaction in the courts. "Hundreds of arrests for horse and cattle stealing and other depredations were made," claimed John Clay, "but the judges of the territory of Wyoming . . . were lenient and the juries in the northern part . . . were friendly to all classes of crime, but more so to live stock depredators. The miscarriage of justice came to be so notorious that in some counties if a prisoner pleaded guilty he was not punished."[16] Homesteaders and other small operators sat on juries and grand juries. These men had been crowded off the open range by cattle barons, and they had no sympathy for absentee owners. Despite the accumulation of evidence and the efforts of WSGA attorneys, few convictions were obtained, and rustlers therefore became bolder.

The Annual Love Feast

During the 1880s the WSGA held its annual meeting each April in Cheyenne. Association members first convened in Laramie County Courthouse, but soon found it necessary to move to the larger Opera House auditorium.

"It was a sort of free for all," described John Clay, who first attended in 1884. "We did not in those days have prepared papers over which the author had labored for days." Instead, committee reports triggered impromptu discussions about such subjects as mavericking, railroads, public stockyards, livestock diseases, and the leasing of the public domain. The most important committee topic was roundup information, diagrammed on large sheets of paper, fixing the date and place of rendezvous for each roundup district.

From 1883 through 1887 Joseph M. Carey, as WSGA president, chaired these meetings articulately and patiently, "in every way an ideal presiding officer." Reports were made by two longtime WSGA officers, Secretary Thomas Sturgis (1876-87) and Treasurer A. H. Reel (1876-89), as well as by the territorial veterinarian.

In addition to ranch owners and managers, a number of cowboys were present, many hoping to find work. There were numerous representatives from railroads, stockyards, and packing plants, along with managers of feed companies and "Chicago commission men."

These men socialized throughout the day in saloons, with Luke Murrin's establishment drawing the greatest patronage. At night the Cheyenne Club "was a brilliant scene," related John Clay. "Wine flowed freely, tongues got limber, the different cliques broke away from one another. It was a sort of love feast; no apple of discord appeared and no cloud hung on the horizon."

The WSGA was staggered by the winter of 1886-87. High interest rates—three percent per month, thirty-six percent annually since the 1870s—forced many ranchers to liquidate under pressure from their creditors. One of many Wyoming cattlemen to go out of business was WSGA Secretary Thomas Sturgis. He was not present at the sparsely attended WSGA meeting in 1887; neither were the president and vice-president. Association membership plummeted, with only 183 paid members by 1888. WSGA revenues simultaneously nosedived—at one point in 1890 the treasury contained merely $29—and services were drastically reduced. It was necessary to cut the detective force, even though in the wake of the devastating winter there were many stray cattle offering temptation to rustlers. "There ensued a great wave of stealing, mavericking, changing brands, and selling beef to the smaller towns and to contractors in public works, after the hard winter of 1886-87," related John Clay. "The cattlemen were poorly organized, the ranges were not carefully worked, for funds were scarce, and so the thief, the rustler and the ne'er-do-well were much in evidence."[17]

WSGA members who requested association detectives now were asked to pay half of the expenses. But few ranchers actually paid anything, and the detective bureau shriveled. Chief of Detectives N. K. Boswell suffered health problems, perhaps in part because of the mounting frustrations of his job. Boswell resigned in the fall of 1887 and was replaced by Frank Canton. But by the end of the year, the WSGA felt compelled to dissolve the detective bureau.[18]

"It has been tried and found to be a failure," declared one association report. "The condition of the treasury makes it impossible to do any detective work." One letter from WSGA headquarters lamented that "when it comes to the *detective* part of the work, it has simply been an aggravation and a mistake." Another lettter explained: "After many years experience, and the expenditure of several thousand dollars, the Association found that it was wasting its time and money." Still another letter emphasized the association's problems with unfriendly juries: "We have thrown away thousands of dollars in the past in sincere efforts to stop thieving on the range, and the only result has been that we have been thrown ignominiously out of court."[19]

"The condition of the treasury makes it impossible to do any detective work even if it seemed advisable to do so," stated the association secretary. The WSGA executive committee decided that the association should maintain inspectors "at the railroad feeding and discharging points," but discontinued the detective bureau. Predictably, rustlers became more active than ever. "Depredations upon stock on the range are becoming so open and notorious," angrily reported the WSGA office, "that concerted action of some kind must be taken, and strong measures resorted to, unless we are to give up the fight entirely, and surrender our properties to the rustlers."[20]

The WSGA members who survived the winter of 1886-87 were not the kind of men "to give up the fight entirely." Ranchers who had built pioneer cattle empires were unafraid of taking "strong measures," and they certainly would not peacefully "surrender [their] properties to the rustlers." Although the detective bureau was disbanded, WSGA members never gave up on the idea of range detectives. Frank Canton stayed on the association payroll, and Wyoming ranchers considered hiring their own special deputies as conditions might dictate. Frank Canton would become an important instrument of

WSGA Officers Through
the Johnson County War

President		Vice-President	
1873-75	M. V. Boughton	1876-81	G. A. Searight
1876-81	A. H. Swan	1882-84	A. H. Gilchrist
1882	N. R. Davis	1885-86	John McShane
1883-87	Joseph M. Carey	1887-88	A. T. Babbitt
1888-89	A. T. Babbitt	1888-95	George Baxter
1890-95	John Clay		

Secretary		Treasurer	
1873-75	Wm. Kuykendall	1873-75	Wm. Kuykendall
1876-87	Thomas Sturgis	1876-89	A. H. Reel
1887-90	Thomas Adams	1890-1903	Henry Hay
1891-95	H. B. Ijams		

the WSGA and a key figure in the Johnson County War. He spent the first three decades of his life as Joe Horner, but by the time he reached Wyoming he had changed his name and concealed an outlaw past. Born in 1849 in Arkansas, Joe moved with his family to Texas, and as a teenager he became a cowboy. Joe herded cattle up the Chisholm Trail, and by his early twenties he had established a small cattle ranch a few miles north of Jacksboro, on the northwest Texas frontier. Adventurous and reckless, he drank freely and never backed away from trouble. Joe stole horses from Indian reservations in Oklahoma, then began stealing livestock from fellow ranchers. [21]

In 1874 in Jacksboro, Joe engaged in a wild shootout with black troopers—"buffalo soldiers"—from nearby Fort Richardson. There was other gunplay, and soon he was charged with several counts of theft and assault. Jailed in Jacksboro in 1875, within a week he was broken out of the flimsy lockup by several riders, probably led by his three brothers. Accompanied by younger brother George, Joe led "The Horner Gang" into outright outlawry. Like other notorious gangs, Joe and his men were blamed for all manner of depredations, not always correctly. In January 1876 the gang executed a successful bank robbery in the frontier town of Comanche. Escaping with about $5,500, the Horner brothers were arrested, separately, a few weeks later in San Antonio. Tried on various charges, Joe was sentenced to ten years at hard labor in the state penitentiary in Huntsville. Incarcerated in San Antonio's infamous jail—the "Bat Cave"—while awaiting appeal, Joe led three other prisoners in digging through a wall and sawing off leg irons. Joe and two others escaped.

Joe and another desperado robbed a stagecoach, then were chased down by a posse and arrested, following a furious exchange of shots. Finally imprisoned at Huntsville in 1877, Joe spent two years behind walls. But the Texas penal system hired out most prisoners as convict labor, and by 1879 Joe was assigned to one of these work gangs. An experienced escape artist, he disappeared from his group in August 1879.

Equipped with a new name, Frank Canton left Texas, determined to make the best of his new chance. Reaching the remote northern range country, Canton found work as a cowboy. He cultivated the friendship of ranch owners and lawmen, and in August 1881 he was called to Cheyenne for an interview with association secretary Thomas Sturgis at WSGA headquarters. Impressed with the quiet-spoken but highly knowledgeable Texan, Sturgis employed Canton as a field inspector, not knowing that he had hired a former stock thief to catch stock thieves.

Frank Canton stood nearly six feet tall, and at 140 pounds he had a hard, lean build. He had blue, piercing eyes, handsome features, and a big moustache. As Joe Horner he had been aggressive and ruthless and unafraid to use a gun, qualities that Frank Canton would use on the side of the law for the rest of his life.

Canton was assigned to vast, sparsely settled Johnson County in northern Wyoming. Johnson County issued Canton a deputy sheriff's commission, so that he could make arrests, and half of his salary therefore would be paid by the county. Filled with new ambition, Canton stayed in the saddle, checking for rustlers and verifying ownership of livestock at roundups and shipping points. His efforts were so impressive that early in 1882, WSGA and Johnson County raised his salary to $150 per month.

Later in 1882, WSGA ranchers persuaded Canton to run for county sheriff against a Republican "granger." Although there were many grangers and small ranchers in Johnson County, with the backing of WSGA members Canton won a close election. As a county sheriff he had to resign from the WSGA, but of course he retained his ties to association members, and his monthly salary now was $250.

Sheriff Canton promptly strengthened the jail in Buffalo, then began populating the facility with inmates. Canton imposed order in Buffalo through the force of his intimidating presence, and he and his deputies scoured the countryside for lawbreakers. The sheriff made numerous arrests, including a great many horse thieves, and he was recognized as a tough, competent peace officer. In 1884 the Democratic Party renominated him unanimously, and he won reelection over his Republican opponent.

Now in his mid-thirties with a well-paid position, Canton could realistically think about marriage and family. In 1885 he married seventeen-year-old Annie Wilkerson, daughter of a Johnson County rancher. During the next three years Frank and Annie became the parents of two daughters. Frank owned a small house in Buffalo, along with a 160-acre homestead ten miles south of town (he later acquired an additional 320 acres). During his second term, he was appointed a deputy U.S. marshal by Marshal T. Jeff Carr.

During four years as sheriff, Frank Canton sent nineteen felons to the penitentiary, all but one for livestock theft. But there was a growing resentment against big ranchers, and it was becoming difficult to convict rustlers, particularly if the stolen animals were from a large spread. Furthermore, complaints about the expenses of the sheriff's office triggered threats to cut salaries. With a good sense of timing and the claim that he needed to spend time with his family and his little ranch, Canton declined to run for a third term. E. U. Snider won a close election, and Frank Canton moved his family to a snug new log cabin on his ranch.

Sheriff Frank Canton (upper right) poses with friends for an 1884 tintype. Early the next year he would marry Annie Wilkerson (seated at left). (Courtesy Bob Edwards, Buffalo)

On his homestead ten miles south of Buffalo, Frank Canton built a three-room cabin for his growing family.
(Courtesy Johnson County Jim Gatchell Memorial Museum)

"The conditions in Johnson County grew from bad to worse," observed the ex-sheriff. Indeed, salaries of the new sheriff and undersheriff were cut in half, while it became "almost impossible to convict a rustler."[22] During the ensuing four years, merely five stock thieves were sentenced to prison. In response to requests for help from WSGA ranchers in northern Wyoming, Chief of Detectives N. K. Boswell appointed former sheriff Canton as chief detective in the north. Canton would police a region that encompassed Johnson and Crook counties, as well as the northern area of Laramie, Albany, Carbon, Uinta, and Fremont counties. Canton was free to operate as he pleased, at an annual salary of $2,500 plus expenses, although Johnson County no longer would pay half the salary of WSGA detectives. Canton's appointment began soon after he turned in his sheriff's badge, on April 1, 1887.[23]

With his customary relentlessness, Canton quickly "secured positive evidence in many cases for cattle stealing." The results of his efforts were frustrating. "The thieves were arrested and brought into court, but it was almost impossible to convict a rustler," complained Canton. "The jury was summoned from the body of citizens of the county and friends and sympathizers of the thieves would always manage to get on the jury and turn the defendants loose as fast as we arrested them." Other "friends and sympathizers" refused to testify against rustlers. Canton contemptuously dismissed the popular term "rustler as he called himself, which was a picturesque, gentlemanly name for a cattle thief."[24]

Maj. Frank Wolcott presented Frank Canton with this .38 Colt double-action revolver, a tangible indication of the esteem in which cattlemen held Canton. (Courtesy L. F. Blake)

Wolcott had the backstrap of this presentation Colt inscribed: "F. M. Canton From His Friend F. Wolcott." (Courtesy L. F. Blake)

Six months after Canton began his second tenure with the WSGA, Boswell resigned and Frank was asked to head the detective bureau. But most of the range detectives were laid off during 1887 by the cash-strapped association, and by year's end the bureau was dissolved. Canton remained on the WSGA payroll until March 1888, when he became an inspector for the newly created Wyoming Board of Livestock Commissioners. This agency assumed many of the responsibilities of the ailing WSGA, while key association members managed to maintain control over the new board, which meant that Frank Canton's duties remained virtually unchanged.

In 1888 Canton hoped to regain the sheriff's office from the inept E. U. Snider. But by this time a majority of Johnson County voters were alienated against the WSGA, and Canton had lost his political support. The Democrats nominated W. G. "Red" Angus, who went on to win the November election. Sheriff Angus then appointed a known mavericker as his undersheriff. Although Canton still held commissions as a deputy U.S. marshal and as an inspector for the Livestock Commission, he could not obtain an appointment as deputy sheriff, which limited his ability to make arrests.

Canton felt a growing resentment against rustlers and Red Angus. His low opinion of Angus was shared by Joe LeFors, who sometimes worked with Canton in northern Wyoming. Locating a herd of cattle with clearly altered brands "and ears cut off close to the head," LeFors sent word to Sheriff Angus. "No officer would even come out to see them," fumed LeFors. "The sheriff's office would not do a thing. ... The sheriff's office showed us very plainly that we could expect no help from that direction. How could we hope for help with the deputy sheriff owning a maverick brand himself?"[25]

In 1889, with rustling rampant on the northern ranges, several ranchers offered a $1,500 reward for the conviction of any stock thief. With rustlers operating throughout the region, Frank Canton intended to capitalize on this opportunity and earn several rewards. ("Canton was out to collect rewards," stated a "Wyoming old-timer" who claimed to have provided information to the lawman. "He was always looking for someone. . . . All he thought about was guns and killing.")[26]

Canton carefully gathered evidence against six suspects, including Jack Flagg and Martin Allison Tisdale, who used the alias "Al Allison" because of a shooting scrape in Texas. Flagg had ridden up the trail from Texas in 1882, working as a cowboy until blackballed by the WSGA in 1887. Regarded by Canton as "the worst rustler in the county,"[27] Flagg stocked his Hat Ranch presumably with stolen cattle. In 1884 Al Allison and his brother, John Tisdale, also had ridden up the trail with Texas Longhorns. John Tisdale was a neighbor of Flagg's, and his murder in 1891 would be widely blamed on Frank Canton.

W. G. "Red" Angus was elected sheriff of Johnson County in 1888, and he would organize defenders against the Invaders of 1892. (Author's collection)

Canton's evidence was sufficient to secure indictments against all six suspected stock thieves in district court. But they were released on bail, and within a few months the charges were dismissed—to the disgust of Canton and the WSGA. Canton had lost potential rewards totaling $9,000, while association members became more convinced than ever that no matter how much evidence was compiled, no matter how skillfully WSGA lawyers performed, justice against rustlers could not be achieved through the courts.

"It seems as if we could not keep a thief in jail after we put them there," complained one of many such letters from the WSGA office. "Unfortunately," went another complaint, "it is almost useless to bring matters to the court even after an indictment has been obtained and the evidence pretty well gathered. There seems to be a morbid sympathy with cattle thieves both on the bench and in the jury room."[28]

Other correspondence sounded an ominous note. "Circumstances have forced cattlemen to look to themselves for protection, outside of any Association," reported one letter, while another made it clear that "matters will continue to get worse, unless concerted action is taken. If the territory does not come to our assistance . . . I expect to see

Red Angus

The man who defeated Frank Canton in 1888 for the office of sheriff of Johnson County would spearhead the 1892 defense of the county against Canton and the other Invaders. William G. Angus, known to everyone as "Red," was born in 1849 in Zanesville, Ohio (also the birthplace, in 1875, of western novelist Zane Grey). In later years Red related the story of his early life to Buffalo businessman-historian T. J. Gatchell, who wrote a short manuscript after Angus died in 1922.

The Angus family moved to Iowa in 1854 but soon pushed west to "Bleeding Kansas." When the Civil War erupted, Red's father enlisted in the Second Kansas Cavalry and served throughout the conflict. In 1862, when he was still twelve, Red talked his mother into letting him join the Thirteenth Kansas Infantry. During the remainder of the war his company was involved in numerous skirmishes. After the war the teenager worked as a government teamster, hauling freight to frontier outposts in Kansas and Oklahoma during Indian campaigns.

Angus finally left government service in 1871, worked with his father for a year in Little Rock, then moved to Texas, lured by the booming cattle business. In 1877, with a large number of other men, Angus went to Guatemala to haul freight from the coast to the capital. A year later he sailed from Guatemala to California, where he worked as a teamster and cowboy.

In 1880 Angus helped trail a herd of cattle to northern Wyoming. After delivering the herd in the spring of 1881, he became a popular saloonkeeper, earning the nickname "Mayor of Laurel Avenue" (Buffalo's red-light district). Angus joined local fraternal orders, was nominated by the Democratic Party for county sheriff, and won back-to-back elections. By 1892 he was a forceful, confident man in his early forties. Tested and shaped by varied adventures, Red Angus was poised to enter into the most notable event of his life.

a stronger combination than ever formed for the suppression of cattle and horse steal-ing." Another correspondent warned that "while I would be sorry to see the return of the old days, when it was necessary to defend your property at the expense of human life I am inclined to believe that we shall come to this." Many big ranchers were near-ing the point of extralegal action: "The existing state of affairs cannot long continue without collisions between the owners of stock and the thieves that seem to infect the entire range country."[29]

But as rustlers seemed to overwhelm the range, big ranchers made a partial come-back. So many cattle died during the winter of 1886-87, and so many ranchers aban-doned their Wyoming spreads, the relatively empty grasslands recovered by 1888. "It was a virgin range we had to stock up," recalled John Clay, although it proved difficult to find loans for restocking. "It seemed as if bankers had long and tenacious memories." Favorable conditions produced successful years for cattlemen in 1888, 1890, 1891, and 1892.[30]

As the ranchers who had survived struggled to reestablish their operations, the ac-celerating pace of stock theft was maddening. By 1889 ranchers and rustlers were on a collision course, and some cattlemen were willing to resort to extralegal action. Livestock theft was not their only problem, but it was one aggravating problem that was subject to direct action—extralegal action that long had been commonplace and gener-ally accepted in America.

Chapter 4

Johnson County: Future Battlefield

"The town itself [Buffalo] has less of that portable appearance so prevailing elsewhere. There are some neat little cottages, and a number of brick buildings, also a flour mill."

OWEN WISTER (JUNE 26, 1891)

Johnson County, site of the West's most famous range war, had its beginnings as a cavalry post in another frontier war, the conflict between Sioux and Cheyenne warriors and the United States Army. During the intensive campaign of 1876, one of the casualties was Lt. J. A. McKinney. Cantonment Reno, a supply depot on the old Bozeman Trail,

Looking west at Fort McKinney, ca. 1884. Officers' Row is on the right, and the barracks are at left, across the parade ground. (Courtesy Johnson County Jim Gatchell Memorial Museum)

was renamed Fort McKinney. In 1878 Fort McKinney was moved fifty miles north to the eastern base of the towering Big Horn Mountains, alongside a beautiful stream named Clear Creek.[1]

A sawmill began to shape pine logs, while a shingle maker provided roofing. As Fort McKinney took form, barracks were erected for three companies of cavalry and four infantry troops. There would be fourteen sets of officers' quarters, along with stables, warehouses, a large hospital, and numerous auxiliary buildings. Civilian workmen were employed to help soldiers with construction, and teamsters found steady work freighting supplies to Fort McKinney. This outpost offered a lucrative market for vegetables, meat, dairy products, and miscellaneous other foodstuffs, as well as oats and hay. In addition, the 300 to 400 soldiers stationed at Fort McKinney needed someplace to spend their pay. By 1879 a town began to spring up about two miles east of the fort. At the suggestion of a former resident of Buffalo, New York, the new frontier community was named "Buffalo."[2]

Buffalo grew up alongside a north-south main street bisected by Clear Creek, flowing eastward. Freight wagons regularly proceeded up and down this street, heading to or from the fort. Freighters also purchased considerable amounts of oats and hay to feed to their oxen, horses, and mules. Homesteaders flocked to the area to take advantage of the opportunities offered by a new fort and military payroll. Each settler would file on a 160-acre homestead claim near Clear Creek or one of the other area streams. But the Desert Land Act had been legislated in 1877, offering settlers a full section—640 acres— if the land were irrigated. So a number of settlers filed Desert Land claims and began digging irrigation ditches. By 1884 more than 10,000 acres had been irrigated along Clear Creek, and by the next year 6,000 acres were irrigated along Rock Creek, north of Buffalo.[3] Fencing in their small claims with barbed wire, the settlers raised oats, wheat, hay, and a few head of livestock.

In 1880 Johnson County was organized, with the new county government taking office in the growing village of Buffalo in May 1881. In addition to present-day Johnson

Buffalo in 1883. The Occidental Hotel is housed in the two large buildings just to the north (right) of Clear Creek. The large structure on the other side of the stream and the opposite side of the street is Conrad's general store, while Foote's general store is the large building at far right. Foote's store faces Fort Road, which angles toward Fort McKinney, the cluster of buildings which may be seen in the distance. At left, the other road angling away from Main Street is Laurel Road, site of the Red Light district. (Author's collection)

County, this 1881 county encompassed all of modern Sheridan County and the regions of modern Big Horn and Washakie counties east of the Big Horn River. Sheridan County was organized in 1887, while the Wyoming Legislature authorized Washakie County in 1890. Western Johnson County was dominated by the magnificent Big Horn Mountains, while the eastern part of the county featured rolling plains and the Powder River, which ran south to north. In broken country to the southwest an isolated canyon became known as "Hole-in-the-Wall." Large ranches, such as Moreton Frewen's Powder River Company, sprawled across the southern expanse of the county, while the northern part was populated with homesteaders and small ranches.

The county seat, Buffalo, was in the north. During the 1880s Buffalo grew into a lively frontier community which offered numerous services and amenities to residents and visitors. "The town is full of life," proclaimed the *Big Horn Sentinel* in 1886, "plenty of gambling and considerable of those who are inclined to sample fire-water quite frequently, and with all this there is very seldom an occasion for arrest."[4] By 1890 there were twenty-three saloons (along with forty-two other businesses), and a red-light district just west of Main Street. But a city ordinance against carrying firearms helped keep rowdyism under control. "There is no necessity for anyone carrying firearms in Buffalo," announced the *Big Horn Sentinel* following an 1885 gunplay involving a gambler. "Lay aside your 'pops' boys, and go it John L. Sullivan Style."[5]

Owen Wister saw Buffalo in June 1891, on his fourth trip west. Reaching town at the end of a forty-mile horseback ride, his first impression was negative and conde-

Buffalo's Occidental Hotel comprised the building complex just north of Clear Creek on the west side of Main Street. (Courtesy Johnson County Jim Gatchell Memorial Museum)

39

scending. "The town of Buffalo, of course, is something horrible beyond words. They all are. ... A general litter of paltry wood houses back to back and side to back at all angles that seem to have been brought and dumped out of a wheelbarrow. You would die in a moment here." But he was "very cordially entertained" at Fort McKinney, deeply affected by the scenic settings, and intrigued by "the motley blackguards I meet." Wister soon regarded Buffalo more favorably. "Buffalo is a shade better in its appearance than most of these towns. ... The town itself has less of that portable appearance so prevailing elsewhere. There are some neat little cottages and a number of brick buildings, also a flour mill. The stages come in from Douglas and from Belle Fourche. Fort McKinney is two miles away to the west, almost against the mountains, whose canons open just above it and whose snow peaks are in plain view behind the lower timbered foothills."[6]

Although no railroad would reach Buffalo until 1918, there was regular stagecoach service, and a telegraph line connected to the military line at Fort McKinney provided communication with the outside world. Stagecoach passengers could stay at the Occidental Hotel, a big log hostelry on the west side of Main Street just north of Clear Creek. Another log structure, McLeod's Saloon, housed Wyoming's first roller-skating rink (proprietress Nettie Wright paid a dollar a pair for forty-five pairs of roller skates in 1883). Two other big log buildings on the east side of Main Street were general stores: John H. Conrad and Company, and Robert Foote, General Merchandise, which boasted a two-story false front. Foote and his store would play a key role in the climactic battle of the Johnson County War. A native of Scotland, Foote was fifty when he arrived at Buffalo in 1882. He had been post sutler at Fort Halleck, Wyoming, and had shot a man dead at Fort Laramie. As a leading citizen of Buffalo, Foote sported a Prince Albert coat, top hat, striped trousers, walking stick, and a flowing white beard.

Another well-dressed civic leader, attorney Charles H. Burritt, was a native of Vermont who had studied at Brown University before coming to Buffalo when he was twenty-nine. The tall, black-bearded Burritt cut a striking figure around town in a black frock coat, vest, and striped pants. When he gestured in a courtroom, a gold ring flashed on his little finger. In 1886 Burritt became Buffalo's second mayor, serving ably for the next eleven years. Major Burritt secured a water works and electric lights for his community at an early date, and he frequently was called upon to represent Buffalo and Johnson County in territorial and state politics. Burritt was attorney for several large ranchers and for John H. Conrad and Company, which supplied the big ranchers.

Robert Foote, on the other hand, did not do business with the cattle barons, catering instead

Attorney Charles H. Burritt, the progressive mayor of Buffalo from 1886 through 1897. A key civic leader, Burritt would find himself endangered because of his identification with the large ranchers. (Courtesy Johnson County Jim Gatchell Memorial Museum)

Buffalo's 1884 courthouse still dominates the north end of Main Street. (Photo by Karon O'Neal)

to the small operators. Burritt and Foote would be on opposite sides when the Johnson County War erupted. Another leading citizen, banker Will Thom, would find himself identified with the big ranchers. Thom came to Buffalo early in the town's existence and successfully promoted the community through progressive leadership of the First National Bank. His contributions to the growth of Buffalo would be ignored to the extent that his life was in danger in 1892.

During the 1880s, however, Burritt, Foote, Thom, and others worked to expand their isolated village into a vibrant, growing community. In 1884 the log courthouse was replaced by a big brick structure. The most impressive building in Buffalo, the new courthouse dominated the skyline from atop a hill on the north end of town and the west side of Main Street. A "Grand Ball" was held in the courthouse when it was completed. In 1886 a two-story brick school was built a short distance west of the courthouse, on Fort Road.

Fort McKinney's surgeon provided Buffalo's first medical services, although doctors and a dentist soon established practices in town. In 1888 Dr. John Howard Lott resigned as army surgeon at Fort McKinney and moved to Buffalo, practicing there for the next twenty-five years. Likewise, the post chaplain, Rev. G. W. Simpson, held the first religious meeting in Buffalo and organized the first Sunday school. But in 1884 a resident minister reached town, and by 1890 citizens could worship with congregations at the First Baptist Church, St. Luke's Episcopal Church, Union Congregational Church, Methodist Episcopal Church, Christian Church, and the Fort McKinney Chapel.

Dinnertime!

Although Buffalo was a law-abiding town, violence occasionally erupted. In 1885, for example, a homesteader named Jake Schmerer was murdered, and his hired hand, Bill Booth, immediately disappeared. An eight-man posse tracked down Booth and brought him back to Buffalo. On the third day of the ensuing trial, prosecuting attorney Charles Burritt extracted a confession from Booth.

A death sentence was handed down, and a proper gallows—complete with thirteen steps—was erected behind the new brick courthouse. A crowd gathered on the morning of February 26, 1886, to view the hanging. James Enoche, who had been one of the arresting posse members, observed that "Booth was by far the best looking man at the hanging!"

Atop the gallows, Booth asked the time and was told it was not quite noon. "I wish it would hurry up," he gamely told his captors. "I want to get to hell in time for dinner."

Citizens also ventured out to the fort for post band concerts, Fourth of July celebrations, and baseball games. During Buffalo's early years, baseball was becoming the National Pastime. Popular among military companies as an outdoor competition, baseball teams flourished on military posts. Buffalo organized a team to play against the Fort McKinney nine, and baseball games also were an exciting feature of the Johnson County Fair. In 1884 a foot race was conducted at a horse track on the south side of town. Betting was heavy among the two hundred spectators that thronged the track, but children were prohibited "so that the innocent ones could not see the racers in their scanty togs."[7]

During the winter, ice skating and toboggan sledding were popular on the hilly inclines of Main Street. A town band was organized in 1882. There was great enthusiasm for theatricals, church socials, parties, and picnics. Although the saloons and sporting houses offered drinking, gambling, and other masculine recreation, innocent diversions—from church services to baseball games—also abounded.

With no rapid connection to the outside world, Buffalo enjoyed a strong sense of community. As in all small towns, everyone knew everyone else, and gossip was a constant pastime. A favorite feature of Buffalo newspapers (*The Big Horn Sentinel*, which soon changed its name permanently to the Buffalo *Bulletin*, and two short-lived publications, the Buffalo *Echo* and the Buffalo *Voice*) was such personal information as births, deaths, marriages, and arrivals and departures on the stagecoach. Any outside threat to such a close-knit community would rally the citizens in a surge of defensive response.

Chapter 5

Vigilante Background

"This cleanup of horse thieves put a stop to horse and cattle stealing in Montana for many years."

GRANVILLE STUART

When the invasion of Johnson County was planned, the organizers were following an extralegal tradition that stretched back into the American past for more than a century and a quarter.

Violence against British authority was commonplace in the colonies for several years prior to the American Revolution. The Boston Massacre of 1770 and the Boston Tea Party of 1773 were the most famous of scores of riots which began during the mid-1760s. In this atmosphere of unsanctioned violence, an outbreak of frontier crime in South Carolina triggered a response by angry citizens which launched the vigilante tradition in America. From 1767 through 1769, respectable citizens organized themselves as "Regulators" and tried troublemakers, flogging and expelling many undesirables. One outlaw gang was cornered, and sixteen members were slain.[1]

This successful Regulator movement would inspire hundreds of similar actions during the remainder of the eighteenth century, throughout the nineteenth century, and into the twentieth century. Many Regulator groups were highly organized and operated on a comparatively large scale, while other men banded spontaneously to deal swiftly with a single criminal. For nearly a century these extralegal groups usually were called "Regulators," but by the late nineteenth century the customary term had become "vigilante."

Another term common to extralegal experiences was provided by Col. Charles Lynch, a prominent citizen of Bedford County, Virginia (the town of Lynchburg was named for Colonel Lynch). By 1780, with the Revolution still raging, Bedford County had become a hotbed of outlawry. Leading citizens formed a court with Colonel Lynch sitting as presiding judge. Regular—if illegal—trials were held, with flogging as the common punishment. This court thereby dispensed "Lynch Law," although in time this term came to mean a far more lethal form of justice than flogging.

During the eighteenth, nineteenth, and twentieth centuries, more than 6,000 men (and a few women) were executed by vigilante activities. In his authoritative study of violence in America, Richard Maxwell Brown described the development of "the ideology of vigilantism," which "gripped the minds and emotions of Americans." Brown concluded that "the vigilantes, knowing full well that their actions were illegal, felt obliged to legitimize their violence by expounding a philosophy of vigilantism." By the mid-1800s, "self-righteous vigilantes ... were routinely invoking 'self-preservation' or 'self-protection' as the first principal of vigilantism." Brown quoted an 1858 resolution of Indiana vigilantes:

"We are believers in the doctrine of popular sovereignty; that the people of this country are the real sovereigns, and that whenever the laws, made by those to whom they have delegated their authority, are found inadequate to their protection, it is the right of the people to take the protection of their property into their own hands, and deal with these villains according to their just desserts. ..."[3]

Such sentiments were vigorously embraced by pioneers, and vigilantism flourished on the western frontiers of the nineteenth century. The westward movement often outraced the establishment of courts, law officers, and even jails. Indeed, vigilante action was quicker and cheaper than any system of courts, judges, juries, attorneys, trials, appeals, and institutional punishment. Wherever lawlessness broke out, prominent citizens encouraged, organized, and usually led vigilantes in establishing order. "A host of distinguished Americans—statesmen, politicians, capitalists, lawyers, judges, writers, and others—supported vigilantism by word or deed," stated Richard Maxwell Brown. Usually their support or participation was when they were younger men, leaders on the rise, "but in later life, they never repudiated their actions." Brown specifically listed two future presidents (Andrew Johnson and Theodore Roosevelt), five U.S. senators, and eight governors of states or territories (including John E. Osborne and Fennimore Chatterton of Wyoming).[4]

When the westward movement leaped across half a continent to the California gold fields, vigilance committees were organized in one community after another. San Francisco's Committee of Vigilance was formed in 1851 to control a soaring crime rate. This committee was revived on a larger scale in 1856 by leading citizens. More than 6,000 San Franciscans joined the Committee of Vigilance in 1856. The committee utilized the local police force and courts in trying and executing four criminals, and in banishing twenty-eight other men. This large-scale, methodical action served as an inspiration and model for future vigilantes in a variety of locales.

In Montana in early 1864, a vicious outlaw gang led by Sheriff Henry Plummer committed thievery and more than one hundred murders in the gold fields around Bannack and Virginia City. Citizens finally banded together as vigilantes and hanged Plummer, along with more than a score of his gang members. Twenty-nine-year-old Wilbur Fisk Sanders served the vigilantes as prosecuting attorney in Virginia City. Later Sanders founded the Montana Bar Association, and when Montana achieved statehood in 1889, he won election as one of the first two U.S. senators. In 1866 Thomas J. Dimsdale, a vigilante participant and editor of Virginia City's *Montana Post,* released the first book ever printed in Montana, *The Vigilantes of Montana; or, Popular Justice in the Rocky Mountains.* Another former Virginia City vigilante, Nathaniel Pitt Langford, the "father

The gallows frame at "Hangman's Gulch" near Bannack, Montana. In 1864 Sheriff Henry Plummer was hanged from his own gallows by vigilantes, who also executed a score of the sheriff's henchmen. (Author's collection)

of Yellowstone National Park," wrote *Vigilante Days and Ways,* which was published in 1890, in time to instruct potential vigilantes in Wyoming.

Texas, which would provide Wyoming with cattle herds, cowboys, and in 1892 more than a score of hired gunmen, also offered frequent examples of vigilante action. Hundreds of men were lynched in Texas, and while many of them were black victims of racial violence, many more were lawbreakers who were executed by aroused citizens. In 1874, for example, outlawry was rampant in Bell County. With the legal system unable to control criminal activity, citizens organized a large-scale vigilante movement which would intimidate desperados throughout the region. Ten rustlers and murderers were rounded up and jailed in Belton, the county seat. One lawbreaker fell ill and was taken to a back room, while the other nine prisoners were incarcerated in a large, iron-slatted cell. The sheriff conveniently left town, assigning only one jailer to night duty. After dark more than one hundred vigilantes forced their way through a fence and into the jail. Fearing a necktie party, the prisoners cowered at the rear of the cell, but the jailer hid the keys. The impatient vigilantes simply inserted the barrels of their rifles and revolvers between the iron slats and opened fire. All nine prisoners fell dead, riddled with bullets.

A similar incident occurred in Meridian in 1878, when vigilantes barged into the jail and gunned down accused murderers Mart and Tom

In 1878 murderers Tom and Mart Horrell were shot to death by a lynch mob in their cell at Meridian, Texas. The Horrell brothers were taken home to Lampasas, where they were buried at Oak Lawn Cemetery. (Photo by Karon O'Neal)

45

Horrell inside their cell. Other lynchings—and there were a great many in nineteenth-century Texas—usually were accomplished by hanging.

Between 1883 and 1898, the number of people lynched each year in the United States easily surpassed the annual total of legal executions. During the two decades between 1882 and 1903, 3,337 people were lynched. More than half of those executions were racial murders in the South, but most of the rest were vigilante actions directed against western troublemakers. During the midst of this vigilante heyday, eleven Sicilians were lynched in New Orleans on March 14, 1891, a spectacular incident that attracted national headlines at the very time that the vigilante action in Johnson County was being contemplated.[5]

It is not coincidental that extralegal activities marked labor relations during this period. Poorly paid workers, who toiled for interminable hours under harsh conditions, began to organize unions and resort to strikes. Between 1881 and 1906, the nation experienced 38,000 strikes. Faced with economic disruption, captains of industry frequently resorted to strikebreakers, which often caused rioting. Miners often used available explosives in defending themselves, helping to label this period of labor relations the "dynamite era." Early in 1892 miners went on strike at the lead and silver mines at Couer D'Alene, Idaho. Faced with strikebreakers, the miners loaded an ore car with one hundred pounds of dynamite and rolled it toward their antagonists, inflicting more than twenty casualties. Federal troops intervened in July—three months after the U.S. Cavalry intervened in Johnson County, Wyoming. Also in July 1892, striking laborers at the Carnegie Steel works in Homestead, Pennsylvania, battled three hundred Pinkerton "detectives." The private army of detectives was driven away, but a few days later the governor sent the state militia into Homestead and the strike was broken by non-union

Federal troops intervene in the Pullman strike at Chicago in 1894, two years after U.S. cavalrymen rescued the Invaders at the TA Ranch. (Courtesy Library of Congress)

On the Road Again

A decade after the Johnson County War, Casper vigilantes took it upon themselves to hang a troublemaker and then pinned a revealing jingle to the dangling corpse:

> Process of law is a little slow
> So this is the road you'll have to go.
> Murderers and thieves, Beware!
> PEOPLE'S VERDICT

workers who were protected by militia. The Johnson County War, featuring a private army and violent resistance, was very much part of the spirit of the times.

By the time of the Johnson County War, Wyoming citizens had been resorting to extralegal justice for nearly a quarter of a century. When the railroad reached Wyoming in 1867, frontier disorder quickly compelled vigilante response. A series of stranglings at Bear River City, a typical railroad "Hell on Wheels," resulted in the arrest of three suspects, who promptly were taken from jail and hanged. When other local criminals rioted, citizens drove them out of town, then requested a military force from Fort Bridger. In 1868 in Laramie more than four hundred citizens organized a vigilante movement that executed seven criminals. In 1868 and 1869 about two hundred people banded together to battle lawless elements in Cheyenne, a movement producing sixteen executions. Malcolm Campbell, a future sheriff who would support the Johnson County Invasion, arrived in Cheyenne just in time to witness four vigilante hangings. "Undoubtedly," he reminisced, "these incidents went far in shaping those trails of danger where I was later to apprehend some of the most dangerous outlaws of the plains."[6]

In 1881 George "Big Nose" Parrott, a notorious rustler, train robber and killer, was lynched in Rawlins. Dr. John E. Osborne, a young railroad physician who would win a two-year term as governor of Wyoming in 1902, skinned the corpse, tanned the skin, and made a death mask of Parrott. Pieces of the outlaw's skin, along with the top of his skull and other Parrott souvenirs, were displayed in various places for decades afterward. Following a brutal murder near Cheyenne in 1883, the killer was captured and jailed in the capital. Unopposed by the sheriff, vigilantes forced the cell door, then took the murderer outside and hanged him from a telegraph pole.

With typical frontier pragmatism, Wyoming community leaders repeatedly organized vigilante groups. Justice beyond the law met with general approval in Wyoming, as in most other sections of the United States. Furthermore, many Wyoming cattlemen, with roots in the East, felt a kinship to captains of industry who battled labor disruptions by hiring private armies of strikebreakers. Certainly there was a long-established pattern of confronting frontier outlawry—including livestock theft—with extralegal force.

For a recent solution to rustling that was congenial to their natural inclinations, Wyoming cattlemen had to look no farther than Montana's open-range country, less than three hundred miles north of Johnson County. Early cattle ranching in Montana was centered in the mountain valleys of the western part of the territory. But Montana pioneer Granville Stuart led a movement to place cattle on the rich grasslands to the east. In 1879 Stuart became managing partner of the DHS Ranch, and he located the new enterprise at the base of the Judith Mountains, well to the east of any previous Montana ranch. Soon, however, numerous other ranchers moved into the region, and within two years 600,000 cattle grazed on the suddenly crowded ranges.

By 1883 the open-range spreads were plagued by cattle and horse thieves. Near the DHS, Stuart "discovered one rancher whose cows invariably had twin calves and frequently triplets, while the range cows in that vicinity were nearly all barren and would persist in hanging around this man's corral." Stuart and other cattlemen visited the ranch and threatened "to hang the man if his cows had any more twins."[7]

In Miles City on April 20, 1884, 429 cattlemen attended the second annual meeting of the Montana Stockgrowers Association. There was a strong sentiment "to make the penalty for stealing so severe that it would lose its attraction." Two ranchers from western Dakota Territory, the Marquis de Mores (an ambitious Frenchman) and Easterner Theodore Roosevelt, vigorously urged "a rustler's war."[8]

Stuart counseled a less obvious approach. "I openly opposed any such move and pointed out to them that the 'rustlers' were strongly fortified, each of their cabins being

At the 1884 meeting of the Montana Stockgrowers Association, Dakota rancher Theodore Roosevelt—Harvard classmate of Owen Wister—urged "a rustler's war." (Courtesy Roosevelt Nature and History Association, Medora, N.D.)

48

a miniature fortress." Stuart went on to warn that "every man of them was a desperado and a dead shot," and that a fight would result in heavy casualties, along with murder trials for the death of any suspects. Although many younger ranchers still wanted to raid the rustlers, the association voted to take no action.[9]

But Stuart and other determined ranchers were cleverly setting up the rustlers, while avoiding any public commitment to violent activities. Learning that the association had decided not to make any decisive move, the "jubilant" rustlers "returned to their favorite haunts and settled down to what promised to be an era of undisturbed and successful operations."[10]

The thieves were busy on unsupervised ranges during the association's roundup, but they were being watched by stock detectives. These men met at Stuart's cabin on the DHS after the close of the spring roundup. Although Stuart's role in subsequent events is hazy, the fourteen vigilantes who sallied forth became known as "Stuart's Stranglers."

On June 25 two rustlers stole seven horses from the string of a cowboy working for J. A. Wells. Rancher Bill Thompson gave chase, fatally wounding one thief, then capturing the other man after a chase of six miles. Incarcerated in a stable, the rustler was seized by vigilantes that night and hanged.

On July 3 word reached the DHS that rustler Sam McKenzie had been sighted nearby with two stolen horses. The entire DHS crew was mobilized, and soon a bound McKenzie was brought to the bunkhouse. After dark he was taken out and hanged, and the next day the swaying corpse was "the center of an admiring concourse of flies."[11]

After hearing of McKenzie's lynching, two other rustlers rode into Lewiston (several miles south of DHS headquarters) the next day, arrogantly spoiling for trouble with Fourth of July celebrants. Red Owen and Rattlesnake Jake Fallon drunkenly ignited a shootout in Lewiston's only street. One citizen was killed and another wounded, but both outlaws were gunned down by an angry populace. Before the shooting stopped, Rattlesnake Jake had been hit more than nine times, while Red Owen took eleven wounds, "any one of which would have proved fatal."[12]

On that Fourth of July, the "vigilance committee" divided into two groups and sought out more desperados. One group confronted rustlers Billy Downs and California Ed at their hideout at the confluence of the Missouri and Musselshell rivers. Evidence at the hideout included butchered meat, a pile of fresh cowhides, and twenty-six horses with familiar brands. Downs and California Ed were hanged in a grove of cottonwoods. The second group of vigilantes found Brocky Gallagher and Red Mike driving a stolen band of horses across the Missouri River. After a ten-mile chase, they were overtaken and hanged.

The vigilantes then decided to assault the principal outlaw stronghold on the Missouri, fifteen miles east of the Musselshell. A large log cabin, loopholed for defense, sat adjacent to a stable and corral, and a tent made of wagon covers was located one hundred yards away beside the riverbank. On the night of July 8 five vigilantes surrounded the cabin and three others covered the tent, while a ninth man held the horses. The vigilantes opened fire at dawn, when a man emerged from the cabin. Six desperados scrambled out of the tent: one escaped clean; the "boss outlaw," John Stringer, was cornered and went down fighting; and four men concealed themselves in the brush, later to fashion a log raft and drift downriver. The five men inside the cabin resisted stoutly, until the building was set ablaze. As the outlaws burst out of the burning cabin, they were shot down.

The next morning the four men on the raft were captured by the military, then turned over to a deputy U.S. marshal. However, at the mouth of the Musselshell a party of masked vigilantes took the prisoners from the deputy. Two log cabins stood nearby, only a few feet apart. A log was placed between the cabins, supported by each roof, and the four rustlers were hanged from the log. Then the cabins "caught fire" and burned to the ground, cremating the four corpses.

Nineteen rustlers had been killed, and stock theft in the area declined immediately. The vigilantes deliberately kept their identities obscure, but they were dubbed "Stuart's Stranglers," and Stuart was elected next president of the Montana Stockgrowers Association. "Once I heard a woman accuse him of hanging thirty innocent men," related Stuart's son-in-law Teddy Blue Abbott. "He raised his hat to her and said, 'Yes madam, and by God, I done it alone.'" [14]

Granville Stuart, noted Montana pioneer and managing partner of the DHS Ranch. After "Stuart's Stranglers" executed a deadly sweep against rustlers in 1884, he was elected president of the Montana Stockgrowers Association. (Courtesy Montana Historical Society, Helena)

Stuart had not done it alone. He later wrote that there were fourteen vigilantes, "and they were all men who had stock on the range and who had suffered at the hands of the thieves." Stuart insisted that not a single victim "was hanged for a first offense," and he scoffed at talk that cattlemen had hired "'gunmen' to ... drive the small ranchers and sheepmen off the range." [15] Other rumors exaggerated the number of lynch victims to "thirty innocent men" [16] or even more. Theodore Roosevelt praised the "clean sweep" of the "'stranglers,' [a] happy allusion to their summary method of doing justice," but he qualified his approval: "several of the sixty odd victims had been perfectly innocent men who had been hung or shot in company with the real scoundrels, either through carelessness and misapprehension or on account of some personal spite." [17] Another rancher placed the "total number of outlaws hung or shot in eastern Montana and western Dakota [at] sixty-three." [18] A cowboy employed by T. J. Bryan, president of the Montana Stockgrowers Association, liked to joke that he "was working for the Montana Assassination. They knew what I meant." [19]

Stuart bristled at accusations of imported gunmen and arrogant ranchers and innocent victims. "There was not one man taken on suspicion and not one was hanged for a first offense. The men that were taken were members of an organized band of thieves that for more than two years had evaded the law and robbed the range at will." Although Stuart described Montana cattlemen as the most "peaceable and law-abiding a body of men as could be found anywhere," they felt forced to take action because the "civil laws and courts had been tried and found wanting."[20]

Similar justifications would be offered by Wyoming cattlemen in 1892. Faced with rampant rustling and unfriendly courts, Wyoming ranchers were tempted to resort to the same extralegal solutions that had worked in nearby Montana in 1884. With a bold, coordinated strike, the Montana vigilantes broke up an epidemic of rustling, while suffering no legal repercussions. Like their Montana counterparts, a few resolute Wyoming ranchers decided to act on their own, instead of taking official action through an association.

Western historian Robert K. DeArment, who wrote about the Johnson County War in his definitive biography of Frank Canton, later emphasized "the importance of the successful Granville Stuart outlaw raid of 1884 in Montana as a blueprint for the Wyoming cattlemen eight years later." DeArment explained his viewpoint in a letter to this author: "I would go so far as to say that had there been no Stuart raid there might never have been a Johnson County War, at least in the way it developed."[21] Certainly the determined and effective operation against rustlers in 1884 was a seductive example to Wyoming ranchers a few years later. In 1892 vigilante action was not an embarrassing relic of a more violent past—it still was commonplace in the East and South, as well as in the West.

But regardless of the expectations of bold success by the Wyoming ranchers, their Johnson County Invasion would become "vigilantism's most famous failure."[22]

Chapter 6

The Killing Begins

"She had to be killed for the good of the country."
Dr. Charles B. Penrose

Murderous extralegal action was committed against two homesteaders by a lynch party of Wyoming cattlemen on Saturday, July 20, 1889. That afternoon six ranchers seized Ella Watson and Jim Averell at their adjoining homesteads along the Sweetwater River in Carbon County. Ella and Jim were taken to an isolated canyon a few miles away and brutally hanged. Their arms and legs were not tied, and they thrashed about wildly as they slowly strangled to death.

Ella usually is referred to as "Cattle Kate," a prostitute who traded her favors to cowboys for stolen cattle. Newspaperman Ed Towse, who would be one of two journalists permitted to ride with the Johnson County Invaders in 1892, wrote a pro-cattleman account of the lynching for the Cheyenne *Daily Leader*. This article appeared three days after the double hanging, on Tuesday morning, July 23, 1889. Subtitles beneath the bold headline "A DOUBLE LYNCHING" emphasized that "They were tireless Mavericks who defied the law" and "The man weakened but the woman cursed to the last." Towse called Ella "a virago" and "a holy terror."

Jim and Ella were accused of stealing cattle "on a large scale," and they were expected to "gather several hundred for shipment this fall." After ignoring several warnings to leave the country, the "thieving pair" was forcibly taken by "amateur executioners." Ella reportedly "exhausted a blasphemous vocabulary upon the visitors," and she "died with curses on her foul lips." When a posse found the dangling corpses, their "faces were discolored and shrunken tongues hung from between the swollen lips, while a film had gathered over the bulging eyes." Despite this grisly execution, "it is doubtful if any attempt will be made to punish the lynchers," concluded Towse expectantly. "They acted in self protection, feeling that the time to resort to violent measures had arrived."[1]

John Clay, who was well acquainted with the incident, insisted that Ella "was a prostitute of the lowest kind, … she was common property of the cowboys for miles around. If they could not pay the price of her virtue in cash, they agreed to brand a maverick or two for her behoof." Although Clay recognized the ultimate risk of extralegal violence, he shared the frustrations of his fellow ranchers: "This of course was a horrible piece of business, more especially the lynching of the woman, and in many ways indefensible, and yet what else are you to do? Are you to sit still and see your property ruined with no redress in sight?"[2]

Dr. Charles B. Penrose, an Easterner who would accompany the Johnson County Invaders of 1892 as surgeon, was told by his friends among the cattlemen about the lynching of 1889. "Ella Watson was known as 'Cattle Kate', and was a receiver of stolen cattle," wrote Penrose, relating the standard perspective of the big ranchers. "Ella Watson was a cowboy harlot, who took her pay in stolen cattle and yearlings. She is without shame, had a vile tongue, and was endowed with physical strength and personal courage. … She had to be killed for the good of the country."[3]

The description of "Cattle Kate" handed down to Dr. Penrose (if not his cold-blooded conclusion) became the common image of Ella Watson, and continued to be repeated decade after decade. For example, in the excellent *Reader's Encyclopedia of the American West*, published in 1977, Ella's entry is listed under "Cattle Kate." She is described as "a notorious prostitute who prospered by establishing a bawdy house in Sweetwater, Wyoming, where cattle was the medium of exchange." Furthermore, "she is known to be good with guns and a pro with a branding iron."[4] Even Helena Huntington Smith, who harbored scant sympathy for the cattlemen, stated that Ella kept "a hog ranch," and described her as "a strumpet with a vocabulary to match" and "a full-bosomed wench" who, Smith admitted grudgingly, was "Not bad-looking in a common way."[5]

But this view of Ella Watson—"Cattle Kate" the foul-mouthed whore, trading sexual favors for mavericks, good with guns and branding irons—was never universally accepted, and may have been incorrect in almost every detail.

Journalistic responses soon countered Ed Towse's Cheyenne *Daily Leader* stories and the word of mouth from large ranchers. In the Casper *Weekly Mail* of August 16, 1889, for example, two stories offered support for Jim and Ella. They were known in the area, and the writer asserted that "there is positive and convincing evidence that neither Averell nor the woman ever stole or assisted in stealing any cattle. Let it be distinctly understood that nine tenths of the people of Carbon County know that these parties were hung for another reason than that charged against them." Another story in the same issue repeated "the opinion expressed by nearly every man in that part of the country: Instead of being anything like the mythical 'Kate,' she was her exact opposite."

Some later historians also rejected "the mythical 'Kate.'" Harry Sinclair Drago, in *The Great Range Wars*, published in 1970, refused to accept the Cattle Kate image, and so did Dan Thrapp in his three-volume *Encyclopedia of Frontier Biography*, published in 1988. In 1993, George W. Hufsmith, whose great-grandparents moved to Wyoming Territory in 1874, offered a complete challenge to the traditional version in *The Wyoming Lynching of Cattle Kate, 1889.*

Hufsmith carefully presented biographical information about Ella and Jim. The first

Ella Watson in a Sunday dress straddles a horse. This pose would become the popular image of "Cattle Kate."
(Author's collection)

of ten children, Ellen Liddy Watson was born on July 2, 1861, on a farm in Canada. In 1877 the family moved to a homestead near Lebanon in north central Kansas, at the geographical center of the United States. "Ellie" (later "Ella") went to a one-room school but always spoke with the thick brogue of her parents (her father was born in Scotland, while her mother was a native of Ireland).

In 1879 Ella married homesteader Bill Pickell. But Pickell drank and beat her, and after two years she returned to her family home. A divorce was obtained in 1886. Meanwhile, she worked as a cook and domestic on a nearby farm for a couple of years. In 1883 she moved twelve miles north to Red Cloud, Nebraska, securing a job as a cook and maid at the Royal Hotel. Within a year, Ella visited a brother in Denver, then ventured north into frontier Wyoming. She found familiar employment as a cook and maid at the Rawlins House, the best hostelry in Rawlins. Ella stood five-foot-eight, tall for a woman of that day, and at 165 pounds she had a strong and buxom physique. She sported auburn hair, blue eyes, and a pleasant smile. By 1886 she had become acquainted with Jim Averell, and in May they obtained a marriage license.[6]

James Averell, like Ellen Watson, was born in Canada, on March 20, 1851. Jimmy was the youngest of seven children. The family moved south into New York State not long after Jimmy was born, but his father soon died. Within a couple of years his mother remarried, and three more children followed. When Jimmy was about thirteen, he became the ward of his sister and brother-in-law, newlyweds Sarah and Able Cole. The Coles took up farming near Eureka, Wisconsin, where Jimmy attended school. At sixteen he went to work at a sawmill near Eureka.

In 1871, when he was twenty, Jimmy left the sawmill and enlisted for a five-year hitch in the U.S. Army. Assigned to Company H of the 13th Infantry, Private Averell was sent to Fort Douglas, Utah, just outside Salt Lake City. Soon he was stationed at Fort Fred Steele, fifteen miles east of Rawlins, Wyoming. A scout at the fort was Joe Rankin, later appointed U.S. marshal in Wyoming; eventually Averell would become friends with Rankin's brothers, Robert and Jim. Private Averell campaigned against hostile warriors, before being transferred with his unit to Louisiana in 1874. He was discharged at Port Gibson, Mississippi, on May 22, 1876.

Returning to the Cole home in Wisconsin, Averell quickly became restless as a civilian. He traveled to Chicago and reenlisted on June 20, 1876. Placed in Company D of the Ninth Infantry, Averell thus returned to Wyoming, which presumably was a principal reason for his enlistment in the Ninth. Promoted to sergeant, he participated in pursuits against war parties and renegades. Sergeant Averell also was assigned to construction duties at a series of new outposts—Cantonment Reno and Depot McKinney—and then was sent to help build a telegraph line from Fort Fetterman to Fort McKinney. Stationed at Fort McKinney, Sergeant Averell bought a small house in Buffalo. Obviously he had saved his meager army pay, and he rented the house to local jailer Robert Rankin and his family. Averell reserved a room for himself, when he was in town, and for a boarder.

He was definitely in town on May 2, 1880, when he fatally wounded Charlie Johnson in a saloon. Johnson apparently threatened and provoked Averell, who fired a warning shot into the air after being called "a cowardly son of a bitch." A big, strong man,

Johnson continued to advance on his smaller opponent (Averell stood only five-foot-seven and weighed just 135 pounds). Averell lowered his aim and pumped two bullets into Johnson, who died eight days later. Averell was jailed, released on bond, then jailed again. (He was in jail in Rawlins when a lynch mob broke in to execute Big Nose George Parrott.) Finally the courts released him to military justice, although the army apparently did not court-martial him. Averell finished his second five-year hitch at Fort Fred Steele, where he was discharged on July 19, 1881. He stayed on for several months, working at the big sutler's store, then sold his house in Buffalo and returned to Wisconsin for a visit with the Coles. There he met and married Sophia Jaeger on her twenty-second birthday, February 23, 1882. Averell brought his bride to a Wyoming homestead, but within a few months their son died following a premature birth, after which Sophia became ill and died.[7]

Saddened, Averell sold his homestead and house in 1885. He filed on another homestead, fifteen miles north of his earlier spread. Averell's new home was located at a beautiful site in the Sweetwater River Valley, on the military road about fifty miles southwest of old Fort Casper. Independence Rock, one of the most famous landmarks on the Oregon Trail, stood a few miles to the northwest. Averell filed a second claim under the Desert Land Act of 1877, and he began to build irrigation ditches and fences for his vegetable gardens. One of the two log cabins he erected became a road ranch for travelers and area cowboys.

Although he shot a man dead while serving the cavalry, Jim Averell later became an industrious homesteader and postmaster. Nevertheless he was accused of rustling and was lynched. (Author's collection)

In 1886 the industrious Averell was appointed justice of the peace, notary public, and postmaster of Sweetwater.

In February 1886, when Averell went to Rawlins to file on his second claim, he encountered Ella Watson of the Rawlins House. Even though Ella was ten years younger and there was a physical mismatch, an emotional attraction quickly developed. In May the couple traveled to Lander to obtain a marriage license, although evidence of a wedding has not been found. Indeed, when Jim and Ella came together to the Sweetwater River Valley, she continued to be called Watson. George Hufsmith believes that they traveled to Lander, where they were not known, and Ella continued to use the name Watson because they wanted to file on two more government claims, which they could not do as man and wife.

Ella Liddy Watson secured land titles in Rawlins and had a one-room log cabin built, about a mile and a half from Averell's road ranch. With four claims between them, Jim and Ella held title to 640 acres. Jim completed four miles of irrigation ditches, Ella fenced in a sixty-acre pasture, and late in 1888 she bought a brand, "LU" (perhaps a brand pronunciation of "Ella"). Ella purchased a small herd of cattle, numbering between twenty-eight and forty-one, and she cooked meals for travelers at the road ranch.

Ella took in an eleven-year-old boy, Gene Crowder, who had an unfortunate family situation, while John DeCorey, about three years older, worked for her. Averell's nephew, Ralph Cole, was employed at the road ranch, and so was a seasoned hand named Frank Buchanan.[8]

George Hufsmith compiled a number of accounts from acquaintances of Jim and Ella which countered their negative image. A teamster who regularly stopped at Jim's road ranch recognized that Averell was not a rancher: "He was never accused of cattle stealing, never owned a single head." Another man pointed out that "her correct name was Ella Watson," not Cattle Kate, and she "was a very pretty woman and I can say I never seen a thing wrong with her or a bad move from her." A trail driver reminisced about arriving at the road ranch on a cold, wet night. Ella provided the crew hot coffee, blankets inside the cabin, breakfast the next morning, "and refused to take any pay." "Ella Watson was a fine looking woman," declared a neighbor. "Nobody went hungry around her." John Fales, who built her cabin, stated, "She was not only a fine appearing woman, but a good woman. Neither of them ever stole a cow. And those who say that Ella Watson slept with cow-punchers, are slandering a good woman's name." Fales praised Ella for adopting the eleven-year-old boy, and he related that she bought her first little herd of footsore calves for a dollar per head from a man headed west on the Oregon Trail. Fales drove the cattle to her place from nearby Independence Rock. "As for her rustling cattle," emphasized Fales, "she didn't."[9]

In addition to establishing a reputation for honesty, generosity, and hospitality for Jim and Ella, Hufsmith explored the origins of the "Cattle Kate" myth. Hufsmith theorized that various cattlemen and newspaperman Ed Towse darkened the reputation of Ella Watson by deliberately confusing her identity with two contemporary women of loose virtue:[10]

> *Ella Wilson* was an illiterate prostitute who was wounded in a wild shootout at the notorious bawdy house at Fetterman in 1884. The attending physician incorrectly recorded her name as Ella "Watson," and she was mentioned in the story of the gunfight in Towse's newspaper, the Cheyenne *Daily Leader*.
>
> *Kate Maxwell* was a madame who had been an entertainer in Chicago and who ran a bawdy house in Bessemer, a little community about ten miles south of Casper. She had shot a man fatally, had robbed a faro dealer, and she often consorted with rustlers, which earned her the nickname "Cattle Kate."

The day after first reporting the lynching of Jim and Ella, Ed Towse fired off another article slandering the victims. The Cheyenne *Daily Leader* of July 24, 1889, identified Ella as Cattle Kate Maxwell, "a poor tramp of the worst type." Formerly "a Chicago variety actress," after relocating to Wyoming she "simply revolutionized ranch life." She maintained bulldogs which fought coyotes and wolves, and she had a stable of racehorses. "A couple of her jockeys were fleet of foot and they were matched against Indian sprinters, defeating the red man with ease." On another occasion, Indians angry over being "fleeced" had to be driven away "with the loss of several braves." Kate supposedly poisoned her husband, Maxwell, but then suffered the theft of their horses and cattle.

When "a colored boy made away with Kate's diamonds," she shot him and recovered her jewelry. But having lost the Maxwell gambling den and livestock, she joined up with Jim Averell to create another frontier dive.

Thus Ella Watson became "Cattle Kate," a fictional hybrid of Kate Maxwell and Ella Wilson. But Ella Watson of Kansas and Nebraska and the Rawlins House had never been called "Kate" or "Cattle Kate" or "Kate Maxwell." She did not have a pack of fighting bulldogs, a stable of racehorses, nor diamond jewelry. She had never poisoned a husband nor shot anyone. She was not a gambler, a prostitute, or a cattle thief. Likewise, Jim Averell was never suspected of stealing livestock. He was serious about his duties as justice of the peace and postmaster, and he worked diligently to improve his property.

That property, although legally acquired, would trigger the lynching of Jim and Ella. Their claims, totaling 640 acres and including fencing and irrigation ditches, stood in the middle of a big pasture that had been pre-empted by an open-range rancher named Albert Bothwell.

Born in 1855 in Iowa, Bothwell moved west as a young man. He first tried his luck in California, before venturing into Colorado in 1880, then Wyoming three years later. Locating a ranching operation in the Sweetwater River Valley, Bothwell ran cattle over a vast range. He identified immediately with the cattlemen who were Wyoming's most influential men. Bothwell liked to wear a red hunting jacket, unaware that his cowboys called him "Little Red Vest." An ambitious promoter, Bothwell tried to launch gold and oil and irrigation schemes, and he attempted to sell town lots beside his ranch headquarters. (Modestly he named his town "Bothwell," but a community did not materialize.) Although he had been ranching in the valley only a couple of years when Averell showed up with a government claim, he considered the industrious homesteader an interloper. Averell's second 160-acre claim was awarded in adjacent forty-acre parcels along Horse Creek, a little tributary of the Sweetwater that was controlled by the claims of Jim and Ella.[11]

Confident and well established in his new home, Jim Averell would not be intimidated by Bothwell or any other cattlemen. On February 7, 1889, he wrote a lengthy letter to the editor of the Casper *Weekly Mail* criticizing "the Sweetwater land-grabbers," with pointed references to Bothwell and Robert Galbraith. Galbraith was born in 1844 in England, but immigrated with his family to the United States when he was five. Raised in Illinois, he moved on to Wyoming in 1867 as a locomotive engineer with the Union Pacific. Within two years he was head of the railroad yards in Laramie. But in 1870 he left the Union Pacific to pursue mining interests in the region of the Sweetwater River Valley. In 1884 he was elected to the upper house of the Wyoming Territorial Legislature.[12]

In clashing with Albert Bothwell and Robert Galbraith, Jim Averell aroused other powerful, self-made men. Another area cattleman, John Henry Durbin, bristled at the presence and attitude of the homesteader. Like Galbraith, Durbin arrived at Wyoming in the late 1860s. Born in Pennsylvania in 1842, he served as a Union officer in the Civil War (he liked his cowboys to call him "Captain"), and, after farming in Indiana and suffering the death of two wives, remarried and opened a butcher shop in Cheyenne. With the help of two brothers, he began to build a ranching empire. The Durbins also made a small fortune with mining investments around Deadwood. A charter member of the WSGA, John Durbin served for a time as a cattle inspector. Like many other cattlemen

Devil's Gate, with Tom Sun's Hub and Spoke Ranch in the foreground. The Sweetwater River runs through Devil's Gate, a landmark on the nearby Oregon Trail. A few miles away, Jim Averell and Ella Watson were lynched by Tom Sun and other ranchers. (Photo by Jim Browning)

across the West, he expanded his herd with the help of cowboy-rustlers, specifically a trio of Texans: Tom Collins (Durbin's foreman, until he was blacklisted by the WSGA), Nate Young, and Clabe Young.[13]

Clabe Young also would work as foreman of Tom Sun's Hub and Spoke Ranch, located in the shadow of Independence Rock. Tom Sun moved to Wyoming as a boy, working with a trapper in the 1850s. Born Thomas de Beau Soliel in Vermont in 1846, his French-Canadian name later was Anglicized. When he was eleven, Tom's mother died and he left home for the West. In St. Louis he was taken in tow by a mountain man who had been trapping in Wyoming since the 1830s. Tom's apprenticeship taught him sign language and Indian tongues, as well as hunting and trapping skills. He trapped furs and prospected in Wyoming until 1869, then worked as an army scout and a hunting guide. He built his first ranch on the Sweetwater in 1872. If anyone might resent a Johnny-Come-Lately homesteader, it could be Wyoming pioneer Tom Sun.[14]

Two other Sweetwater Valley ranchers proved capable of drastic action. The first, forty-year-old Bob Conner, a native of Pennsylvania, had begun his Lazy UC Ranch in 1881 and had served on the Executive Committee of the WSGA for the period 1884-87. Suspected of building his herd illegally, Conner employed two successive foremen who were notorious rustlers. The second, Ernie McLean, had a small dairy spread, the EM Bar Ranch, which featured 150 purebred Durham milk cows and a few beef cattle.[15]

On Saturday morning, July 20, a stock detective brought word to Albert Bothwell about the small herd of freshly branded cattle in Ella Watson's pasture. The scruffy

Tom Sun's hat, chaps, and saddle on display in the Carbon County Museum in Rawlings. (Photo by Jim Browning)

calves wearing Ella's new LU brand might have been construed as mavericks which had just been branded so that they could be moved and sold. Bothwell hastily sent word for his neighboring ranchers to meet in his former hay pasture, now the property of Jim Averell. John Durbin, Robert Galbraith, Bob Conner, and Ernie McLean soon rode up, while Tom Sun arrived driving a buggy. Bothwell angrily accused Ella and Jim of gathering and branding mavericks, urging his friends to accompany him for an impromptu inspection of the little herd in Ella's enclosed pasture. Tom Sun and one of the other men reportedly expressed opposition, but reluctantly tagged along.[16]

At Ella's cabin they found only her eleven-year-old ward, Gene Crowder. When the ranchers examined her cattle, they became agitated, and John Durbin furiously began dismantling her barbed wire fence. Gene Crowder came out to protest but was threatened. Ella soon walked back to the cabin with young John DeCorey, and immediately she was accused of cattle theft.

Ella responded that she had bought the livestock from a westbound traveler on the Oregon Trail and that she had deposited the bill of sale in the bank in Rawlins. She was not believed and was ordered into the buggy. Bothwell threatened to tie her to the vehicle and drag her to death. Little Gene Crowder vaulted onto his pony and tried to ride for help, but the boy was thrown to the ground by Bothwell. The ranchers shoved Ella into Tom Sun's buggy, then proceeded on until encountering Averell at his gate, preparing to drive a wagon to Casper to buy supplies for his store. Caught unarmed, he was forced at rifle point into the buggy. Several witnesses saw part of these events from a distance.

Gene Crowder and John DeCorey raced to the road ranch. There they found Ralph Cole and Frank Buchanan. Cole saddled up and rode to the nearby Bothwell ranch for help, but soon returned empty-handed. Buchanan strapped on his gunbelt and trailed the buggy and riders.

Meanwhile, the lynching procession traveled southwesterly up the riverbed for about five miles, before struggling into a rocky canyon called Spring Creek Gulch. Halting a few hundred yards into the little canyon, Bothwell threw his lariat across the limb of a pine tree, then tightened a noose around Averell's neck. While Jim shouted their innocence, Ernie McLean tossed his lariat across the same limb, then struggled to place a noose over Ella's head. Jim and Ella finally were manhandled onto a boulder.

By this time Frank Buchanan had dismounted and climbed into the rocks to a vantage point about fifty yards away. Seeing what was about to happen, he desperately opened fire with his revolver and managed to hit John Durbin in the hip. Buchanan was answered with rifle fire, but gamely he reloaded and squeezed off six more rounds.

During this uneven duel—rifles vs. a sixgun—Bothwell and McLean shoved their victims off the boulder. They dropped only a couple of feet, not enough to break their necks. Their legs and arms had not been tied, so they struggled wildly to save themselves. As the supple limb bent downward, their death throes gradually lessened. Outgunned and outnumbered, Buchanan was forced to retreat to his horse, then gallop away from the canyon. The killers also departed the canyon, leaving behind Jim and Ella, faces grotesquely distorted, swinging from a bent limb.

Although it was late afternoon when Frank Buchanan emerged from the canyon, he reined his horse toward the Oregon Trail. Determined to find law officers, he rode northeast toward Casper, fifty-five miles away. Buchanan pushed thirty miles through the night, until arriving at the log cabin of E. J. "Tex" Healy at about three o'clock in the morning. Exhausted, Buchanan roused Healy from his bed and blurted out his awful tale. Healy demanded that Buchanan go to bed, while he caught a fresh horse and finished the ride to Casper. Arriving on Sunday, Healy found Deputy Sheriff Phil Watson (who was unrelated to Ella Watson). Watson deputized a posse and set out for the scene of the crime.

Watson and his men arrived at Jim Averell's road ranch a couple of hours after midnight. The boys were there asleep, along with Frank Buchanan, who had ridden back from Tex Healy's after a few hours of rest. Although his posse was tired after their forced ride, Watson insisted on proceeding to the murder site. Buchanan found two kerosene lanterns, saddled up, then led the posse to Spring Creek Gulch. After an hour's ride, moonlight and lantern light revealed the corpses, which had been dangling from the pine tree for two nights and a day. The bodies, with hideously twisted faces, were cut down and taken back to Averell's place.

A Casper attorney and justice of the peace conducted a coroner's inquest. Frank Buchanan and Gene Crowder testified, and it was officially stated that Jim Averell and Ella Watson were hanged by Albert Bothwell, Robert Conner, John Durbin, Robert Galbraith, Earnest McLean, and Tom Sun. A large grave was dug southeast of the road ranch cabin, and Jim and Ella were buried beside each other.

Deputy Watson led the posse to Tom Sun's nearby ranch. Sun "admitted he was one of the lynchers and readily gave the name of the others." He also related that John Durbin had been wounded in the hip. The lawman took Sun into custody, then rode on to round up the others who had been named. Bothwell also openly admitted his participation, and threatened Buchanan and Healy with the same fate "if they did not leave the country." Bothwell then belligerently warned Deputy Watson that on the way back to Casper "he would be likely to find six or eight more cattle rustlers hanging by the neck."[17] Only John Durbin was not taken into custody. Durbin had left the ranch to seek medical help for his wound, and soon he was recuperating at his handsome home in Cheyenne, where he remained untroubled by the law.

Deputy Watson took his five prisoners to Rawlins and delivered them to Sheriff

Frank Hadsell. By this time the Cheyenne *Daily Leader* had commenced the journalistic campaign to brand Jim Averell as a rustler and "Cattle Kate" as a prostitute. Furthermore, the WSGA and individual cattlemen surely were beginning to exert influence behind the scenes. A makeshift court was assembled in a stable. There were no witnesses for the prosecution, and the offense was labeled manslaughter instead of murder. Manslaughter being a bailable offense, the accused men were freed on $5,000 bail—and were even permitted to post bail for each other. Following these questionable legalities, they left Rawlins and rode back to their ranches. A second inquest was quickly convened, with the conclusion that the deceased were executed by unknown parties. Concurrently, and presumably upon the advice of legal counsel, the five ranchers recanted their earlier admissions of guilt.

Although various newspapers began to challenge the accusations against Jim and Ella, witnesses to the events of July 20 soon sensed menace. Manslaughter? Bail? Unidentified parties? It seemed clear that the type of men who lynched Jim and Ella, the type of men who controlled Wyoming, had taken charge of matters. If witnesses were not present to testify, no legal action was possible, and the type of men who would lynch women would have no reservations about bribing—or killing—witnesses.

Ralph Cole remained at the Averell road ranch in the weeks following the lynching. But the twenty-year-old began to suffer symptoms of some mysterious malady, and on September 9, 1889—less than two months after the lynching—the young man died. There were strong rumors that strychnine had been slipped into his medicine. The day after Cole died, Phil Watson was arrested on charges of horse theft. Shortly after the cattlemen he had arrested were released, Watson wisely left the area and became city marshal of Sundance, in northeastern Wyoming. But he and a man named Jess Lockwood were taken into custody, and ten days later Tex Healy also was arrested for the same offense. All these men were convicted and sentenced to prison. Gene Crowder and John DeCorey disappeared. Reportedly Gene soon died, and rumor held that he, too, had been poisoned.[18]

In October a twelve-man grand jury was convened in Rawlins to rule on the original accusations against the five cattlemen. An excellent legal team was assembled to defend the ranchers—a process that would be duplicated in 1892. The prosecution's key witness was Frank Buchanan, who was placed under a $5,000 bond. But Buchanan's friends among the homesteaders raised $500, and he was—perhaps unwisely—released from custody. Buchanan was seen in the company of cattlemen, which led some to believe that he had been bribed. It was rumored that he was given a great sum and sent to the British Isles. But it was also rumored that he was murdered. When a skeleton was discovered nine miles north of Rawlins a few years later, the knot in a surviving bandana convinced many that the remains were those of Frank Buchanan. Dr. Charles Penrose related what he was told by cattlemen about this mystery: "It was said that a man named Buchanan, who ... was the only witness, had to be put out of the way so that he might not testify."[19] Asa Mercer wrote that he "was hunted like a wild beast, and as he failed to appear before the grand jury, and has never been seen or heard from ... , the supposition is that he sleeps beneath the sod in some lonely mountain gorge."[20] In any event, when Buchanan forfeited his bail and vanished, the prosecution's case effectively was

Owen Wister Meets a Good Solid Citizen

In the fall of 1889, Owen Wister visited Wyoming for the fourth time. After his initial stay with Frank Wolcott in 1885, he returned in 1887, 1888, and 1889. In 1887 Wister had ventured all the way to the West Coast, traveling through Canada, the Pacific Northwest, and California, before hunting in the Yellowstone region (he killed a grizzly at Jackson Hole). In 1888 he traveled by train to Rawlins, then headed northwest by stagecoach 140 miles to Fort Washakie, from where he would commence another hunting expedition. He repeated this itinerary in 1889.

On October 11, 1889, he rode the train from Cheyenne to Rawlins. In the smoking car he gravitated, as usual, to a fellow member of the upper class. This cattleman provided Wister a firsthand connection with the highly publicized lynching and its aftermath. On October 12, at a stop on the stagecoach route from Rawlins toward Fort Washakie, Wister recorded the encounter:

> Sat yesterday in smoking car with one of the gentlemen indicted for lynching the man and the woman. He seemed a good solid citizen and I hope he'll get off. Sheriff Donell said "All good folks say it was a good job; it's only the wayward classes that complain."

Wister heard the sheriff's name incorrectly. It was Sheriff Hadsell, not Donell, and the officer proved by actions, as well as words, that, like many other public officials, he sympathized openly with the cattlemen. Wister's train companion probably was John Durbin, because in mid-October he was the only member of the lynch gang who would have been free to make the trip from Rawlins to Cheyenne and back on a regular basis.

The "wayward classes" seethed when the "good solid citizens," as Wister hoped, "got off." The lynching of Jim and Ella helped set the stage for class warfare in Johnson County.

ended, and the accused cattlemen soon were no-billed by the grand jury. (In 1892 key witnesses to violent events of the Johnson County War would also disappear, and the rumor was that they had been bribed or murdered.)

But the accused ranchers—as well as cattlemen in general—were stigmatized for killing a woman. Even the Cheyenne *Daily Leader* article that launched the journalistic assault on Jim and Ella closed with an unintentionally damning one-sentence paragraph: "This is the first hanging of a woman in Wyoming." She would remain the only woman ever to be executed in Wyoming.

Ironically, twenty years before Ella was lynched, Wyoming women became the first in the United States to be granted the right to vote, hold office, and serve on juries. In addition, it was customary for men in range country to treat women courteously. The hanging of Ella Watson brought widespread journalistic criticism upon Wyoming. Even newspapers which accepted the "Cattle Kate" image remained critical of the lynching of a female, whatever her shortcomings. And throughout Wyoming, homesteaders—grangers and nesters and small operators of every label—were incensed that two of their own had been summarily executed, and the executioners had utilized wealth and influence and high-handed methods to elude justice. Although none of the rancher-executioners was directly involved in the Johnson County War of 1892, their murderous action and subsequent acquittal in 1889 was a significant step toward a more violent confrontation. The summary execution of accused rustlers, with a subsequent escape from consequences, further emboldened Wyoming cattlemen, while the growing resentment of homesteaders was fueled to combative levels.

Even though the members of the lynch gang escaped legal consequences, it was not as easy to evade public disapproval and, perhaps, private demons. Ernie McLean, who had jammed a noose around Ella's neck and shoved her off the boulder to her doom, soon sold his EM Bar dairy ranch and dropped out of sight. Rancher-politician Robert Galbraith also sold out quickly and moved away from Wyoming. The sale price of his large operation helped him to become a prominent banker in Little Rock, and he died in Arkansas in 1939 at the age of ninety-five. Bob Conner likewise sold his Lazy UC Ranch for a good price and moved away from Wyoming. Returning to his native Pennsylvania, Conner became noted for his philanthropy. He died in 1921 at seventy-two.[21]

In 1891 John Durbin became the fourth member of the lynch gang to sell his ranch and leave Wyoming, even though he had been appointed a member of the Executive Committee of the WSGA a year earlier, not long after the lynching. Moving his family to Denver, he opened a chain of slaughterhouses and long was associated with Francis E. Warren and Joseph M. Carey. Durbin died in 1907 at sixty-four. But Tom Sun, a Wyoming pioneer since before the Civil War, refused to leave his home. He stayed on the Sweetwater, dying at sixty-five in 1909, and the Hub and Spoke remains in family hands.

Albert Bothwell, who instigated the lynching, also refused to leave the ranch he had killed to maintain. Indeed, he quickly acquired through extralegal means the 640 acres claimed by Jim and Ella, and Bothwell and Durbin took possession of her small herd of cattle. In 1889 Bothwell, like Tom Sun, was appointed to the WSGA Executive Committee. Bothwell served until 1902, while Sun remained a committee member until his death in 1909. Aware of the animosity against him, Bothwell habitually took careful precautions, and Tom Sun appeared to be his only friend in Wyoming. There was a family home in Los Angeles, where his wife spent most of her time. The house-keeper was a lovely young lady who presented Bothwell with twin daughters. A divorce resulted, then Bothwell married his housekeeper, who later gave him another daughter and son. He finally sold his ranch holdings in 1916 and moved permanently to California, where he died in 1928 at seventy-two.[22]

The year following the lynching, another par-ticipant was shot to death. George B. Henderson had been employed as a stock detective by John Clay, who found him to be "a most fascinating man." Henderson had worked for the Pinkerton Detective Agency, had traveled to South America to apprehend "a famous criminal," and had been involved in the Molly Maguire labor difficulties. "He was a born sleuth," testified Clay, "and it had become the mania of his life. He would rather hunt a thief than eat. He had no thought of fear. It was left out of his make-up." Henderson hounded rustlers who preyed on Clay's vast ranch, hauling one horse thief back from Idaho. "The bad men began to disintegrate under his watchfulness from our outfit," stated Clay, "but they hired off to other parts of the country."[23]

Noted cattleman John Clay served as WSGA president during the Johnson County War. Clay hired George Henderson as a stock detective, but in 1890 he was killed by rustlers. (Author's collection)

Historian George Hufsmith believes that Henderson was the stock detective who checked the cattle in Ella Watson's pasture on the morning of the lynching. After relating his information to Albert Bothwell, Henderson would have had to ride hard fifty miles to Rawlins, then catch a train to Cheyenne, another 150 miles. Ed Towse reported on July 23, 1889, in his initial *Daily Leader* story about the lynching, that George B. Henderson, "who happened to be in the capital," had received a telegram from Rawlins with news of the fatal event. Henderson presumably was interviewed by Towse and by reporters from other newspapers. All that John Clay, his employer, would say was that although "Henderson was not a party directly to this business, he was indi-rectly connected to it."[24]

Henderson was killed by John Tregoning in 1890. Acting as foreman for John Clay's Seventy-One Quarter Circle ranch, Henderson fired Tregoning, who was labeled "a rustler" by Clay. When the story was related to Owen Wister the following year, he was told that Henderson had run off several rustlers. But when Henderson later entered his cabin unarmed, six of these men were waiting for him, and "he was shot through the heart." Tregoning was tried and convicted of second-degree murder. Although sen-tenced to life in prison, Tregoning "escaped through the influence of the jailer's daugh-ter," according to Clay.[25]

But the violence had only begun. During 1891 and 1892, Wyoming would suffer an escalation of shootings, ambushes, another lynching, and vigilante action on a far larger scale. Like their 1889 counterparts, cattlemen in 1891 and 1892 determined to protect their interests boldly, confident to the point of arrogance in their ability to control events. As in 1889, excellent lawyers would be engaged, witnesses would disappear, and extralegal violence would be employed at every level that was deemed necessary.

Chapter 7

The Troubles of 1891

"It is believed the same fiend killed both men. ... "
BUFFALO *BULLETIN*, DECEMBER 10, 1891

Owen Wister returned to Wyoming in June 1891 for his fifth visit since 1885. He spent a week at the TTT Ranch in Johnson County, forty-four miles south of Buffalo. Wister's host was Bob Tisdale, whose brother John was a state senator and a partner in the ranch. Both Bob and John Tisdale would ride with the Johnson County Invaders the following year.

For a few days Wister enjoyed the company of his host. Then, while they were riding together, Tisdale began to curse his tiring horse. He kicked and beat the animal, then gouged out an eye. Horrified, Wister soon learned that Tisdale was notorious for his cruelty to horses, especially for his disgusting habit of gouging out their eyes. Wister soon departed the TTT, riding to Buffalo with cattleman Chester Morris, who pointed out the site where he had last seen George Henderson before he was killed the previous year. Morris also talked about Frank Canton, following a chance encounter with the lean lawman. "Very quiet," observed Wister about Canton. "Very even voice. Does less shooting than any officer in his position, but is feared by all hands."

Wister enjoyed the hospitality of the officers of Fort McKinney. He found the scenery stunning, going into "ecstasies over the sunrise," and he decided that Buffalo was a cut above most hardscrabble Wyoming towns. After a week Wister and Morris left Buffalo, but during the past fortnight the writer had recorded rich experiences in his journal. In Cheyenne Wister visited Dr. Charles Penrose, a fellow Philadelphian, and other friends, then journeyed with them to northwestern Wyoming for hunting and sightseeing in Yellowstone.[1]

Penrose would ride with the Johnson County Invaders the following spring. By this time Wister had met in Wyoming, or had previously known in the East, numerous participants in the forthcoming Johnson County War, including Penrose, the Tisdale broth-

Eastern Wyoming, 1891–92

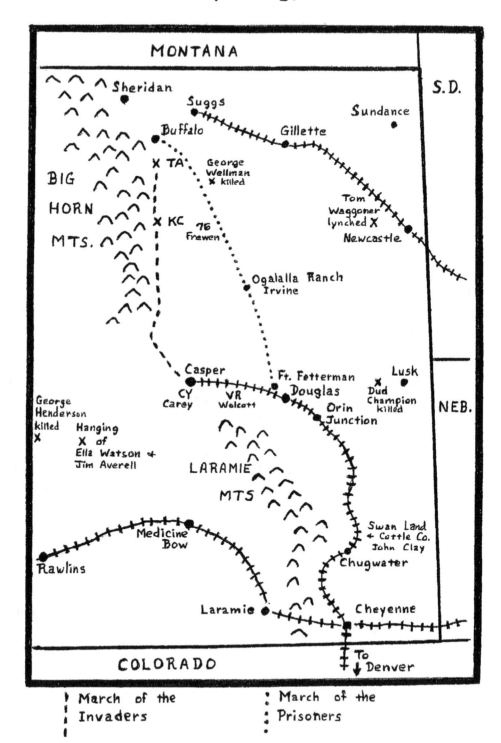

MONTANA

S.D.

^ ^ ^ Sheridan

Suggs

Sundance

^ ^ ^ Buffalo

Gillette

BIG

HORN

MTS.

X TA

George
Wellman
X killed

Tom
Waggoner
lynched X

Newcastle

X KC

76
Frewen

Ogalalla Ranch
Irvine

Casper

Lusk

CY
Carey

VR
Wolcott

Ft. Fetterman
Douglas

Dud
Champion
killed

NEB.

George
Henderson
killed
X

Hanging
X of
Ella Watson +
Jim Averell

Orin
Junction

LARAMIE

MTS

Medicine
Bow

Swan Land
+ Cattle Co.
John Clay

Rawlins

Chugwater

Laramie

Cheyenne

COLORADO

To
↓ Denver

March of the
Invaders

March of the
Prisoners

ers, Frank Canton, Frank Wolcott, William C. Irvine, Fred Hesse, Hubert E. Teschemacher, Frederick O. de Billier, and Acting Governor Amos W. Barber. Wister identified and sympathized with such men, as proved by entries in his diaries and by his later publicized fiction, most notably *The Virginian*.

The same month that Wister arrived in Wyoming, June 1891, another lynching occurred. Soon after Wister departed in September to return to Philadelphia, a series of shootings erupted. During this round of violence in 1891, Frank Canton would become even more "feared by all hands" than Wister had suggested.

Thomas J. Waggoner, widely regarded as a horse rustler, was lynched near his home on June 4, 1891. Tom Waggoner had moved to Wyoming in the late 1880s from his family home in Nebraska City, Nebraska. He started an isolated horse ranch about twenty miles west of Newcastle in eastern Wyoming, and rapidly prospered. He kept upwards of 1,000 horses in fenced pastures, was known to carry $1,000 or more in cash, and had bank deposits totaling at least $17,000. Waggoner shared his two-room log cabin with Rosa Chuler and their son and daughter. On April 11, 1891, when their little girl was one month old, Tom and Rosa were married.[2]

Waggoner's prosperity was generally attributed to stock theft, and many thought that his spread was a relay ranch for a large gang of horse rustlers which operated across several states.

During 1891 Thomas G. Smith suffered considerably from horse theft. He held a U.S. deputy marshal's commission, but he had tried to establish two stagecoach lines, including one into Buffalo. Smith lost a great deal of money, partially due to horse theft, and it was easy to blame Tom Waggoner.

In addition to Thomas G. Smith, Tom Waggoner aroused the ire of another dangerous man. Joe Elliott, a deputy sheriff of Weston County, also was a stock detective hired by the WSGA to engage in lethal actions against rustlers. But Elliott's problem with Waggoner was personal. In the spring of 1891 a team of Elliott's horses had disappeared. The animals returned wearing Waggoner's brand. Elliott investigated, learning from some of Waggoner's cowboys when and where his horses were rebranded. Elliott soon encountered Waggoner in a saloon at Merino, a little end-of-track town twenty miles north of Waggoner's ranch. Trying to provoke gunplay, Elliott slapped Waggoner in the face with his hat. Waggoner wisely refused to be provoked, and Elliott angrily uttered a threat.[3]

In early June, Deputy Sheriff Joe Elliott picked up a prisoner in Buffalo and rode east with him to-

WSGA stock detective Joe Elliott played a leading role in the 1891 hanging of suspected rustler Tom Waggoner. (Group photo, courtesy Wyoming State Museum)

ward Newcastle. The prisoner was George Burns, a rustler who had helped steal 100 horses from the Burlington Stage Company—managed by Thomas G. Smith. Roger Hawthorne, who researched the Waggoner lynching, concluded that "Elliott and Smith assuredly met" on June 3 on the road which led to Tom Waggoner's cabin. Hawthorne pointed out that three men arrived at the ranch on Thursday morning, June 4, but one never dismounted. Rosa Waggoner later said that the men's features could not be discerned because they were wearing bandanas and eye goggles, along with facial hair that might have been fake. The Waggoners were not alarmed because the spring roundup camp of the big 101 Ranch was nearby, and cowboys often wore bandanas and goggles as protection against the dust. But the two dismounted men jammed handcuffs on Waggoner, told Rosa they were taking him to Sundance (the seat of Crook County) for stealing horses, and rode off with him.[4]

Malcolm Campbell, sheriff of Converse County and a sympathizer of the cattlemen, related that Waggoner "was hanged by three strangers who went to his ranch, and, in the presence of his wife and two children, arrested him." Campbell went on to comment about the hostile and dangerous atmosphere that was spreading throughout Wyoming. "Bands of rustlers armed to the teeth had often called out settlers from their homes, to ask them whether they sided with the cattle-owners or the rustlers. ... The law-abiding people who lived in the rustler-infested regions were obliged to keep quiet, and overlook what went on."[5]

About two miles north of the cabin, at a location where Elliott and Smith and their prisoner may have camped the night before, Tom Waggoner was hanged from the limb of a tree. (Charles Penrose was told that Waggoner—"a most prosperous thief"—was "hanged on his own rope.")[6] Thinking that her husband was in custody in Sundance, about fifty miles to the northeast, and perhaps aware that he was guilty of horse stealing, Rosa Waggoner did not become alarmed until his mount finally wandered home.

Meanwhile, Elliott deposited his prisoner in jail at Newcastle late on June 4, while Smith rode to Buffalo. On June 14 another lawman and John Waggoner, Tom's brother, asked Elliott if he knew anything about the missing man. Elliott frankly stated that Waggoner had been lynched because of a conspiracy. The next day, eleven days after his death, Waggoner was found still hanging from a tree. Although his horse presumably had been slapped out from under him, the rope had stretched so far that his feet now touched the ground. Deputy Elliott was part of an official party that cut down Waggoner's corpse and buried him on the site. A three-man coroner's jury held a perfunctory inquest, ruling that Waggoner met his death at the hands of unknown parties.[7]

A member of the coroner's jury, Deputy Sheriff Fred Coates, was appointed executor of Waggoner's estate. Coates then designated Joe Elliott to supervise Waggoner's horse herd. It was rumored that Tom Smith soon acquired enough of Waggoner's horses to start another stagecoach line. The Burlington Stage Company suffered no further loss of horses after Waggoner's lynching. In September 1891 a jury acquitted George Burns, and he promptly disappeared. The 101 Ranch soon moved its cattle onto Waggoner's range, and his fences were taken down.[8]

Deputies Joe Elliott, who had ridden for the 101 a year earlier, and Fred Coates would team up in November 1891 to perform deadly work for the WSGA. The following April Elliott would ride into Johnson County with the Invaders, alongside Richard Allen, foreman of the 101.

Another member of the Invaders, George Dunning, was told by H. B. Ijams, WGSA secretary from 1891 to 1895, that "Smith and party read a bogus warrant to Wagoner and took him a short distance from home and hanged him."[9] Ijams was referring to Thomas C. Smith, a deputy U.S. marshal from Texas hired by the WSGA. But Smith did not arrive in Wyoming until November 1891—five months after the lynching. Roger Hawthorne speculates that when Joe Elliott reported to Ijams about the lynching, he mentioned the participation of "Tom Smith," a deputy U.S. marshal. The WSGA secretary assumed that Elliott was referring to the recently hired Thomas C. Smith, instead of Thomas G. Smith.

George Dunning further related that "Mr. Ijams gave me to understand that the men who were employed by the Wyoming Stock Growers Association to do the killing last fall in Johnson county, Wyoming, were Frank Canton and Joe Elliott and Tom Smith and another man whose name I forgot [Fred Coates?]. ..."[10] Thomas C. Smith, a veteran Texas lawman and a deadly shootist, was a newcomer to Wyoming. Recruited by the WSGA late in 1891, he would be a key figure in the dramatic events of the next few months.

Nate Champion, doomed hero of the Johnson County War. (Courtesy Johnson County Jim Gatchell Memorial Museum)

Another key figure from Texas was Nathan D. Champion, born near Round Rock in 1857 into a large and respected family. Nate became a cowboy, and after apparently accompanying a herd up the Goodnight-Loving Trail in 1881, he and his brother, Dudley, decided to stay in Wyoming. The Champion brothers became top hands on several Wyoming ranches, and Nate earned widespread respect for his cowboy skills and leadership abilities. Johnson County rancher A. L. Brock admired Nate for his integrity. Even Frank Canton, who was instrumental in pursuing and killing Nate, grudgingly conceded that "Nate Champion was the only man among the rustlers that I considered a dead-game man. He was an expert shot with a rifle," added Canton, and others also remarked that he was good with a gun.[11]

Nate eventually acquired about 200 head of cattle, and he turned them onto the protected range of the Middle Fork—a thirty-mile canyon flanked by red bluffs which soon would become famous as Hole-in-the-Wall, hideout of rustlers and outlaws, notably Butch Cassidy's Wild Bunch. The Bar C Ranch had utilized the canyon grazing until going belly up in 1889. Then about 2,000 Tisdale cattle from the nearby TTT Ranch were shoved into the canyon, soon to be joined by Champion's smaller herd. Bob Tisdale was unhappy about the intrusion, but Champion insisted on keeping his cattle on open range.

Bad blood quickly developed. When the Tisdale herd was moved, a number of

Champion cattle reportedly were driven out with them. Champion was accused of rustling cattle, and soon he joined the growing list of blackballed cowhands. Champion also had trouble with Mike Shonsey, a native of Canada who came to Wyoming in the early 1880s as a teenaged employee for WSGA stalwart W. E. Guthrie. A cowboy of exceptional skills, Shonsey was working as a roundup foreman when Nate Champion cut out a few head of his own cattle. During a roundup being conducted by TTT cowboys, Nate and several cowboys, "armed to the teeth," rode up, roped and tied the calves, then scattered the remainder of the 1,500 head of Tisdale cattle. With his cowboys unwilling to offer fight, "Tisdale was quite powerless in the face of desperate odds." According to Malcolm Campbell, Champion and his men returned the next morning, branded the calves, and rode off with them. Dr. Charles Penrose, arriving in Cheyenne about this time, was told by his cattlemen friends that Nate Champion, although "quiet and brave," was "a very active rustler and one of their leaders." Malcolm Campbell came to a similar conclusion: "Fearless in the face of any odds and with the reputation for being the quickest man with a sixgun in this country, he was a typical leader for as hard a lot of rustlers as could be found anywhere in the West." [12]

At about this same time, another small rancher from Texas who was good with a gun, Al Allison, also raided a big roundup. Rumored to have left Texas because of a shooting scrape, Al had spent a couple of years as a partner of Jack Flagg and other blacklisted cowboys. Unintimidated by big Wyoming ranchers, in July 1891 Al led a band of armed cowboys into a roundup camp and cut out thirty calves. [13]

Al Allison and Nate Champion and the riders who backed them may well have been collecting calves that otherwise would have been lost to them. They were not permitted to participate in the big roundups, but all unbranded calves would be gathered and sold to WSGA members. Indeed, cowboys working for big ranchers were paid five dollars per head for

Martin Allison Tisdale, brother of murder victim John A. Tisdale. Known as "Al Allison," he reputedly used an assumed name because of a shooting scrape in Texas, and in Wyoming he was regarded as a rustler. (Author's collection)

branding mavericks, while men with small herds could not legally claim their own calves. Frustration and defiance among small ranchers not only was understandable—it should have been expected. Every homesteader with a few head of cattle cheered the audacity and courage of Nate Champion and Al Allison in riding boldly into WSGA roundups.

Big ranchers, of course, regarded such actions as an armed threat. There was immediate talk of meeting such impudent challenges with extralegal violence. On the Fourth of July in 1891, John Clay was visiting Frank Wolcott at the beautiful headquarters site of the VR Ranch. "At that time like many other cowmen I had thrown discretion to the winds," revealed Clay, "and was quite willing to draw a rope on a cattle thief if necessary." [14]

Wolcott, sensing an opening with the influential Clay, emphasized that "there was an urgent necessity for a lynching bee," then began to explain "a plan he had in his mind." Clay was taken aback by Wolcott's drastic proposals: ". . . his scheme was so bold and open that I told him it was an impossible one, and that, so far as I was concerned, to count me out." After reflecting on Wolcott's plan overnight, "I talked again to him, and strongly advised against any such action." Clay soon left Wyoming for a lengthy overseas holiday, "and the matter left my mind."[15]

But the matter did not leave Wolcott's mind. Other cattlemen were more receptive, and support grew for a plan that involved hired gunmen and the killing of numerous "rustlers" and troublemakers. Then the toughest of the "stock detectives" employed by the ranchers were told by someone to go after Nate Champion. Cattlemen had lynched Jim Averell and Ella Watson in 1889, and enough influence had been invoked to spare them any legal consequences. Horse rustler Tom Waggoner had been lynched in 1890, again with no legal consequences. Why would there be legal consequences for the execution of rustlers in 1891?

Four, or perhaps five or six, of the stock detectives located Nate Champion in the fall of 1891. Champion had decided to winter in the Hole-in-the-Wall country, renting a homesteader's one-room log cabin secluded in a small canyon. On the last night of October, Champion and a cowboy named Ross Gilbertson bunked together in the cabin's only bed. Champion warily draped his gunbelt over the bedpost before going to sleep.

Just before dawn a party of gunmen stealthily approached the cabin. Champion would recognize Joe Elliott. Others later named included Frank Canton, Mike Shonsey, Fred Coates, Bill Lykens, and somebody called Woodbox Jim. Tom Smith also was sus-

Cabin where Nate Champion routed half a dozen predawn attackers. (Courtesy Johnson County Jim Gatchell Memorial Museum)

pected by some, but he may not yet have arrived from Texas. Word soon spread among the cattlemen's faction that "the stock association" had offered their detectives "$1,500 for each man killed." At daybreak on Sunday, November 1, the hired gunmen "intended to hang Champion and Gilbertson in their cabin."[16]

Two of the gunmen slipped inside the unlocked door and leveled their revolvers at the bed in a back corner of the low room. A third man stood just behind the door. "Give up, boys," demanded one of the gunmen, "we've got you."[17]

"Who are you," asked Champion, "and what do you want?" Champion turned over slowly—then snatched his revolver from its holster. The two gunmen near the bed immediately fired, and Nate was powderburned as a bullet ripped trough his blankets and slammed into his pillow. Another slug punched into the bedding near Gilbertson's feet, but Champion snapped off a shot in reply. As the dim little room rocked with explosions and filled with clouds of gunsmoke, the gunmen scurried outside, shutting the door behind them. Champion triggered another round through the door, then scrambled out of bed. Peering out a little window, he "saw a short dark little fellow going into the brush, holding his stomach."

Having been awakened by gunmen shooting at him, "Gilbertson didn't seem much interested in fighting . . . ," but Champion made him take his gun and cover the window. Looking out of the doorway, Champion spotted a new .38-56 Winchester leaning against the cabin wall. Since Champion and Gilbertson were armed only with sixguns, the rifle would be invaluable if the cabin came under siege. Slipping outside, Champion grasped the Winchester in his left hand, then spotted another rifle lying on the ground. Suddenly, Joe Elliott appeared at the corner of the cabin with a revolver in his hand. Perhaps not expecting Champion to be outside, Elliott seemed to freeze.

"I jumped inside and fired a shot through the chinking of the cabin," related Champion. "When I got outside again, I saw a man going through the brush some distance from the cabin, but he disappeared before I had time to get a shot at him."

With his assailants now in retreat, Champion persuaded the reluctant Gilbertson to join him in pursuit. A short distance from the cabin they discovered four overcoats, three silk handkerchiefs, and a couple of other items that had been abandoned during the hasty and unexpected withdrawal. Champion pressed on to the old Bar C Ranch headquarters, where a young man named Tommy Carr was milking cows in the barn. Brandishing one of the rifles he had retrieved, Champion asked Carr "if there was anybody hiding around the ranch." Carr responded negatively, and Champion told him about the dawn violence.[18]

The next day Champion, reinforced by two friends—fellow cowboys Nick Ray and homesteader John A. Tisdale—found a deserted camp in Beaver Creek Canyon. Six horses were still tethered, a pair of goggles was fished from the remains of the campfire, and bedding that had been left behind included a tarpaulin-ground cloth that was smeared with blood. When the party encountered Mike Shonsey, Tisdale "cornered" him "and made him talk." Shonsey admitted to being in the party, along with Elliott, Canton, Lykens, and Woodbox Jim. Rumor held that Bill Lykens, wounded by Champion, had been carried in a wagon to Casper for medical treatment, then moved to Missouri, where he soon died.

Except for Woodbox Jim, these men were veteran stock detectives who each had been on the WSGA payroll. Word about their attack spread rapidly across Wyoming's cattle country, helped considerably by Champion. In an interview with a Buffalo newspaper reporter, Nate pointed out proudly "that this crowd came to my cabin to kill Gilbertson and myself, but met with the wrong kind of reception to suit them." He drove the point home: "they were scared off." Champion listed the horses and clothing and guns and other property he had retrieved, "which the owners can have by calling for it," he taunted.[19]

The owners did not call for their abandoned possessions. Joe Elliott, the only attacker who could be positively identified by Champion, was arrested for attempted murder. But Ross Gilbertson disappeared, which was becoming a common occurrence for witnesses who might testify against WSGA interests. It began to be rumored that such witnesses were murdered, or run out of the country, or perhaps bribed. In any event, without Gilbertson to confirm Champion's accusation against Elliott, the case was dismissed. It appeared that once again the WSGA had done whatever was necessary to evade the consequences of another extralegal action.

Tensions mounted between the cattlemen and the small operators. First, ranchers hanged two homesteaders, including a female; then commissioned peace officers lynched a horse rustler. Now WSGA stock detectives had assaulted a blacklisted cowboy. The big ranchers had the support of politicians, judges, law officers, and the strongest organization in Wyoming. "In 1891, we made up our minds to do something," wrote cattleman Billy Irvine.[20] WSGA secretary H. B. Ijams told George Dunning, after hiring him to participate in the Invasion, "that last fall the Wyoming Stock Growers Assn. made a contract with certain parties to kill fifteen men who were considered by the Stock Association to be the leaders among stock thieves in Johnson County, Wyoming. Mr. Ijams gave me to understand that the men who were employed by the Wyoming Stock Growers Association to do the killing last fall . . . were Frank Canton and Joe Elliott and Tom Smith and another man whose name I forget, who Ijams said got off all right to Montana." But Ijams admitted that "the Stock Association was mistaken in regard to the effect produced by killing off a few thieves. . . . That, instead of terrorizing the Rascals, that the thieves were . . . getting more on the war path every day of their rascally lives." Ijams confessed that this murderous policy "had bitterly prejudiced a great many ranchers and business men and other people who never owned any stock, against the Stock Association."[21]

It was becoming evident that the small operators—homesteaders, maverickers, blacklisted cowboys—would not buckle. People who settled the frontier West faced hardships and dangers unflinchingly, as a part of pioneer life. Even though Wyoming achieved statehood in 1890, the population of this vast area was sparse, and a frontier atmosphere still prevailed. Those who were easily cowed did not stay long in the West. Threatened by the cattlemen and their stock detectives and the powerful WSGA, Wyoming settlers—like generations of frontiersmen before them—defiantly prepared to resist danger, to defend themselves if necessary.

Earlier in the year, in May 1891, the WSGA strengthened its authority in Johnson County with the organization of the Northern Wyoming Protective Association.[22] In

December 1890 the first Wyoming State Legislature nullified the infamous Maverick Law, but this change proved merely cosmetic. The WSGA fully intended to operate during roundups as though the law still was in effect. The Northern Wyoming Protective Association would be an instrument of this unwritten policy, which the WSGA clearly felt could be enforced.

Fred G. S. Hesse was elected president of the new NWPA. Like many big Wyoming ranchers, Hesse was a native of England, but he had to work his way from modest beginnings to a position of prominence. He rode up from Texas with a trail herd for Moreton Frewen, then became foreman of Frewen's famous 76 Ranch, at an annual salary of $3,000. Hesse was selected as foreman of the memorable spring roundup of 1883, in which twenty-seven chuck wagons, 400 men, and 1,400 horses gathered at the head of Crazy Woman Creek. After the 76 Ranch folded five years later, Hesse was granted the Crazy Woman range as payment of debts owed to him. Headquartering his new 28 Ranch on a homestead on Crazy Woman Creek, he built a house, barn, fencing, and irrigation ditches and bought

Fred G. S. Hesse, a native of England who became a Texas cowboy. Hesse was hired as Moreton Frewen's foreman, then built his own spread in Johnson County. (Frank Leslie's Weekly, June 2, 1892)

mowing machines, gang plows, a self-binding reaper, and other equipment. The vast herds of the Frewens had been preyed upon by rustlers, and there were those who said that Hesse built up his own herd with cattle which belonged to his employers. These rumors perhaps were started by his enemies. Hesse certainly had a host of enemies after he began to build a substantial ranch, because no one was more outspoken against livestock thieves. The "boldest operators," according to Hesse, were Nate Champion, Ross Gilbertson, J. A. Tisdale, Ranger Jones and his brother John, Nick Ray, Henry Smith, Jack Bell, Ed Tway, Billy Wallace, Al Smith, and Ed Cherpillod, along "with quite a following of men who were afraid to work so boldly."[23]

Hesse refused to let any of these men work at his fall roundup, saying "they repeatedly threatened to take my life." Friends in Buffalo sent word "that I must be very careful how I traveled through the country," and he began riding with great caution.[24]

With Hesse in charge of the Northern Wyoming Protective Association, the homesteaders and small ranchers and mavericks decided to counter with their own association. Communal efforts, from log rollings to barn raisings to cattle roundups to quilting bees, were commonly practiced on any frontier. In late October 1891—two nights before the attack on Nate Champion's cabin—the Northern Wyoming Farmers and Stock Growers Association was formed. After a series of meetings, the new organization offered a $500 reward for the capture of anyone found shooting livestock on the range (a response to charges against mavericks). Two murders by ambush would spur the new association to far greater defiance within a few months.

The escalating violence next was directed at Ranger Jones, who was on Fred Hesse's list of "bold operators." Orley Everett "Ranger" Jones was twenty-seven, and during the past few years he had made a name for himself as a gifted cowboy and bronc rider. He had come to Johnson County from Nebraska in 1887, then returned home in the winter when there was no work. The following spring he came back to work for the EK Ranch. Margaret Hanson described: "He was a splendid rider and was a valuable man in an outfit; his greatest delight was in riding a pitching horse, and as the outfit had a great many of them, he had his hands full. It was really wonderful to see him ride, he had such a grip in his knees that he could fairly make a horse groan, and a horse could only pitch a short while until he would have to stop to get his breath. His strength was so great that he could handle the most vicious 'bronc' as easily as an ordinary man could a Shetland pony."[25]

Ranger's older brother, John "Curley" Jones, claimed a homestead on the Red Fork of the Powder, where he would bring his family. Ranger then filed on a homestead adjoining his brother. He became engaged and started building a house. Because Ranger was a skilled cowboy who owned a small spread, plus the fact that he and Nate Champion had worked together on the EK, he became regarded as a rustler by the cattlemen. Perhaps he fell victim to disastrous timing, exposing himself alone in the countryside just when the cattlemen determined to press their attack.

On Friday, November 20, 1891, Ranger told his brother that he was traveling to Buffalo for flooring lumber, and that he would be back in four or five days. Ranger headed north in a vehicle drawn by two horses. He took considerably longer than expected, finally starting for home with his lumber on Saturday, November 28. Jones wore two coats against the cold. D. A Kingsbury, riding north toward Buffalo on the county road, crossed the bridge over Muddy Creek and noticed an armed man up the stream bed. Thinking that he was "looking for horses," Kingsbury continued on, stopping to talk with Ranger Jones after another couple of miles. Also encountering Jones was a Mrs. Washburn and her son, who were traveling north in a wagon into Buffalo. After crossing Bull Creek, they encountered a rider with a bandana covering part of his face. They were further alarmed when they saw another rider, and later they surmised that these men were setting a trap for Ranger Jones.[26]

Tracks indicated that two or perhaps three men concealed themselves beneath the Muddy Creek bridge, which was fourteen miles south of town. After Jones drove over the bridge, the gunmen emerged from cover and opened fire at his back. One slug was deflected by a large cartridge belt he wore. But two other bullets slammed into his torso, and he slumped dead in his seat. The frightened team stampeded, but the pursuers caught the buckboard as it labored uphill. The team and buckboard were taken up the creek about half a mile, and the horses were unhitched and set free. The buckboard was wheeled behind the creek bank out of sight of the road, with the corpse still in the seat.[27]

A few days later John Jones arrived in Buffalo, concerned about his overdue younger brother. By that time another fatal ambush had taken place south of town, so a heavily armed search party quickly retraced Ranger's route. The frozen body of Jones was found on Thursday, December 3, five days after he was murdered. His two horses were grazing in a nearby pasture. On Sunday, December 5, Ranger Jones was buried in the cemetery just south of Buffalo, near the fresh grave of John Tisdale.[28]

After his murder on November 28, 1891, Ranger Jones was buried in Buffalo. (Photo by Karon O'Neal)

John A. Tisdale was from Round Rock, Texas, about twenty miles north of Austin. He was born in 1855, two years before Nate Champion's birth, also near Round Rock. Although Tisdale attended college, soon he took up work that seemed to be irresistible to adventurous young men in post-Civil War Texas. Quickly mastering the cowboy's skills, he also proved to be an able leader. Tisdale bossed at least three cattle drives from Texas, he was a roundup foreman in 1883, and after delivering cattle to eastern Montana, he met Theodore Roosevelt in Mingusville (later renamed Wibeaux). Tisdale was hired as foreman of Roosevelt's nearby Elkhorn ranch. In 1885 he married Kate Powers in Mingusville. An avid reader, she discussed books with Roosevelt, and when the first of her four children was born in 1887, the future president offered a high chair as a baby gift. When Roosevelt withdrew from ranching after the devastating winter of 1886-87, he helped Tisdale secure an appointment as superintendent of the Northern Pacific at Mandan, North Dakota.[29]

After a couple of years, Tisdale decided to establish a cattle ranch in Wyoming. He moved his family to a homestead on the Red Fork of the Powder River, about sixty-five miles south of Buffalo. He was joined by his brother, Martin Allison Tisdale, who called himself "Al Allison," reportedly because of "a shooting scrape with some Mexicans out on the border prior to leaving Texas." A few months earlier Al had stirred up trouble by leading armed riders into a roundup and cutting out thirty calves.[30]

THE MURDERS OF
JONES AND TISDALE

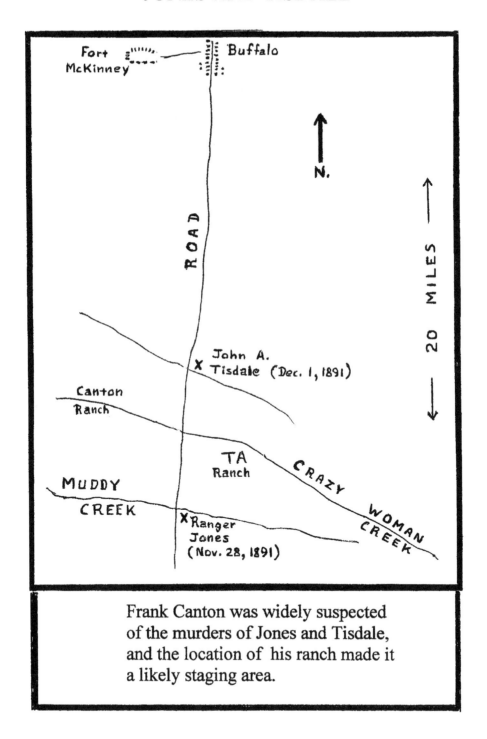

Frank Canton was widely suspected of the murders of Jones and Tisdale, and the location of his ranch made it a likely staging area.

John Tisdale accumulated a small herd of cattle and horses, and he may have been regarded as a mavericker. But there was talk that he had confronted Mike Shonsey over the attack against Nate Champion and Ross Gilbertson. According to this story, Tisdale had intimidated Shonsey into listing the attackers, which would have bitterly angered members of the cattleman faction. Another story suggested that Tisdale had known Joe

Horner in Texas. By the time they again met in Johnson County, Joe Horner had become Frank Canton. Although Tisdale kept the secret of Joe Horner to himself, Canton—according to the rumor—regarded Tisdale as a threat to the new identity he had worked to establish.[31]

Tisdale certainly felt a threat from someone, or perhaps from the general poisoned atmosphere. Late in November he took the long journey into Buffalo to buy supplies and Christmas presents for his three children (his wife was pregnant with their third son, who would be born the following March). In Buffalo he bought flour, sugar, beans, bacon, and Christmas gifts. He also spent several days drinking in Buffalo's saloons. "It was the first time the people of this city had ever seen him in his cups." Tisdale reportedly overheard Frank Canton say to Fred Hesse, "Never mind this part of it. I'll take care of Tisdale."[32] Alarmed over this or some other threat, Tisdale "told several friends here that he was afraid to start for home alone, as he felt that he was shadowed and that an effort would be made to kill him." Already armed with a revolver, which he carried in a shoulder

John A. Tisdale, a cowboy from Texas who worked as foreman for Teddy Roosevelt. Tisdale knew the secret of Frank Canton's outlaw past, and he was drygulched in 1892. (Courtesy Johnson County Jim Gatchell Memorial Museum)

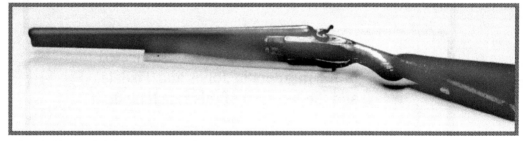

This double-barreled shotgun was purchased by John A. Tisdale shortly before he was murdered. (Photo by Karon O'Neal from the Johnson County Jim Gatchell Memorial Museum)

holster, he purchased a double-barreled shotgun and ammunition from a hardware store. When Tisdale left Buffalo at about noon on Monday, November 30, the shotgun was on the wagon seat beside him. The winter roads were difficult, so he stopped for the night at the Cross H Ranch, about six miles south of Buffalo. To Elmer Freeman, in charge at the Cross H, Tisdale voiced his concerns. "Tisdale expressed fear for his life and shut down the window curtains," recalled Freeman.[33]

After breakfast the next morning, Tisdale drove away from the Cross H. Heading south on the county road, he stopped for a brief conversation with mailman Sam Stringer. After driving three miles Tisdale braked his wagon and dipped down into Haywood Gulch—soon to be renamed Tisdale Gulch. As the horses then began to climb the hill on the other side, an assassin stepped from behind a clay abutment. At a distance of no more than twenty or twenty-five feet, the killer opened fire at Tisdale's back. One bullet ripped through his left arm, glanced off the gun in the shoulder holster, then struck one of the horses in the side of the neck. The fatal slug slammed into the left side of his back, tore through his body, and emerged under his right nipple. Tisdale slumped in his seat and died, while his blood spilled over the groceries and Christmas toys.[34]

The killer led the team into the gulch about eight or nine hundred yards, then shot both of Tisdale's horses in the head. He began riding toward Buffalo, followed by Tisdale's dog. The gunman shot the dog, then continued toward town.

Charles Basch, whose ranch was near Frank Canton's, was riding north into Buffalo that morning. From a distance he saw Tisdale's team and, he later testified, Canton and

Haywood Gulch, south of Buffalo, was renamed Tisdale Gulch soon after the ambush of John A. Tisdale.
(Photo by Karon O'Neal)

81

his sorrel horse Fred. Basch soon heard two shots, then encountered both Sam Stringer and Elmer Freeman on the road. Freeman and Basch rode into town together, arriving before noon. Basch told Freeman about hearing shots and seeing Canton, and Freeman, concerned about Tisdale, went to the sheriff's office. Sheriff Red Angus asked Freeman to lead a search party consisting of Undersheriff Howard Roles and two other men.[35]

At Haywood Gulch these men found blood from Tisdale's wounded horses. Following a broad trail, they soon found the wagon with Tisdale's corpse and the dead horses in harness. They also found tracks back and forth from the assassin's hiding place to the top of the gulch, as he watched for Tisdale's approach. Tom Gardner, search party member who was close to the Tisdales, rode up the road to notify Mrs. Tisdale, while Elmer Freeman proceeded to town with the news. He soon returned with Coroner F. H. Eggleston, who examined the site, then returned to Buffalo with Tisdale's body.

Tom Gardner pushed hard into the night. At midnight he stopped for a brief rest at Jack Flagg's cabin. As Flagg turned out to spread the word, Gardner finished his ride, awakening Kate Tisdale to tell her she was a widow. At dawn on Wednesday, Gardner led Kate and her three children toward Buffalo. At Flagg's they were met by a large party of sympathizers. The men were heavily armed, and this grim procession continued toward town.

That same day, while everyone in Buffalo viewed Tisdale's corpse, an inquest was held behind closed doors. A local physician, one of the three members of the coroner's jury, examined the body. Charles Basch would say nothing about Canton for the record. That afternoon the jury ruled "that the deceased came to his death from a gunshot wound at the hands of some party or parties unknown." The next day, Thursday, the Buffalo *Bulletin* denounced the "dastardly, cold-blooded, deliberate murder" and reported that feelings in town were "pretty high." The newspaper urged restraint: "Let matters rest in the hands of the officers who are doing everything in their power to unravel the mystery surrounding this dastardly deed." The editor cautioned against extralegal violence: "There is not the least doubt about the murderer, as he is believed to be known at the present time."[36]

This suspect was Frank Canton. The off-the-record statements of Charles Basch were enough for an angry populace. On Wednesday afternoon the coroner's jury made their conclusion about "parties unknown." But the next evening the body of Ranger Jones was brought to town. "HORRORS ACCUMULATE," blared the Buffalo *Bulletin*. "ORLEY E. JONES FOULLY MURDERED." Two murders by drygulching infuriated the citi-

Frank Canton was widely suspected of ambushing John A. Tisdale and Ranger Jones. (Courtesy Johnson County Jim Gatchell Memorial Museum)

zenry. Blame was "directed chiefly against Deputy Marshal Frank M. Canton and Fred G. S. Hesse, active members of the stock association upon whom was laid the blame for the assassinations." About noon on the day of the Tisdale murder, Mrs. Sophia Rothwell and Mrs. C. J. Hogerson saw Canton's horse, Fred, and a mount belonging to Hesse. The Rothwell home, at the south end of Main Street, was next door to the house of Bill and Julia Wilkerson, parents of Frank Canton's wife. Annie Canton and her little girls were staying at the family home, and Frank headquartered there when he was in town. Mrs. Rothwell and Mrs. Hogerson were walking down a neighborhood alley when they noticed the lathered horses in a barn. They assumed that Canton and Hesse had just reached town after a hard ride. But after learning of the murder, the ladies prudently decided to keep the story to themselves, telling only family members.[37]

Canton met the accusations head on. He quickly realized that "the rustlers and their friends ... at once decided upon a plot to assassinate me, which failed to materialize." He boldly arranged a meeting with "leaders of the rustlers" on Friday night in a general store. Canton "demanded that they prefer charges against me in order that I might meet and refute the slander."[38]

On Monday, December 7, Martin ("Al Allison") Tisdale filed charges against Canton for the murder of his brother. Canton surrendered to Sheriff Angus and was placed under guard in the building near the courthouse where he had lived while serving as county sheriff. The next day the district courtroom was packed as Judge Carroll Parmalee called the hearing to order. Canton was represented by attorney Charles Burritt, Buffalo's highly capable mayor. The testimony of Canton and more than two dozen witnesses took all day and continued into the evening.

Charles Basch, now willing to identify Canton and his horse Fred, testified at length about the rider he had seen at the murder site. He also testified that Canton had cornered him on the previous Wednesday in a livery stable: "he asked me what was this he heard about his horse; ... he said it was a very serious matter to get out on a person."[39] At first intimidated, Basch apparently decided he could count on Canton's good will. A longtime neighbor who had known Canton for several years, Basch had performed an invaluable service to the Canton family in June 1891. About a mile from the Canton ranch, a buggy team ran away with Frank's wife and two little daughters. Basch and his son-in-law galloped to the rescue and caught the team. But Frank's wife and youngest daughter were injured, so Canton asked him to ride for medical help on his speedy horse Fred. Basch raced twelve miles into town astride Fred in thirty-five minutes. Fortunately, Annie and little Ruby Canton recovered rapidly, and Frank said to Basch that "he would always remember this." Basch "several times" told his stepgrandson, John Washbaugh, in later years "that he thought there was only one thing that saved his life"—Canton's gratitude for the rescue.[40]

But a dozen Buffalo citizens testified on Canton's behalf, establishing his presence in town at the time of the murder. Canton detailed his activities throughout a busy day in Buffalo. Judge Parmalee finally adjourned the hearing at ten o'clock and retired to consider his decision. The next morning he announced point by point his conclusion that there was not "sufficient ground to hold this defendant to answer to the district court."[41]

Canton still clearly enjoyed solid friendships in Buffalo from the years he had spent as a conscientious sheriff. Released from custody, he asked Joe DeBarthe to publish a public "commendation" in the *Bulletin* for Sheriff Angus' courteous treatment.[42] But Canton knew his acquittal had not satisfied those who considered him guilty of both murders: "they wanted some excuse for getting me out of the way, and I knew they intended to do it the first time they got the drop on me. They also wanted to kill Fred Hesse, because he had taken a prominent part in having them prosecuted."[43] Dr. Charles Penrose was told that the death of Ranger Jones "was credited to Fred Hesse of the cattlemen's party."[44] Since Penrose's principal source of information was the cattlemen, apparently some of the ranchers "credited" Hesse with the ambush. Asa Mercer said that while "it was generally believed" that Canton had slain both Tisdale and Jones, "a few persons thought Fred Hesse was the guilty party" in the first killing. Mercer pointed out that this theory was based on Tisdale's claim of overhearing "Canton tell Hesse that he would 'take care of Tisdale,' thus implying that that was his share of the bloody work, and that others were to do their share."[45]

Canton and Hesse decided to leave Wyoming ahead of any retribution. Already they had sent their families to Chicago, securing their safety shortly before the murders began. On November 21, Annie, Ruby and Helen Canton bundled up in a wagon driven by Annie's father and went to the nearest railroad depot, 110 miles to Gillette. The Canton ladies took a train for a long visit with relatives in Chicago. This departure has the appearance of an incriminating coincidence. On Thursday, December 17, after learning that more evidence was being gathered for another legal attempt at Canton, he and Hesse left Buffalo for Gillette. They were accompanied by Sam Sutherland, Hesse's brother-in-law and a future Invader who would bring the horses back to Buffalo.[46]

Canton and Hesse headed east on a Burlington train for Chicago. But at Crawford, Nebraska, Canton left Hesse to travel by rail to Cheyenne, where he checked into the Inter Ocean Hotel on Christmas Eve. Canton received a telegram from Charles Burritt "advising him not to go" to Buffalo. He was interviewed about the recent killings in Johnson County and the new charges against him. Recanting his recent public praise of Sheriff Red Angus, Canton stated that it would be "suicidal" for him to return to Buffalo "unarmed in the custody of a friend of the rustlers and a personal enemy."[47]

Almost certainly Canton met with prominent WSGA members. He would have reported everything he knew about the recent killings. Whether or not Canton was the trigger man, he needed good legal counsel to combat charges that he was. Canton was extended the expert services of two former chief justices of the Wyoming Supreme Court, John W. Lacey and Willis Van Devanter, who represented the WSGA.[48]

Canton also surely was brought up to date on the evolving plans for further action against "rustlers." Already widely suspected of using his guns on behalf of big cattlemen, he certainly would be a key figure in any large-scale action. On December 26, as Canton finally boarded a train for a belated Christmas with his wife and daughters in Chicago,[49] he would reflect back on a troubled and violent year. And Canton knew that even more trouble and violence promised to take place in 1892.

Chapter 8

Organizing the Expedition

"[WSGA Secretary H. B.] Ijams did not seem to get mad or excited during our conversation in Nampa, but seemed to talk about the matter of murdering 30 or more men in much the same manner that many people would talk about taking a picnic excursion."

IDAHO GUNMAN GEORGE DUNNING

For Frank Canton, 1891 ended with accusations of murder and the tensions of pending legal action. But 1892 began with grief. "When I reached Chicago I found my wife and two little daughters all down with diphtheria." He helped to nurse them during their dangerous illness and long recovery. Annie and six-year-old Ruby survived. But on January 16, the family lost three-year-old Helen. It was a grim way to start a grim year.[1]

Back in Wyoming, events accelerated toward a violent confrontation. In February Nate Champion and Joe Elliott again faced off against each other—this time in the district courtroom in Buffalo's brick courthouse. "It was a remarkable scene," reported the Buffalo *Bulletin*, "and few who saw it will ever forget it."[2]

During Elliott's incarceration, "certain persons in this city" had taunted him "with the information that the rustlers were thirsting for his blood—that they were only awaiting a favorable opportunity to take him from the officers and embellish some telegraph pole ... with his body." The prisoner "became terribly worked up" and asked the judge to let him remain in the comparative security of his cell rather than be exposed in a courtroom. Once inside the courtroom, Elliott dramatically faced his accuser, Nate Champion. Champion testified under the questioning of the county attorney. As Champion spoke, his "piercing steel gray eyes were riveted on Elliott's face. He was not looking at, but through him. Elliott sat four feet away and busied himself knocking off ashes off the end of a half-smoked cigar." Finally, the county attorney asked if Champion recognized any of the men who attacked him.

"Yes," said Champion, inclining his head toward Elliott, "that man."

The following tense scene was described by the *Bulletin*: "As he spoke the words 'that man,' Elliott looked him straight in the eye. For ten seconds, while these two men looked at each other's faces, there was a sickening stillness. Then somebody coughed, and the spell was broken. Elliott's face had not paled, but a sallow color had crept over it."[3]

But without the testimony of the vanished Ross Gilbertson, the case boiled down to one's man word against another. Attorney Charles H. Burritt helped secure bail,[4] and Elliott reported to Cheyenne for further assignment.

Nate Champion, who had not made himself any safer by facing down Joe Elliott in public, soon had a new assignment of his own. Virtually all small stockmen on the northern ranges had been blackballed in 1891 by the Northern Wyoming Protective Association. Therefore, these small operators anticipated that the spring roundup of 1892 would result in the confiscation of virtually all of their unbranded calves. So the newly organized Northern Wyoming Farmers and Stockmen's Association held a series of meetings and decided upon a bold move. They would conduct their own roundup, and it would begin on May 1—one month before the roundup of the Northern Wyoming Protective Association. Selected as roundup foreman was the man who defied the cattlemen's faction with the greatest success—Nate Champion. The day following the attack on Champion and Ross Gilbertson, Nate had ridden to the home of John A. Tisdale to enlist his help. "There's going to be trouble," Champion predicted accurately. "If it comes to fighting I can fight, but I can't lead a fight."[5] Although Champion was right about his abilities as a fighting man, these combative qualities inspired others to rely upon him. He may not have wanted a leadership role, but when it was thrust upon him, a sense of responsibility compelled him to accept. Although he already had fought off one attempt on his life, and even though Ranger Jones and John Tisdale had been treacherously murdered, Champion would not duck a fight.

The announcement of the May 1 roundup was an open challenge to the cattlemen. They reacted by putting into effect an audacious plan that had been evolving for several months. Although John Clay disapproved of the plan and was out of the country during this period, he was aware that "there were numerous meetings during the fall and winter that followed." The leaders who pushed for the most extreme course of action were Frank Wolcott, WSGA Secretary H. B. Ijams, and WSGA Vice President George W. Baxter, a former territorial governor of Wyoming. "They were backed by every large cattleman in the state," said Clay, "and behind them they had the moral influence of the two Senators, Warren and Casey." Dr. Charles Penrose also felt "confident they knew all about the whole thing." Penrose further pointed out that attorney Willis Van Devanter, former chief justice of Wyoming and future member of the United States Supreme Court, "knew all about it." Clay and Penrose agreed that "Governor Barber knew all about the expedition."[6]

Acting Governor Amos W. Barber clearly was a key ally of the cattlemen. Dr. Barber had graduated from the Medical School of the University of Pennsylvania one year ahead of Dr. Penrose. After working at the Pennsylvania Hospital, Dr. Barber came to Wyoming in 1885 to take charge of the hospital at Fort Fetterman, which had been established by cattlemen for their sick and injured cowboys. Because of this duty, concluded John Clay, "he knew a lot about the inside workings of the range." Clay also pointed out that "he gave Owen Wister many a story which was incorporated in the 'Virginian,' that thrilling tale of cowboy life." Dr. Barber was physically impressive, personable, and popular. On September 11, 1890, he was elected first lieutenant governor of the state of Wyoming. Francis E. Warren won election as governor, but he soon resigned to accept appointment from the state legislature as U.S. senator. On November 24, 1890, Dr. Barber became acting governor.[7]

Acting Governor Barber surely was aware of Article XIX, Section 1, of the Wyoming State Constitution:

> No armed force, or detective agency, or armed body, or unarmed body of men, shall ever be brought into this state for the suppression of domestic violence, except upon the application of the state legislature or the executive, when the legislature cannot be convened.

But Barber knew that an "armed force" was being assembled to "be brought into this state." Indeed, after the cattlemen calculated that the state militia totaled 309 officers and men, Governor Barber was requested to make certain the militia offered no opposition. Consequently, on March 23, 1892, a telegram was sent to the commander of the Wyoming National Guard, Col. DeForrest Richards:

GENERAL ORDER No. 4

Colonel DeForrest Richards, Commanding First Regiment Infantry, Wyoming National Guard, is hereby directed to instruct his company commanders that they shall obey only such orders to assemble their commands as may be received from these headquarters, to assist the civil authorities in the preservation or enforcement of the laws of the State of Wyoming.

By order of the Governor and Commander-in-chief.

FRANK STITZER
Adjutant General

Colonel Richards soon communicated to his company commanders around the state "General Order No. 7," which demanded compliance with General Order No. 4. General Order No. 7 reached the company captains at Buffalo and Sheridan on April 4, just two days before the cattlemen's expedition left Cheyenne for Johnson County.[8]

The cattlemen had assigned Mike Shonsey and Phil DuFran, formerly a ranch foreman, to scout around Johnson County. The ranchers had decided to send an armed force into Johnson County to kill rustlers and their allies. "The cattlemen then selected 19 men who they thought should die for the good of the country," admitted Dr. Charles Penrose. Other sources elevate the number of targets on the death list as to as many as seventy who "should die for the good of the country."[9]

The ranchers held one of their meetings that spring in Omaha, Nebraska, a location that might aid in keeping their deadly plans secret. The ranch owners had not yet decided if they should accompany the gunmen they intended to hire from Texas and elsewhere. Billy Irvine was surprised when John Winterling, who ran the Big Red Ranch in Sheridan County, offered a motion "that all owners and managers who could possibly do so should go" on the expedition. Winterling pointed out four good reasons the owners and managers should ride with their hired guns: "To show them the way; to point out those we wanted; to give the expedition prestige; and last, to prevent mistakes."

Rancher W. C. "Billy" Irvine, future president of the WSGA, was a principal leader of the Invasion. (Author's collection)

Irvine eagerly seconded the motion, which carried after a discussion. "The moment it carried," Irvine wrote, "I personally put the question to every man in the room, 'Will you go,' and received a reply that they would from every man there, except old Col. Pratt and George W. Baxter."[10]

Billy Irvine would accompany the expedition, then, and so would Maj. Frank Wolcott. Since Wolcott had pushed for the expedition for months, and since his duties as a Civil War major a quarter century earlier presumed command experience, he would be considered the field commander. The Tisdale brothers, Bob—notorious for his cruelty to horses—and John N., also would go. John had been elected to Wyoming's first State Senate, but recently he had sold his interests in the TTT Ranch to Bob and moved to Salt Lake City. Perhaps stung by criticism for having left Wyoming, Senator Tisdale returned to Cheyenne to take a place in the expedition.

Also returning, from Chicago, was Fred G. S. Hesse, ready to march back toward his home.

Marching together would be two Harvard men who were partners in the big Duck Bar Ranch on the Platte River, Frederic O. de Billier and Hubert E. Teschemacher. Handsome, polished, and well-educated, de Billier resided in Cheyenne. Teschemacher, one of Wyoming's most influential citizens, had served on the WSGA Executive Committee since 1883, the longest tenure of any committee member. Another prominent rancher was W. E. Guthrie, a member of the Wyoming Legislature. He was a partner in the Guthrie and Oskamp Cattle Company of Converse County, and for years he employed Mike Shonsey.

Englishman Richard M. "Dick" Allen, general manager of the British-owned Standard Cattle Company, participated in the expedition. Allen lived in Cheyenne, but his company's range was near the horse operation of the de-

W. E. Guthrie, prominent rancher and longtime employer of Mike Shonsey. (Frank Leslie's Weekly, June 2, 1892)

ceased Thomas Waggoner. Also residing in Cheyenne was Scot-Canadian C. A. Campbell, a Converse County rancher. Campbell lost his herd in the disastrous winter of 1886-87, but he remained in the cattle business as an associate of his friend, John Clay. H. W. "Hard Winter" Davis, who owned a ranch at the mouth of Salt Creek on the Powder River, also agreed to go, but harbored serious misgivings.

Other ranch owners and managers readied themselves to ride into Johnson County. A. R. Powers was the managing partner of the Powder-Wilder Cattle Company, a comparatively small operation on Crazy Woman Creek and the Powder River. Arthur B. Clarke owned the DE Ranch in southern Wyoming. Frank H. Laberteaux was resident manager of the Hoe Ranch, which was owned by Henry Blair of Chicago. W. J. Clarke, formerly a WSGA foreman, now ranched on Crazy Woman Creek. Lafayette H. Parker was manager of the Murphy Cattle Company on Piney Creek, north of Buffalo. Tall Charles Ford was resident manager of the TA Ranch south of Buffalo. Owned by Dr. William Harris, the TA would become a key site of the Johnson County War.

The oldest member of the expedition was E. W. "Pappy" Whitcomb. He went west

in 1857, working for several years for Russell, Majors & Waddell before becoming a rancher along Hat Creek. He joined the WSGA in 1875 and later was selected to the Executive Committee. Now sporting a flowing white beard, Pappy lived in Cheyenne and was financially obligated to John Clay. A. D. Adamson, a stout Scotsman who managed the Ferguson Land and Cattle Company in southern Wyoming, was assigned to ride near Pappy Whitcomb.

Governor Barber "advised" his friend and former schoolmate, Dr. Charles Penrose, to go with the cattlemen. Dr. Penrose would act as surgeon of the expedition, and would borrow Dr. Barber's medical bag. Penrose reflected that Barber realized "that he, the Governor, could not control things, and that the cattle men could not by any process of law obtain protection, he approved the plan that they proposed, of taking the matter into their own hands."[11]

Charles Ford, manager of the TA Ranch south of Buffalo, was one of several foremen who felt compelled to support the Invasion. (From group photo, courtesy Wyoming State Museum)

In addition to a surgeon, the cattlemen also brought along a couple of newspapermen to provide favorable publicity. A natural choice was Ed Towse, who had flacked so effectively for the cattlemen during the aftermath of the lynching of Ella Watson and Jim Averell. A reporter for the Cheyenne *Daily Leader* in 1889, Towse now was city editor for the Cheyenne *Sun.* Along with Towse, Sam T. Clover of the Chicago *Herald* talked his way onto the expedition.

In his autobiographical *On Special Assignment,* Clover related that while at the Chicago stockyards he received a tip from a livestock inspector about "a band of regula-

Therapy for the Doctor

Dr. Charles Penrose of Philadelphia, a friend of Owen Wister's and of Wyoming's governor, would ride with the expedition as a surgeon. A graduate of the Medical School of the University of Pennsylvania, Dr. Penrose was diagnosed with pulmonary tuberculosis in the fall of 1890. He traveled to health resorts in Florida, Wyoming and Colorado, but there was no improvement. Then the acting governor of Wyoming, Dr. A. W. Barber, who had graduated a year before Penrose from the University of Pennsylvania, invited his friend to Cheyenne.

Dr. Barber secured for Penrose a room at the Cheyenne Club and introduced him to numerous citizens, including the city engineer, who agreed to help with a therapy program. Dr. Penrose was provided a pick and a shovel, and every morning after breakfast he worked for two hours helping to fill in a trench that had been dug for a new water line. After lunch Dr. Penrose rode horseback for two or three hours, and following supper he read or played cards. "I ate enormous meals of beef, mutton, pork, eggs, and milk, and took codliver oil," he said, and soon he gained twenty pounds.

"During my residence at the Cheyenne Club I met many of the cattlemen of Wyoming, and became familiar with the depressed state of the cattle business and the difficulties with which the cattlemen were contending." When his new friends organized the Johnson County expedition, Dr. Penrose was asked to come along as surgeon. He consented, "because the men who asked me were my friends, and I was glad of the opportunity to take part in an adventure of this kind." (Penrose, *The Rustler Business*, 5-7)

tors organized to clean out the cattle rustlers up in the Big Horn country." Clover was told to travel to Cheyenne by April 1 and sell himself to "a few of the big cattle-owners there." Clover's managing editor provided expense money, and the correspondent took a train to Cheyenne and checked into the Inter Ocean Hotel. A letter from Henry Blair— a fellow Chicagoan who owned the Hoe Ranch on the lower Powder River and whose foreman, F. H. Laberteaux, was riding with the expedition—provided Clover access to cattlemen in Cheyenne. During an appointment with Maj. Frank Wolcott and Billy Irvine "at a lawyer's office not far from the hotel," Clover persuaded the expedition leaders that he would be useful. Wolcott told Clover of a "place of rendezvous" where he could send his "blankets, saddle and bridle, and commissary outfit," and "the major graciously" offered to provide a horse. Clover purchased the necessary gear, and on Sunday, April 3, he telegraphed his editor in Chicago: "Have succeeded in undertaking, and am to join party. Will start in few days. Ought to be able to send in big story later."[12]

When the expedition began to take shape, the leaders decided to purchase supply

Expedition Participants from Wyoming

RANCH OWNERS AND MANAGERS

Maj. Frank Wolcott★	William C. Irvine★
A. D. Adamson	F. H. Laberteaux
Richard M. Allen★	L. H. Parker
C. A. Campbell	A. R. Powers
Arthur B. Clarke★	Sam Sutherland
W. J. Clarke★	H. E. Teschemacher★
H. W. Davis★	Bob Tisdale★
Fred de Billier	John N. Tisdale
Charles Ford	W. B. Wallace
W. E. Guthrie★	Elias W. Whitcomb★
Fred G. S. Hesse★	

★*current or future members of the WSGA Executive Committee*

STOCK DETECTIVES

Frank Canton	Ben Morrison
Scott Davis	Mike Shonsey
Phil DuFran	W. H. Tabor
Joe Elliott	

MISCELLANEOUS

Dr. Charles Penrose
Sam Clover, Chicago *Herald*
Ed Towse, Cheyenne *Sun*

TEAMSTERS

Charles Austin
William Collum
George Helm

wagons, provisions, horses, guns, and equipment. Funding was provided by substantial contributions from the cattlemen. Donations to the war chest reportedly averaged $1,000, and a total of at least $100,000 was raised. This vast sum would be utilized for expedition purchases, for paying hired gunmen, and, quite likely, for legal fees. With ample funds available, three new Studebaker wagons were bought, and WGSA member R. S. Van Tassel journeyed to Colorado to purchase horses. He acquired a sizable remuda near Longmont, and when he returned, Englishman W. B. Wallace came with him. When the expedition sallied forth in April, Van Tassel elected to stay at home in Cheyenne, but Wallace adventurously rode with the Invaders. Three teamsters were hired to drive the wagons and tend the draft animals: Charles Austin, William Collum, and George Helm. [13]

 Preparing to go into action, the cattlemen summoned Frank Canton back from Chicago. "In April I was requested by the Wyoming Stock Association to return to Cheyenne," he reported. Although Canton had been charged with first-degree murder in the death of John A. Tisdale, his attorneys negotiated a bail-bond agreement. In Laramie on Monday, April 4, Judge John W. Blake set bail at the staggering sum of $30,000. But twenty-one prominent men had been lined up as bondsmen, including WSGA secretary H. B. Ijams, and Canton was free to report for duty in Cheyenne.[14]

Joining Canton in Cheyenne were fellow stock detectives Joe Elliott, Ben Morrison, W. H. Tabor, and Scott "Quick Shot" Davis. A former shotgun guard for gold shipments on the Deadwood to Cheyenne stagecoach line, Davis was hired by the WSGA in 1890. Morrison had become a WSGA stock detective in 1879, and he and Tabor "said they had worked for the stock association so long that the association thought they owned them."[15] These five detectives would be reinforced by Mike Shonsey and Phil DuFran, who still were scouting in Johnson County and would join the expedition in the field.

There was another stock detective, a dangerous man from Texas who was an essential figure in the plans of the cattlemen. Tom Smith was an experienced law officer who was noted as a courageous shootist. It was said that "in one battle he killed seven men without removing the Winchester from his shoulder."[16] This exaggeration emanated from the same public respect that enhanced the reputations of various western mankillers—Wild Bill Hickok, Billy the Kid, John Wesley Hardin, and other gunfighters.

Thomas Calton Smith was the son of a Texas sheriff and pioneer, Thomas Jefferson Smith. The elder Smith, born in Virginia in 1808, went to Texas to fight in the revolution against Mexico. Wounded and captured by the Mexicans, he escaped and settled in Richmond. He opened a blacksmith shop, operated a hotel and livery stable, and won election as sheriff of Fort Bend County. His son Tom—one of eight children—was appointed deputy sheriff. Sheriff Smith retired and died in his eighties in 1890. But by that time Tom Smith had been appointed chief deputy by a

Scott "Quick Shot" Davis was a former shotgun guard who was hired as a stock detective by the WSGA in 1890. (From group photo, courtesy Wyoming State Museum)

Texan Tom Smith earned his reputation as a fearless gunman during the Jaybird-Woodpecker Feud in Fort Bend County. (From group photo, courtesy Wyoming State Museum)

new sheriff, his brother-in-law, J. T. Garvey. Therefore, Tom held a position of authority when the murderous Jaybird-Woodpecker Feud erupted in Fort Bend County.

The feud, with political and racial conflicts that originated during Reconstruction, was waged by factions that derisively nicknamed each other "Jaybirds" and "Woodpeckers." Chief Deputy Tom Smith was a Woodpecker, but he was not involved in early shootouts around the county. In August 1888 a Jaybird leader was ambushed and killed by a shotgun blast, and the next month another Jaybird leader was badly wounded. A subsequent flurry of threats and brawls caused a contingent of Texas Rangers to be dispatched to Richmond to try to maintain peace. But in June 1889 Woodpecker Kyle Terry killed L. E. Gibson, then the following week Terry was slain by Volney Gibson.[17]

This escalation of violence exploded into the "Battle of Richmond" at dusk on Friday, August 16, 1889. Deputy Sheriffs Tom Smith and H. S. Mason were standing in front of the courthouse when they saw Sheriff Garvey escorting a prisoner up the street. Sheriff Garvey had arrested a Jaybird for making a disturbance, but Volney Gibson and other armed Jaybirds suddenly appeared. Finding himself under fire, Sheriff Garvey ran for the safety of the courthouse. Deputies Smith and Mason drew their revolvers, but Garvey collapsed on the courthouse lawn, riddled with bullets. Then Deputy Mason caught a slug in the shoulder and dropped near the dying sheriff.

From beside his fallen fellow officers, Tom Smith opened fire at enemies across the street. His only targets in the gathering darkness were gun flashes and moving figures that were little more than shadows. When his gun clicked on empty, Smith began using the revolvers of Garvey and Mason. Two Texas Rangers inside the courthouse warned Smith to take cover, but he refused as long as Garvey and Mason were exposed. The two Rangers came out to help, but while pulling Garvey and Mason inside, one of the Rangers caught a bullet in the leg. Smith provided covering fire until all available revolvers were empty, then he retreated unscathed into the courthouse. He found a loaded Winchester and marched back to the door, but the Texas Ranger leader, Sgt. Ira Aten, persuaded Smith to stay inside, and the firing subsided.[18]

During the Battle of Richmond in 1889, Chief Deputy Sheriff Tom Smith made a one-man stand in front of the Fort Bend County courthouse. (Courtesy Fort Bend County Historical Museum, Richmond)

The Battle of Richmond produced eight casualties, including four dead. The next day Governor Sul Ross and two militia units arrived to restore order. Governor Ross stayed for several days, supervising the reorganization of county government. With Sheriff Garvey dead, Chief Deputy Tom Smith became acting sheriff, but his brief tenure lasted only until the current Fort Bend County officials were suspended. The displaced officials soon moved to other communities.

But Tom Smith's courageous stand over his fallen comrades established his reputation as a lethal shootist. Apparently this exploit was the source of the story "that in one battle he killed seven men without removing the Winchester from his shoulder." Smith moved his family to Taylor, Texas, where he became city marshal and "where he is said to have killed two men."[19]

Perhaps feeling that he could earn more money by collecting fees and rewards while working as a deputy U.S. marshal, Smith left his family in Taylor and centered his professional activities in Paris. But Smith was one of several deputies who made arrests in the jurisdiction of the northern district of Texas, which headquartered in Dallas. Complaints from the U.S. marshal in Dallas resulted in an investigation led by an official named McDougal, sent to Texas from the office of the U.S. attorney general in Washington, D.C. McDougal "laid off" Tom Smith and other officers, although George Tucker, one of the Paris deputies most deeply involved in the controversy, retained his commission. The discharged officers felt free to meet Tucker at the train depot and claim part of his fee when he brought in a prisoner. "All in fun, they would threaten to take the money from me if I didn't hand it over," reminisced Tucker. "I usually did, for the poor devils had to live, and with many of them I'd already gone through hell. Tom Smith was one of these old partners. He was a fine, brave, big fellow. I would usually divide with him."[20]

But Tucker did not need to divide with Smith for long. Smith soon accepted employment with the Wyoming Stock Growers Association. According to Tucker, Smith's initial contact with the WSGA came through Texas cattlemen who had ranching interests in Wyoming. Smith was an experienced manhunter with a reputation as a deadly gunman—exactly suited for the job description of stock detective for the big Wyoming ranchers. By November 1891 Tom Smith was in Wyoming, learning about the cattle thieves of Johnson County. But when the cattlemen decided to employ a large number of gunmen, someone suggested—perhaps Smith himself—that if other deputy marshals were hired, the expedition might acquire a greater air of legality. Tom Smith knew such men in Texas, and he was dispatched back to the Lone Star State as a recruiter.

Another recruiter of gunmen was WSGA Secretary H. B. Ijams, who wrote to officials of stock associations in Idaho, where there had been range difficulties in recent years. A man named Stearns contacted George Dunning, who had worked in ranching and mining in Idaho. Stearns told Dunning what he knew about the proposition. Dunning suspected that "the whole business was crooked," and insisted upon meeting Ijams in person. Ijams soon caught a train for Idaho, meeting Dunning at the Nampa office of Stearns on Monday, March 7, 1892. Dunning had been asked to "bring four or five of my friends along," but even though he came alone, Ijams talked about matters with total candor. He described "the lynching of Averell and Cattle Kate" and of Tom

H. B. Ijams, secretary of the WSGA (1891-95), was an enthusiastic recruiter for the Invasion of Johnson County.
(Author's collection)

Waggoner. Ijams related details about "men who were employed by the Wyoming Stock Growers Association" assaulting Nate Champion, Ranger Jones, and John A. Tisdale. But Ijams emphasized that there was a need for action on a larger scale, so WSGA employee Tom Smith, a former deputy U.S. marshal, had been dispatched to Texas to recruit twenty-five men. "Mr. Ijams said that the latest scheme of the stock association was to publicly wipe the thieves in Johnson County, Wyoming, out of existence; the way he said the stock association of Montana did in that state eight or nine years ago." Ijams felt that it would take about a month for the force to find and execute the thirty or so key rustlers in Johnson County who were on a list he showed Dunning. Then Ijams planned to divide the gunmen into five-man squads "and have them ride over the country for several months and kill the thieves whenever they run on them." Dunning was assured that the courts, the military, and the politicians, from Mayor Burritt of Buffalo to Senator Carey, were solidly behind the operation.[21]

Ijams promised five dollars per day and expenses, plus "$50 for every man that was killed or hung by the mob on the raid." He asked Dunning to line up a few more men, and promised to keep in touch by mail. Dunning was amazed at what he had been told. He reflected that Ijams "seemed to talk about the matter of murdering 30 or more men in much the same manner that many people would talk about taking a picnic excursion." Despite serious misgivings about the expedition, Dunning became so financially strapped that he had to pawn his revolver. Ijams wrote to Dunning twice with updates, then wired travel money. Dunning retrieved his sixgun from the pawn shop, then boarded a train for Cheyenne, having failed to enlist a friend named Bob Gunnell.[22]

Dunning arrived in Cheyenne on Saturday night, April 2, on the five o'clock train. He quickly spotted Ijams, who had hoped to greet a squad of men from Idaho. Ijams offered to put his new gunman into the Inter Ocean or Metropolitan Hotel at WSGA expense, but Dunning was self-conscious that he had only his work clothes, and he checked into "the Dyer house, a 25-cent hotel." Ijams told him that the Texans would not arrive for a few days, until after the annual WSGA meeting, scheduled for the following day. That night Ijams put Dunning in the company of WSGA stock detectives Ben Morrison and W. H. Tabor, who talked at length about recent violence and the upcoming expedition. The next day Ijams told Dunning that a new .45-90 Winchester awaited him at a gun shop where "the stock association would foot the bill." A day later Dunning put a saddle and other gear on WSGA accounts.[23]

On Monday, April 4, the Wyoming Stock Growers Association conducted its twentieth annual meeting in the county courtroom. The previous Saturday evening, Secretary Ijams told George Dunning that this session "would be the most important meeting of its kind ever held in this Western country." Ijams emphasized that it was "necessary" for every WSGA member to be present "or to be represented by proxy, and that it would be necessary for every one of them to endorse the general plan of campaign."[24] A WSGA historian wrote that "the attendance at the 20th annual meeting in 1892 was the largest in the history of the organization."[25] But another association historian, writing a decade later, stated that "only 43 members answered roll call." President John Clay still was abroad, so the presiding officer was Vice President George Baxter, the former governor who was one of the leaders in planning the expedition. There is no record of what was decided in the brief meeting, although Secretary Ijams told George Dunning that "the stock association had approved of the general campaign ... of killing rustlers." Furthermore, the WSGA Executive Committee notebook declares: "No meetings of the Executive Committee were held in 1892."[26] WSGA leaders left no official records that would legally connect the association to the extralegal expedition.

However, many WSGA members obviously approved of the expedition—contributing substantial money to the war chest, influencing their contacts, and, for more than a score of men, riding with the armed column into Johnson County. On Sunday, April 3, when George Dunning went to the gun shop to pick up his new Winchester, he "saw a number of stockmen getting guns and ammunition," including H. W. Davis and Bob and John Tisdale. On Monday, April 4, the day of the WSGA meeting, Dunning helped brand the horses from Colorado, burning an "AL" on the left shoulder.[27]

The next day, with R. S. Van Tassel giving orders, Dunning helped to load the three new supply wagons onto a flat car, the freshly branded horses into three stock cars, and the personal belongings of the participants into a baggage car. Railroad officials, who did a great deal of business with WSGA members, had agreed to cooperate, and assembled a special train—which also included a passenger car—at the Cheyenne stockyards. Dr. Penrose learned that the expedition would depart that day: "The word was passed for us to meet at the Cheyenne Stock-yards at five o'clock in the afternoon." The cattlemen "walked singly and in twos and threes to the stockyards and gathered in the horse stable there." Maj. Frank Wolcott had traveled to Denver to meet a train from Texas.[28] Tom Smith and the Texas gunmen were on their way to Cheyenne.

Chapter 9

The Texas Gunmen

"I ... became a member of the Texan army that was going to free Wyoming from the rustlers."

DEPUTY U.S. MARSHAL GEORGE TUCKER

Texas was an obvious place to recruit gunmen. Texas Rangers had been instrumental in popularizing Sam Colt's revolving pistols, while battling Comanche war parties during the 1840s, then while campaigning in Mexico with the United States Army. Texans soon began using revolvers against each other, in bloody feuds, individual altercations, and clashes between outlaws and lawmen. During the era of western gunfighting, from the 1850s until early in the twentieth century, far more shootouts erupted in Texas than in any other state or territory. By the 1890s Dodge City and other Kansas cattle towns were tranquil, and so were Tombstone and Lincoln and many other former trouble spots across the West. But gunplay remained commonplace in West Texas, and shootists still congregated in El Paso and Fort Worth.[1]

However, Tom Smith did not seek recruits in El Paso or Fort Worth. He journeyed from Wyoming to Paris, in northeast Texas, about eighteen miles south of the Red River. While Paris was the home of cattle baron John Chisum (Chisum was buried in a small family cemetery within the city limits, following his death from cancer in 1884), the town hardly was famous in western lore as a haven for gunfighters.

Originally called Pinhook, the town was organized during the 1840s, when Texas still was a republic. Soon renamed after the world-famous French city, Paris became the seat of Lamar County. The little farm community experienced rapid growth after the Texas and Pacific Railroad reached town in 1876. Brick buildings began to go up in downtown Paris, and within a few years the population reached 4,000. Two more railroads—an east-west and a north-south line—met in Paris in 1887, stimulating a population jump to 8,264 by 1890. Impressive Victorian homes were erected, along with numerous churches.[2]

Such a growing, bustling little city was a logical choice as seat of a new federal judicial district. In anticipation of opening Oklahoma reservation lands to settlers, Congress reorganized and expanded the area's federal judiciary in 1889. As part of this reorganization, the Eastern Judicial District of Texas was created, with court headquarters in Paris. But jurisdiction included the Chickasaw Nation and a large portion of the Choctaw Nation, and deputies operating out of Paris would find most of their action across the Red River in Indian Territory.[3]

The Paris courthouse was a brick structure built in 1874 for $50,000. The jail at the rear of the building was expanded in 1884. After a federal court was established in Paris, deputy U.S. marshals (as many as seventy-five deputies worked out of this court)[4] and hopeful possemen hovered around the courthouse. These lawmen lined up for the opportunity to serve warrants, thereby collecting arrest fees, travel expenses, and posted rewards.

Deputy U.S. marshals and possemen regularly congregated around the courthouse at Paris, hoping to receive warrants to serve. (Courtesy Aiken Regional Archives at Paris Junior College)

Tom Smith arrived in Paris to promise such men warrants to serve on cattle thieves in Wyoming. His promise was that the pay would be good and "that the job would soon be over." In Idaho, George Dunning was promised a wage of five dollars per day, with all expenses paid and a bonus of fifty dollars per victim if it proved necessary to kill any rustlers. Similar promises from Tom Smith attracted more than a score of adventurous men willing to carry their guns to faraway Wyoming.[5]

Smith's proposal intrigued a trio of brothers who had served as deputy U.S. marshals during the 1880s for the large and dangerous jurisdiction of the famous "Hanging Judge," Isaac Parker. Parker conducted his court in Fort Smith, Arkansas, which was the home area of the Barling brothers. Indeed, the family farm was at the little community of Barling, a few miles southeast of Fort Smith.

Frank Rector Barling was born in 1859, and by 1880 he had pinned on a deputy U.S. marshal's badge. Frank married Mamie Snyder in 1882, but they divorced after the couple had two children. In 1886 Frank married Kate Euper in Fort Smith, where he and his brothers became involved in the saloon business.[6]

Jerry Kannady Barling, born in 1862, married Mary Alice Euper in 1885. Mary Alice and Kate were sisters who married brothers. Three weeks before her first anniversary, Mary Alice died following childbirth. Within a few days her baby boy also died. Devastated, Jerry eventually would develop a drinking problem. In 1888 he was sworn in as a deputy U.S. marshal.

Robert Gibson "Bob" Barling was born in 1865, and in 1889 he married Clarence "Clara" Surratt, daughter of a former police chief of Fort Smith. Bob and Clara had the

BARLING'S MINT SALOON.

N. E. Corner Square.

Paris. Texas, _Aug 22 1891_

Left: Bob Barling, a Paris saloonkeeper and former deputy U.S. marshal, enlisted with Tom Smith, along with his brother Jerry. (From group photo, courtesy Wyoming State Museum) Above: Letterhead of the Barling saloon in Paris. (Courtesy James F. Barling, New Boston, Texas)

first of their five children in 1889, and by that time he had traded in his badge for a bartender's apron. Bob bought the Silver Dollar Saloon in Fort Smith.

The Barling brothers were attracted to the opportunities afforded by booming Paris. By 1891 Frank owned Barling's Mint Saloon on the northeast corner of the courthouse square. Frank wrote his father that Bob "is doing splendid." Like Jerry, Bob imbibed too freely, but Frank told his father that "Bob promised not to drink a single drop."[7]

In addition to their saloon enterprises, the brothers also were engaged in farming. But when Tom Smith circulated his Wyoming offer, the Barlings—who had ridden against Indian Territory outlaws—saw an opportunity to earn cash in Wyoming. It was decided that Frank would stay behind to run the Mint Saloon and other family interests, while Bob and Jerry would enlist with Tom Smith.

Another pair of brothers, Buck and J. A. Garrett, also signed on with Smith. Buck Garrett was only twenty, but he already had developed a fascination with law enforcement that would dominate the direction of his life. Born in Tennessee in 1871, Buck moved to Texas in 1878 with his parents, Larkin and Clara Garrett, and his three siblings. Larkin was a bartender who found work in Cooper, about twenty miles south of Paris. After Clara died in 1881, Larkin relocated to Paris, where he tended bar and his children shifted for themselves.

Left: Young Buck Garrett was six-two and 200 pounds and an experienced posseman. He hoped to earn a wedding stake in Wyoming. Right: J. A. Garrett went along with his brother, Buck, on the Wyoming adventure. (From group photo, courtesy Wyoming State Museum)

Young Buck drifted away from school, selling newspapers and working at other odd jobs. He ventured into Oklahoma to visit an older sister, who had married a farmer living near Boggy Depot, and he soon found a job on a ranch in the vicinity of Ardmore. In Ardmore he met his future wife, Ida May Chancellor, daughter of Deputy U.S. Marshal J. M. Chancellor. The strapping young cowboy impressed Chancellor, who recommended him to U.S. Marshal J. J. Dickerson. A deputy U.S. marshal was required to be twenty-one, so eighteen-year-old Buck was utilized as a posseman. For the next couple of years he rode against lawbreakers and courted Ida May.[8]

But he had not yet married in the spring of 1892 when Tom Smith came down from Wyoming. Buck was free to go, and so was J. A. The Garrett boys were big—Buck stood at six feet two and weighed two hundred pounds—and they shared the same features. They even wore their hats alike, tipped back, with a shock of hair showing on their foreheads. Buck and J. A. hastily prepared to share a Wyoming adventure.

Among other recruits was Jim Dudley. His full name was James Augustus Greenberry Dudley, and in Wyoming he used the alias "Gus Green." Dudley was a heavy man who was regarded as an expert rifle shot.[9] Thirty-year-old Kinzie A. Pickard was a family man who needed the cash offered for the Wyoming trip. He had married in Paris on December 2, 1888, one day after his twenty-seventh birthday; his bride was seventeen-year-old Lucille C. "Lou" Bedford.[10]

David E. Booker was a quiet-spoken but deadly officer who responded to Tom Smith's offer. A forty-one-year-old native of Kentucky, Dave Booker had moved to Texas when young. He wore a badge for most of his life, riding into Indian Territory in pursuit of fugitives "when lawlessness was ... rampant."[11]

Another veteran lawman who answered Smith's call was Jeff D. Mynett, "one of the best deputies that ever wore a badge," according to a fellow officer. Mynett had married a young woman from "a very good family" from Palestine, Texas, and he earned a living as a deputy U.S. marshal headquartered at Paris. A big man with a volatile temper, Mynett would sail into combat with fists or guns. When a Gainesville newspaper reporter named Walker published "a rather coarse insult," Mynett immediately traveled to Gainesville. "I'm going to whip somebody if a retraction is not made," he fumed. Mynett was accompanied by fellow deputies

Jeff Mynett, "one of the best deputies who ever wore a badge," also was known for his volatile temper. (From group photo, courtesy Wyoming State Museum)

Jim Chancellor and George Tucker, who intended to back their friend. In Gainesville Chancellor attended to some business while Mynett and Tucker went into a saloon. Aware of his temper, Mynett handed his revolver to Tucker, took off his coat, then marched to the newspaper office. Finding Walker, Mynett knocked him unconscious with one blow. Then Mynett delivered a series of vicious kicks to his fallen foe, knocking out most of Walker's front teeth. One of the printers started for Mynett with a club, but Tucker drew a revolver "and told him I'd bore him if he didn't stand back." Tucker allowed "that Jeff had been a little too harsh with Walker." But, after all, "Walker had insulted him, and Jeff had a right to protect his honor." All three lawmen were arrested. "Several rich fellows of the town went upon our bond," and the officers went back to work until their trial. They were assessed heavy fines, but U.S. Marshal James J. Dickerson arranged loans through the City National Bank of Paris, where he was a shareholder.[12]

Mynett's friend and colleague, Deputy U.S. Marshal George Tucker, was perhaps the most formidable gunman recruited by Tom Smith. When he was an old man, Tucker wrote a lengthy and thoughtful memoir of his half-century in law enforcement. "I have hunted men, killed men, good men, bad men, innocent men, and men who could instruct the devil in the ways of crime," he said. "I have killed men who had forfeited the right to live and other men who were not bad at all. I may have shot too fast on certain occasions, but those who were a second too slow are not left to tell the tales of their adventure. It was, in those days before 1900, a dangerous calling. Life was much cheaper, and blood was spilled with abandon. It wasn't so bad to kill a man then."[13]

George Tucker was born in 1855 in Franklin County, Arkansas. When he was a boy he attended a log cabin school near his home. In 1864, after Confederate Arkansas had fallen to Federal troops, the Tucker family joined a neighborhood wagon train bound for Texas, the home state of George's mother. She died the next year, however, and young George lived variously with a married sister and a married brother. Like most frontier boys, he was taught to shoot. "I can scarcely remember when I couldn't shoot," he recalled. "I grew up with a gun in my hands." Involved in a brawl and a fatal shootout in Arkansas when he was a teenager, George fled back to Texas. He finally settled down on a farm near Spanish Fort, just south of the Red River in Montague County. Nearby Indian Territory swarmed with lawbreakers, "and when the thieves and gunners came across into Spanish Fort, they were not in the habit of acting as church members."

By 1878 the office of town marshal in Spanish Fort was vacated.[14] Several townspeople came out to George Tucker's farm, offering him five dollars per day to keep the peace in Spanish Fort. The money was far more than he could earn from the grind of farming, and at the age of twenty-three George Tucker became a peace officer.

The Hired Gunmen

Tom Smith	Alex Lowther	Will Armstrong
M. A. McNally	Bob Barling	Bob Martin
Jerry Barling	Jeff Mynett	John Benson
Kinzie Pickard	Dave Booker	Cliff Schultz
Jim Dudley (Gus Green)	George Tucker	Buck Garrett
Starl Tucker	J. A. Garrett	B. S. Willey
Alex Hamilton	W. A. Wilson	Jesse Johnson
George Dunning (Idaho)	Bill Little	

Soon a young hardcase named Jim Melton became drunk in a Spanish Fort saloon. He harbored a grudge against Tucker, and after Melton mounted his horse, he fired a shot at the startled lawman. Tucker and another man quickly mounted up as Melton spurred out of town. The pursuit lasted only a mile. Tucker and his companion blazed away with Winchesters, tumbling Melton out of the saddle with a fatal neck wound. Tucker deeply regretted the killing, but after all, Melton "had tried to kill me." Tucker began to develop a pragmatic approach to law enforcement: "It doesn't help matters for a police officer to get soft with tough fellows."[15]

Not long afterward, a rugged character from Indian Territory known as Old Man Dayton was thrown out of a Spanish Fort saloon by the bartender. Bent on revenge, he crossed the Red River to arm himself, then returned to town. Tucker, backed by a brother and a cousin, tried to arrest him, but Dayton pulled a revolver and shot Tucker's brother in the arm. Old Man Dayton promptly was slain by a return fusillade of bullets.[16]

When a robber band called the Watson Gang rode into Spanish Fort from Indian Territory, Tucker gathered three men and armed his little posse with shotguns. The gang began carousing in a saloon, and one member rode his horse inside. Tucker called out for the gang to surrender, but the answer was, "Go to hell!" A street fight broke out, and buckshot from the posse peppered three members and five of their horses. One of the horses fell dead, and the gang retreated back into Indian Territory.[17]

Tucker did not offer pursuit, because the gang badly outnumbered his small force. Soon, though, he eagerly joined a sixteen-man posse formed to go after the Watson Gang in Indian Territory. "Most of us wanted a good crack at the Watson Gang anyway," remarked Tucker. Shortly after encountering their prey, the lawmen opened up with shotguns and revolvers. "We wanted to kill them anyway," admitted Tucker. "There wasn't much harm done in killing a man in those days, and especially not if he was a member of the Watson Gang."[18]

When a gang member named Trowbridge went down, the other outlaws scattered. The lawmen loaded a cache of stolen goods into wagons, then returned to Texas. But Trowbridge survived and charged each posse member with assault to kill and the theft of $7,000 worth of goods. Tucker and the others evaded conviction in a local court, but they were indicted by a federal grand jury at Judge Parker's court in Fort Smith. They were taken into custody at Spanish Fort by U.S. Marshal Charles Garrison.[19]

The resulting trip would foreshadow Tucker's experience in Wyoming. Marshal Garrison transported his prisoners in wagons, camping out at nights during the month-long journey to and from Fort Smith. But the "prisoners" were not shackled or hand-cuffed, and they were permitted to wear their revolvers and gunbelts. Upon arrival at Fort Smith, the accused officers received bond money from three prominent citizens. Released from custody, they returned for trial six months later, establishing a camp on the outskirts of Fort Smith. Marshal Garrison asked them not to wear their guns inside Judge Parker's courtroom. Each day before reporting to court, the officers piled up their guns in camp, leaving one man to guard the weapons. After court adjourned, they buckled on their guns again.[20]

Tucker was impressed by Judge Parker, but the prosecuting attorney ripped into the accused. "I had never realized before how very mean I was," recalled Tucker, "until I listened to his argument." But the officers were ably defended, and the jury acquitted everyone. Vindicated, Tucker groused that "there was never any real reason for having been tried. We were carrying out the law against tough law violators. . . . However, as it turned out, I suppose that law enforcement was furthered, since the courts had upheld us in both of the trials."[21]

Tucker resumed his duties in Spanish Fort, and by this time he also carried a commission as a Montague County deputy sheriff. When Tucker and another deputy spotted accused cow thief L. L. Lamb astride a horse in the main street of Spanish Fort, they walked over to arrest him. Ordered to surrender his pistol, Lamb tried to fight. The officers opened fire with their revolvers, hitting Lamb twice in the face. But Lamb somehow stayed in the saddle and galloped out of town. Tucker emptied his revolver, but a man dashed from a saloon offering a loaded pistol. Tucker emptied this gun, too, but Lamb made good his escape and recovered from his wounds. Four or five years later Tucker encountered Lamb on a train. Lamb thanked the officer profusely for turning his life around. Afraid that "I was headed straight for hell," Lamb repented and became a preacher.[22]

After learning that a trio of rustlers had fled Indian Territory, Tucker gathered five possemen and located the fugitives eight miles from Spanish Fort. The rustlers were arrested and handcuffed, but Tucker's party soon was intercepted by six irate citizens bent on discouraging rustlers. Tucker turned over his prisoners without a fight: "I would not have killed one of those decent fellows for all of the thieves in the Territory." Finding that they only had two ropes, the vigilantes asked Tucker for his. One of his prisoners was therefore lynched with his rope. But Tucker had the foresight to retrieve the three sets of handcuffs before the hanging. "I lost three prisoners and a good rope," reminisced Tucker with little regret. "However, those times were far different from the present, and especially in the attitude toward thievery."[23]

On another occasion, Tucker was equally pragmatic when three members of the Barlow Gang were shot to death: ". . . the very character of the men who had been killed didn't fill me with any desire to catch the killers. It was good riddance, the killings!" In August 1885 Tucker and a posse pursued a badman called "Peg Leg" all the way to Kansas. When Peg Leg attempted to flee the posse, they opened fire, killing him on the spot. "We might have captured him," explained Tucker about the long pursuit, "but it was August and, therefore, too hot for a lot of physical exertion."[24]

In 1889, after more than a decade of enforcing the peace in Spanish Fort, the hardbitten Tucker read in a newspaper that the U.S. marshal in Paris needed deputies. Tucker was tired of "the petty work of a policeman," and he knew that he could earn "a great deal more money" through arrest fees and travel allowances. By this time Tucker had acquired a formidable reputation as a lawman, and his application was accepted.[25]

Deputy U.S. Marshal Tucker worked out of Spanish Fort for a time, then moved to Paris to be in closer touch with the marshal's office. Tucker now spent most of his time as a manhunter, coming to relish "a certain exhilaration that one gets out of it. It is different from any other kind of hunting, this manhunting." When Tucker and two other officers tracked down Charley Bowie, the seventeen-year-old fugitive holed up in a light frame house and opened fire. Blasting away with their Winchesters, the officers shot seventeen holes in the flimsy walls, inflicting a fatal wound. Tucker was indicted for the killing, but "I knew that there wasn't any danger of being convicted on the charge." The prosecutor and judge both were friends of his who understandably supported law enforcement in an unruly land. The judge refused to allow testimony from various "tough characters," then directed the jury to return a verdict of not guilty.[26]

Early in his tenure as a federal officer, Tucker was one of twenty-five deputies dispatched to South Texas in the wake of the Battle of Richmond. There were forty warrants to serve to participants of the Jaybird-Woodpecker Feud, after which the officers policed the legal proceedings in Galveston. Everyone finally went free, but perhaps this was when Tucker met Tom Smith. The oppressive humidity caused Tucker to regard residents of "swampy countries" as unhealthy—"Their livers are out of fix." Habitually alert for danger, he concluded: "You don't want to fool with a fellow whose liver is out of fix—he'll kill you before you know it."[27]

Also in 1889, while tracking a lawbreaker in Indian Territory, Tucker saw some of the first Land Rush participants racing to stake out claims, "riding all sorts of animals and vehicular contraptions imaginable." He was glad of the chance to be an eyewitness: "It was frantic, so hectic, so seemingly crazy and hurried!" Another welcome experience was the opportunity to see "the North" by transporting prisoners to northern penitentiaries. Hoping "to see the country," he joined a platoon of deputies who escorted sixty prisoners to Detroit, then he helped transport eighty-five convicts to Brooklyn, returning by way of Washington, D.C. "I enjoyed both of the trips, but I would not like a steady diet of that sort of thing. I much preferred to work in the field. There was more spice to it."[28]

The "spice" involved more manhunts and more shootouts, including one that claimed the life of a young bystander. All too often this risky work resulted in the legal release of lawbreakers. Following the release of three culprits, Tucker complained that "as was the case with so many of the damned crooks that we caught, they were after pardoned."[29]

By the time he was contacted by Tom Smith about working in Wyoming, therefore, George Tucker was a hard man with broad experience in law enforcement. At the age of thirty-seven he had served for fourteen years as a town marshal, deputy sheriff, and deputy U.S. marshal. He was a blooded veteran of numerous shootouts and countless pursuits. He had been robbed of rewards, and he had watched in disbelief as scoundrels that he had risked his life to capture were freed by the legal system. Indeed, he had been brought up on charges several times by criminals. Accordingly, he felt few qualms about summary justice. More than once he had received financial and legal help from big ranchers and other prominent men more interested in justice than legalities.

Now such men were offering good pay to arrest cattle thieves in Wyoming. "That was just to our liking," said Tucker, speaking for himself and other experienced frontier officers. "We'd been doing it for years. Nobody liked a cattle or horse thief."[30]

Therefore Tucker told Tom Smith that he would go to Wyoming. So did Jeff Mynett and Dave Booker and Bob and Jerry Barling. Tom Smith bought tickets for a westbound train out of Paris. Buck and J. A. Garrett came aboard, along with ill-fated Jim Dudley and Alex Lowther. Nearly a dozen other men boarded the train, wearing sixguns and carrying Winchesters.

But when the train pulled out of Paris, George Tucker was not on board. After Tom Smith arrived in Paris and began enlisting gunmen, Tucker rode northwest into Indian Territory in pursuit of two fugitives. He made the arrests, then brought his prisoners back to Texas, jailing them in Gainesville. He knew that the train from Paris was scheduled to stop in Gainesville. Even though Tucker now had to take his prisoners back to Paris, he went to the depot "to see the boys." They urged him to come along, and Smith was insistent. When Tucker explained that he had spent about fifty dollars on this manhunt, Smith pledged to pay the fifty dollars and to arrange for a deputy to transport the prisoners to Paris. A deputy named Reynolds was on the train, and he agreed to get off and take charge of Tucker's captives. Tucker then boarded the train, "and thus became a member of the Texan army that was going to free Wyoming from the rustlers." [31]

Tucker was struck that Smith's recruits formed "a pretty tough-looking bunch of hombres." Tucker knew most of the men on board: "There were some good men, and some who were worse than no men at all." He regarded Bob and Jerry Barling, Jim Dudley, Alex Lowther, Cliff Schultz, and John Benson as "mere saloon bullies" rather than gunmen. Puzzled at some of Smith's selections, Tucker "never could explain why he chose so many fellows who knew nothing at all of gun fighting." Such men "were more dangerous than helpful." An experienced peace officer, Tucker was familiar with the type: ". . . they were brawly, always getting into arguments and personal altercations. If one of them could get to a man with his fists, he would give a good account of himself." In Wyoming, however, guns would be the primary weapons—not fists. "We would have been better off if those fellows had been left in Texas." [32]

Tucker was further dismayed when the train pulled into Henrietta, about sixty miles west of Gainesville. His seventeen-year-old half-brother, Starl Tucker, came aboard. In Paris Starl had asked George if he could join the expedition. "I told him that it was no place for a boy," the lawman said. Of course, such a blunt statement would irk any teenager—especially Starl Tucker. "He didn't have a bit of sense," explained George Tucker. "He was mean and always wanting to kill somebody." [33]

That night as the train hurtled northwestward toward the Texas Panhandle, Tucker asked Tom Smith for the fifty dollars. Smith said that he had only been kidding, that he had promised the money merely to entice Tucker onto the train. "I didn't like it very much," Tucker later recalled, "but then Tom was too good a friend of mine for me to raise a squabble with him over so paltry a sum." [34]

The Union Pacific route angled five hundred miles from Paris to the northwest corner of the Panhandle, then another eighty miles to Raton Pass on the border of New Mexico and Colorado. Two hundred miles to the north was Denver, where the Texans were met by their employers. The Texans had tried to sleep in their seats, but they were "pretty tired" by the time they reached Denver. [35] Their stamina and endurance—and courage—soon would be stretched to far greater lengths. The Texans were about to earn the pay they had been promised.

Chapter 10

Invasion: The First Four Days

"The next morning at breakfast, [Wolcott] made a very manly speech, resigning command of the expedition for the sake of peace and harmony. . . ."

BILLY IRVINE

When a train from Texas pulled into Denver on Tuesday, April 5, 1892, it was met by several Wyoming ranchers. They had traveled from Cheyenne to welcome Tom Smith and a score of weary Texans.

The Texans all carried revolvers and Winchesters, mostly in .44 caliber. But their Wyoming employers brought them new and more powerful rifles: some of .45-90 caliber and some of .38-55. "It looked like a war, to see them handing out the new guns," said George Tucker. "They were dandies, to be sure."[1]

But Tucker soon grew uneasy, because as the train pulled out the cattlemen "pulled down all of the blinds and locked the doors of the coach." The Texans said little about this precaution, because most of them wearily fell asleep in their seats. When the train rolled into Cheyenne late in the afternoon, the blinds remained drawn and the Texans stayed aboard. Their car was backed to the stockyard and coupled onto the special train. A passenger car, baggage car, three stock cars, and a flat car, along with an engine and tender, pulled out of Cheyenne before six o'clock.[2]

Frank Canton was impressed with the hired gunman, particularly the "brave and experienced officers from the Indian Territory." Chicago *Herald* reporter Sam Clover "found the Texas contingent a picturesque lot of men," while Dr. Penrose observed that the "Texans were a good-looking body of men, who were well able to take care of themselves." But Dr. Penrose was concerned that the Texans "were not very warmly clad for April in Wyoming—their clothes were more for the Texas climate." Big Gus Green "arrived clad in nothing but a summer undershirt, trousers and shoes, with his six-shooter on his right hip." Frank Canton pointed out that "April weather in Wyoming is always bad," a reality that soon would become painfully clear to the Texans.[3]

Tom Smith was in charge of the Texans, while Major Wolcott "was ostensibly in command of the expedition." On the train Wolcott's command post was the baggage car, where there was considerable sorting and organizing to be done, in order to facilitate a rapid departure. Wolcott "ordered every one out of the baggage car except those he wanted to help him." But Frank Canton soon entered the baggage car, "and was promptly ordered out," according to Billy Irvine. Canton was a dangerous man to boss around, particularly with the customary brusqueness of Frank Wolcott. "This was the start of a bitter feeling between the two," related Irvine, "which gave us considerable trouble later."

The train halted at tiny Orin Junction, about 120 miles north of Cheyenne. Wolcott stepped off and asked the telegraph operator to wire a message to Buffalo. After several unsuccessful attempts, the operator informed Wolcott that the wires were down. "This was what we wanted to learn," revealed Dr. Penrose.

Ed David, ranch manager for Senator Joseph M. Carey, had been assigned to cut the wires into Buffalo. With David obviously carrying out his plans, Wolcott stopped the train again after another twenty miles. David was waiting at old Fort Fetterman with two saddle horses for Wolcott's use. The horses were loaded onto a stock car, but David remained behind to thwart telegraph repairmen and keep the wires cut.[5]

Soon the tracks turned westward. It was sixty miles from Orin Junction to Casper, located near the confluence of the North Platte River and Casper Creek. The train arrived before dawn, about four o'clock, and stopped at Casper's stockyards, on the eastern edge of the community. "Casper is a small town on a sage brush flat," noted Dr. Penrose. "We all tumbled out of the cars where we had spent an uncomfortable night trying to sleep sitting up."[6]

The men began unloading wagons, horses, and equipment. Saddling their horses, the riders were told to carry large quantities of ammunition in their saddlebags. The sun was nearly an hour in the sky when the Invaders headed out of town and, according to George Dunning, several Casper citizens "seemed to be watching the mob closely." Billy Irvine stayed behind with a few men to finish loading supplies and equipment into the wagons. The others rode along Casper Creek for about six miles, then stopped in the

Center Street, Casper's main thoroughfare. The expedition's special train stopped on the outskirts and spent considerable time unloading the cars and setting out to the north. (Author's collection)

Guns of the Invaders

The Cheyenne gun shop favored by Wyoming cattlemen was exceptionally busy during the days preceding the invasion of Johnson. A good number of newly purchased Winchesters were presented to the gunmen from Texas. Several days later the Invaders were compelled to surrender their guns to the U.S. Cavalry, but Major Wolcott insisted that a careful list be made, in expectation that these weapons eventually would be returned to the owners. The list, which included serial numbers—a boon to gun collectors—was discovered in the army records of the National Archives by historian Robert A. Murray and published in the July 1967 edition of *Shooting Times*.

The guns of forty-three men are inventoried. Missing from the list are the firearms of Texans Gus Green and Alex Lowther, who died of wounds. Also missing are the weapons of Tom Smith and of a few of the Wyoming ranchers, some of whom were released from custody almost immediately.

Forty-two handguns and forty-six shoulder guns were listed. Major Wolcott, Billy Irvine, and W. B. Wallace carried no revolvers, only Winchesters. Everyone else packed a handgun, while two men carried a brace of revolvers. L. H. Parker had a Colt .45 and a Colt .38. Only four men carried a Colt .41 double-action, which was not as reliable as the single-action Colt .45. There were twenty-eight Colt .45s and four Colt .44s, as well as two Colt .38s and two "pistols" of unknown type. John Tisdale had a .44 Smith and Wesson, A. B. Clarke had a .44 Webley, and W. H. Taylor had a .42 revolver. A number of cartridge belts and scabbards were taken up, but several men apparently shoved their revolvers into pockets or waistbands.

Most of the rifles were Winchesters. Seven of the Texans, along with two of the Wyoming men, carried their old model 1873 .44-40 Winchesters into battle. Four more Texans stuck with their Model 1873

The 1886 Winchester boasted numerous improvements by master gunsmith John Browning. The octagonal barrel was 26 inches long. The .45-caliber rifle loaded eight cartridges. (Author's collection)

.38-44 Winchesters, despite the offer of newer models. The other Winchesters included two .38-56 caliber, four .40-82 calibers, along with a dozen large-bore Model 1886 rifles: eight .45-90 calibers and four .45-70 calibers. (Beginning with the Model 1886 guns, master gunsmith John Browning engineered various improvements in Winchester products.)

Joe Elliott and Pappy Whitcomb carried .40 caliber Sharps carbines. Charles Ford was armed with a shotgun, a .45-70 Winchester, and a Colt .45 revolver. George Tucker had two Winchesters, a .40-60 and a .40-82, along with his Colt .45. Four Wyoming men carried Martini rifles: Fred de Billier, H. E. Teschemacher, and A. R. Powers had .44 Martinis, while C. A. Campbell had a .38 Martini.

Principal calibers purchased for the expedition. Rifle ammunition cost roughly two dollars per 100 cartridges. Three thousand rounds were loaded onto the supply wagons, in addition to cartridges stuffed into pockets and saddle bags. (Author's collection)

shelter of an array of bluffs. The horses were unsaddled, and several were unbridled and picketed to sagebrush while breakfast cooked.

About nine o'clock Irvine arrived with the wagons. The teamsters unhitched their horses and turned them out to graze along the creek bottom. However, the unpicketed horses soon spooked, and as they cavorted several other animals broke free and joined the stampede. About fifteen horses galloped into the countryside. Several men saddled up and rode in pursuit, but it was five or six hours before they returned. In addition to the long delay, three or four of the horses could not be caught. Dr. Penrose lost his mount ("I should have kept the bridle on, or should have picketed him by the foot"), and so did Sam Clover. Clover "immediately took a Texan's horse and insisted it was his." Irvine, who would be consistently paternalistic toward the Texans, returned the horse and ordered Clover to ride in one of the wagons. "The reporter was a fresh young man with a disposition to take other people's things," pointed out Dr. Penrose. "The next day he took my bridle—an unusually fine one—and never returned it."[7]

About noon, while the expedition still awaited the return of the runaway horses, a rider was sighted. Several men rode out and took the unarmed man into custody. The captive, Joe Todd, was headed for Casper to shear sheep, and he knew several of the riders, including Frank Canton, who was his neighbor. Todd had spent his first night out with Nate Champion and Nick Ray at the KC Ranch, "but somehow [he] got a little brainstorm" and did not mention this dangerous fact. Although Todd was forced to come along when the march was resumed, Frank Canton soon rode up and said, "We don't want this boy. Let him go." Todd was released, after being warned "to say nothing about seeing the mob in the country."[8]

Two other riders, also encountered during the noon stop, were disarmed, offered lunch, then compelled to join the march. Twenty-year-old Billie Martin and Charlie Negus, still in his teens, claimed that they wanted to join the hunt for rustlers, while actually looking for a chance to escape. During the first couple of days of the journey, other individual riders were encountered, and these men were released with warnings not to talk about the column of riders.[9]

During the afternoon march, a band of Senator Joseph Carey's saddle horses was encountered. Carey, whose open-range ranch was in the vicinity, was known to support the expedition, and replacement mounts were provided for all of the dismounted men except Dr. Penrose, who chose to stay in the wagon. It was cold, and the men rode into a spitting snow from the north. "I thought that I'd freeze to death," recalled George Tucker, one of the lightly clad Texans. "My Texas blood was too thin for a Wyoming May [sic] winter."[10]

Running increasingly behind schedule, the expedition rode into the night, finally pitching camp about twenty miles north of Casper. A young steer was shot and butchered, and supper was dished out about ten o'clock. Two Sibley tents, which would sleep half a dozen or more men each, were pulled from a wagon and set in place. Several Wyoming cattlemen bedded down in the tents, along with Dr. Penrose. Before ducking inside to his sheltered bedroll, the doctor watched with admiration as Tom Smith tended to his men. "It was a cold night, and before turning in himself, Captain Tom Smith went around in a fatherly way to all the Texans to see that they were comfortable," Penrose recalled.[11]

The antagonism triggered on the train by Major Wolcott with his curt orders to Frank Canton festered throughout the day. That night, Hubert Teschemacher "and others" approached Billy Irvine "and said I would have to talk to Wolcott in regard to the trouble that was brewing." Of course, Wolcott's arrogant personality rendered him easy to dislike, which probably was a personal motivation of Teschemacher and the others. Irvine realized that Smith and Canton were friends, "and the Texans naturally followed Smith." Probably he also recognized that most members of the expedition disliked Wolcott and were not inclined to accept his leadership.

Irvine bedded down that night alongside Wolcott and had a frank talk with him. The next morning, Thursday, April 9, the men were called together and Wolcott "made a very manly speech, resigning command of the expedition for the sake of peace and harmony; that we were out for a distinct purpose, and that the feelings and wishes of no one man should be allowed to stand in the way of our success." It was announced that Tom Smith would continue to direct the Texans, while Frank Canton would exercise field command.[12]

Canton intended to march to Buffalo as rapidly as possible, seize control of the Johnson County seat, then clean out those regarded as rustlers. But the snow and frigid north wind continued to slow the expedition, and the wagons repeatedly bogged down in the muddy gumbo of the roads. "Four abreast the cavalcade faced the storm," wrote Sam Clover, "the animals pushed along to the extent of their limits." The growing blizzard "coated every horseman with a white rime of frost from head to foot." Clover managed to stay warm by donning his slicker, then draping himself in a used cavalry overcoat that he had bought in Cheyenne. But Clover's fellow journalist, Ed Towse, was miserable, tormented with bleeding hemorrhoids as well as vicious weather. Towse rode in the rear of the column, slumped over his saddle horn and moaning through clenched teeth. The snow "made it difficult for fast marching," grumped Frank Canton impatiently, "and the men and horses were soft."[13]

About noon the column stopped for lunch. Then the riders pushed ahead, leaving the wagons to follow at a slower pace, although it was a dangerous tactic to separate the men from their supply train. Even Dr. Penrose left his wagon to mount a little white horse that had been found. "He was old and weak and looked as though he had survived his last winter," complained Penrose. As the snowstorm worsened, however, Penrose returned to the wagons. At dark the teamsters made camp, but the riders continued on toward the Tisdales' TTT Ranch, sixty-five miles north of Casper. Frank Wolcott became lost after dark, finally stopping to sleep in a haystack. When the column at last rode up to the TTT, the hired gunmen bedded down in the bunkhouse, while Bob and John Tisdale led their Wyoming friends to the ranch house.[14]

About ten or twelve miles before reaching the TTT, the column was joined by Mike Shonsey. Shonsey had been scouting the countryside, and he reported that about fifteen rustlers[15] were at the KC Ranch, sixteen miles north of the TTT on the Middle Fork of the Powder River. The Wyoming men met to discuss the next move. Canton's first priority was to march in force to Buffalo, then pursue individual rustlers (until killing occurred, it was perfectly legal for the expedition to march to Buffalo or anywhere else). But the cattlemen—who were Canton's employers—had wanted to go after rustlers as soon as they rode into the countryside. There was a vigorous disagreement. "Hesse was thoroughly angered by Wolcott," observed Sam Clover, also reporting that Hesse disliked Tom Smith, who "threatened to draw on Irvine." When Dr. Penrose arrived the next day with the wagons, he observed, "There seemed to me to be some lack of harmony in the party while we were at Tisdale's ranch."[16]

The decision was made to attack the rustlers at the KC Ranch. The ranch house was a stout log cabin, so Canton wanted to use dynamite to flush the prey. Since the dynamite was loaded in the wagons, there would be a further delay while the teamsters drove toward the TTT. But a day of rest would be good for the horses, not to speak of their riders. "The Texas men were about played out," noted George Dunning.[17]

Frank Wolcott left his haystack bed and rode into TTT headquarters during the morning of Friday, April 8. About ten o'clock a cowboy arrived from Billy Irvine's Ogallala Ranch with two pack horses loaded with ammunition, which later was transferred to the supply wagons. That afternoon the men were called together and told that they would ride that night for a dawn raid on a rustler hideout sixteen miles away. The wagons arrived about five o'clock in the afternoon. Because the riders expected to stay ahead of the wagons, everyone was directed to draw blankets and a day's rations and ample ammunition from the supply vehicles. During the evening the leaders "gave orders for the mob to kill every man on this ranch they proposed to raid, and to leave no man alive about the ranch to tell any tales afterward no matter who he might be."[18]

The Tisdale cowboys told the Texans that "a big dance" at the KC had brought together the rustlers. Sam Clover reported that Mike Shonsey "had brought in the important news that two of the most notorious rustlers of the Powder River country, Nick Ray and Nate Champion, were camped at Nolan's 'K.C.' Ranch on the middle fork." According to Clover, Shonsey related that there were stolen cattle at the KC, which Ray and Champion would take to a railroad extension camp near Gillette, about seventy miles cross-country to the northeast. "This opportunity to catch two ringleaders who were on the 'wanted' list was not one to be neglected, and in defiance of the storm, it was decided to make an all-night ride to the Powder River, surround the ranch house, and let Judge Lynch do his work at daylight."[19]

After arriving with the wagons, Dr. Penrose treated Ed Towse for "acute piles." Now that killing was imminent, both Penrose and Towse decided that they had gone far enough. "I was directed to stay with Ed Towse, and to follow with the wagons the next morning," claimed Penrose. But Sam Clover wrote that Dr. Penrose "flatly refused to fall in" when the men mounted up that night. Also staying was rancher H. W. Davis, who claimed "that his horse was played out." Unconvinced, his fellow ranchers "thought that Davis lost heart," according to Dr. Penrose, "and for long afterwards they held this desertion against him."[20]

About seven o'clock that evening Mike Shonsey rode out with three Texans—Dave Booker, Kinzie Pickard, and Jesse Johnson—to scout the KC Ranch ahead of the main body. George Dunning, who later claimed he intended to warn the men at the ranch, persuaded one of the Texans "to let me go in his place." But Frank Wolcott, who was giving orders again, saw Dunning saddling up "and said I could not go along with the party to investigate matters." Wolcott directed the original scouts to ride, then—with his usual tact—added "that us fellows would have to learn to obey orders better and ask less questions."[21]

A few hours later Major Wolcott gave the word for his men to head out for the KC. Each rider strapped a blanket behind his saddle and wrapped a ration of crackers and bacon into his slicker.[22] At eleven o'clock they mounted up and rode into a cold and stormy night.

Hard Winter Davis Writes His Wife

On April 5, 1892, the day that the Invaders left Cheyenne for Johnson County, rancher H. W. "Hard Winter" Davis sent a letter to his wife attempting to explain his participation in the expedition. The letter is written on the stationery of Cheyenne's Inter Ocean Hotel. Discovered by Bob Edwards in the archives of the Jim Gatchell Museum, the letter was first published in the April 2005 issue of *The Sentry*, the publication of the Gatchell Museum Association.

My own dear precious wife

I write you this letter to explain all in case of any serious injury befalling me. When I left Buffalo I had no idea of any such undertaking being contemplated but was lately asked to come here and hear the formulated plan. Since here I know to my surprise how intense the feeling is and that a large number would participate, you will learn of those that have acted. I feel my responsibility is as great as that of others, I have prayed for guidance and cannot see that I will ever be able to return to my home unless the gang are driven out besides Webb and Taylor have sworn to shoot me on sight. A man that will not protect himself & home is a coward, I could do nothing alone except to sacrifice my life. I hope precious you will not think hardly of me and that I have not thought of you and the babies. There are times when one has to act decidedly in this life, I realize that that time has come to me. There is no use in any longer hoping to make the rustlers believe that I am innocent, they are no doubt determined to drive me from my home and property, they have sworn to kill me, I must act.

I love you darling with my whole heart, kiss the babies for their papa & do not let them forget me.

My God bless you & forgive me   With my whole heartful of love to you & our babies

> *Your faithful husband,*
> *Winter*

One object I have is to prevent if in my power, the unjust shedding of blood. To save the innocent & to prevent extreme measures in those guilty of nothing greater than sympathy for the rustlers.

Chapter 11

Last Stand at the KC

"By God, [Nate Champion] may be a rustler, but he is also a HE MAN with plenty of guts!"

THE TEXAS KID

On Friday evening, April 8, Mike Shonsey and three Texans swung into their saddles and headed into the cold night. They rode for the KC Ranch, sixteen miles to the north. Their mission was to scout this supposed rustler haven, then backtrack and meet the other members of the expedition at a point four miles south of the KC.[1]

A few hours later[2] the main party of riders headed into a blowing snowstorm. There was almost no talk as each man huddled in his saddle against the cutting wind. "The frigid snow dashed with savage violence in their faces," recalled Sam Clover vividly, "blinding their eyes so that it was impossible to see a foot beyond their horses' heads, while beards and mustaches quickly became solid masses of snow and ice."[3]

The icy column plodded through the miserable night for hours. Four miles from KC headquarters, the shivering riders descended into a gulch. Dismounting, they hastily built several fires from sagebrush. Confessing that "he was two benumbed to remove his feet from the stirrups," Sam Clover had to be lifted from his saddle by Tom Smith. For an hour the men crowded around the fire in the shadow of the gulch. Some of the Texans were talking themselves into a killing mood, probably thinking about the fifty-dollar bonus promised for each dead rustler. Billy Irvine, aware that the Texans did not know their prey by sight, told the hired gunmen that "rather than kill an innocent man we preferred to let a rustler get away . . . ; and I tried to impress upon their minds that not a man was to be fired on by them until they were ordered to do so by some Wyoming man who knew what he was doing." Mike Shonsey and the other scouts rode in with the news that they had heard fiddle music from the KC cabin. Finally, "with circulation partially restored, the word was passed to mount. . . . Within moments the men rode again into the freezing gloom."[4]

Before dawn the column pulled up in the brush half a mile south of the KC Ranch buildings. The men dismounted and, following "a short consultation," the cabin was surrounded. Half a dozen Texans, reported to be good shots, were deployed in a ravine south of the cabin that was an obvious escape route. Several men stationed themselves along the riverbank about 100 yards above the bridge, while several others clustered inside and near the log stable which stood close to the river, about seventy-five yards below the cabin. A small party stayed with the horses.[5]

The first light of dawn revealed a spring wagon, "which Mike Shonsey said did not belong there." It was concluded that someone was inside the cabin "that we did not want, … so we just laid around keeping quiet and out of sight until some time after the sun was up. …" Joe Elliott had carried about ten pounds of dynamite behind his saddle, so that the cabin could be destroyed with a surprise explosion. But Irvine and one of the Tisdales refused to kill "strangers," and the dynamite "was placed aside." It was decided to let any rustler "come out as far as possible and then … shoot them down."[6]

As the sun rose, the Texans and anyone else who had never seen the KC viewed a modest ranch headquarters situated in an open pasture south of the clear waters of the Middle Fork of the Powder River. The KC had begun as a line camp of Moreton Frewen, before cowboy Johnny Nolan homesteaded the location. A line of bluffs ran west and south of the ranch buildings. A road angled across the bluffs from the southwest, crossed a wooden bridge near the stable, then pointed north toward Buffalo. In addition to the low log stable and pole corral, there was a stout four-room cabin built of milled pine logs—with a clear field of fire on all sides. "The rustlers had cut portholes along each side," Frank Canton glumly observed. "A few men with a supply of ammunition, plenty of water, and something to eat could stand off a large force on the outside indefinitely."[7]

Inside the cabin were ammunition, water, food, and four men, including the redoubtable Nate Champion. Big Nick Ray was with Champion. As a cowboy for Billy Irvine, it was said that Ray had mavericked for his employer, then had begun to steal cattle from the rancher. The Wyoming men told Sam Clover that Ray was "one of the most energetic rustlers in the country."[8] Instead of fifteen or so "rustlers" at the KC, Champion and Ray were the only men on the "death list" of the Invaders.

For the previous few days there had been five suspected rustlers at the KC: Champion, Ray, Billy Hill, Ed Starr, and Jack Long. Late in the afternoon of Friday, April 8, a passing cowboy had delivered a note from an area rancher that about forty head of Hill's cattle had strayed into his pasture. Although it soon would be dark, Hill saddled up and rode downriver to retrieve his cattle. Starr and Long also left, "to undertake certain operations under cover of darkness in the Ogallala country to the east." After dark, two ranchers, George Peterson and J. Brown Parker, arrived separately at the KC. Parker was driving a wagon loaded with lumber bought in Buffalo. He asked if he could spend the night, but when Champion and Ray pointed out that they had no hay or feed for his team, Peterson invited Parker to stay at his ranch, eight miles away.

As Peterson and Parker headed into the night, two trappers drove their wagon to the river to water their team.[9] The trappers were gray-haired Bill Jones and a younger man, William Walker. Champion and Ray strolled over and offered the shelter of their cabin and barn. Gratefully the trappers accepted the hospitality of the KC, stabling their

Siege at the KC, April 19, 1892

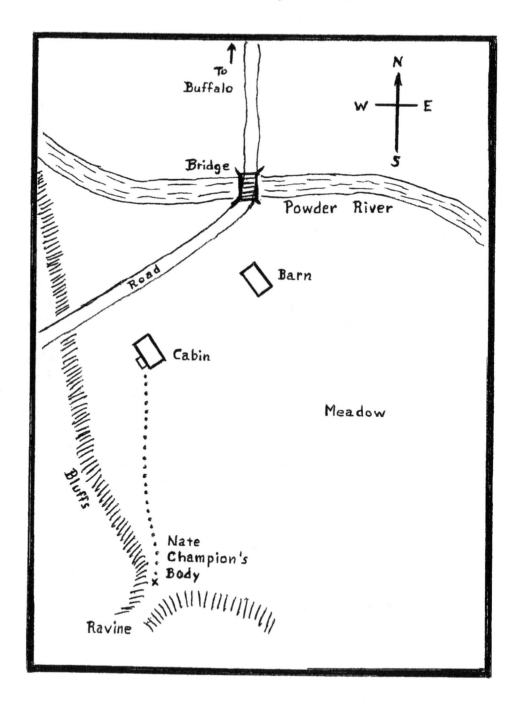

The KC barn, pictured from the south. The cabin, another low, log structure, stood to the west, or left. The Middle Fork of the Powder River runs left to right behind the barn, and may be seen above the horses at right. (Courtesy Johnson County Jim Gatchell Memorial Museum)

horses, then lugging their bedrolls into the cabin. The trappers bedded down on the floor, and the four men slept through the cold night, oblivious to the quiet approach of more than forty armed antagonists.

The gunmen shivered at their positions for two hours, until the cabin door finally opened after sunrise. A man came out, then quickly went back inside, probably after relieving himself. About fifteen minutes later "an old man—Bill Jones—ventured outside. "Tin bucket in hand," Jones headed toward the river to get water for breakfast. When he passed the stable, "the moment he was out of sight of the house two Winchesters were poked in his face, and he was ordered to make no outcry." Jones convinced his captors that he was an innocent traveler. He said that Nate Champion and Nick Ray were asleep in the cabin, but that his partner, William Walker, was awake.

Two Texas gunmen were assigned to guard Jones behind the riverbank.[10] Perhaps half an hour passed before Walker emerged from the cabin. Despite frigid temperatures, he did not wear a coat or vest, and his galluses hung over a thick shirt. Yawning, Walker made his way slowly to the stable, presumably searching for Jones. According to Sam Clover, when confronted by Winchesters Walker "turned sulky and showed his teeth" and reached for his pistol. But Tom Smith alertly seized Walker's weapon, then brandished his own revolver in the trapper's face. "Against such persuasive argument he had nothing to offer," related Clover, "and without a word he was led to the river-bank to join his side-partner."[11]

There was another long wait before Nick Ray finally stepped outside to urinate.

Seventeen-year-old Starl Tucker was the youngest of the hired gunmen. "The Texas Kid" had a mean streak, and he eagerly shot down an unsuspecting Nick Ray. (From group photo, courtesy Wyoming State Museum)

Inside the stable, Starl Tucker, positioned beside George Tucker, "begged" his older brother for permission "to let him kill him." Tom Smith overheard Starl, and asked George in a whisper, "Do you think the kid could hold steady enough to get him?"[12]

Knowing that Starl was a crack shot, George replied, "I reckon he could."

"Let him go ahead, then," directed Smith.

"Starl pulled down on him and knocked him down," reported George Tucker. "But he didn't kill him, and when he began to wriggle about, we all began to shoot at him."[13]

"The big man staggered and fell," said George Dunning. Sam Clover remembered that Ray struggled to his feet, but "with a quavering curse, again fell to the ground." As Ray crawled toward the door, rifle bullets "bit the dust all around him." Suddenly, Nate Champion appeared in the doorway and emptied his Winchester rapid-fire at the stable. Ducking back inside, he reloaded, then again stood in the doorway and provided covering fire. With Ray now just a few feet from the door, Champion tossed his empty rifle inside, then clutched his wounded partner and man-handled him into the shelter of the cabin.[14]

The concealed riflemen, who had not displayed impressive marksmanship, expressed admiration for Champion's heroism. Billie Martin thought that "Champion kept the gang firing at him in order to let his wounded comrade draw nearer the open doorway." Starl Tucker, "who boasted uncontradicted, that he had fired the shot that brought Ray down," also shouted, within Martin's hearing, that Champion was "a HE MAN with plenty of guts!" Listening to the men in the stable express agreement, Martin observed, "That was the thought of all."[15]

Champion began pumping rifle bullets at his antagonists "as fast as he could burn ammunition." Aware that slugs were thudding into the cabin walls from all sides, Champion shifted from room to room to hold his attackers at bay. "Several of the invaders were wounded," testified Billie Martin, "but none seriously injured, slight flesh wounds, alone, being received." Sheriff Malcolm Campbell was told that when Nate Champion first opened fire from the cabin doorway, one of his bullets "grazed the cheek of the Texas Kid, drawing blood." According to Campbell, Champion later nicked one other antagonist, then "he wounded one Texan in the arm seriously, and another was creased deeply in the thigh before the raiders learned to be more cautious." Champion's return fire was sufficient to keep the riflemen behind cover. The attackers maintained a heavy fire for hours, but no one left his position to charge the cabin. Picket riders were assigned to guard the nearby road.[16]

Inside the cabin Champion took time to try to tend the mortally wounded Ray. The partners had been preparing breakfast when Ray stepped outside, triggering the initial barrage. Perhaps Champion was able to wolf down a few bites of food during the siege. He already had pulled on a pair of trousers, a collarless shirt, and a vest. Champion collected and arranged the guns and ammunition belonging to Nick Ray and the trappers. He produced a red pocket notebook and pencil—standard articles for stockmen, who frequently had to tally animals and jot down brands—and at intervals he composed a diary of his desperate stand.[17]

> Me and Nick Ray was getting breakfast when the attack took place. Two men here with us—Bill Jones and another man. The old man went after water and did not come back. His friend went out to see what was the matter and he did not come back. Nick started out and I told him to look out, that I thought there was someone at the stable and would not let them come back.
> Nick is shot but not dead yet. I must go and wait on him.

Sam Clover tried to change positions, but a bullet cut the air above his head, and he dove for cover. He remarked that "if a man was exposed for a second a bullet quickly whistled in his direction from the shattered window-frame of the house."[18]

> It is now about two hours since the first shot.
> Nick is still alive.
> They are still shooting and are all around the house.
> Boys, there is bullets coming in like hail.
> Them fellows is in such shape I can't get at them.
> They are shooting from the stable and river and back of the house.

A few months earlier Champion successfully had fought off a morning attack on another cabin. Although outnumbered, he had driven off his attackers with a bold counterattack. But during the morning of April 9, Champion soon realized that the odds were far longer, and that this time a counterattack was unlikely. He was cornered, pinned down by dozens of gunmen. And all too soon he was alone.

> Nick is dead. He died about 9 o'clock.
> I see a smoke down at the stable. I think they have fired it. I don't think they intend to let me get away this time.

The stable was not ablaze. The chilled Invaders apparently built a fire for warmth. "After wasting considerable ammunition," reported Sam Clover, a council of war was convened where the horses were being held. While eight riflemen stayed in position and continued firing at the cabin, everyone else withdrew to discuss tactics. There was no support for a direct assault against the sharpshooting Champion. It was decided that "burning the house was ... the most practicable, and four men were dispatched to the nearest rancher's for a wagonload of hay, under cover of which it was proposed to steal up and fire the cabin."[19]

After the hay wagon squad departed, the balance of the men returned to their firing positions. Champion noticed their temporary withdrawal, and for a time he hoped that his attackers might be preparing to leave.

It is now about noon. There is someone at the stable yet. They are throwing a rope out at the door and drawing it back. I guess this is to draw me out. I wish that duck would go out further so that I could get a shot at him.

Boys, I don't know what they have done with them two fellows that staid here last night.

Boys, I feel pretty lonesome just now. I wish there was someone here with me so we could watch all sides at once. They may feel around until I get a good shot before they leave.

After an absence of two hours, the hay wagon "squad returned empty-handed, no wagon being obtainable, and another council was called, at which nothing definite was decided." The picket riders guarding the road were called in for this second council.[20] But while the road was unguarded, a wagon and rider approached the KC from the south. A lull in firing during the second council of war gave Nate Champion a chance to write in his notebook. It also allowed the two travelers to close in on the besieged ranch without the warning of gunshots.

The unsuspecting travelers were Jack Flagg and his seventeen-year-old stepson, Alonzo Taylor. Flagg's Red Fork Ranch was eighteen miles west of the KC. That morning Flagg and Alonzo left their home for a journey of more than 130 miles to Douglas. Flagg rode horseback, while Alonzo drove a wagon and a team of horses. Flagg and Alonzo approached the KC about two-thirty or three o'clock in the afternoon, when the shooting had stopped and there were no pickets on the road. Alonzo was about fifty

Bridge spanning the Middle Fork of the Powder River near the KC buildings. Jack Flagg and Alonzo Taylor galloped across this bridge under fire from the Invaders. (Courtesy Johnson County Jim Gatchell Memorial Museum)

yards ahead of his stepfather as he passed close to the ranch buildings and neared the bridge. The Texans did not recognize Jack Flagg, regarded by the Wyoming ranchers as "the most notorious rustler in the county."[21] Since the Texans had been told not to shoot at anyone until authorized, they let the travelers pass.

But as Alonzo drew abreast the stable, someone—presumably one of the Wyoming men—ordered him to halt. Startled, Alonzo urged his team forward, and when a rifle was discharged nearby, the horses "stampeded across the bridge and on up the road." Several men closed in behind Flagg, and he was told to stop and raise his hands. Instead, he spurred his horse to a gallop. Charles Ford, foreman of the TA Ranch, recognized Flagg and snapped off a Winchester shot. As the other men opened fire at Flagg, "I threw myself on the side of my horse and made a run for it."[22]

By the time Flagg caught the wagon, seven men had mounted up and were in pursuit. Flagg seized his rifle from the wagon, but he had only three cartridges. The pursuers tried to close a distance of 350 yards, "but as soon as they saw I had a rifle, they stopped." One of the bay horses had been wounded, and Flagg told Alonzo to cut the unwounded horse free. When Alonzo vaulted bareback aboard the animal, they headed north, in the direction of Buffalo. The pursuers stayed out of rifle range, then broke off the chase and returned to the KC. They told George Tucker that the "last they saw of Flagg and the boy was that they were flying up the road toward Buffalo."[23]

It was about 3 o'clock now. There was a man in a buckboard and one on horseback just passed. They fired on them as they went by, I don't know if they killed them or not. I have seen lots of men come out on horses on the other side of the river and take after them. I shot at the men in the stable just now. Don't know if I got any or not. I must go and look out again. It don't look as if there is much show of my getting away. I see twelve or fifteen men. I hope they did not catch them fellows that run over the bridge toward Smith's. They are shooting at the house now. If I had a pair of glasses I believe I would know some of those men. They are coming back. I've got to look out.

Champion not only would have recognized several of his attackers—he also would have known the "one on horseback," Jack Flagg. But Nate remained alone inside the cabin, except for the stiffening corpse of Nick Ray. Although Champion increasingly felt there was not "much show of my getting away," it seems never to have occurred to him to request a truce—perhaps because he suspected that he would receive no mercy from his attackers. As bullets continued to slam into the stout walls of his cabin, he detected an even more ominous sound.

Well, they have just got through shelling the house like hail. I heard them splitting wood. I guess they are going to fire the house tonight. I think I will make a break when night comes, if alive.

The wagon abandoned by Alonzo Taylor and Jack Flagg was exactly what the search party had sought—unsuccessfully—earlier in the day. The vehicle and remaining horse

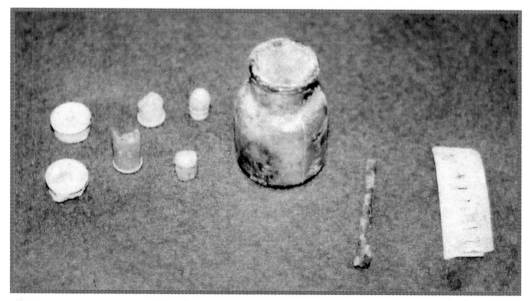

Artifacts excavated at the site of the KC Ranch include shell casings, bullets, bottles, square nails, and a harmonica. (Photo by Karon O'Neal)

were brought down to the KC. But "we were all so mad and chagrined at Flagg's escape that we came near fighting among ourselves," related Billy Irvine. Frank Canton, Fred Hesse, and the others who hoped to take control of Buffalo were already impatient with numerous delays. Now, realizing that Flagg would spread the alarm, Canton and the others feared "that the rustlers would kill their friends in Buffalo; and they wanted to strike that minute for Buffalo." But Major Wolcott imperiously announced that "we will do one thing at a time." Wolcott's commanding manner carried the argument. "We will get these fellows first while we are at it," he directed, "and then we will go on to Buffalo as fast as we can."[24]

To convert the wagon into an assault weapon, according to Frank Canton, the Invaders "took off the front wheels, fastened the coupling pole on tight, got some posts and tied them onto the hind axle, in an upright position for breastworks." This work was done behind the stable, out of Champion's view. "We cut down some pitch pine posts which were around the hay corral," described Billy Irvine, "and as there was a little old hay there, we put a layer of hay, then a layer of pitch pine (having split the posts), then another layer of hay and pine, built out wide and high." Intending to shove the fire wagon against the window on the northwest side of the cabin, Major Wolcott told Irvine to take six riflemen and have them methodically fire bullet after bullet into the window, so that Nate would have no chance to shoot at the approaching wagon. Wolcott then picked up the wagon tongue, asking for the help of four other men, "two on each side of the double tree." John Tisdale, Tom Smith, A. B. Clarke, and Jim Dudley joined Wolcott.[25]

With revolvers and matches at the ready, these five men began backing their incendiary vehicle toward the cabin, seventy-five yards from the stable. Irvine's squad of riflemen triggered a steady stream of bullets, keeping Champion away from the window.

Wolcott and his men shoved the wagon "right up against the window, and set it on fire, staying there with his men until the load was burning well."[26]

> Shooting again I think they will fire the house this time. It's not night yet.
> The house is all fired. Good bye, boys, if I ever see you again.

Champion placed the notebook in a pocket, and he jammed a revolver into his waistband. Then he picked up his Winchester. As the cabin filled with smoke and flames, he retreated to a ten-by-six-foot dugout storeroom off the kitchen. With the north wind blowing dense smoke across the meadows, he decided to sprint through this cover toward an opening in the bluffs about a hundred yards or so south of the cabin. Champion would run in his stocking feet—perhaps because it was faster, or perhaps because he had fought all day in his socks, and now the fire blocked him from his boots.

"Just as the roof was falling in," recalled George Tucker, "Major Whitcomb [*sic*] came to me and told me to get on a horse." Wolcott wanted someone ready to ride down Champion. "'When he comes out, kill him,' Major Wolcott told me." But as Tucker was mounting up, Champion made his break.[27]

"There he goes!"

Rifle in hand, Champion bolted from the rear of the burning cabin. With rifles blazing behind him, Champion raced through the smoke across the meadow and toward the gulch—apparently unaware that Texans had been stationed there since before dawn. As he ap-

At the Hoofprints of the Past Museum in Kaycee, rancher Brock Hanson holds part of the stove excavated from the site of the burned KC Ranch cabin. Hanson helped conduct the dig in 1997. (Photo by Karon O'Neal)

proached the gulch, Champion may have hoped for an instant that he could at least clear the perimeter where he had been trapped throughout the long day. But unexpectedly he was met at the gulch by point-blank rifle fire. Champion squeezed off one shot as he toppled onto his back in the grass and died.[28]

"He ran into two of our best men, who killed him," said Billy Irvine, even though more than two Texans had been assigned to guard the gulch. Big Jim Dudley struck him first in the arm, according to Sheriff Malcolm Campbell. But George Tucker emphatically stated that Jeff Mynett fired the shot that killed Champion. All of the attackers admired

The site of the KC Ranch cabin is just beyond and to the right of the modern storage building. Nate Champion sprinted from the burning cabin toward the ravine at left of the center tree, but he was gunned down as he reached the ravine entrance. (Photo by Karon O'Neal)

their adversary for his raw courage against impossible odds. "Champion was determined not to surrender," emphasized Frank Canton. "He came out fighting and died game."[29]

Men emerged from the stable and from behind the river embankment, crossed the meadow, and gazed down at the valiant adversary who had held them at bay all morning and throughout most of the afternoon. The dead man's rifle and revolver were confiscated. Tom Smith went through Champion's clothing and found the battle diary, moist with blood. But there were no names mentioned in the diary, and Billy Irvine reasoned that since Champion stated that Nick Ray died at midmorning, the Invaders could not be blamed for intentionally incinerating him. Major Wolcott directed Sam Clover to pin to Champion's shirt a sheet of note paper declaring: "CATTLE THIEVES, BEWARE!"[30]

Nate Champion's ring. (Photo by Karon O'Neal from Johnson County Jim Gatchell Memorial Museum)

During the latter stage of the siege the supply wagons arrived, and Wolcott ordered the cooks to prepare supper. By four o'clock the Invaders were wolfing down their first meal of the day, "which

124

we were badly in need of." The trappers, Bill Jones and William Walker, were paid "one hundred dollars for burning up their bedding," then told to go "on their way." Preparing to ride hard through the night to Buffalo, almost fifty miles away, each man drew "a large supply of ammunition" from the wagons, which again would lag behind the riders. Joe Elliott, John Tisdale, and Scott Davis agreed to accompany the wagons, but once more the column would be separated from its supply of food and ammunition.

The services of the absent Dr. Penrose were missed by the men who had been gouged by Champion's bullets. The two Texans who were hit in the arm and leg "had their wounds roughly cauterized." Able to ride, they were given "plenty of bandages and ointment" and were directed to ride to Douglas or even "to Cheyenne where friends would help them on out of the country."[31]

The column rode out after dark, with what remained of Nick Ray's badly charred body having been pulled free from the smoking ruins of the cabin. Nate Champion's corpse remained where he fell. "We left him lying for the coyotes," shrugged a hard-bitten Texan, for whom Champion and Ray represented $100 in bonuses.[32]

Chapter 12

Siege at the TA

"The whole affair had been blundered from first to last."

JOHN CLAY

At midafternoon on Saturday, April 9, Jack Flagg and Alonzo Taylor had raced away from the besieged KC Ranch and the half-hearted pursuers who turned back after spotting Flagg's rifle. Flagg and Alonzo had pushed for thirty miles before reaching tiny Trabing after dark, at about nine o'clock. Three men were willing to ride back with them in hopes of relieving the siege. Flagg acquired additional cartridges—he had only three in the magazine of his Winchester—while a weapon was provided for the unarmed Alonzo. These five men rode until midnight, when they reached the ranch of Dick Carr, seventeen miles from the KC.[1]

Flagg and Alonzo were preceded in spreading the word by rancher Terrence Smith, who had heard distant gunfire Friday morning from his ranch a few miles to the north. After carefully scouting the KC from a nearby hill, Smith rode all the way to Buffalo, sounding the alarm along the route. A dozen men armed themselves and headed toward the KC. In the meantime, the Invaders were marching away from the KC after dark, intending to ride through the night for Buffalo. An advance guard rode ahead, while the supply wagons would pack up and lumber along behind the column. After a march of six or seven miles, the riders changed horses at former governor George Baxter's Western Union Beef Company, where Mike Shonsey was foreman, then immediately resumed their trek. "We had no moon to guide us," pointed out Frank Canton, "and the night would have been very dark had it not been for the snow on the ground." In the light of the snow, the column was spotted in open country near Poison Creek by the twelve men riding toward the KC, who quickly decided to set an ambush. But young Al Smith dropped his gun, and the quiet of the night was broken by an accidental gunshot.[2]

It was nearly midnight when Will Guthrie and another outrider sighted the "dim forms of horsemen ahead of us." The Invaders immediately dismounted, sent out a few skirmishers, then formed a firing line. But there was no attack. With their ambush revealed by the unexpected shot, the impromptu—and outnumbered—posse rapidly pulled out, retiring to the nearby Carr ranch headquarters. Shortly afterward Jack Flagg and his four companions arrived at the ranch. In the midnight dimness the column had looked "100 strong," so the men at the ranch decided to get a few hours' sleep, then pick up the trail of the column the next morning.[3]

When the Invaders realized that their potential ambushers had gone "to the bush," they mounted up and proceeded with caution. Guided by Fred Hesse, Frank Canton, and others who knew the country, the column left the road, shifted to the west, cut a wire fence, then rode through a large field before returning to the road. "We made a hard ride that night," remarked one participant. The column halted at Fred Hesse's 28 Ranch, "where we got some coffee and bread and took two hours' rest in the loft of the stable." The imported gunmen rested in the stable, while Hesse led the other Wyoming men into the ranch house.[4]

Now twenty-two miles from Buffalo, the cold, weary riders mounted up before dawn and again headed north. Eight miles and two hours later, the column neared the TA Ranch, thirteen miles from Buffalo and about a mile off the main road. One of the Wyoming men, tall Charles Ford, was foreman of the TA, and he wanted to break off and see his wife and little boy. Jim Dudley, the 225-pound Texan, had worn out his horse and needed a new mount. "Charlie Ford loaned him an old gentle gray horse that had never been known to buck," recalled Billy Irvine. Dudley saddled the horse, and part of his rig was a rifle scabbard that was strapped to the saddle horn. But when the heavy Texan swung his bulk into the saddle, the gentle old horse that never bucked—did exactly that! Dudley stayed aboard, but his rifle was jarred from its scabbard. The butt hit the ground, and the loaded gun discharged, sending a slug into Dudley's knee. The wound was painful and dangerous, and it was decided to send Dudley to the post surgeon at Fort McKinney. The big man later was placed in a ranch wagon, and two TA cowboys set out to take him to the fort.[5]

The Invaders proceeded up the road to Buffalo. But at least two sympathizers of the ranchers—Billy Irvine named Jim Craig, while Frank Canton mentioned Craig and John Pierce—had ridden from Buffalo to intercept the column. The Invaders were informed that Terrence Smith had reached Buffalo with news that an armed force was fighting its way through Johnson County. Sheriff Red Angus was organizing resistance, and large numbers of men were arming themselves for a counterattack. Craig and Pierce asked their friends not to come to Buffalo "for fear of a battle in the town that might result in women and children getting hurt."[6]

The column halted, and while the hired gunmen sagged in their saddles, the Wyoming men held a council of war. Frank Canton, who was convinced—erroneously, as events would prove—that "two thirds of the people of the town were our intimate friends," pressed his case to "get into Buffalo as soon as possible." Although Fred Hesse, Charles Ford, and a few others agreed with Canton, others argued for a retreat to the TA. "We had only one meal in thirty-six hours and some of our men were very badly worn out," conceded Canton. "The party voted to stop at the ranch."[7]

Rancher Dick Allen announced his intention to ride, "alone and unarmed," into Buffalo, then to travel to Denver. He explained "that he had large payments on

Southern cattle coming due, and it was imperative for the sake of his credit that he should do so." Against the advice of his friends, Allen proceeded on toward Buffalo, accompanied by Sam Clover. The newspaperman wanted to file his sensational story over the military telegraph at Fort McKinney, and he pointed out to the cattlemen "the possible advantages that might accrue . . . if he managed to send out a version of the expedition." He was permitted to leave with Allen, although Billy Irvine felt that "Clover deserted the party." As Allen and Clover rode north toward Buffalo, the rancher began cursing himself for "the fool notion that had led him to embark in such a venture." Allen and Clover even concocted plans to avoid trouble after reaching the hostile environment of Buffalo.[8]

Despite losing two more members of their party, the Invaders soon were reinforced by John Tisdale, Joe Elliott, and Scott Davis, who had decided to leave the slow-paced wagons and race ahead to join the main column. The Invaders rode several miles back to the TA, dismounted, unsaddled, and turned their tired mounts into the corrals beside the log and frame barn. About one hundred yards east of the barn stood a large log cabin with a front porch facing south. The ranch complex also included three small structures to the north, an ice house, hen house, and a dugout potato cellar. The rippling waters of Crazy Woman Creek curled around the TA headquarters to the north, east, and south. Although the ranch buildings today are shaded by a large grove of cottonwoods, there were no trees on the site in 1892.

The TA was the property of an absentee owner, Dr. William Harris of Cheyenne, who grazed about 8,000 acres. His foreman, Charles Ford, lived in the cabin with his wife and son. Ford, at the age of twenty-nine, had married twenty-year-old Nellie Sutherland in 1888, at the home of Robert Foote—who would play a prominent role in the siege of the TA.[9]

View of the TA Ranch from the west. Crazy Woman Creek flows in the foreground. At right are the barn and corrals. Beyond is the cabin, while the ice house is in the center of the photo. (Author's collection)

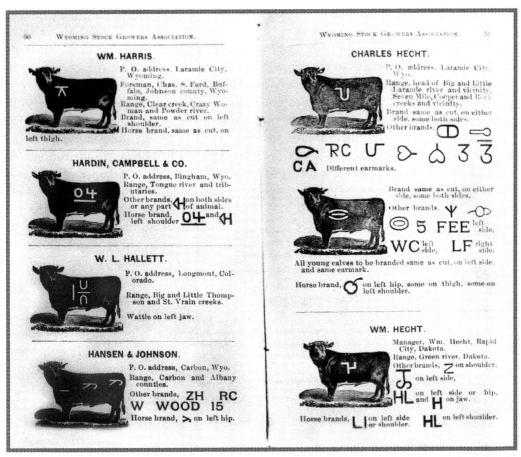

This 1887 brand book, on display at the Jim Gatchell Museum in Buffalo, is turned to the page displaying the TA brand of William Harris. (Photo by Karon O'Neal from the Johnson County Jim Gatchell Memorial Museum)

When the column pulled up, only a few miles from Buffalo, and then withdrew to the comparative safety and comfort of the TA, the Invaders completely lost their momentum. The expedition suddenly switched from the offensive to the defensive—the Invaders now became the Defenders. "The leaders claimed that we were safer fortified at the TA ranch than anywhere," reported George Dunning. "They said the sheriff at Buffalo would deputize several hundred settlers for the purpose of arresting the mob."[10]

Now that the leaders of the invasion of Johnson County feared attack from "several hundred settlers," it seemed prudent to strengthen the defensive capabilities of the ranch headquarters. Accordingly, a long day of manual labor ensued. A gentle hill rose one hundred yards or so west of the barn, and from this nearby height enemy riflemen could dominate the TA headquarters area. "We all got busy and dug trenches on this hill," related Frank Canton. There were four trenches about four feet deep, forming a square about twelve feet long on the interior of each side. Timbers for future construction at the ranch had been stacked inside one of the corrals. Some of these timbers were used to reinforce the redoubt on the hill with a three-foot-high breastwork, complete with loopholes. Three-foot-high breastworks were also erected on the north, east, and south sides of the cabin (the stable and redoubt were on the west side), and planking was nailed across the cabin windows.[11]

About noon a party of fifteen or twenty riders was sighted west of the ranch on the road to Buffalo. Leaders of the expedition thought that the riders might be Sheriff Red Angus and a posse. The Defenders quickly concealed themselves, and orders were passed to open fire if the riders descended to the ranch headquarters. This party did not leave the road, however, and the digging and carpentry work resumed. Then, within an hour or so, two other riders approached the ranch—WSGA employee Phil DuFran and Sam Sutherland, brother-in-law of Fred Hesse. They had been in and around Buffalo, and they brought confirmation that the area was rising up in defiance of the Invasion.

DuFran and Sutherland "informed us to get ready to fight 250 men, as that number would be out to see us the next day." DuFran and Sutherland, "being afraid to return" to Buffalo, became part of the TA garrison.[12]

The Defenders redoubled their efforts at fortifying the TA. With an augur, loopholes were drilled in the loft of the barn and in the ice house. Two barrels were filled with water from Crazy Woman Creek and placed in the cabin. The stream flowed inside

Left: Marriage license of Charles Ford and Nellie Sutherland. Ford was foreman of the TA, and during the siege Nellie and their little boy stayed under cover in the cabin. (Courtesy office of Johnson County Clerk, Buffalo)

Right: Sam Sutherland, brother-in-law of Fred Hesse, rode into the TA Ranch with news that Buffalo citizens were on the attack. (From group photo, courtesy Wyoming State Museum)

130

TA ranch house, with the barn in the background. The Invaders forted up in these two log buildings. (Courtesy Johnson County Jim Gatchell Memorial Museum)

The TA barn after the siege, showing the loopholes that were augured out by the Invaders. (Courtesy Johnson County Jim Gatchell Memorial Museum)

one of the corrals, so the horses also would have water. A steer was killed and butchered, and the meat was taken to the cabin, along with potatoes from the cellar and some coffee and flour. Tom Smith was asked to station himself in the barn with a dozen Texans, while John Tisdale and fifteen men were assigned to the hillside redoubt nicknamed "The Fort." There had been little rest for several days, "and after getting supper we sent out outposts on guard duty and the rest of us rolled up in our blankets on the floor and were soon lost to the world," said Frank Canton. "We were all tired," remembered Texan George Tucker, "and retired early to our blankets." But while the Defenders caught up on badly needed rest, aroused citizens were converging on the TA for an all-out assault.[13]

The countryside had first been alerted that a force of gunmen was on the move by Terrence Smith on Saturday, April 9. After viewing the siege from a safe distance, Smith rode north, spreading the alarming news at every ranch and to every rider he encountered. Pushing hard for almost fifty miles, Smith reached Buffalo about seven-thirty Saturday evening. He found Sheriff Red Angus, who promptly went into action. The sheriff sought out Captain Menardi, commander of the local National Guard troop, Company C. But when asked to assemble his company and assist the sheriff "in repelling invasion and arresting criminals," Captain Menardi declined, citing the recent order he had received from Adjutant General Frank A. Stitzer. The order, which was published in the newspaper, forbade companies of the Wyoming National Guard "to assist the civil authorities in the preservation or enforcement of the laws of the state of Wyoming" unless directed from the adjutant general's office. Undeterred, Sheriff Angus assembled a posse. Although he could raise only half a dozen men on short notice on a Sunday night, Angus led the small party south, toward the KC.[14]

While Angus conferred with Captain Menardi and put together a posse, word of the attack on the KC swept through the small town, confirming rumors that had been swirling for days around Wyoming. The activities of the ranchers in Cheyenne a few days earlier had been noticed, along with the loading and departure of the special train. Casper citizens had observed the arrival of the train in their little community, as well as the unloading and early morning march of the armed expedition. By Saturday, April 9, "many wild rumors ... have prevailed" in Cheyenne, while "Douglas, Casper and Glenrock were all considerably excited." The Cheyenne *Leader* declared on April 9: "Nothing else was discussed and little else thought of." On Friday, April 8, a reporter asked Governor Barber "if he had taken any action with reference to the armed body of men which entered and passed through the state on Tuesday evening." The governor replied that he had taken no action. "'The matter has not been brought to my attention officially. I only know of the matter through newspaper reports which as you know,' he added with a smile, 'are somewhat conflicting on the subject.'" Of course, he could have added—with another smile—that he knew a great deal more about the expedition than any newspaper.[15]

On Sunday morning Jack Flagg and his fellow riders arrived in Buffalo. They confirmed and added to Terrence Smith's information, then reported that the invading party was at the TA Ranch, only thirteen miles away. (At this point the Invaders had passed the TA, but after proceeding to within six or seven miles of Buffalo, they returned to the ranch and began to fort up.) Riders left Buffalo in every direction to alert the countryside and summon combatants to defend the town.

The response was immediate and reflexive. Men seized their guns and rode to Buffalo, ready to do battle. A newspaper reporter somewhat flippantly asked a man he knew if he was a rustler. "No," the citizen growled with deadly seriousness, "but I am fighting for my home and property."[16]

News that an assault force was marching into Johnson County did not intimidate the citizens of Buffalo. In Western movies and television shows, a vicious gunfighter or an outlaw gang often would "tree" a town—citizens would cower until the hero successfully confronted the villains and made the town safe again. But such fiction ignored reality. Settlers who willingly braved frontier hardships and dangers were not intimidated by hostile Indians or outlaws or gunfighters. When the James-Younger Gang in 1876 tried to rob the bank in Northfield, Minnesota, citizens seized firearms and shot the gang to pieces, then rode in pursuit of the surviving thieves. In 1884 Henry Brown and three other criminals killed two bankers in Medicine Lodge, Kansas. They were chased down by an impromptu posse, which forced their surrender after a gun battle, then took them back to Medicine Lodge—and a lynch mob. The Dalton Gang tried to loot two banks in Coffeyville, Kansas, in 1892, but townspeople took up arms and gunned down all five would-be robbers.

The citizens of Buffalo and the surrounding area reacted with the same spirit of warlike defiance. Like the colonials who swarmed to do battle with invading British soldiers at Lexington and Concord in April 1775, the citizens of Johnson County promptly armed themselves and rode out to go to war in defense of their homes in April 1892.

Throughout Sunday, April 10, the streets of Buffalo filled with men who talked angrily about the invasion of their county. Friends of the Invaders, mostly men who did business with the big ranchers, wisely kept a low profile. "The business men of Buffalo as a rule took no part in the controversy," observed a journalist. "Many of them are against the rustlers and some are almost bursting with suppressed excitement and anxiety."[17]

With a volatile mood growing around town, it certainly was prudent of these businessmen to suppress their approval of the invading party. Men who were friendly with the ranchers, as well as strangers in town, were regarded with open suspicion. When Sam Clover and Dick Allen rode into Buffalo on Sunday, they went directly to the Occidental Hotel, but before they could register they were approached by a wary deputy sheriff. Clover pointed out that he was from Chicago and that he was a friend of Maj. Edmond Fechet from Fort McKinney, while Allen claimed that he was an unemployed cowboy named Cameron. But a surly crowd had noted that Allen's horse bore the brand of the Western Union Beef Company. Within moments the deputy was escorting Clover and Allen to the county jail. Clover whined that he "got into bad company," but he persuaded his captors to send for Major Fechet, who vouched for his old friend. Clover was released into the custody of Major Fechet, leaving behind a morose Allen to languish in his cell.[18]

When the wagon carrying Jim Dudley reached town, the badly wounded Texan was allowed to proceed to the military hospital at Fort McKinney. Although Dudley admitted that he was from Paris, Texas, he gave his name as Augustus Green. "He says thirty-five of them were hired in Texas to punch cows at $5 a day," reported a newspaper skeptically. His leg was amputated, but his condition rapidly worsened. By Wednesday the outlook was bleak for the Texan, who "will die tomorrow the doctor says."[19]

Buffalo on Sundays typically was a quiet town, but April 10 was not a typical Sabbath. Men rode into town, armed and in dangerous moods. A few bold scouts brought word that the invading force was fortifying the TA Ranch. The Invaders were thought to number more than forty or fifty—or even sixty. Nevertheless, by nightfall forty-nine men had decided to advance on the TA under cover of darkness. Since Sheriff Angus had gone to the KC at the head of a posse, the men who decided to sally forth from Buffalo elected as "their leader" A. S. Brown. A strapping, unkempt man who operated a local grist mill, Brown's past was rumored to have included violent encounters and Indian connections, and he was called "Arapahoe" or "Rap." Arapahoe Brown and the others rode south, approaching the TA about midnight and setting pickets "at a safe distance" from ranch headquarters.[20]

About an hour later Sheriff Red Angus and his posse wearily returned to Buffalo, having ridden well over one hundred miles since the previous night. At the KC on Sunday the posse had discovered the horribly burned remains of Nick Ray in the charred ruins of the cabin, and the corpse of Nate Champion in the gulch to the south. With darkness gathering, Angus led his posse back toward Buffalo, intending to send the county coroner with a party to retrieve the bodies. Returning to town an hour after midnight, Sheriff Angus learned that half a hundred armed citizens already had marched toward the murderous invading column, which had forted up at the TA Ranch. Although Arapahoe Brown had been elected leader, the citizens' party had no official sanction, and they were no more than equal in number to the men they would oppose. Sheriff Angus therefore recruited another force, soon leading about forty armed riders south toward the TA, and assuming command after he arrived. While it was still dark, a number of riflemen crept to within several hundred yards of TA headquarters.[21]

During the predawn hours of Monday, April 11, there was activity at the ranch headquarters. Although some of the men slept deeply, Billy Irvine and a few others "worked most of the night" to prepare the ranch for a possible attack. About four o'clock, according to Frank Canton, one of the guards entered the cabin and awakened

Two .44-caliber Winchesters used by participants at the TA battle. (Photo by Karon O'Neal from the Johnson County Jim Gatchell Memorial Museum)

TA Ranch, The Last Day
From the Report of Col. J.J. Van Horn

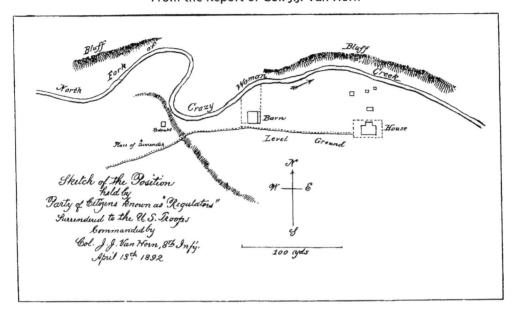

Sketch of the Position
held by
Party of Citizens known as "Regulators"
Surrendered to the U.S. Troops
commanded by
Col. J. J. Van Horn, 8th Infy.
April 13th 1892

100 yds

Major Wolcott to report that eighty men had ridden through the front gate of the TA. The guard related that the riders "had all disappeared in the darkness, and that he thought they were getting positions in the low hills surrounding the ranch." The cook was told to prepare breakfast "with plenty of black coffee," and some of the men were "quietly aroused from sleep" so that they could dress and eat. About that time George Dunning came down from the hillside redoubt for food. "After I had finished my breakfast at the house I took some grub and coffee up to the men at the fort," he said. The outlying guards were brought in and "relieved from duty, that they might get the much-needed rest." But there would be little rest. At dawn the Invaders-turned-Defenders, still in their blankets at the TA, were startled by bullets ripping into the log ranch buildings. "At daylight, we were surprised to hear gunshots," recalled George Tucker. "And bullets began to drop around the ranch house and stables."[22]

"We did not know how many there were of them," said Tucker, "but it was not long before we discovered that we were surrounded. And from the number of shots that came our way, there seemed to be a large force of the rascals." The firing came "from the hills in every direction at long range," related Frank Canton, "from six hundred to eight hundred yards, and continued constantly for about half an hour." The Defenders did not return this initial fire, "as we were in no hurry to waste our ammunition and could see nothing to shoot at except a puff of smoke from the black powder that they used." Utilizing field glasses (of course, field glasses had been included in the equipment inventory), the Defenders examined the positions of their attackers. "They had dug holes in the soft bank of the bad lands around the ranch and were keeping well under cover." Despite their heavy long-range barrage, they caused "no damage except they occasionally dropped bullets in the corral among our horses and wounded several

135

of them." One of the horses that was struck was Billy Irvine's, causing him to have the remuda crowded into the barn, to be released into the corral at night for watering.[23]

At about nine o'clock on Monday morning the Invaders' three supply wagons, slowly trying to catch up to the main party, were intercepted and captured. The wagons were loaded with provisions, bedding, personal effects, 3,000 rounds of ammunition, coal oil, two cases of "giant powder" (dynamite), and "poison." It was speculated that these "poison tablets" were intended by the Invaders "to poison the food and water of the rustlers and poor settlers." But these tablets were found among the medical supplies that had been brought on the expedition. "They were the usual bichloride tablets," explained Dr. Penrose, "each of which was marked 'poison,' that were found in my surgical outfit." The three teamster-cooks—Bill Collum, George "Tex" Helm, and Charlie "Shorty" Austin—were questioned, then released and told to stay in Buffalo, in case they were needed. The wagons were driven to the forward firing positions, where the besiegers would happily dine on the provisions and fire off the ammunition which matched their guns. And by the next day a use was devised for the wagons.[24]

The besieging party was growing by the hour. The riders who had been sent out from Buffalo had rapidly spread the alarm. "It was remarkable how quickly rumor traveled in such a thinly settled county," observed Dr. Penrose. "Sympathy was with the rustlers," he noted. As armed men swarmed into Buffalo, longtime community leader Robert Foote opened his general store to any potential besieger for guns, ammunition, or anything else that might be needed. Dressed in his trademark black coat, Foote mounted his black horse and rode up and down Buffalo's main street, shouting out his offer. Sheriff Angus soon returned to Buffalo in order to coordinate recruitment of newcomers. The Sheridan *Enterprise* would compliment Angus for his command efforts, emphasizing that "few men could have controlled a crowd of citizens as he did." Women of the community promptly went to work, and later they were thanked publicly for "supplying food to the hungry" and for "the eagerness of all to be of service to those men who had left their homes in defense of life and liberty." Buffalo's First Baptist Church was converted into "a kitchen and dining room for the many ranchmen who were in town" during the next several days.[25]

Buffalo merchant Robert Foote provided rifles, ammunition, and supplies to the besiegers of the TA. (Courtesy Johnson County Jim Gatchell Memorial Museum)

A great many Johnson County men left their homes that day, ready to do battle. "Dozens of grangers who do not own a steer left their plows to take their rifles and went to the front," reported the Omaha *World Herald* in a story that was headlined, "SURROUNDED." By Monday morning at least 175 riflemen had swarmed to the perimeter surrounding the TA fortifications. Sheriff Angus directed traffic from town, while Arapahoe Brown remained in command in the field, assisted

Robert Foote's big general store, located on the east side of Buffalo's main street. (Courtesy Johnson County Jim Gatchell Memorial Museum)

by E. U. Snider, an early settler who had served as sheriff between the tenures of Frank Canton and Red Angus. The besiegers set up headquarters at the Convention Ranch, half a mile from the TA.

On Monday evening a reporter from the Cheyenne *Leader* arrived in Buffalo. "Men were coming and going from the scene of the action," he observed. At eleven o'clock he accompanied fifteen men to "the camps." He found "able bodied men, mere boys and gray haired old men." He was told that about 125 men were ranchers, while another twenty-five were workingmen and mechanics. "The other twenty-five are rustlers, gamblers, and men about town."[26]

Throughout Monday the besiegers banged away from long range, while the Defenders—deprived of 3,000 rounds of ammunition confiscated with the supply wagons—conserved cartridges and did not return fire. Emboldened, "about a dozen men were seen riding along the slope of a hill about six hundred yards away in plain view," according to Frank Canton. "We thought this a good time to remind them that we were still living." About two dozen riflemen loosed a volley which dropped a couple of horses. The exposed besiegers "scattered to the hills for cover and they were very careful after that to keep out of range of our guns."[27]

Although the distant barrage continued to rain upon the TA, the Defenders remained "relatively safe" as long as they stayed behind cover. "There wasn't much that we could do except keep out of the way of the bullets," related George Tucker. "We couldn't see anything to shoot at." Frank Canton explained that the best Winchesters available "in those days" had a range of six to seven hundred yards (although Winchesters with open sights were accurate in the hands of most men to only two hundred yards or so). "But some man of their party had a rifle of large caliber and greater penetration. The reports sounded to me like the old Sharps fifty-caliber that we formerly used on the plains and called the buffalo gun." Several rounds from this rifle "penetrated our breastworks, but did no particular harm." Sheriff Malcolm Campbell was told that a citizen nicknamed "Dan" Boone "was using an old buffalo gun which

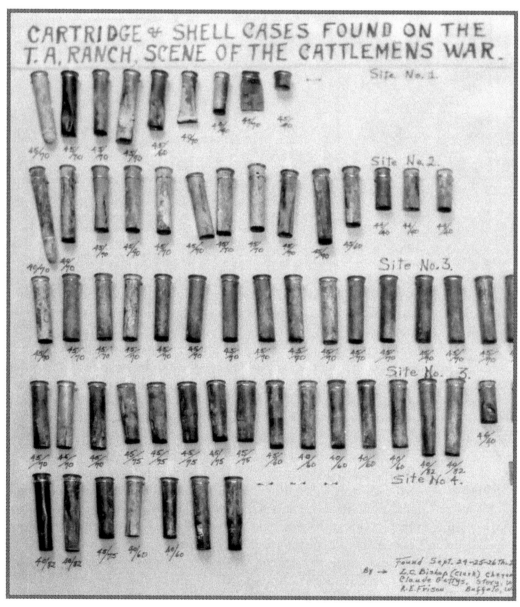

Cartridges and shell cases dug up from the positions around the TA Ranch headquarters are on display at the Jim Gatchell Museum. A great many whiskey bottles also were found. (Photo by Karon O'Neal from the Johnson County Jim Gatchell Memorial Museum)

Above: Harmon Fraker (Malcolm Campbell was told the sharpshooter was named Boone) blazed away at the TA ranch buildings with a Sharps .40-70 which boasted an octagonal barrel. The eighteen-pound buffalo gun probably was the most effective weapon used by the besiegers.

Left: When the TA ice house was torn down in 1949, a rafter was cut to reveal the penetration of this heavy slug. (Photos by Karon O'Neal from the Johnson County Jim Gatchell Memorial Museum)

needed for each charge a cup-full of powder and a bullet the size of a clothespin." Boone was positioned on a hill a thousand yards from the TA, happily banging away with his powerful rifle. "Every few minutes," said Campbell, "everyone in the valley would hear Boone's gun roar, and an instant later a chunk of lead would knock a large slice out of the door or window of the buildings."[28]

A favorite target was the cabin, "which was considerably shot up," recalled Billy Irvine. "They finally got the range of the doors, and it was dangerous to go in or out." Although the windows were boarded up, rifle bullets could penetrate the planking. "I remember finding Teschemacher standing with his back to a window and told him to get away." An instant after Teschemacher moved away from the window, a bullet crashed through a plank. A similar incident involved a teenaged ranch hand who "was keen to be in on the fighting." He tried without success to borrow a gun, before he "finally found an old shotgun in the loft of the ranch and cleaned it up." But suddenly "a bullet came in one of the windows and creased him across the neck just enough so the blood would ooze out of the wound. This soon quieted the boy, who went and laid in a corner, and it was the last we heard of him."[29]

Two other noncombatants were the wife and son of TA foreman Charles Ford. Throughout the two-day siege, Nellie Ford kept her son beneath a table in the cabin.[30]

That evening John Tisdale and George Tucker emerged from cover at the redoubt to sit on a log. "Things had quieted down, and we had been cramped up all day," explained George Tucker. "We were sitting there chatting about our fine predicament."

Their conversation was interrupted when a rifle bullet clipped off part of the brim of Tisdale's hat. "Tisdale crawled back into our burrows," Tucker reported.[31]

When a few cows ambled over looking for feed, two of the animals were shot and killed by the besiegers. After dark the Defenders, conscious of their limited larder, slipped out and butchered one of the dead cows. Although there was a heavy snowfall Monday night, citizens braved the weather to man their perimeter. Throughout the stormy night "the flashes of their guns could be seen from the gullies and hills surrounding the regulators."[32]

That night "Wolcott, who had a foolish idea that the rustlers would not fight," revealed Billy Irvine, "wanted to take twenty men on foot and make a night attack on about three hundred [sic]. This I opposed. He became very angry and called me a damned mutineer." Irvine insisted that everyone should go, or no one. "He finally agreed to leave it to the Wyoming members of our party, and they all agreed with me; result, we did not go."[33]

On Tuesday the growing number of citizens worked at "digging their ditches nearer and nearer the evidently doomed cattlemen." Around ten o'clock Frank Canton spotted a daring rifleman who "had crawled up a gulch and dug a hole in a bank in which he concealed himself, about three hundred yards from the ranch. None of them had ever ventured that close before. This fellow commenced firing at the east end of our breast-works and shooting uncomfortably close to some of our men." Canton asked the nearby Defenders to hold their fire until he could provide direction. He took an augur into the cabin's low attic and drilled a hole in the roof, which gave him "a good view of the sharpshooter in the hills. I could see his head very plainly through the sights of my rifle." Calling out instructions to a dozen riflemen below, he counted to three, then joined in triggering an unexpected volley. "We literally covered the fellow up in dirt and dust, and he went out of sight." The Cheyenne *Leader* reporter noted that "one bullet threw dirt in a citizen's face." But the smoke from Canton's rifle drew a return barrage, and the attackers "soon shot the shingles all to pieces. I was lucky to get down from this place without getting hit."[34]

Major Wolcott directed Billy Irvine to pick fifteen men and relieve Jack Tisdale and his fifteen men in the redoubt. Irvine selected seven men from the crowd in the cabin, but the eighth man refused to go. Irvine told Wolcott he had only seven replacements, and asked him to send along the balance. But Wolcott, learning of the refusal, brusquely ordered the reluctant replacement to go with Irvine. Again the man refused, pointing out that he would be killed in the 100-yard crossing from the cabin to the redoubt. "Which do you prefer," shouted Wolcott furiously, "being killed going up the hill, or being killed right here, as you white-livered son of a B. you will either do as I order or I will kill you myself." As a result of this verbal onslaught, the man joined Irvine's squad, which made their way up to the redoubt "without accident."[35]

By Tuesday, recruits from Sheridan County were arriving to swell the ranks of the besiegers to more than 300 men. As their numbers mounted and their trenches grew closer to the TA, the besiegers became confident of overwhelming the trapped riflemen. Wagons from town began bringing bales of hay to be piled atop the breastworks and used as protection for diggers to extend the trenches. Regarding their determination to prevail, Arapahoe Brown grimly stated, "If we are whipped, there will be none but cattlemen left, for we will all be dead." But many of Brown's younger men boasted that "the white caps shall all be killed."[36]

Despite their bravado, there was no interest in a massed charge upon more than forty riflemen protected behind log breastworks and sturdy buildings. It was thought that it might "cost 100 lives to drive the stockmen from their entrenchments." So on Tuesday afternoon a detail of citizens began digging post holes to the north of the ranch. "I think their plan was to stretch barbed wire around the ranch so that we could not get out," speculated Frank Canton. "Our men from the trenches on the hill then opened up on them with such a hot fire that they went to cover like a lot of quail and abandoned their plan of stretching the wire."[37]

With no one inclined to launch a direct assault, the besiegers decided to employ a version of the rolling device that the Invaders had utilized to flush Nate Champion at the KC. Two of the captured wagons would be used, along with dynamite. The plan was to construct "a movable breastwork" which would protect as many as forty men, who would advance far enough to hurl the confiscated dynamite into the redoubt. The men who constructed this war wagon assigned it two nicknames: "Go-Devil" and "Ark of Safety."[38]

Two of the Studebaker wagons were brought up just behind the trenches on the west side of the ranch, facing the redoubt and the stable. The wagons were lined up several feet apart, "then fastened together with a frame work of logs." A breastwork more than six feet tall was erected across the rear of the wagons. This fortification was built of two thicknesses of eight-foot logs, fastened together with wire. There were five loopholes. "Five men could slowly move the ingenious contrivance, fifteen could move it easily, and it would protect 40 men," according to one onlooker.[39] The observation that the Ark of Safety could shelter forty men while advancing may have been optimistic; it seems likely that men on the edges of such a large group would have been exposed to rifle fire.

Frank Canton, who saw the Go-Devil the next day, offered another description. The breastwork was wide enough for sixteen men to stand behind, while a large tongue extending to the rear was designed for a team of horses facing the front. Protected by the breastwork, the team would push the vehicle forward. "I understand it was invented by Arapahoe Brown and built under his instructions and that he had a lot of bombs manufactured himself and a good supply of dynamite with fuse attachment," wrote Canton.[40]

The construction effort went on within earshot of the Defenders, although they could only guess about what was being built. "During the night we could hear men working with axes, saws, and hammers about three hundred and fifty or four hundred yards west of our trenches. At one time we heard a loud explosion where the rustlers were working that sounded like the bursting of a shell or bomb." (A request to Fort McKinney for the loan of an artillery piece was denied, so some of the besiegers had put together a homemade siege gun from a piece of pipe—which promptly exploded.)[41]

Billy Irvine, now stationed in the redoubt, also heard construction sounds, on Tuesday afternoon. "We could not see them, but could plainly hear them pounding and working, and when it was finished a great cheer went up." Writing many years later, Irvine hoped to clear up a matter he regarded as a misconception. "Much has been said and done about what they could have done to us with this instrument of war had not the soldiers come and prevented it." Irvine insisted "that the Ark of Safety was completed about 3 o'clock" on Tuesday afternoon. "They pushed her up toward us until we could just see a little of one corner of her, and then their hearts failed them; they could not get the men to man her. They had plenty of time to use her had they had the courage."[42] Perhaps the Go-Devil was not yet deemed ready for combat, which is why construction continued during the night. By morning, the vehicle was ready to go to war.

Under cover of darkness the Defenders, anticipating an attack on the redoubt, worked to improve their position. "We dug a trench through the soft sand extending from the bottom of our old trench in a westerly direction towards the enemy," related Frank Canton. "This trench ran along the edge of a bluff and was about fifty feet long and deep enough to conceal fifteen or twenty men." Anyone assaulting the redoubt would come under sudden fire from the flank. "We would have them in the open and at close quarters," emphasized Canton. "After we had finished this job we gathered tumble weeds and dry sagebrush . . . and covered up the new trench so completely that it could not be seen even in daylight."[43]

An animated discussion took place at the TA about attempting a breakout during the night. "There was not a time either in daylight or night but what we could have cut through their lines and come out with our entire party, and we all knew it," blustered Frank Canton. Major Wolcott apparently agreed. After consulting with several of his fellow ranchers, Wolcott sent for Billy Irvine. "We have decided to go out of here at 2 A.M.," Wolcott said. "What do you think of it?" Irvine replied that his opinion mattered little "if the move has been decided upon. I am going with you. I am damned sure I do not want to stay here alone." But soon the moon came out, reflecting brightly off the snow and removing the camouflage of darkness. Wolcott postponed the breakout until the next night.[44]

Rifle fire continued throughout the night. The besiegers had whiskey, no doubt to fight the cold, and this lubrication obviously spread to their trigger fingers. (Decades later, two brothers who lived at the TA dug in the rifle pits for cartridges, and found not only shell cases but whiskey bottles.) "The rustlers' bullets were not so bad," declared George Tucker. "We could stand them. But we could have put up with them in a little better humor if we had had more to eat." There was no shortage of water, and "enough good beef the first day, but by the third day we were reduced to raw-potato rations. And I don't care how good a fighter a man may be, he simply can't do his best on such a diet." The loss of the supply wagons was proving critical. Nearly half a hundred people were under cover at the TA, and the available food was quickly consumed. By Wednesday the only chuck that could be found "was one loaf of corn bread and the hind quarters of a calf."[45]

Following another long night, the cold, hungry Defenders prepared to receive the expected attack. Early on Wednesday morning, Billy Irvine and Will Guthrie were assigned guard duty at the east side of the cabin. Because of the frigid temperature, Irvine dragged a mattress outside to sit on, and he and Guthrie also wrapped a blanket around their legs. Suddenly, Irvine felt something strike his foot, and he went inside to investi-

Interior view of the hayloft above the stable shows bullet holes and loopholes fashioned by auguring all four corners. (Photo by Karon O'Neal)

gate. "When I took off my overshoes and boot I found the bullet in the boot, which had passed through the soles of both shoes, but did not break the skin of the foot. It bruised it, however, so that in about thirty minutes it was much swollen, and the next day the front end of the foot was as black as my hat. I did not wear a boot for three or four weeks after that."[46]

All of the long-range sniping had produced nothing worse than a bruised foot and "dirt in a citizen's face." But when Texan Alex Lowther replaced Irvine at the east end of the cabin, he took the precaution of crawling outside on his hands and knees. Somehow his revolver was dislodged—from a pocket or waistband or holster—and when it struck the ground it discharged. Apparently Lowther had loaded all six chambers, rather than using "five beans in the wheel." (With no safety, a Colt revolver was dangerous to its owner, unless the hammer rested on an empty chamber.) By carelessly dropping his revolver, Lowther "shot himself in the stomach," reasoned Billy Irvine. With the condition of "Augustus Green" steadily worsening following his amputation, Lowther now was the second Texan who accidentally had self-inflicted a life-threatening wound. Again the services of Dr. Penrose—who was trying to make his way back to Cheyenne—were sorely needed.[47]

Throughout Tuesday-Wednesday night more besiegers had come out from Buffalo, including Rev. Marvin Rader, and early in the morning the Go-Devil was set in motion. The awkward vehicle appeared over the hill and advanced slowly about two hundred feet. The fifteen men in the redoubt searched their rifle sights for targets, intending to unleash a volley at close range. But Texan Dave Booker, at one end of the rifle pit, became "anxious to send them a challenge and could not resist the temptation to take a shot." He triggered three rounds "in rapid succession" from his .45-70 Winchester, "and each shot could be heard plainly to strike their breastworks." Although Booker "was severely censured," his action stopped the advance and probably saved lives. "In a few minutes the rustlers had drawn the machine from sight," remembered Frank Canton, "and never attempted to show up with it any more."[48]

Actually, no time remained for further use of the Go-Devil or any other assault tactic. At 6:45 A.M., while the besiegers blazed away with their rifles at the ranch fortifications, three troops of the Sixth Cavalry from Fort McKinney rode onto the scene, bugles blaring. The authorized strength of a cavalry company was one hundred men and three commissioned officers. But during the nineteenth century, troops were chronically understrength, so there were 107 uniformed men who rode up to the TA early Wednesday morning—definitely the most impressive force on the field. Sheriff Red Angus accompanied the cavalrymen, and he "ordered his posse to cease firing."[49]

The gunfire halted. Col. James Van Horn rode toward the ranch, along with Maj. Edward Fechet, Capt. C. H. Parmalee of the Wyoming National Guard, Sheriff Red Angus, two orderlies, and three color sergeants carrying a guidon of each of the companies. The advancing color guard brandished a flag of truce. George Tucker expressed the reaction of most of the Defenders: "It was with a feeling of relief that I saw the soldiers coming."[50]

Bread for the Besiegers

Bill Adams of Buffalo related that his grandfather worked at Robert Foote's General Merchandise during the Johnson County War. According to Adams' grandfather, while the TA Ranch was under siege, several local ladies each agreed to bake ten to fifteen loaves of bread each evening. A couple of hours after midnight, a wagon would drive through the streets collecting the bread for dawn delivery to the hungry men on the siege lines.

Chapter 13

Surrender

"All of the besieged looked haggard and care worn."
Cheyenne *Leader*, April 14, 1892

Since the beginning of their expedition, the Wyoming cattlemen had boasted to their hired gunmen that they could rely on support from the most powerful political officials. When WSGA secretary H. B. Ijams recruited George Dunning as a gunman, he assured his new employee that Buffalo mayor Charles Burritt and two dozen or more "friends" would provide help and join the expedition when it invaded the town. "Ijams said the governor [Dr. Amos Barber] and Judge [John W.] Blake were back of this movement to wipe the thieves in Johnson county out of existence," related Dunning. "Ijams told me about the United States marshall [Joe Rankin] helping him plan the raid and said the stock association had some very warm friends in Congress and the United States Senate, among whom he said was Senator [Joseph] Carey, a man of great influence and worth."[1]

After the expedition was besieged at the TA Ranch, the Wyoming cattlemen repeatedly urged the hired gunmen to keep fighting "until Governor Barber, Senators Carey and Warren could send troops at McKinney to the rescue of the mob." George Tucker came to realize that "the higher officials of the state were on the side of the ranchers, and fortunately so for us."[2]

Governor Barber knew when the expedition left Cheyenne; indeed, his medical bag was present, carried by his friend, Dr. Penrose. Not only was there anticipation in the governor's office—the WSGA office also anxiously awaited word after the special train departed Cheyenne. It further may be assumed that Senators Carey and Warren had been notified in Washington, D.C., and were expecting information or requests for assistance. But part of the plan was to cut telegraph wires, so that information about the invasion could not be sent to Buffalo, and so that calls for help could not be telegraphed from the town. Ed David, ranch manager for Senator Carey, was assigned to cut the lines. The area repairman promptly put the line back in operation, but soon the wire again was cut. For days the wire south of Buffalo was alternately cut and repaired. But the northern line, from Fort McKinney, was never interrupted. By Tuesday communication between Buffalo and Cheyenne was restored. "Telegraphic communication is again established and news is beginning to flow in here very freely," reported the Cheyenne *Leader* on Wednesday morning, April 13. "The single wire to Buffalo has been kept redhot all night."[3]

Governor Barber had begun to receive information on Tuesday morning. A lengthy telegram was delivered to the governor from C. J. Hogerson, chairman of the board of Johnson County Commissioners and "acting mayor" in the absence of Mayor Charles Burritt, an attorney who had to be in federal court in Cheyenne. Hogerson reported that "about sixty men have invaded this county in defiance of law," killing two men before fortifying themselves on the nearby TA Ranch. Hogerson described the early skirmishing, then stated his belief that the Invaders "cannot be arrested without a good deal of skirmishing now." Asserting that "the gravest fears are entertained by all loyal citizens," Hogerson requested "that the commanding officer at Fort McKinney be ordered to assist in putting down this rebellion." Later in the day Governor Barber replied that he had "directed state militia to assist in restoring order and have called upon president to direct United States troops to assist in suppressing insurrection and restoring order."[4]

Governor Barber's telegram to President Benjamin Harrison described the "insurrection" against the state government. "Open hostilities exist and large bodies of armed men are engaged in battle," the message announced. Governor Barber insisted that the state militia could be of no immediate aid, since "the scene of action is 125 miles from the nearest railroad point." But Fort McKinney was nearby, and Governor Barber urgently requested the intervention of United States troops. Governor Barber then wired Gen. John R. Brooke, commander of the Department of the Platte, headquartered in Omaha, Nebraska. Although asking for more information, General Brooke was encouraging: "I think I have troops enough at McKinney for all purposes in case the president orders me to act." Governor Barber also wired Col. James Van Horn, commander at Fort McKinney, again describing the situation and requesting "every possible assistance" from the troops.

The telegraphic traffic on Tuesday included an exchange of four telegrams between Governor Barber and Capt. C. H. Parmalee of the Wyoming National Guard. Judge Parmalee had acquitted Frank Canton of murder charges in December 1891, while Captain Parmalee was aide-de-camp to Governor Barber. Parmalee notified the governor about the combat at the TA, estimating that the Invaders were "sixty strong" and passing on the rumor that six of the invaders had been killed, while two were wounded. "Order can be restored in no other way except by fight to finish." He recommended that Buffalo's National Guard troop, Company C, should be placed "on duty to keep the peace in Buffalo," and that the president should be asked "for use of troops at Fort McKinney." Governor Barber directed Captain Parmalee to deliver orders to the combatants to cease hostilities, but there was no compliance.

There was compliance, however, when Governor Barber ordered Parmalee to muster Company C: "Use all the militia at your command to restore order, and at all other persons." The militia, then, was expected to protect—presumably from lynch mobs—any prisoners from the cattlemen's expedition. On Tuesday "the call" was issued for Company C to assemble, and soon four commissioned officers and thirty-eight enlisted men reported for duty. Placed "under the mayor's order for the protection of life and duty," the uniformed soldiers were stationed around town.[5]

A more imposing military force received its marching orders Tuesday night. The telegrams of Governor Barber to Washington during the day were followed up by a noc-turnal visit to the White House by Senators Carey and Warren, accompanied by the acting secretary of war, Frederick Dent Grant, son of the former president (Secretary of War Stephen B. Elkins happened to be absent from Washington). President Harrison already had retired to bed, but he responded to his fellow Republicans. The president's friendship with Carey dated back to the 1880s, when they served together in Congress: Harrison as senator from Indiana, and Carey as territorial representative from Wyoming. Carey and Warren impressed upon the drowsy president the urgency of the situation in Wyoming, pleading the case for the cattlemen, as well as the need to halt the violence. President Harrison began to dictate telegrams, which were wired to the West shortly after eleven o'clock. The president informed Governor Barber that he had "ordered the secretary of war to concentrate a sufficient force at the scene of the disturbance and to co-operate with your authorities." At the same

President Benjamin Harrison, strongly influenced by Wyoming Senators Carey and Warren, ordered federal intervention in the Johnson County War. (Courtesy Library of Congress)

time General Brooke in Omaha received orders from Acting Secretary of War Grant. General Brooke in turn telegraphed Colonel Van Horn at Fort McKinney, then wired Governor Barber that the colonel had received marching orders.[6]

At Fort McKinney Colonel Van Horn promptly went into action. A native of Ohio, James Judson Van Horn was a West Pointer, Class of 1858, and a Civil War veteran who received a brevet for gallantry and courage at Cold Harbor. In September 1891 he was promoted to colonel of the Eighth Infantry, and he assumed command of Fort McKinney. Three companies of the Eighth were stationed at McKinney, along with the regimental band and headquarters company, and three companies of the Sixth Cavalry. Although a cavalry detachment had just returned from forcing a band of troublemakers back onto the Crow Reservation, Van Horn turned out the entire garrison on a cold night to ready all three cavalry troops for immediate departure. At two o'clock on

Wednesday morning, April 13, Colonel Van Horn and Maj. Edmond Fechet, the ranking officer of the Sixth Cavalry at the post, led Companies C, D, and H—eleven officers and ninety-six enlisted men—out of Fort McKinney. The column rode two miles to Buffalo, then turned south toward the scene of the conflict. Captain Parmalee and Sheriff Red Angus joined the soldiers, and Sam Clover inevitably tagged along, riding a horse borrowed from a friendly officer at Fort McKinney. En route the column encountered riders coming and going from the TA positions. They brought rumors of "a desperate encounter" in which most or all of the cattlemen had been killed. Other stories suggested a planned ambush of the soldiers, or of a raid intended to seize the prisoners from the column.[7]

The column arrived at the TA about 6:45 Wednesday morning. The Go-Devil had just been advanced and fired upon, and return rifle fire rained upon the ranch buildings. "The besiegers had increased to probably 400 persons," stated the Cheyenne *Leader* reporter, "some of whom had come from adjoining counties."[8] The Defenders, now outnumbered nearly ten to one, experienced "a general feeling of relief" when the cavalry rode into view.[9] It has been commonly assumed that the timely arrival of the cavalry saved the Defenders from imminent annihilation. But the attackers had greatly outnumbered the Defenders for two days, and although some of the younger attackers had boasted about how many gunmen they would kill, there had been no move to attack the TA fortifications. And if the hundreds of besiegers had charged the TA *en masse*, they would have presented open targets to men firing repeating rifles from protected positions. Since the attackers were not organized as a trained military force, their charge would not have been skillfully coordinated, and it may be assumed that if they took casualties their attack would have been broken. Although the TA riflemen also were untrained as a military force, it is far easier for amateur soldiers to defend a prepared position than to attack one. In fact, the TA defenders realized that they could not break out

TA cabin after the siege. Note the boarded-up windows and the breastwork on the right side of the porch.
(Courtesy Barb and Earl Madsen, TA Ranch)

148

and that they faced eventual starvation, but they were unwilling to submit to an overwhelming mob. George Tucker flatly stated that "most of us had decided to stick it out until we were killed."[10]

Supposition about an attack on the TA defenders became meaningless when the U.S. Cavalry arrived in force. Colonel Van Horn told Sheriff Angus and Arapahoe Brown to order their men "to cease firing" and asked if he would let "the regulators" surrender to an army force. "Yes," said Brown, "if the military will agree to turn them over to the civil authorities." Sheriff Angus agreed, since he knew that his 400-man posse could not force a surrender without trying to storm the fortifications.[11]

Angus ordered his "posse" to stop firing, and Colonel Van Horn rode toward the redoubt under a flag of truce. The colonel was accompanied by Major Fechet, Captain Parmalee, Sheriff Angus, two orderlies, and a color detail. Colonel Van Horn asked Billy Irvine, "Who is in command of this party?"[12]

"We have no one in command," replied Irvine. "We are simply an outfit of cattlemen up here trying to protect our property." Colonel Van Horn did not believe that there was no commander, and he curtly repeated his question. "We have no one in command," insisted Irvine, "but Major Wolcott is acting as our foreman."[13]

Colonel Van Horn asked to see him, and Irvine sent a man to summon Major Wolcott. "I shall always remember this incident with pleasure," reminisced Irvine to Dr. Penrose. "The old man came out of the house with as much dignity and assurance as if he had a thousand men." Colonel Van Horn explained that he had been sent to halt the bloodshed, and that the best way to avoid further violence was to have Wolcott's men surrender. "Do you surrender, Sir?" Wolcott wanted to know if the surrender would be to the army or to the civil authorities. "If the former, we will surrender; if the latter, we will NOT surrender," he stated.[14]

Colonel Van Horn gave assurances that they would be in military custody; Sheriff Angus would have to rely upon process of law to recover the prisoners from the military at a later time. The discussion was "rather long," but Colonel Van Horn had "assured [Wolcott] that they would receive protection in the event they surrendered." Tired and hungry and trapped by a superior force, the cattlemen decided that by entrusting themselves to the security of the military, they would buy the necessary time for their political connections to go to work. At last "the stockmen sent forward another flag of truce with the information that they would surrender to Col. Van Horn."[15]

Van Horn and Major Fechet had their men ready. While two companies stayed in formation in full sight of the besiegers, the other troop "quickly surrounded the buildings" and disarmed the Defenders. "A complete tally was made of all the prisoners," and their weapons. While collecting and tallying ordnance, the soldiers counted 5,000 rounds of ammunition. Had there been an assault, the Defenders would have been able to lay down a curtain of fire. The officers inspected the fortifications with grudging admiration. Major Fechet stated that the redoubt "was so well planned, and so solidly built, that four hundred men could not have carried it without losing half their number, and that a cannon was the only thing that could possibly have dislodged the defenders." In addition to providing names and turning over their guns, members of the expedition collected their personal possessions and saddled their horses. The severely

Prisoners Taken from the TA
to Fort McKinney

A. D Adamsom	*Texans*
C. A. Campbell	Will Armstrong
Frank Canton	Bob Barling
Arthur Clarke	Jerry Barling
W. J. Clarke	John Benson
Scott Davis	Dave Booker
Fred de Billier	Buck Garrett
Phil DuFran	J. A. Garrett
Joe Elliott	Alex Hamilton
Charles Ford	Jesse Johnson
Fred Hesse	Bill Little
W. E. Guthrie	Alex Lowther
Billy Irvine	M. A. McNally
F. H. Laberteaux	Jeff Mynett
Ben Morrison	Kinzie Pickard
L. H. Parker	Cliff Schultze
A. R. Powers	George Tucker
Mike Shonsey	Starl Tucker
Sam Sutherland	B. S. Willey
W. H. Tabor	W. A. Wilson
H. E. Teschemacher	
Bob Tisdale	
John Tisdale	
W. B. Wallace	
E. W. Whitcomb	
Frank Wolcott	

wounded Alex Lowther was made as comfortable as possible; an army ambulance would be sent out from Fort McKinney. "All of the besieged looked haggard and care worn," observed the Cheyenne *Leader* reporter. "They had evidently not slept much for the previous four days and looked dirty and worn out." Sam Clover described them as "hollow-eyed, begrimed, and half-frozen. … But they were game to the end, and not a murmur ever was heard from them."[16]

It took two hours, but finally forty-four prisoners were mounted and arranged in a column (the forty-fifth prisoner, Alex Lowther, could not ride). Company H would lead the procession; Company D flanked the prisoners in two files; and Company C rode as a rear guard. When the column moved out at 8:45, the besiegers were kept at a distance, but jeers and taunts were shouted out, and the identities of various captives were spoken aloud. "General bitterness was manifested toward a few who seemed the objects of undisguised hatred."[17]

Despite this ominous mood, the column proceeded without incident, other than being pelted by sleet. "The troops, who had looked for trouble, were pleasantly disappointed." Some of the besiegers rode along near the column, but most of the men began to disperse. Before riding toward their homes, however, most members of the huge posse toured the TA. The buildings were pockmarked with bullet holes, and the redoubt impressed onlookers as "well nigh impregnable." As the sightseers wandered through the TA grounds and structures, they found a great variety of discarded items. "Coats, belts, extra clothing, field glasses and even guns lay scattered about in disorder and disarray." When a reporter tried to interview Alex Lowther, lying on a makeshift bed of hay, the wounded Texan refused even to give his name. There was talk of burning the cabin, but the would-be arsonists were turned away by the soldier who had been assigned to guard Lowther. There was relief in the attic, where George Dunning had concealed himself to avoid capture.[18]

Colonel Van Horn set a brisk pace, and the column skirted Buffalo and rode into Fort McKinney at 12:45 that afternoon. More than one hundred riders had gathered outside the post to view the arrival of the procession, and many of them would pitch camp there. A rumor had circulated that at the TA "the dead body of W. C. Irvine was found there, while Maj. Wolcott was fatally wounded." But the spectators saw both Irvine and Wolcott ride into Fort McKinney, where "all of the men were formally placed under arrest." The prisoners were quartered in the "up-stairs of the bath-house," said Irvine, "where we were very comfortable." The exhausted prisoners yearned for "rest and sleep," and they headed for their bunks "at the earliest moment possible."[19]

MIA

On the day of the surrender, Wednesday, April 3, the Cheyenne *Leader* reported that the previous Monday, when the growing posse began to close in on the TA, "one of the regulators escaped, they say." Reports persisted that at least one or two Defenders managed to slip past the encircling besiegers.

When the list of prisoners was compiled, two Texans were missing: Tom Smith and Bob Martin. The inventory of guns recorded no weapons belonging to Smith or Martin. Probably Smith, and perhaps Martin, too, had been dispatched to get word to Cheyenne that the expedition was trapped. Martin disappeared, and was seen no more in Wyoming. But Smith reached Cheyenne, then rejoined his comrades in time to be included in the famous group photographs.

Fort McKinney parade ground. Officers' Row is at right, while the barracks stand at left. Quartermaster and commissary storehouses are just to the right of the flagpole, and one of these structures still stands. (Courtesy Johnson County Jim Gatchell Memorial Museum)

With his prisoners secured, Colonel Van Horn telegraphed Governor Barber at 4:52 in the afternoon:

> Received the surrender without bloodshed, of Major Wolcott and forty-five men, at 6:45 this morning. I have them now under my charge at this post. One man was seriously wounded on the 12th inst.; name unknown. He will be brought to the post hospital.

The colonel also telegraphed his superior officer, General Brooke at Omaha. And Captain Parmalee telegraphed Governor Barber, succinctly relating the cavalry's timely march and the surrender at the TA: "Arms and ammunition and prisoners brought to Fort McKinney to await instructions for disposal. Small bodies of armed men followed the troops to the fort, the sheriff's party disbanding."[20]

Sheriff Angus soon obtained warrants and asked Colonel Van Horn to turn over the prisoners to the civil custody of Johnson County. But Colonel Van Horn had orders that traced all the way to President Harrison. Rebuffed at Fort McKinney, Sheriff Angus telegraphed Governor Barber on Thursday, April 14, pointing out that warrants had been issued for Van Horn's prisoners. "Make a request on General Brooke to have the commanding officer at Fort McKinney to surrender the 44 men, now held by him as prisoners, to civil authorities for trial under the charge of murder." Governor Barber replied the next day that the prisoners would remain at Fort McKinney for the time being. "They will not be delivered until order and quietude are so fully restored as to convince me that no further violence will be offered them and that the civil authorities of that county are entirely willing and able to give them the protection which the law requires to be given to all prisoners." The subjective judgment regarding the "order and quietude" of Johnson County and the safety of the prisoners would be made by Governor Barber—who had helped the prisoners plan and execute the expedition.[21]

So the prisoners remained at Fort McKinney. Since they were incarcerated in a brick bath house, the men were able to enjoy the comforts of bathing. They were escorted under guard to the mess hall for meals. The oldest prisoner, E. W. "Pappy" Whitcomb, telegraphed his wife in Cheyenne: "Am under arrest by the U.S. troops. Am well. Will write you." Colonel Van Horn gave permission for the prisoners to make purchases at the sutler's store, although alcoholic beverages were off-limits. L. H. Parker and Frank Laberteaux bought cigars from the sutler, then "violated their parole by indulging in a few drinks of whiskey." Parker and Laberteaux were punished with close confinement, while all of the prisoners lost "various other privileges."

E. W. "Pappy" Whitcomb was the oldest member of the expedition. The rancher's home was in Cheyenne, and from Fort McKinney he telegraphed his wife that he was "under arrest" but "well." (From group photo, courtesy Wyoming State Museum)

Although a few of the cattlemen enjoyed individual friendships with certain officers of Fort McKinney, most of the officers "gave us the cold shoulder," said Billy Irvine. Irvine claimed that a soldier was offered $500 to set off "a bomb" beneath the bath house. Although the explosives "would have blown us all to Kingdom come had it been touched off," the soldier supposedly backed out when he could not collect his money in advance. (Sheriff Malcomb Campbell heard that a soldier named Keyser rigged a bomb of dynamite, but when his 500-yard detonation cord malfunctioned, he "then gave up the job.")[22]

After their arrival at Fort McKinney on Wednesday, the prisoners learned that their wounded comrade, Jim Dudley (alias Gus Green), had been buried that morning. On Sunday Dudley had been accidentally wounded in the knee with his own rifle. Two TA cowboys agreed to take him to Fort McKinney for medical care, but their wagon was stopped in Buffalo by "perturbed citizens." Various theories were advanced that he had been wounded by Nate Champion or Jack Flagg, or that "he was playing sick in order to get to the fort to ask for assistance." But it was obvious that he was severely injured, so the wagon was permitted to proceed. The post commander, Col. J. J. Van Horn, did not want to receive the suspicious stranger, "but he was too ill to be sent back to town." By the next day his wound was gangrenous, and after his leg was amputated he became delirious. "He babbled of Texas and of a little woman down in Paris who was anxiously awaiting his return." Periodically "he upbraided himself for joining such an expedition and several times begged 'Capt. Tom' to pay him off and let him go home." Finally he fell quiet, until an hour after midnight on Wednesday morning. Then, "just as the sentry called across the parade ground that all was well, Jim suddenly sat up in bed, looked wildly around," and cried out for his wife: "Gypsy! Gypsy!" He stretched his arms out to embrace her, but "fell back on the pillow dead."[23]

Jim Dudley was buried on Wednesday without ceremony or mourners, "the procession consisting of the hearse and one carriage containing men to lower the body into the grave." The surviving members of the expedition took up a collection and quickly raised

A wing of Fort McKinney's hospital survives today as a visitor center for the Wyoming Veterans Home. Wounded Texans Jim Dudley and Alex Lowther were taken to the post hospital, but both died. (Photo by Karon O'Neal)

The commissary building at Fort McKinney, still standing more than a century after the Johnson County Invaders were brought to the outpost. (Photo by Karon O'Neal)

Dr. John C. Watkins. The highly regarded Buffalo physician was considered a casualty of the Johnson County War. (Courtesy Johnson County Jim Gatchell Memorial Museum)

$125, arranging for a headstone, floral wreaths for the grave, and a white picket fence to be erected around the burial plot. Late on Wednesday the army ambulance arrived bearing Alex Lowther, also accidentally wounded with his own gun. Shot in the abdomen, Lowther lingered for a month before dying on May 12 in the post hospital. "He was unconscious most of the time since his removal there and his end was painless." Like Dudley, Lowther was buried in the post cemetery, far from Texas.[24]

On Friday there were two dramatic funerals in Buffalo. At ten o'clock services were held for the town's first doctor, John C. Watkins. In addition to his practice, Dr. Watkins served as coroner for Johnson County. On Tuesday he had set out with a coroner's jury for the KC Ranch to view the remains of Nate Champion and Nick Ray. But at Carr's ranch, thirty miles south of Buffalo, Dr. Watkins was stricken fatally with "apoplexy." The sudden death at the age of fifty of this beloved citizen was another blow to the shocked community. Reared in New England, Watkins served in the infantry during the Civil War, then became a clerk in the War Department. While in Washington, D.C., he attended Georgetown Medical College. Following graduation in 1868, Dr. Watkins served for a year with the army in Nevada. Returning to the East, he married and later had two sons. In 1880 he took his family to Wyoming, moving to Buffalo in 1883. Until his arrival, the citizens of Buffalo and the surrounding countryside had to rely on the surgeons at Fort McKinney. Dr. Watkins endeared himself by riding long distances to deliver babies and attend emergencies.

A large crowd turned out for his funeral. The services were conducted by the organizations to which Dr. Watkins belonged: the Masonic Lodge, the Knights of Pythias, the Grand Army of the Republic. With eight

The charred remains of Nick Ray were placed in a coffin, decorated with flowers, and placed on display in Buffalo before burial. (Courtesy Johnson County Jim Gatchell Memorial Museum)

members of Company C of the Wyoming National Guard as a military escort, the doctor's flower-draped coffin was taken from his home to the Congregational Church, where a sermon was preached and many mourners stood outside and looked in through the windows. Then, while the church bell tolled, the coffin was escorted to the cemetery and taps was played over the grave. "By his sudden demise Johnson county has lost one of her best citizens, always unassuming, courteous, kind to a fault."[25]

An even more traumatic funeral was held a few hours later in a vacant store on Main Street. Ladies were seated first, and few men could be squeezed inside for the services of Nate Champion and Nick Ray. "The handsome coffins were beautifully and profusely decorated with flowers." A Baptist minister, Rev. W. J. McCullom, read passages from the Bible and led a prayer. Then Rev. Marvin Rader delivered brief remarks. "These men have been sent to eternity," he said. "We know not why. They were not criminals. They were of Christian parents. Ray leaves five brothers and three sisters. His parents could not be notified as the wires were cut. But the same honors have been paid as if they were here."[26]

Many members of the crowd were reduced to tears. The bodies had been on display since Thursday afternoon, but those who had not yet viewed the remains were allowed to approach the coffins. Nick Ray's "black and charred trunk" was camouflaged "with a floral surrounding." Reverends McCullom and Rader led the procession to the cemetery. The horse-drawn hearse was followed by carriages, wagons, pedestrians, and at least 150 mounted men. Someone counted 483 participants, and timed the procession at eight minutes to pass a given point.[27]

The day before these funerals, the Buffalo *Bulletin* editorialized "that this band of invaders should not be bailed out and turned loose to work their devilish plans of vengeance." There was growing concern in Buffalo that the prisoners incarcerated at Fort McKinney were not going to be delivered over to Johnson County officials. "Will they be brought to justice to answer for their crime?"[28]

Not only did the prisoners remain at the fort: Sheriff Angus was forced to relinquish the only member of the expedition that he held in custody in Buffalo. Dick Allen had

Nate Champion and Nick Ray are buried side by side in Buffalo's Willow Grove Cemetery. (Photo by Karon O'Neal)

156

deserted the expedition on Sunday, April 10, and had ridden into Buffalo, where he promptly was thrown into jail. A few days later, however, Governor Barber ordered that Allen should be delivered to Fort McKinney. Although Allen's removal from the jail was "bitterly contested" by Sheriff Angus, "the governor's orders prevailed." On Saturday, April 16, a corporal and a private reported to the jail in a wagon, and Allen was placed in their custody. When Allen and the two enlisted men emerged from the courthouse, "a crowd of more than one hundred people" had gathered. Allen must have been nervous, but the trio of men was allowed to pass unmolested. At Fort McKinney the prisoner finally was safe from the possibility of lynching, and "the happiest one in the barracks was Allen."[29]

Rev. Marvin Rader. Soon after manning a position overlooking the TA, the preacher returned to Buffalo to help bury Nate Champion and Nick Ray. (Courtesy Johnson County Jim Gatchell Memorial Museum)

Another defector from the expedition stayed at large for several days before being captured. When the expedition departed the Tisdale Ranch during the night of Friday, April 8, Dr. Charles Penrose stayed behind, along with rancher H. W. "Hard Winter" Davis and reporter Ed Towse, who was crippled with hemorrhoids. On Saturday morning the three supply wagons left for the KC, where the attack on Nick Ray and Nate Champion already had commenced. Throughout the day neighboring ranchers "dropped in" at the Tisdale Ranch. "They were all apprehensive and obviously scared," observed Penrose, "and were armed." There were rumors about the killing of Ray and Champion, and some passersby saw the smoke from the burning KC cabin. That night trappers Bill Jones and Bill Walker arrived. "They were harmless, simple-minded men; very much alarmed by their experience, afraid to talk, and anxious to get out of the country as fast as possible."[30]

Appalled by events at the KC, Dick Allen deserted the expedition and rode with journalist Sam Clover into Buffalo, where they were arrested. (From group photo, courtesy Wyoming State Museum)

Everyone at Tisdale's slept "in the same room with our firearms beside us" that evening. On Sunday morning Davis persuaded Penrose and Towse to ride with him to his ranch on the Powder River, about twenty miles northeast of Tisdale's. Although the traveling was rough, the three men considered it prudent to ride cross-country. Arriving late in the afternoon, they found four men, a teenaged girl, and the foreman's wife and child at the ranch. The entire party took the precaution of sleeping together in the bunkhouse, while the men took turns on guard duty outside. On Monday morning one of the men rode out to scout for information. He returned to tell about the killing of Ray and Champion, then reported that the expedition was trapped by hundreds of citizens at the TA Ranch. "Realizing that the game was up," related Penrose, "we decided to hunt cover."

Davis tried to persuade Penrose and Towse to stay and help defend his ranch. But Towse wanted to head for safety in Nebraska, while Penrose determined to travel to Douglas, about one hundred miles to the southeast, then take a train to Cheyenne. The Davis foreman, "anxious to get his wife and child away," decided to travel part of the way with Penrose. On Monday afternoon, April 11, the foreman climbed into a buggy with his wife and child, while Dr. Penrose settled into a buckboard with the seventeen-year-old girl. Avoiding the main road, the party headed for Billy Irvine's Ogallala Ranch, thirty-five miles away, and arrived at nine o'clock that night. Penrose introduced himself as "Dr. Green from Fort McKinney," and slept with the cowboys in the bunkhouse. Awakening to a heavy snowfall, Penrose spent all day Tuesday at the Ogallala, as ten or twelve inches of snow covered the ground. "The following morning was beautiful and sunny," and "Dr. Green" left alone in the buckboard. Barely able to make out the road, Penrose encountered no other travelers. After a ride of forty miles, he stopped for the night at Mike Henry's road ranch at Brown Springs.

That evening a young Englishman who had a nearby spread came to the road ranch for his mail. Although the Englishman and Penrose had been acquainted in Cheyenne, neither man gave any sign of recognition. "I thought at the time that he should have invited me to come to his ranch," mused Dr. Penrose, "as he knew that I had been with the cattle men, who were his friends and were protecting his interests." But suddenly it was dangerous to associate with the cattlemen's faction, and Dr. Penrose experienced a chilling ostracism from a fair-weathered friend. "If I had gone to his ranch I would probably have succeeded in getting into Nebraska," Penrose later reflected with regret.

Penrose drove his buckboard away from the road ranch on Thursday morning. Douglas was a half-day's drive away, and when he reached town he planned to take a train to Cheyenne or, if it seemed prudent, head toward Nebraska in the buckboard. When Penrose crossed the Platte River bridge at Fort Fetterman, he tossed into the running water "everything about me that might be compromising and bore my name, as I was still Dr. Green from Fort McKinney. I here threw away the telegraph code with which I was to have communicated with Judge Vandevanter and Governor Barber." But all precautions proved useless when Penrose drove into the little town of Douglas. The townspeople "just looked at me. There was an apparent air of suspicion and antagonism." No one spoke to him when he put his horse in a stall of the livery stable. On the street Penrose saw Sheriff Malcolm Campbell, and in the bank he found Col. DeForest Richards—both Cheyenne acquaintances. Colonel Richards, commander of the Wyoming National Guard, told Penrose he "should have avoided the town." And Sheriff Campbell, who had received a telegram from Sheriff Angus "to be on the lookout for stragglers from the north," soon entered the bank and arrested Penrose, relieving him of "a fine revolver [and] plenty of cartridges."[31]

The jail was a square brick structure with a three-cell cage standing in the middle of the building. There already were two prisoners, and Penrose was tossed into the third cell. "This was very unjust," he complained, "as I was confined purely on suspicion." When a large crowd surrounded the jail, Campbell warned Penrose to stay out of view of the windows "for fear of being shot." The sheriff also sent for a carpenter to reinforce the door. Penrose began playing cards with his "cage mates." Food was "scraps from the sheriff's table," and was served in a basket on the floor with no plates, knives, forks or spoons. Penrose was denied permission to buy food with his own money. One of the prisoners grumped that the jail was "a tough jug to live in, but all that could be expected on a sage brush flat.'" When told that he would be returned to Johnson County "to be tried for conspiracy," Penrose "declared earnestly that he had left the raiders before they made their first killings." He was permitted to send telegrams to friends in Cheyenne and Philadelphia, "and his illustrious brother took legal steps immediately to assist him in regaining his liberty."

That evening Penrose was visited by Colonel Richards, who brought a couple of novels and reassurances that the townspeople had been calmed. But, after his medical bag was returned, Penrose injected himself with half a grain of morphine, "so that I might face anything that arose during the night with equanimity."

The night proved uneventful, and following "a cold breakfast on the floor," the card game resumed. That afternoon a special locomotive brought U.S. Marshal Joe Rankin, who presented Sheriff Campbell with a writ of habeas corpus for Penrose. Within a few minutes Rankin and Campbell hustled Penrose onto the locomotive, "which had the cabin door closed in behind with canvas." Governor Barber, informed by telegraph of Penrose's arrest, had obtained a writ that he was held in jail without a warrant and was deprived of his due process of law. Penrose was whisked out of Douglas before anyone realized what was happening. Marshal Rankin and Dr. Penrose stepped off the locomotive at Orin Junction, then caught a southbound train, arriving in Cheyenne around midnight. "I resumed my residence at the Cheyenne Club in the nominal custody of Rankin, who also lived there," the doctor reported.

Like Penrose, another member of the expedition blundered into custody. After all of the sightseers finally rode away from the TA, and after the army ambulance arrived and departed with Alex Lowther, George Dunning climbed down from his hiding place in the loft of the cabin. Trying to escape after dark, Dunning wandered into Buffalo, "where he was immediately suspected of being an invader." Dunning was incarcerated and secluded—there would not be another invader lost to Fort McKinney. Six months later, Dunning produced a forty-four-page confession, transcribed and sworn to before T. P. Hill, clerk of the District Court of Johnson County.[32]

When stories about the invasion began to reach Texas newspapers, there was great concern in the community of Paris. A Paris journalist reported on April 16 that eleven of the men involved in the Wyoming difficulties

Live in this city and have at one time or another been in the service of the state and federal governments as deputy sheriffs or deputy marshals. They left this city about ten days ago in rather a mysterious way. It was given out and generally believed that they had gone to the Cheyenne and Arapahoe country to assist in the opening of that country. It has leaked out later that they had gone into the cattle business in Wyoming. That was in a sense correct. The large ranchmen in that territory were overwhelmed in numbers by rustlers or small cattlemen and their pals. They were making it unpleasant and unprofitable for the large ranch owners and it became necessary for them to appeal to the president for protection.

The marshals in Texas were communicated with and forty-three bold and adventurous men were dispatched from this state to preserve the peace. The matter was kept a profound secret, and the eleven men in this city went away without letting any one, even their own families, know where they were going.[33]

It was easy for Texans to side with the Wyoming ranchers against "rustlers or small cattle owners and their pals." And certainly the image of "bold and adventurous men" sallying forth from Texas "to preserve the peace" in Wyoming was readily believable.

On April 20 a long story in the Dallas *Morning News* headlined: "Four Texans Killed in the Great Cattle War in Wyoming." A man named Linvell, on his way from northern Wyoming to Cheyenne, stopped in Douglas long enough to report that he had toured the TA two days after the siege ended. Linvell claimed that he had seen the corpses of three Texans, "dead men who had probably been overlooked," although it was not explained how the bodies could have been overlooked by the hundreds of people who had swarmed all over the ranch. The fourth Texan was Lowther, whose accidental shooting and subsequent death were correctly reported.[34]

By the next day, after this news story reached Paris, it was speculated—incorrectly— that the dead Texans were Frank "Cannon," Buck Garrett, Bob Barling, and—correctly—Alex Lowther. In Paris, Frank Barling sent telegrams to Fort McKinney, Buffalo, and Douglas, but received no replies. Since the Barling family home was in Arkansas, Barling also wired for help from a senator and the governor of Arkansas. A prominent citizen of Paris telegraphed the governor of Texas, James S. Hogg, asking him to wire Governor Barber "to save Texas boys from mob law. Some of them are my personal friends and are honorable men. It is sincerely hoped that our boys will be protected against violence and will at least be given a fair trial." Governor Hogg, on the eve of launching his re-election campaign, promptly telegraphed Governor Barber. Barber immediately wired his assurances: "Troops will protect them against violence."[35]

Governor James Hogg tried to intervene on behalf of his fellow Texans who were incarcerated in Wyoming. (Author's collection)

Indeed, by the time the governors of Wyoming and Texas exchanged telegrams, the U.S. Cavalry once again was escorting the Texans and the other prisoners to friendly confinement at a more advantageous location than Fort McKinney. George Dunning was the sole member of the expedition to remain in custody in Johnson County. The other prisoners, again safeguarded by three cavalry troops, departed the area, so that their legal battles could be conducted far from Johnson County.

Chapter 14

Escape from Johnson County

"The invaders looked like tramps."
SHERIFF MALCOLM CAMPBELL

"The sheriff was working like fury to get us turned over to him," said Texan George Tucker, "but all of his telegrams were futile." On the same day that the Invaders surrendered to the military and were taken to Fort McKinney, Sheriff Red Angus filed murder charges and obtained warrants for their arrest, hoping to incarcerate the forty-four prisoners somewhere in Buffalo. But Col. J. J. Van Horn, following instructions from his superiors, refused the sheriff's demands that the Invaders be released to his custody. Sheriff Angus then telegraphed Governor Barber, requesting that the prisoners be turned over "to the civil authorities for trial under the charge of murder." Governor Barber not only denied this request; he soon ordered that Sheriff Angus release rancher Dick Allen to the custody of Colonel Van Horn. The governor telegraphed Colonel Van Horn "that there seems to be too much danger of the civil authorities not being able to give the men adequate protection against violence." To make certain that Sheriff Angus did not somehow prevail, Governor Barber wired Colonel Van Horn's immediate supervisor, Gen. John R. Brooke, in Omaha. General Brooke replied that he had directed Colonel Van Horn to "hold the Wolcott party until he gets his orders from me."[1]

Governor Barber was a physician, not a lawyer, and he had little experience as a politician. But he remained in contact with Senators Carey and Warren in Washington, while conferring closely with WSGA attorneys, who insisted that the prisoners should "be re-

Dr. Amos W. Barber, acting governor of Wyoming during the Johnson County War, and a partisan of the cattlemen. (Author's collection)

161

moved to a place of entire safety and there kept in custody until the time of trial." Legal maneuvers would concentrate on moving the trials to "the Southern part of the State." On Friday afternoon, April 15, Secretary of War S. B. Elkins wired Governor Barber with welcome news: "Orders have been sent to Gen. Brooke to deliver to you as soon as he can do so, the captured party under Wolcott." The prisoners were to be transferred to Cheyenne, where most of the Wyoming ranchers had friends and family, and where Governor Barber and the WSGA could provide on-site assistance.[2]

It was decided that Maj. Edmond Fechet and all three cavalry troops stationed at Fort McKinney would escort the prisoners to the closest rail connection, at Douglas, where troops from Fort D. A. Russell would meet the column, take custody of the prisoners, then return by train to Cheyenne. The 160-mile march to Douglas would proceed along the old Bozeman Trail and was expected to take a week. Harsh weather was anticipated, and a large wagon train would carry provisions and camp equipment. To discourage possible mob violence or snipers, a Hotchkiss gun would be packed on a mule and carried at the front of the column. A 1.65-inch two-pounder "mountain rifle" capable of rapid and accurate fire up to 4,000 yards, the Hotchkiss gun "insured a peaceful journey for the cavalcade."[3]

These preparations and the normal contact between Fort McKinney and Buffalo alerted citizens that the prisoners were about to be taken out of Johnson County to a friendlier location. Word spread rapidly—as it had about most other developments of the unsuccessful expedition—and citizens felt considerable frustration that the prisoners were soon to leave Johnson County. On Saturday, April 16, the telegraph wire again was cut.

"The State authorities are apparently powerless," complained General Brooke to the War Department, "and the only conservator of the peace is the garrison at Fort McKinney." Billy Irvine was told by a friend "that the rustlers intended to bushwhack us from brush as we left the Post." Irvine called on Colonel Van Horn, told him the rumor, "and requested that our arms be returned to us for the trip south." Although Colonel Van Horn refused this request, "without our knowledge" he concealed inside one of the supply wagons the prisoners' weapons, "to be used in case of an emergency."[4]

The large column formed up in a cold rain on the morning of April 17, Easter Sunday. There were ten wagons pulled by four- or six-mule teams with rations and grain for a week, Sibley tents, and miscellaneous army equipment; three wagons pulled by four-horse teams with the supplies and gear of the prisoners; and an ambulance. Counting a surgeon and four members of the hospital corps, along with a telegrapher and a four-man infantry detail to serve the Hotchkiss gun, the soldiers totaled ten officers and 140 enlisted men. The mounted prisoners were lined up two abreast, with one cavalry troop flanking the captives, one leading the column, and one riding as a rear guard. The prisoners rode their own horses, a few of which had been wounded at the TA Ranch, and during the coming week some of these mounts would play out, with replacements secured along the way at cattlemen's expense. As the column took shape, a number of civilians drifted onto the post, while many others began to ride out from town. A concerned Major Fechet "ordered all strangers out of the post."[5]

At ten o'clock Major Fechet directed the column to advance. The road out of the fort was crowded on both sides with buggies, carriages, wagons, and riders. At the orders of Major Fechet, the leading troopers bumped the riders and teams, and the roadway quickly was widened. But half a mile from the post a couple of dozen cowboys rode near the column, until Major Fechet ordered the troopers to draw their carbines. Then, as the column approached the bridge across Clear Creek, three men brandishing rifles blocked the road—until Major Fechet ordered a dozen dismounted skirmishers forward. Past the bridge the road narrowed through a dense stand of willows. Although concerned about an ambush, the column had to ride single file until reaching an open plain, where the group reformed unscathed—except for shouted taunts. Sheriff Angus and several other riders watched from a knoll, then wheeled their mounts toward Buffalo.

After skirting the town there seemed to be little danger to the column. But the rain turned to sleet, and a full-scale blizzard began to develop. During the day, as trail conditions worsened, the struggling wagon train fell behind the mounted troopers and prisoners. The soldiers wore winter overcoats and slickers, but the prisoners had lost their camp equipment and some heavy clothing when the expedition's three supply wagons were confiscated. They resorted to binding gunnysacks around their feet, wrapping their torsos in blankets, and drawing bandanas or other cloth over their faces. "It was a sorry lot of soldiers and prisoners that crouched over brush-fires that night while waiting for the belated wagon-train to get to camp," observed the ubiquitous Sam Clover.[6]

The first night's camp was along Crazy Woman Creek, after a march of twenty-five miles. The column had not brought hay for the horses, expecting to graze the livestock. But new snow already covered the grass, and by the next morning another three inches had fallen. Since there were tents only for the officers, "the soldiers and prisoners had to shift for themselves." Predictably, Sam Clover had "arranged to mess with Captain Scott and Lieutenant Lindsley, of D troop, two of the finest types of Uncle Sam's West Pointers. Their tent, their blankets, their good-will—everything they had—was" shared with the reporter. As the hardships of the march mounted, the officers became less charitably disposed toward the prisoners who were the cause of their discomfiture. Major Fechet "was no friend of ours," remarked Billy Irvine, who also disliked Capt. Edwin Stanton, commander of C Troop. These two cavalry officers had begun their long military careers as enlisted men in the infantry early in the Civil War. After the war, Fechet served for a quarter of a century as an officer in the Eighth Cavalry, before accepting a promotion to major in the Sixth Cavalry in 1891. Stanton was transferred to the Sixth in 1877 and promoted to captain in 1886. Both men were combat veterans who had spent three decades in the service of their country. Major Fechet and Captain Stanton had friends in Buffalo, and they were offended by the extralegal march into Johnson County, but they resolutely performed their duty toward men they disdained.[7]

The march resumed "in a whirling snowstorm" early Monday morning. After struggling another twenty-eight miles, a wet camp was pitched at Powder River Crossing, "every rider being pretty well exhausted," remembered Sam Clover. "Tuesday's ride was a repetition of the previous for discomfort and physical suffering," according to Clover. But the Chicago reporter watched with admiration as the ill-clad prisoners stoically endured the vicious weather: "with all their physical suffering and distress of mind, not a murmur escaped them." In his reminiscences, George Tucker did not even mention the difficult march. Frank Canton, whose frontier hardships included two years in Alaska, likewise ignored the travails of the journey when he wrote his autobiography. "The trip was a very cold and unpleasant one," admitted Billy Irvine, "as we had a regular blizzard nearly the whole way." But Irvine could take consolation in the anticipation that soon he would literally enjoy the comforts of home. His Ogallala Ranch headquarters stood near the Bozeman Trail, although he had taken the precaution of sending his family out of state. The column camped at Seventeen Mile Ranch on Tuesday night, but Irvine expected to spend Wednesday night in his own bed.[8]

On Wednesday morning, however, "the storm seemed to take a new lease on life." Sam Clover described "an attack of rain, hail, and sleet," followed by "a sudden change to driving snow, that continued with terrific fury all day." The frigid wind and whirling snowflakes "enveloped the luckless horses and riders until every drop of blood seemed to congeal." Despite this ordeal, the column labored on for twenty-five more miles. As darkness fell, the frozen riders neared the comforts promised by Billy Irvine at the Ogallala Ranch.[9]

While the column plodded on toward Douglas, frustration and resentment were expressed by the citizens who had rallied to defend their town, their county, their homes. The Buffalo *Bulletin* published a list of "THE MURDERERS." Reprinting these names several days later, the Sheridan *Enterprise* indignantly pointed out "a number of prominent citizens and officials of the state—W. C. Irvine, member of the board of live stock commissioners; W. J. Clarke of the board of water control; F. M. Canton, deputy U.S. marshal; J. M. Tisdale, senator from Johnson County, and other well known people. Preserve the list and frame it." Emphasizing that these were "men who had sworn to guard and maintain the constitution and laws of the state," the *Enterprise* voiced outrage that these officials and "the most prominent stockmen of the state" had "banded together in a murderous attempt to override and trample under foot every vestige of law and order." The *Enterprise* pointedly editorialized: "If a man murders, punish him according to law for his crime whether he be a 'rustler,' a cattleman or a state official." A party of angry citizens rode south of Buffalo a few miles and cut the telegraph line. As a repairman wearily set out to find yet another severed wire, authorities in Cheyenne lost track of the progress of the soldiers and their prisoners.[10]

Late Wednesday afternoon, at the end of the fourth day of a tortuous trek, the column finally reached Billy Irvine's Ogallala Ranch. Irvine claimed that "Fechet kept us standing for hours in the storm." While Major Fechet sternly disapproved of the Invasion, it was inconceivable that the prisoners—and their military guards—stood "for hours" in a snowstorm while a hot meal and a warm ranch house and bunkhouse awaited. Irvine disliked Fechet and clearly exaggerated the incident, although several minutes of standing in a blizzard might seem like hours. The delay was caused by the presence of about sixty armed cowboys, including several who had been targeted by the Invaders. To head off any trouble, Major Fechet ordered the Hotchkiss gun unpacked and mounted near the barn, then he "gave an exhibition of what it could do."[11]

Irvine reportedly extended western hospitality, inviting Major Fechet to dinner inside the ranch house. "Not by a damn sight," retorted Fechet. "We pay you for every oat and wisp of hay we get just like any other person." While the military pitched tents beside the ranch house, the prisoners "enjoyed the warmth and food" provided by Irvine, who had a beef slaughtered. A sergeant asked for some of the meat for his men, but he was refused by Irvine, who thought the sergeant had been sent by Capt. Edwin Stanton. Stanton shared Fechet's open disdain for the prisoners, but the sergeant represented a troop commanded by a different captain. "Hell, that makes a difference," reported Irvine. "I'll kill another beef."[12]

Restored by a hot meal—and presumably by liquid refreshments—under Irvine's roof, "we made a night of it singing and playing the piano." Around midnight a soldier sought out Irvine with the message that Major Fechet "desires to inform you that your men are disturbing his rest." With brashness unbecoming a prisoner, Irvine asked the messenger to "tell him the piano is mine; that I have turned it over to the boys for the night and that they can do what they damn please with it." At least, that was Irvine's version of the evening decades later.[13]

Sam Clover asserted that at the Ogallala Ranch "partial relief was found from the horrors of the preceding four days." Because of the condition of the men and horses, it was deemed wise to spend a day recuperating at the ranch. "Thursday was passed in resting and in burnishing the arms and equipment," reported Clover. By the next day the skies had cleared, and the column set out for Brown's Springs, twenty-five miles to the south. "This day's march was made under scorching sun that landed everyone in camp with blistered faces and sore necks," recalled Clover with vivid memory, "while not a few suffered greatly from inflammation of the eyes, caused by the glare of the sun on the sea of snow."[14]

During the Friday march, the column reached Collins Station, a stop on the stagecoach road which afforded the first telegraph connection with the south since the expedition had departed on Monday. Major Fechet learned that on Thursday morning at 5:30, a special train had left Cheyenne to pick up the prisoners. The Cheyenne and Northern locomotive pulled five passenger cars, two baggage cars, and a livestock car for horses. Companies A, B, and C of the Seventeenth Infantry stationed at Fort D. A. Russell were aboard, commanded by Maj. Harry C. Egbert and including nine officers and 109 enlisted men. Also aboard were "a number of friends and relatives of the invaders." Provisions were loaded for several days, since it was uncertain when the mounted expedition would reach Douglas. Following a northern journey of 130 miles, the train parked on a siding at Orin Junction, twelve miles from Douglas, awaiting further instructions and setting up a camp beside the tracks.[15]

Major Egbert was the commander of Fort D. A. Russell, and shortly before the special train departed, Secretary of War S. B. Elkins telegraphed permission to incarcerate the prisoners at the fort. Governor Barber had conferred with Major Egbert, who had acknowledged that at Fort Russell there were "barracks not now occupied for the use of the garrison and which these prisoners can be conveniently and safely confined." Governor Barber expressed concerns to Gen. John R. Brooke that "there still exists much danger of attempted assassination and violence to members of the Wolcott party." General Brooke forwarded Governor Barber's request to Maj. Gen. J. M. Schofield, commander of the army, who passed it on to Secretary of War Elkins. Elkins, who surely was being pressured by Senators Carey and Warren, immediately telegraphed instructions to Brooke to hold the prisoners at Fort Russell "temporarily" and on condition that "the expense of their subsistence shall be borne by the civil authorities or by the prisoners." Significantly, the secretary of war added: "There will be no objection, for the time being, to the party occupying the vacant barracks even after they are in charge of the civil officers if desired." Major Egbert therefore would house the prisoners "indefinitely at Fort Russell."[16]

After learning the whereabouts of the special train, Major Fechet led his column on to Brown's Springs, camping for the night at Mike Henry's ranch. Once more the Sibley tents went up, while the prisoners huddled beneath a makeshift shelter of tarpaulins. Troopers stood guard duty through the night exposed to a new snowstorm and vicious winds which threatened to dismantle the tents. Meanwhile, Major Fechet tapped into the nearby telegraph line to communicate a change of plans to Major Egbert. Fechet

To and from Chicago

One of the first men to meet the weatherbeaten column from Fort McKinney was James Keeley of the Chicago *Tribune* (see Linn, *James Keeley, Newspaperman*, 46-51). When word of the Wyoming conflict reached the *Tribune*, the city editor gave Keeley $300 and dispatched him to Johnson County. But by the time Keeley linked up with the column and began filing stories, Sam Clover of the rival Chicago *Herald* already had been with the expedition since it had departed Cheyenne.

After arriving at Fort D. A. Russell with the prisoners, the resourceful Clover soon was on a train for Chicago. He brought with him Nate Champion's bloodstained diary, which he had obtained within a couple of hours after Nate's death. Champion's riveting words were published in the *Herald*, while Clover loaned the diary to Chicago banker Henry A. Blair, absentee owner of the Hoe Ranch. Clover also provided Blair a "private report," which he referred to in a letter dated May 15, 1892. In the May 15 letter, Clover thanked Blair for returning the diary. Clover also mentioned that "Irvine had already threatened me and I am not fool enough to think his threats idle." He was worried that, like "the two trappers [Jones and Walker]," he might disappear. "My next assignment, I hope will be in Ceylon, Bangkok or Tibet—as far away from Wyoming as possible."

But W. C. Irvine later looked up Clover in Chicago and demanded the diary. Although Clover insisted that he had destroyed the diary, Irvine did not believe him (Penrose, *The Rustler Business*, 34-36). If the diary still exists, however, it has not been seen in well over a century.

One of the structures still standing at old Fort Fetterman, where the prisoners boarded a special train. (Photo by Karon O'Neal)

remembered the threatening crowd that awaited him at the Ogallala Ranch, and he also "was as suspicious of the invaders' friends in the south half of the state as he had been of Angus' in the north." Correctly anticipating that a large crowd would descend upon Douglas, Fechet arranged for the train to meet the column at old Fort Fetterman, about ten miles north of Douglas.[17]

Fort Fetterman had been abandoned a decade earlier by the army, and even though civilians had moved into some of the deserted structures, by 1892 the old post was dilapidated. When the special train arrived on Sunday, April 24, the infantrymen descended to the ground and were aligned into formation. The passengers also alighted, anxious to see the Wyoming cattlemen who were loved ones and friends. Large numbers of spectators from Douglas streamed into Fetterman on horseback and in buggies and wagons.

The column arrived a little before four o'clock. Sam Clover pushed his mount ahead of everyone else, hurrying toward a reunion with a fellow journalist (the previous night Clover had paid a cowboy to ride to Fetterman and file his story at the telegraph office). About ten minutes later the bedraggled column rode to within a few hundred yards of the train. Troop C led the way, Troop H flanked the prisoners on both sides, Troop D was the rear guard, and the wagon train and ambulance followed the riders. The riders showed the ill effects of their arduous journey. "The troopers were so black from exposure that they resembled Indians as they came across the plain, ... their white hats bobbing above their blistered faces," observed Sheriff Malcolm Campbell from Douglas. "The invaders looked like tramps. Unshaven, with the skin already peeling from their noses and faces, and clad in gunny-sacks, red scarfs, slickers, army blankets, with their trousers in rags and with a wild assortment of hats on their heads, they presented a truly terrifying sight."[18]

Major Egbert happily approached Major Fechet, and the two officers shook hands. The friends and relatives of the cattlemen were permitted to come forward, and a warm round of handshakes and embraces ensued. During these moments "a few bottles of liquor" were slipped to grateful prisoners for imbibing on the train. Most of the Wyoming cattlemen had met and liked Major Egbert in Cheyenne, and there were eager greetings for the officer Billy Irvine called "that most beloved soldier." Other friendly reunions took place between ranchers and various officers of the Seventeenth.[19]

After ten minutes the prisoners moved toward the train, while the cavalrymen wheeled and rode to "a commanding position" atop nearby bluffs. Each prisoner unsaddled his horse, then tossed his saddle, bridle, blanket, and warbag into a baggage car, which "was soon filled to the roof with the equipment." The prisoners then formed a line in front of the passenger cars. Major Fechet produced an official list and called the names of the prisoners in alphabetical order. As each man answered "Here," he was assigned a seat in car three or four. When all of the prisoners had climbed into the cars, Major Egbert signed a receipt and Major Fechet ordered his cavalry to ride north to a predetermined campsite. Fechet would travel all the way to Cheyenne, and both majors boarded the train. At about six o'clock, with onlookers firing their revolvers into the air, the train pulled out for Douglas.[20]

As bottles were passed from prisoner to prisoner, spirits quickly rose, "and they were singing at a furious rate." Wolcott boasted of the sirloin steaks he intended to eat in Chicago within a few weeks. After a short journey the train reached Douglas and a crowded depot platform. The train rolled to a stop at the same siding as the previous night, while soldiers brandishing carbines stood guard on the steps of the coaches. Prisoners happily extended their heads out of the windows. "There were a number of tearful reunions," reported Sheriff Campbell. "Women hurried through the crowd, Mrs. Shonsey among them, and greeted their husbands eagerly, with endearing words often checked by sobs of

The special train which transported the prisoners and their military escort from Fort Fetterman to Fort D. A. Russell. The train is shown traveling carefully through the long Platte River Canyon. (Courtesy Johnson County Jim Gatchell Memorial Museum)

happiness at having their loved ones restored again to safety." The families of Frank Wolcott, Frank Canton, Billy Irvine, and others had been sent out of state before the Invasion began, while some families awaited in Cheyenne.[21]

Major Fechet telegraphed Department headquarters in Omaha that the prisoners had been successfully delivered to Major Egbert. Although the prisoners were confined to the train, Major Egbert escorted Major Wolcott into town to arrange meal delivery to the prisoners. Major Egbert was told of a threat to derail the train as it passed through twelve-mile-long Platte River Canyon. After consulting with his officers, Egbert directed that the train would not travel in the darkness, but would wait until the next day. Arrangements were made for an engine and caboose to precede the prisoner train. Two men with field glasses would ride in the caboose top, scanning the rails ahead, while a section crew with repair tools would ride below.

The prisoners had to sleep in their seats, but Sheriff Campbell noted that they "were plentifully supplied with reading material and choice morsels to eat." The two trains pulled out of Douglas at seven o'clock on Sunday morning. En route the prisoners dozed or read newspapers recounting their recent adventures. Stops were made at several stations, and invariably there were "telegrams of sympathy and support" from Cheyenne. The train proceeded slowly down the length of the Platte River Canyon before finally emerging about one hundred miles south of Douglas. With the likelihood of danger regarded as past, the train sped at normal speed toward Cheyenne. There was one more stop, at little Uva, where H. E. Teschemacher's wife had prepared "a wonderful barbeque dinner." For an hour "all soldiers, stockmen and train-crew ate their fill."[22]

Thus fortified, everyone was ready to finish the journey. Safely delivered from Johnson County, the prisoners had every hope that once in Cheyenne, any legal repercussions from their violent expedition could be resolved in their favor. At midafternoon, the orderly buildings of Fort D. A. Russell came into sight across a rolling plain.

Looking west across the vast parade ground of Fort D. A. Russell. The Invaders were incarcerated in a structure probably located out of sight to the south, or left. The brick officers' quarters in the center once housed Gen. John J. Pershing, who married the daughter of Wyoming Senator Francis E. Warren, one of the most powerful men involved in the Johnson County War. In 1930 Fort D. A. Russell was renamed Fort Francis E. Warren, and today the one-time frontier outpost is F. E. Warren Air Force Base. (Photo by Karon O'Neal)

Chapter 15

The Violence Continues

"I have been notified that I am on the list to be killed. I am in hourly danger...."

Buffalo Mayor Charles Burritt

Although the Invaders were in custody, harsh resentments festered in Buffalo and Johnson County, soon erupting into more killings. The comparative handful of rustlers continued their usual activities, preying especially on the livestock of the arrested cattlemen, and depending on the general hard feelings against these men. But honest citizens also reacted with understandable outrage against those who had attacked their homes, and their anger was compounded by the likelihood that the "prisoners" in Cheyenne somehow would be exonerated. A frustrated Sheriff Red Angus was overheard belligerently expressing "a desire to go to Cheyenne himself, taking with him a sufficient force to bring back the prisoners whether they were turned over to him or not." General indignation first was expressed in insults and taunts to prisoners and their supporters, then escalated to physical intimidation and property damage, and all too soon to another murder and another gun battle.

Sheriff Malcolm Campbell stated that Mat Laberteaux, younger brother of Invader-prisoner F. H. Laberteaux, "was cuffed around the streets" of Buffalo by angry citizens. Campbell also heard that various men in Buffalo who were friends of the cattlemen were intimidated by threats to their lives or property. Maj. Charles Burritt, who was in Cheyenne on legal business during the Invasion and did not return to Buffalo until April 28, was dismayed to find "that this entire community is intimidated" and that "lawlessness is supreme here." A man named Dunn, who clerked for merchant Fred Hasbrouck, a friend of the cattlemen, had his eyes blackened and was "successfully thumped." Hasbrouck angrily informed his "would be intimidators" that this "experiment tried on him would be dangerous ... and the first man that made a break toward him would be killed on the spot."[1]

Major Burritt, who performed a great deal of legal work for big ranchers (and who quietly accepted a retainer to join the defense team for the Invaders), was "notified that I am in hourly danger—my family are in Nebraska—and I dare not bring them home." Burritt's friend and associate, banker Will Thom, sent his family to his wife's home in St. Louis, and he carried a rifle back and forth to the bank. Burritt lamented that "our best citizens [are] sending their families away from the County and getting ready to follow them as soon as possible." Newspaper editor T. J. Bouton was persuaded to sell out to Jack Flagg, a negotiation transacted by Burritt and Thom. "Bouton and his family will immediately leave this country," related Burritt, while Jack Flagg would turn his Buffalo *Bulletin* into an anti-cattleman newspaper. Other men were threatened or roughed up, and A. C. Cobel of the U.S. Land Office feared a riot and sent to Fort McKinney for soldiers to guard federal property.[2]

Nearly a month after the Invasion, Major Burritt was dismayed that Jack Flagg and his comrades "are carrying pistols with them all the time." Burritt was astounded that Robert Foote continued his practice of "feeding the thieves" on credit "—how he expects to get even I can't imagine unless he is figuring upon taking his pay in stolen cattle. ... Foote has taken the Fort McKinney beef contract at $5.48. How is this? Does it not seem to indicate that he intends to fill that contract with 'Rustler Beef Cattle,' taken at a nominal figure by him to balance rustler accounts?" Such threatening conditions continued to cause solid citizens to leave Buffalo, with negative effects on Burritt's potential income. "The ranks of my friends and clients are being daily thinned out by departures and many more are getting ready to join the exodus," he wrote.[3]

During the first weeks in May a rancher named Devoe heard "a large number of shots" at nightfall. Investigating the next morning, Devoe found several cattle dead and several more wounded, all wearing the 28 brand of Fred Hesse. Sheriff Malcolm Campbell reported that a party of "rustlers" raided Hesse's ranch headquarters, "shot the piano to pieces, destroyed all the furniture, and looted the place generally." Such vengeful attacks on Invader ranches "became quite general the following two weeks." Furthermore, continued Campbell, there was "much feeling against the foremen as a class, especially those who had known of the intended raid, and had given no warning to the rustlers." E. W. Whitcomb's foreman, George P. Bissell, abandoned his job because he "feared death." W. Linville, foreman for H. B. Ijams, was "notified" to leave, and he did. Billy Irvine's foreman, a man named Chambers, received the same notification, and he promptly departed for Cheyenne. With Charles Ford, foreman of the TA, incarcerated indefinitely, Dr. Harris hired Charles Carter to manage the ranch. But Carter, who also was a friend and longtime employee of Fred Hesse, "was waited upon by a committee and given two days to settle his business and leave the country and he went within the prescribed time."[4]

F. H. Laberteaux, foreman of Henry Blair's Hoe Ranch, also was incarcerated in Cheyenne. Blair, who lived in Chicago, engaged thirty-three-year-old George Wellman as the new foreman of his big ranch on the Powder River, about forty miles south of Buffalo. A native of Canada, Wellman had come to Wyoming in 1880 and had worked as a cowboy ever since. He had ridden for the Hoe the past five years. Quiet and well liked, he was a member of Buffalo's Masonic Lodge. Wellman had encountered H. W. "Hard Winter" Davis after the rancher deserted the Invasion prior to the attack on the

KC. Davis was trying to leave the country, and Wellman helped him on his way. Wellman similarly assisted newspaperman Ed Towse, who also had left the expedition and hoped to return to Cheyenne. Wellman took the ailing and frightened Towse to Gillette, where he could find a rail connection. Deciding that it was an excellent time to leave the turbulent region, Wellman took an eastbound train. He visited his sweetheart, in Martha, Wisconsin, and they were married on April 21.[5]

Perhaps because he did not yet have a proper residence, or perhaps because of the unrest in Johnson County, Wellman returned alone to Wyoming, stepping off the train in Cheyenne on Thursday, May 5. At this point Henry Blair was in the process of selling part of his vast spread to Robert Gibson, who operated the Hoe Ranch near Gillette. With the arrest of his foreman, Frank Laberteaux, Blair immediately needed a new ramrod. George Wellman, experienced and dependable, was an obvious choice. But Wellman's promotion to foreman also brought an appointment as a deputy U.S. marshal—a position almost as unpopular in Johnson County as foreman for an absentee ranch owner who clearly had supported the Invasion.

Marshal Joe Rankin had been handed injunction papers which would halt the roundup that had been scheduled to precede the WSGA spring roundup in Johnson County. Needing deputies to help him serve writs on thirty-three men, Rankin reported that "at the request of the cattlemen and invaders, I deputized three men, Wellman, Craig and Gibson, to assist serving the writs. These men were to meet me in Buffalo on May 10th and receive instructions. They had all been, and were at the time, in the employ of the large cattlemen, and were selected for this work at the request of the parties who were interested; and also because they knew the parties against whom the injunctions were issued, and where to find them."[6] Apparently, then, Henry Blair was at least partly responsible for the appointment of his new foreman as a deputy U.S. marshal.

The cattlemen's faction had obtained legal assistance in blocking a rival roundup, and they had arranged for three of their employees to assist Wyoming's federal marshal in enforcing their latest action against the small ranchers and rustlers. But the atmosphere in Johnson County had been poisoned by the recent Invasion, and by the subsequent delivery of the Invaders out of the county. With the citizens of Johnson County fearful of some other action, and with lawlessness on the rise, the intrusion of law officers intending to force cattlemen's justice represented a threat that could easily trigger more violence.

Newlywed George Wellman, although popular, became foreman for a decidedly unpopular absentee ranch owner. After being appointed a deputy U.S. marshal, Wellman was assassinated. (Courtesy Johnson County Jim Gatchell Memorial Museum)

Tourists

William Martin, in "PART TENTH" of his typed memoirs (69-75), described a visit to the TA and KC ranches shortly after the famous battle. Martin and his friend, Charles Solon, were rounded up by posse members but easily convinced Sheriff Angus that they had been forced to ride with the Invaders. They spent a week in Buffalo before setting out for Laramie on Wednesday, April 20. "We had filled our belts with shells, purchased at Foote's store, and had flour, bacon, salt, sugar and coffee, rolled in our blankets and tied behind our saddles."

Like many other sightseers, they stopped to look over the TA Ranch. "Relic hunters and passers by had made away with about everything in the way of relics"; however, Martin managed to find a pearl-handled dagger "of Spanish workmanship, which we presumed, had been dropped by some member of the Texas contingent."

Martin and Solon reached the KC Thursday afternoon. After a careful investigation of the site, they built a fire near the river and camped for the night. Arising at four o'clock, they cooked breakfast and tended and saddled their horses. Before they could depart, however, they were surrounded by ten "armed stockmen," who brandished Winchesters and threatened to hang them as rustlers.

As Martin told the story, he had saved the life of one of the cattlemen a few winters earlier. Of course, this grateful rancher vouched for Martin, thus repaying "the great debt I owe you." Martin and Solon swore an oath not to return to Johnson County, and never to reveal the cattleman's name. "With this we shook hands, and, waving at the others, we rode off."

Before leaving Cheyenne for volatile Johnson County, George Wellman took the precaution of insuring his life for $3,000. He reached the Hoe Ranch on Monday, May 9, following a stopover in Gillette to receive instructions from an associate of Henry Blair. At the ranch Wellman, as directed, paid off four cowboys. The next day Wellman was scheduled to meet Marshal Joe Rankin in Buffalo, a fifty-mile ride from the Hoe Ranch. Tom Hathaway, one of the unemployed Hoe cowboys, asked to ride along with Wellman. On Tuesday morning, April 10, the two men mounted up, after Hathaway packed his bedding and other belongings on the extra horse. At about ten o'clock in the morning, as Wellman led Hathaway's pack animal through the Nine Mile Divide, concealed drygulchers suddenly opened fire. A .44 slug from a Winchester carbine slammed into Wellman's back "— the spinal cord was severed and his death was instant and painless."[7]

The sudden gunshots stampeded the horses. Hathaway was unseated, but remounted and quickly caught the other horses. While he unsaddled these two horses and turned them loose to graze, Wellman's bushwhackers swung into their saddles and left the scene. Hathaway rode toward Buffalo, leaving Wellman's body lying in the road. Arriving in town at about four in the afternoon, Hathaway was "unarmed, wild-eyed and excited." He told the story of Wellman's murder to Sheriff Angus, then to just about everyone else in town. Mayor Charles Burritt directed the city marshal to watch Hathaway, who "told several conflicting stories" before retreating to Laurel Avenue and "the Place of 'Widow' Brown." The city marshal arrested Hathaway and placed him in the county jail.[8]

While Sheriff Angus and two deputies prepared to ride out to the murder site, Mayor Burritt made further arrangements. Burritt employed the local undertaker to bring Wellman's body into town, and he arranged with the county coroner to release the corpse to the undertaker. Since Burritt had no "confidence in the ability or anxiety of Angus to examine carefully," he engaged three men to conduct a thorough examination of the site. Sheriff Angus and his deputies rode south late in the afternoon, spent the night at Trabing, then pushed on to Nine Mile Divide the next morning. After finding Wellman's body, Angus made a perfunctory inspection of the site. The sheriff then set out for Buffalo with the body, reaching town about five o'clock Wednesday afternoon.[9]

But at the scene of the murder, the three investigators hired by Burritt arrived and pored over the site. Tracks which Angus had assumed were made by Hathaway provided a more complex scenario when examined scrupulously. "As the road where the murder occurred had not been lately traveled," reported the Buffalo *Bulletin*, "and as the ground from the recent incessant rains was very soft, it was an easy matter to find trails and measure footprints." The three-man posse discovered that three riders had pulled up in a gulch. Leaving one man with the horses, the other two dismounted and walked to an embankment overlooking the road. Here the investigators found a cigarette butt and a .44 caliber cartridge hull. After the ambush, the drygulchers had returned to their horses and ridden off to the southwest.[10]

The tracks also indicated that Hathaway, as he claimed, had chased down his horses. He rode to within sixty yards of Wellman's body, then headed toward Buffalo. Burritt's three investigators followed the trail to the southwest for ten or twelve miles, but "from lack of food and horses had to give it up and returned to Buffalo."[11]

Buffalo was rife with rumors. Soon after Sheriff Angus had left for town for the murder site, "the rumor gained ground that Wellman was not killed at all; that it was a clearly designed scheme to get Angus out of town" and ambush him. About ten o'clock that night "a relief party" rode out to reinforce the sheriff, but late the next day Angus returned to town with Wellman's body. It was suggested that the despised cattlemen had murdered Wellman, but since the victim was foreman of one of the most influential ranchers, this rumor soon was dismissed. Sheriff Angus accused Thomas Hathaway on scant evidence. On Thursday, May 12, Col. J. J. Van Horn notified his superiors of the latest violence, remarking that Wellman was killed "by rustlers it is supposed."[12]

That same day, at ten o'clock Thursday morning, the coroner commenced his inquest. The coroner, who had probed for the bullet before turning the body over to the undertaker, attempted to hold the inquest in secret. But mayor-attorney Charles Burritt, employed by Wellman's boss and serving "as counsel for the family of the murdered

Funeral services for George Wellman were conducted at Buffalo's Episcopal Church. (Courtesy Johnson County Jim Gatchell Memorial Museum)

man," maneuvered to play a role in the hearing and to provide a stenographer to record a precise transcript of the proceedings. "I subjected all the witnesses to a close cross-examination and especially Hathaway," reported Burritt to his employer. At five o'clock in the afternoon, Burritt "demanded that the men from the ranch and the discharged employees be subpoenaed ... and the inquest was adjourned until Monday."[13]

Meanwhile, Burritt and other friends of Wellman made funeral arrangements. Because Wellman was killed in his range clothes, a suit and other appropriate items were purchased. The undertaker had no embalming fluid, and since the only casket available was a wooden coffin, Burritt had "a galvanized iron lining put in the rough box." The body was moved to the Episcopal Church, where funeral services were conducted by Rev. C. A. Duell at ten o'clock in the morning. Foes of the cattlemen created "an ugly undercurrent" against a church funeral or Masonic services for Wellman. But Reverend Duell reportedly "carried arms in his vestments," while Wellman's lodge brothers concealed guns beneath their Masonic aprons. An outpouring of sympathy for the murdered newlywed was reflected by numerous "floral tributes" at the church, and no one caused any trouble. A grave was dug at Buffalo's cemetery, but a telegram arrived from Wellman's family requesting that the corpse be shipped to Bay City, Michigan. E. B. Mather, Past Master of the Masonic Lodge, agreed to accompany the body to Michigan.[14]

Burritt, along with a great many other people, soon became convinced that "Wellman was murdered by the 'Red Sashes,'" a gang of cattle thieves headed by "Wild Charlie" Taylor. Burritt said that these rustlers "distinguish themselves by wearing red sashes," which seems like a dead giveaway. Others said that members of the Red Sash Gang lined their gunbelts with red flannel to protect their trousers from cartridge grease, or that only Taylor wore a sash, a colorful touch effected by many cowboys. According to Burritt, Taylor had announced a "threat that for every man killed among his friends a life should be taken on the other side." Burritt was convinced that "Wellman is the first" and that "there are many of us marked."[15]

It was generally thought that three members of the Red Sash Gang—Charles Taylor, Ed Starr, and "Black Henry" Smith—had ambushed Wellman. Owen Wister had met Smith in Buffalo in June 1891, and regarded him as "the only unabridged bad-man I ever had a chance to know." A Texan, Smith "has been 'run out' of every country he has resided in." Wister noted that "Smith is at present stealing cattle, or, more politely, mavericking." Wister was captivated by the tall, black-haired badman, and described him in detail in his notebook: "His voice is unpleasant. Very rasping, though not over-loud. The great thing is his eyes. They are of a mottled yellow . . . , large and piercing, at times burning with light. They are the very worst eyes I have ever looked at. Perfectly fearless and shrewd, and treacherous. . . . He is just bad through and through, without a scruple and without an affection. His face is entirely cruel, and you hear cruelty in his voice." Floyd Bard knew Smith and described him as "a rough sort of man, [who] looked more like a bullwhacker than a cowboy."[16]

Burial Expenses

In his May 14 letter to Henry Blair, Charles Burritt submitted the expenses he had paid for the burial of George Wellman:

Masonic Lodge, transportation	**$100.00**
F. J. Hasbrouck, shirt	**2.00**
suit of clothes	**30.00**
underwear	**3.00**
collar and cuffs	**0.50**
cuff and collar buttons	**3.00**
tie	**0.50**
slippers	**2.50**
J. A. Jones, metallic casket	**150.00**
digging grave	**5.00**
transportation of body from murder site	**25.00**
M. G. Metcalf, shaving Wellman	**5.00**
Buffalo Hardware, lining box	**20.00**
	$346.50

"George Wellman was much beloved and esteemed here by all of us," wrote Burritt. "We may have made more expenses than you can approve—if so we will cheerfully make it up here."

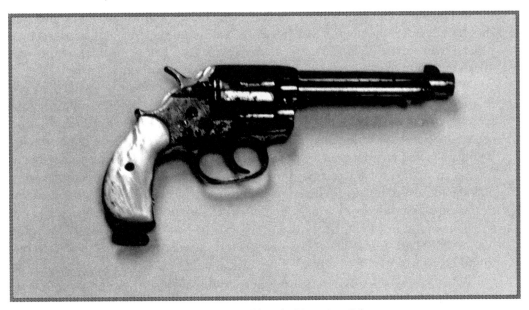

George Wellman's revolver, a nickel-plated, .45-caliber, double-action Colt. (Photo by Karon O'Neal from the Johnson County Jim Gatchell Memorial Museum)

Such a hard-bitten character would have been a logical candidate for a bushwhacking assignment. But in later years it was determined that Ed Starr fired the shot that killed Wellman. In 1895 Jim Potts, who had come down from Montana to work as foreman of a sheep ranch near the Wellman murder site, discovered a double-action nickel-plated Colt .45 revolver hidden in a five-pound baking powder can. Not knowing anything about the gun, he cleaned it and kept the weapon. The double-action revolver was distinctive in a land where reliable single-action Colts remained the preferred handgun. Wellman's gun featured pearl handles on a bird's beak style of grip, as opposed to the plow handle style on single-action Colts. Furthermore, a metal lanyard ring was attached to the bottom of the gun butt. Wyoming men in the 1890s had an eye for guns and certainly would have noticed Wellman's unique weapon. But when Jim Potts wore the double-action revolver with a lanyard ring, no one made any comments to him. Jim's son, Joe Potts, who later became a Johnson County official, theorized "that probably people were afraid to mention recognizing the gun for fear of being implicated with the murder of Wellman."[17]

In 1938, forty-six years after Wellman's murder, "Black Billy" Hill returned to Johnson County to revisit sites made notable in 1892. In 1892 Hill was a small rancher known to be friendly to rustlers, and after Wellman was drygulched Billy deemed it prudent to leave Wyoming and settle in Canada. Late in life Hill decided to visit the dramatic scenes of his youth. Sheriff Mart Tisdale—son of the murdered John Tisdale—agreed to let Hill accompany him on a trip to Kaycee. When they reached the site of the Wellman murder, according to J. Elmer Brock, "Hill pointed to a high sandstone cliff and said that Ed Starr had once taken him over there and showed him a fine six-shooter which he had concealed there." Starr told Hill that he had taken the gun from Wellman's body after the killing, then had hidden the incriminating weapon. "When Tisdale told me of Hill's trip and the story," related Brock, "I knew immediately who had this six-shooter." Brock remembered that Jim Potts had found the gun, and he asked two old-timers, mail carrier T. F. Carr and noted lawman Joe LeFors, to look at the weapon. "Both said it was Wellman's gun as they had seen him wear it many times."[18]

While Brock was a young cowboy, he became friends with Austin Reed, "a cowboy of the old school." The old school apparently included a little rustling in Johnson County during the 1890s, and Reed told Brock a chilling story. Reed said that he and other associates of Wild Charlie Taylor "drew lots to determine who was to kill Wellman." Reed was not worried that he would be chosen to pull the trigger, because it had "been framed for Ed Starr to draw that ticket." Reed *was* concerned that he might pick the lot to accompany Wellman on the murder ride, but Tom "Hathaway drew this ticket and as a result spent a long time in jail at Buffalo." While on the subject of the lethal drawings, Reed told Brock that previously he had drawn the lot "to accompany a man to kill Hard Winter Davis . . . , but when they went to perform their mission they found Davis had left the country."[19]

Reed flatly stated that "Starr was a killer and would as soon shoot a man as a coyote." He told Brock that "he had often heard Starr imitate Wellman's cry when he saw he was going to be killed." After listening to Reed, and after the 1938 visit of Black Billy Hill, Brock became convinced of the identity of Wellman's murderer: "There is no doubt but that Ed Starr fired the fatal shot." Following the murder, Starr and other rustlers "strongly intrenched" themselves on Crazy Woman Creek, where they were given "constant aid and assistance by a very large number of sympathizers," according to U.S. Marshal Joe Rankin. On July 12 Rankin received warrants for the arrest of nine suspects, and assembled a ten-man posse in Johnson County. Only one suspect, Kid Donnelly, was apprehended, while Ed Starr eluded arrest and left the country. He crossed the Montana line, went to the northern part of the state, and hired out to a ranch as "Tom Dunn." The WSGA posted a $1,000 reward for Ed Starr, but no one was able to find Tom Dunn.[20]

Although Tom Hathaway was released from custody after Wellman's inquest, he remained in Buffalo and continued to utter conflicting stories. Benjamin F. Fowler, U.S. attorney for Wyoming, was unwilling to give up on the Wellman case. On June 28 Hathaway again was arrested in Buffalo, then he "was taken out of the country quietly and immediately taken to my office in Cheyenne where he made a voluntary confession implicating Frank ["Black Henry"] Smith and others with the murder of George Wellman." Hathaway expressed fears "that parties had followed him out of the country" with the intention of killing him before he could confess. And on June 30 Black Henry Smith arrived in Cheyenne, but "was at once arrested before he had an opportunity of seeing Hathaway." Smith immediately was arraigned, and Fowler worked diligently for more than a year to have him convicted. But in November 1893 Smith won acquittal, and no one was ever convicted for the murder of George Wellman.

Wellman's assassination in May 1892 further encouraged lawlessness in Johnson County. "No one knows who will be next," wrote a worried Charles Burritt. Fearing that they might be next, Bob Gibson and Jim Craig, whom Marshal Joe Rankin had deputized along with Wellman, wasted no time turning in their badges. "Gibson and

Craig came into Buffalo," reported Rankin, "and there refused to take any action, or serve any papers." Gibson "came out of Johnson county with me," stated Rankin, "left the country, and has not returned since. He said to me, his life was not worth a cent in that county. Craig also left Johnson county, but remained in the state. However, he refused to do any work as a deputy."[22]

One week after Deputy Marshal George Wellman was murdered, lawless elements were emboldened to lash out at Fort McKinney, which had sheltered the prisoners until they could be transferred to Fort D. A. Russell. There was considerable resentment that the military had interfered in civilian matters, and an arson attack audaciously was directed against Fort McKinney. Before dawn on Wednesday morning, May 18, arsonists crept up to the post from the south. Seven sets of single-story company barracks were aligned on the south side of the parade ground, across from officers' row to the north. A two-story sutler's post exchange stood between four sets of infantry barracks, to the west, and three sets of cavalry barracks, to the east.

"The alarm sounded at about 4:20 A.M.," reported Col. J. J. Van Horn, "and the fire was found to be in the kitchen of the Post Exchange building, where it had made considerable progress when discovered." With the loud report of the alarm gun and the shout of "Fire!," the entire garrison rolled out of their bunks. A strong wind was blowing toward the east, however, and the wooden structures were located only a few feet apart. "The exchange building was soon a mass of flames which immediately spread to the barracks of Troop H which were to the leeward," continued Colonel Van Horn. Three employees of the canteen were sleeping upstairs, but they scrambled outside. Soldiers hurriedly carried out as much merchandise as they could, along with the post telegrapher, who was sleeping downstairs and had to be revived from smoke inhalation by a hospital steward.[23]

When the Company H barracks caught fire, eighty pounds of gunpowder were exploded to destroy the building and halt the flames. But before the debris could be cleared, the wind whipped the blaze to the next barracks. Attempting to blow it up, Lt. Charles B. Gatewood—who had ridden with the cavalry to the TA Ranch—was directing the replacement of powder kegs when burning rafters suddenly collapsed. A keg of gunpowder exploded, hurling Gatewood against a wall. Gatewood and two injured privates were helped outside, while the flames spread to the Third Cavalry barracks. The soldiers managed to protect the cavalry stables, which were "separated by a considerable interval" from the blazing barracks. The infantry barracks adjacent to the canteen on the

Lt. Charles B. Gatewood, a noted hero of the Apache Wars, was severely injured during a blaze set by arsonists at Fort McKinney. (Courtesy Arizona Pioneers Historical Society)

179

west twice caught fire, but both times the garrison put out the flames. Within an hour the sutler's store and all three cavalry barracks were smoldering ruins. The cavalrymen "at once pitched a row of tents on the parade ground near their burnt barracks and went into camp."[24]

Lieutenant Gatewood's left arm was shattered. The thirty-nine-year-old officer had graduated from West Point in 1877, then "embarked upon a singular career in the Apache country as commander of Indian scouts," according to Dan Thrapp, distinguished historian of the Apache wars. "His experience in the numerous Apache outbreaks was perhaps more extensive and more indispensable than that of any officer." Gatewood's distinguished service was climaxed in 1886, when he courageously crossed into Mexico, found Geronimo's camp, and persuaded the lethal chieftan to reenter the United States and surrender. During this bold exploit, Gatewood was suffering from acute rheumatism, which worsened with the passing years. Then, at Fort McKinney, his left arm was disabled in the explosion, and in November 1892 Gatewood was sent home to Denver, Colorado, to await discharge. But the army kept him on its roll, moving him to Fort Monroe, Virginia. Although Gatewood never was promoted to captain nor awarded the Medal of Honor for which he was recommended, when he died in 1896 he was buried in the military cemetery at Arlington, Virginia. The active duty career of this superb officer was ended, and his premature death probably was hastened, by the arsonists at Fort McKinney.[25]

The day after the fire the Buffalo *Bulletin* headlined "A HOLOCAUST! AT FORT MCKINNEY." Incredibly, one night later arsonists again assaulted the post. About an hour after midnight on Friday, May 20, "an attempt was made by an incendiary to fire the quarters occupied by the band, 8th Infantry," reported Colonel Van Horn once more, "but the fire was discovered by a sentinel and extinguished before any damage had been done." A warrant was issued charging Charles Taylor and Henry Smith, along with another hardcase, Johnny Long, with burning a barrack building at Fort McKinney, but Marshal Joe Rankin was unable to serve the papers.[26]

The astounding insolence that emboldened men to try to set fire to Fort McKinney suggested a deep bitterness against the military that might trigger further violence. And within four weeks troopers and civilians would be shooting at each other.

Chapter 16

The Battle of Suggs

"We all know how anxious the imprisoned cattle barons are to have martial law declared in Northern and Central Wyoming, and a few more rows between soldiers and citizens will have the desired effect."

SHERIDAN *ENTERPRISE*, JUNE 25, 1892

When the cattlemen who invaded Johnson County proved influential enough to secure the intervention of the U.S. Army and to have themselves and their hired gunmen transferred to their power base at Cheyenne, citizens of Buffalo and outlying areas felt betrayed and vulnerable. It was clear that the cattlemen still controlled the state government and exercised pressure that extended to national authorities and the federal military. In the turbulent, violent atmosphere that now prevailed in Johnson County, citizens were apprehensive about what might happen next.

Lt. G. H. Preston of the Ninth Cavalry visited Buffalo in June, a few weeks after the murder of George Wellman. "At present everything is quiet, and the only fear of the people is that they are again to be attacked by hirelings," he reported. Incidentally, Lieutenant Preston, who apparently was assigned to evaluate the situation in Buffalo, noted the presence of several rustlers. "I also found from ten to fifteen desperadoes, reputed as refugees from justice and at large in the State, of these I can recall only Jack Bell, [Charles] Taylor and [Henry] Smith."[1]

Despite Lieutenant Preston's observation that "the only fear" harbored by citizens of Johnson County was that they might once more be "attacked by hirelings," there was another growing concern. Early in June the Buffalo *Bulletin* published an editorial which began: "Those who pretend to know predict a declaration of martial law at an early date in Johnson, Converse and Natrona counties." Although the *Bulletin* editor disagreed with this premise, worries about martial law had been triggered by the recent announcement that twelve cavalry troops would be deployed in two nearby "summer camps," os-

181

tensibly to drill and practice marksmanship in preparation for appearances at the 1893 Chicago World's Fair. But every fort had a firing range and a large parade ground for drilling, so it hardly seemed coincidental that a substantial cavalry force would be moved into the troubled Johnson County region. "The people of Johnson county view the presence of a large body of troops with apprehension only of what might lie behind," remarked the *Bulletin*, acknowledging the assumption that cattle barons were behind the troop transfer. "The troops themselves are welcome visitors and will find nothing to fight when they get here." Echoing this last sentiment was a deputy U.S. marshal named Hale, who presumably kept his face straight when he said: "There is as much necessity for martial law in this county as there is in heaven."[2]

Wyoming cattlemen indeed had launched a recent and highly presumptuous attempt to engineer major troop transfers that would lead to martial law. On June 1 Senator Joseph Carey in Washington received a telegram from cattlemen Frank Wolcott, Henry Hay, George Baxter, Henry Blair, John Clay, and Judge Willis Van Devanter. The telegram wasted no time in getting to the point: "We want changes of troops made as follows." Dissatisfied with the friendly ties between the officers and men of Fort McKinney with the citizens of Buffalo and the settlers of Johnson County, the cattlemen wanted the Eighth Infantry companies transferred to Fort Sidney, Nebraska, and Maj. Edmond Fechet and his cavalrymen to Fort Niobrara, Nebraska, or "anywhere else out of that country." There was a strong mutual dislike between the cattlemen and Major Fechet. "He and his men have relations with the sheriff and his gang that make the whole command very undesirable for us. Send six companies of Ninth Cavalry from Robinson [Nebraska] to McKinney. The colored troops will have no sympathy for Texas thieves, and these are the troops we want." This wholesale transfer out of Fort McKinney would provide the cattlemen with a more agreeable commanding officer. "We want cool level headed man whose sympathy is with us." They also wanted this large-scale transfer of troops between various outposts to occur immediately. "It is important that action should be taken at once. We urge that time is everything. This is preliminary to declaration of martial law. Advise us when order is made." Also on June 1, Senator Warren, who had returned to Cheyenne, sent a telegram to Senator Carey. "Declaration of martial law seems inevitable," he began hopefully. Warren asked his senatorial counterpart to remind the War Department about the arson at Fort McKinney, and about the repeated requests from leading citizens such as Maj. Charles Burritt "imploring" martial law.[3]

That same day Senator Carey had a "very satisfactory talk" with President Harrison, and he met with Gen. John Schofield, commander of the Army. "General Schofield believes in concentrating troops in the disturbed district of Wyoming" in two "summer encampments," but he did "not consider it necessary to change officers or regimental headquarters." General Schofield—or the president or the secretary of war—also declined to impose martial law. Evidently it was felt that the presence of twelve additional cavalry troops would have a pacifying effect upon the region. And if further violence were to erupt, martial law could be more readily declared. In an effort to reassure an apprehensive public, the War Department sent a dispatch to the Cheyenne *Leader* stating "that the moving of these troops was simply in the execution of a project decided upon long ago to put them in summer camp and drill them for the part they are going to take at the world's fair opening." The War Department denied "that this movement contemplates the placing of Johnson, Natrona and Converse counties under martial law."[4]

Replying to a June 3 inquiry from General Schofield, General Brooke recommended the establishment of two camps: "one to be between Douglas and Casper," and the other "near where the Burlington and Missouri Railroad will cross Powder River." General Brooke suggested the use of rail transportation as far as possible, because heavy precipitation had "made the country very difficult." He also emphatically stated: "The garrison at McKinney should not be disturbed." General Schofield approved these recommendations. Six troops of the Sixth Cavalry from Fort Niobrara would encamp near old Fort Fetterman, while six troops of the Ninth Cavalry from Fort Robinson would spend the summer at the Powder River crossing, near the railroad community of Suggs.[5]

Suggs was a typical "end of tracks" town, except that in the summer of 1892 the tracks had not yet reached the Powder River from the southeast. As the Burlington and Missouri built across northern Wyoming, a large construction crew was sent to erect a bridge across the Powder River, near the confluence of Wild Horse Creek. A ramshackle town sprang up on the east bank of the river, in Sheridan County, about seven miles north of the Johnson County line. As the men began moving great amounts of dirt with teams and fresnos to support the bridge on both sides of the river, tents and log or frame structures were built in the midst of a sagebrush prairie. There was a post office dubbed Suggs, after the nearby ranch of the Suggs brothers. Suggs became a stopover for the stagecoach traffic that ran between Buffalo and Sundance, and a station was constructed. A ferry operated on the river, and a Chinese section developed just across nearby Wild Horse Creek. Liquor and gambling establishments were among the first businesses, and prostitutes quickly arrived, including girls from Buffalo's Laurel Avenue. This raw community attracted other riffraff, including such rustlers as Wild Charlie Taylor and Black Henry Smith. Jack Bell, another hardcase, was hired as town marshal, in the frontier practice of pinning on badges on tough gunmen to control other rugged characters.[6]

Such an officer was Phil DuFran, who had served as a Nebraska deputy sheriff in 1878 and as city marshal of Buffalo in 1885-86. DuFran's checkered career in the West included riding for the notorious rancher-gunman Print Olive, working for the army as a civilian courier, running various saloons, operating as a foreman for Horace Plunkett, and, according to rumor, engaging in shootouts in Texas and Nebraska. In 1886 in Buffalo, DuFran married Christie Lopez, who periodically left home "to lead an open

Phil DuFran, stock detective, Invader, and troublemaker. (Group photo, courtesy Wyoming State Museum)

notorious life of shame as an inmate of houses of prostitution in Buffalo" and various other locations—as stated in the divorce petition he filed in 1888.[7]

DuFran hired out to the WSGA as a range detective, and intercepted the Invaders with news that a posse was riding out from Buffalo. Retreating with the Invaders to the TA Ranch, DuFran was arrested and taken to Fort McKinney, then to Fort D. A. Russell. But since they had not participated in the attack on the KC, DuFran and Sam Sutherland were released from custody in May. Then someone in the cattlemen's faction recommended DuFran, who had worked for the army during the Wounded Knee troubles in 1890-91, as a civilian guide to Suggs. "The man Philip DuFran was sent by me as a guide to Major Ilsley," stated Gen. John Brooke, "he being represented as thoroughly familiar with the Powder River country."[8]

DuFran met with Maj. Charles S. Ilsley when the troop train from Nebraska reached Gillette. Ilsley's command totaled more than 300 officers and men from the Ninth Cavalry. In addition to six troops of the famous "buffalo soldiers," the command included the regimental band and an assistant surgeon and four other members of the hospital corps. Two Hotchkiss guns were packed along, while the troopers were armed with carbines and revolvers, and carried 200 rounds of ammunition apiece. Major Ilsley and his men left Fort Robinson on Wednesday morning, June 8, traveling by train to Gillette, where the tracks ended. The troopers camped for a day and a night, while offloading horses, wagons, and provisions.[9]

When the column had marched about halfway to Suggs, "I noticed that the citizens of the country appeared suspicious and angry at the presence of this command," reported Major Ilsley. After inquiry, "I learned that a belief prevailed amongst these people that the troops were sent into this section solely in the interest of the ... large cattle owners, and that they were accompanied by United States Marshals with warrants for sundry arrests." Capt. John F. Guilfoyle stated that he and other officers made a similar observation: "... it was noticeable that on our march here the citizens generally avoided us, contrary to their usual habits. This ill feeling was prompted ... by rumors ... that our mission to the country was to arrest certain individuals at the instance of one Philip DuFran."[10]

When Lt. G. H. Preston was sent to Buffalo shortly after the column reached Suggs, residents "informed me that DuFran personally had sent out notice that he (DuFran) accompanied the troops commissioned as Deputy United States Marshal with warrants for the arrest of forty two (42) citizens of Wyoming, charged with preying upon the herds of large cattle owners." DuFran took mess with the lieutenant's Company G, and Preston conversed intimately with him. "He took no pains in concealing his hostility to the people of this country," revealed Preston. "He told me that his friends in Cheyenne would soon be out of hock and that then martial law would be declared and the fun would begin."[11]

As soon as DuFran learned that he would accompany troops into the area, he began spreading rumors about martial law and deputy marshals and wholesale arrests. DuFran diabolically claimed that he held a deputy U.S. marshal's commission, and otherwise agitated the rustlers and small ranchers whom he despised. After arriving at Suggs on Sunday, June 12, Major Ilsley began to learn the cause of the general unrest: "I took every occasion and special care to inform the citizens that we came up here merely seeking a summer camp, that DuFran held no official position, that there were no United

States Marshals accompanying us, that their civil law was supreme, and we had no authority or desire to arrest or interfere with any of them."[12]

But these reassurances had little effect on the unsavory characters in Suggs, who "repeatedly threatened" the life of DuFran. It became evident to both officers and men that the population of Suggs was "composed of two distinct elements, the towns people proper, and a floating population called rustlers, whose sympathies are with recent movement against cattlemen in this state, and which is made up of the worst types of western life." The merchants and other businessmen, who undoubtedly were elated at the economic boon brought by more than 300 new customers, welcomed the military. But the rustlers were "in an ugly mood and viewed their arrival with distrust and hostility. These feelings were undoubtedly intensified by race prejudice, and probably also by the knowledge of the presence in the 9th Cavalry camp of one Philip Du Frand [*sic*], … who was an active agent in the cattlemen's party," concluded three officers of the Ninth. "The animosity on the part of the rough characters of the town was shown by their following officers and enlisted men, who were present in town to make necessary purchases, from store to store, and by dropping insulting remarks in their hearing."[13]

Major Ilsley promptly decided to transfer the encampment away from Suggs, "knowing that town to be headquarters of a class known as 'Rustlers,' as well as containing many notorious outlaws and gamblers." On June 13, after just a day and night at Suggs, Major Ilsley ordered a move four miles south, alongside the Powder River. The major contemplated moving still further, to a point eleven miles to the west, but after conferring with his officers, he decided that his orders dictated establishing the permanent camp beside the river. So Camp P. A. Bettens—named after a recently deceased officer—took shape only a few miles north of the Johnson County line. Tents were arranged along orderly military streets, and sagebrush was scraped away to establish a firing range. "I gave verbal instructions to the troop commanders that their men should remain in camp," stated Major Ilsley. For the first few days, only men accompanied by officers could go into Suggs, either to collect mail or to haul purchases back to Camp Bettens.[14]

Of course, the presence of prostitutes and saloons was an irresistible temptation to some of the men stationed at an isolated encampment. In fact, the troopers already were acquainted with Suggs prostitutes who previously had worked at Buffalo's Laurel Avenue. "There were in [Suggs] at this time a number of prostitutes who had been intimately known by members of the 9th Cavalry while stationed at Fort McKinney, Wyo., and elsewhere," a Board of Inquiry declared; "the action of these women in receiving the soldiers served still further to increase the hard feelings already engendered." On Thursday evening, June 16, Pvt. Abraham Champ "without authority" slipped into town on foot to visit a woman he had known in Buffalo. But at her house Champ was turned away. He then went to a saloon, where he joined Pvt. Emile Smith, who had ridden into town to post advertisements for proposals for freighting to Camp Betten.[15]

Within moments of his arrival, Champ was angrily confronted by the prostitute's "white lover," who brandished a cocked pistol. Private Smith whipped out his service revolver, but immediately was covered by guns in the hands of several bystanders. The saloon owner, Mack Thompson, separated the adversaries, persuading both parties to leave the premises. Thompson then conducted the two soldiers through the back door and on a roundabout detour to the edge of town. Warned by the saloon owner "that they might be waylaid," the soldiers climbed onto Smith's horse. Suddenly "they were fired upon by parties concealed in some houses on the outskirts." A bullet cut through Smith's hat, but the two troopers pulled their revolvers and returned fire, then "hastened to camp." The only damage inflicted by the exchange of gunfire was a bullet hole in a campaign hat.[16]

Safely back at Camp Bettens, Smith and Champ began telling their story. As word spread, the agitated soldiers milled angrily in their troop streets and "at once wanted to go in a body to town." At one-thirty in the morning, Major Ilsley was awakened to hear the news from Private Smith, that he and Champ were in Suggs at a bar "when a cow boy rushed into the saloon and thrust a cocked pistol into the face of Champ, insulting and abusing by threatening and indecent language." After hearing the rest of the story, "I immediately got up," Major Ilsley said. He ordered his men to go to bed, then assembled his ranking officers. The number of sentries was increased, and Ilsley and the two captains who were squadron commanders stayed up the remainder of the night to supervise the camp.[17]

But the next day, Friday, June 17, was payday. Flush with cash, soldiers always wanted to go to town for liquor, gambling, and women. With Suggs now a flashpoint, Major Ilsley issued a circular decreeing that no more than four passes per troop per day would be issued, and those passes would be granted only from eight in the morning until noon, or one until four in the afternoon. As an inadequate consolation, the troopers were to be freely permitted to go hunting.[18]

Additional precautions on payday included a doubling of the guard, mounted patrols to ride around the camp perimeter, and company roll calls, announced for eleven o'clock in the evening and two hours later. Although a few soldiers enjoyed brief payday passes, mail was carried and supplies were purchased and carried by civilian teamsters instead of troopers, and lieutenants were in town to oversee their men. 1st Lt. G. S. Bingham testified that he saw about a dozen soldiers in town on pass. "They seemed to be very orderly and quiet," said Bingham. On the morning of June 17 Lieutenant Bingham encountered City Marshal Jack Bell, who complained that some of the soldiers had threatened the man who had waved his revolver in front of Private Champ's face. "I assured him that if the people would not molest them," related Bingham, "there would be no further trouble."[19]

But there would be trouble, despite all of Major Ilsley's precautions. That night, with extra sentries and all officers on duty, more than thirty troopers slipped out of camp and walked toward Suggs, carrying their revolvers and carbines. Most of these AWOL men were from Troops E and G, to which Privates Champ and Smith belonged. During an era when an army recruit spent his entire enlistment in the same troop, company loyalties ran deep, and the comrades of Champ and Smith followed them to Suggs looking for reprisal. With their weapons at the ready, the angry soldiers reached town a little after ten o'clock. About twenty men deployed behind the railroad grade outside Suggs, while another fifteen soldiers made their way toward the town's main street.[20]

Marshal Bell met them as they reached the outskirts of town. Reportedly he "at-

Buffalo Soldiers

More than 200,000 black soldiers served in the Union army during the Civil War. Black units were dependable and fought with distinction. In 1865 the Thirteenth Amendment ended slavery in the United States, and in 1868 the Fourteenth Amendment guaranteed citizenship to former slaves. As citizens with a proven record of military service, black Americans were eligible for the post-Civil War army, although racial attitudes dictated that they would serve in segregated units. The frontier army was reduced to ten cavalry regiments and twenty-five infantry regiments. The Ninth and Tenth Cavalry and the Twenty-fourth and Twenty-fifth Infantry were all-black regiments, with white officers.

These four regiments served continually in the West for more than a quarter of a century. Impressed with their black adversaries from the Tenth Cavalry, plains warriors called them "buffalo soldiers" because the texture of their hair was similar to the fur between the horns of the animal that was their staff of life. A nickname born of respect, "buffalo soldier" was proudly adopted by all black soldiers.

In his classic study of the Indian-fighting army, *Frontier Regulars* (p. 28), the distinguished historian Robert M. Utley described the "high reenlistment rates and low desertion rates" of the buffalo soldiers in contrast to their white counterparts. "Moreover, unit pride and espirit de corps ran high in the black regiments, the product, in part, of this personal continuity, but also of increasing professionalism, superior performance, a solidarity born of prejudice, and a determination to demonstrate the potential of the black race."

The prejudice mentioned by Utley was encountered by buffalo soldiers everywhere in the West, even though the troopers braved hardships and danger to provide protection to frontiersmen. There were countless incidents, and sometimes the black men were provoked to retaliate.

During a ten-day period in January 1881, for example, two Tenth Cavalry troopers from Fort Concho were shot to death in saloons at nearby San Angelo. John M. Carroll, in *The Black Military Experience in the West* (pp. 462-68), recounted the outrage of the buffalo soldiers. A handbill was printed and circulated in town, concluding: "If we do not receive justice and fair play ... some will suffer, if not the guilty, the innocent. Justice or death." Justice was not forthcoming in the courts, and soon a large number of angry troopers sallied into San Angelo and shot up the town. No one was killed, but eleven years later another band of outraged buffalo soldiers followed their example into another frontier town, this time in northern Wyoming.

tempted to dissuade them from going any further, but they compelled him to retreat and advanced down the Main street." A trooper acting as leader—probably one of the three noncommissioned officers who were AWOL—fired a shot into the air, apparently a signal to open fire. The soldiers triggered a volley from their carbines, targeting the nearest buildings. "There were only seven or eight of the boys around," reported someone from Suggs, but they immediately began firing Winchesters from a "saloon called the 'Rustlers' Headquarters.'"[21]

Pvt. William Thompkins was hit: "I was shot in the hand at the first volley." The soldiers flattened onto the ground and continued firing from prone positions, and the troopers located behind the railroad grade also opened fire. Nine business structures or tents were hit. Thirteen bullet holes later were counted in the hotel: "five through Buffalo Bill's place"; three or four in other structures; and one apiece in four buildings.

A citizen named Jim Bennett was shot in the arm, and two horses were killed, including Marshal Jack Bell's mount. "Henry Smith got the closest call, a bullet having passed through his hat close enough to cut the hair."[22]

Within moments "ten or fifteen determined men had their Winchesters in hand and began to fire back." Probably at least a few of the bullets that struck Suggs structures were triggered by citizens defending the community. Private Champ was hit in the shoulder, and Pvt. Willis Johnson was struck in the back of the head. Johnson dropped dead, but in the darkness his fellow troopers may not have seen him fall. (Later it could not be determined if he had been shot by friendly fire from behind him, or by a citizen.) Firing on the move, the soldiers in town withdrew to the railroad embankment, then retreated toward their camp.[23]

When the shooting stopped, "the people of Suggs expected the soldiers to return in greater force to renew the attack and all firearms were gotten in readiness." Someone revealed that a case of Winchesters being shipped to a store in Buffalo was in the stagecoach station awaiting transportation. The box was confiscated and pried open, and the rifles were distributed. "Pickets were then posted in all directions and a second attack awaited."[24]

At Camp Bettens, the officers, sentries, and anyone else who was awake heard a distant gunshot at 10:30, "immediately followed by rapid firing to the number of fifty shots, at least." Upon the orders of Major Ilsley, "each troop was instantly paraded by its troop officers" and roll calls were conducted. Thirty-eight men were absent, although four later were located in camp, and all horses and mules were present. Major Ilsley ordered Capt. John Guilfoyle to mount Troops A and I and, accompanied by the ambulance and surgeon, to march into town. Captain Guilfoyle was directed "to arrest all soldiers found on the road," to investigate the cause of the shooting, and to remain in town "with his command until quiet was restored and the citizens felt willing that he should return." The other soldiers were deployed in a skirmish line around the camp.[25]

After Troops A and I saddled up and armed themselves, Captain Guilfoyle led them down the dark road toward town. Soon the column encountered their unmounted comrades, who were disarmed and taken into custody. The two wounded privates were tended at the ambulance. Guilfoyle arrived at Suggs about 11:30 and "surrounded the town, the army sentinels being but a rod or two from the town pickets." A citizen pointed out the body of Private Johnson to Captain Guilfoyle, who had the corpse

Panic

In the Suggs hotel, a recently arrived family named Potts was startled awake by the sudden gunfire. Potts put his wife and baby daughter on the floor and covered them with the mattress. Telling his wife "to stay there," Potts pulled on his pants and boots and ran outside with his guns.

From the shouts she heard, Mrs. Potts "figured the Colored Troops had attacked the town, and if they took over, the women ... would be victims of the troops." She wrapped her baby, Sadie, in a blanket, slipped out of the hotel in her nightgown, and ran barefooted down the street to Wild Horse Creek, intending to seek refuge with the Chinese there. But the Chinese also had fled. Mrs. Potts waded across the creek, then "walked and ran for an unknown distance and finally hid in the brush." (These events were told to Glenn Sweem in 1967 by Sadie Potts Wagner.)

At dawn Mrs. Potts ascended an embankment and looked toward Suggs: "All she could see was the Colored Troops sitting on their horses surrounding the town so she knew that the troops had captured the town and probably Daddy and the rest had all been killed." Mrs. Potts continued to hide near the river, where she and her baby were plagued by mosquitoes.

After the shooting stopped in town, Mr. Potts could not find his wife and daughter. Following a frantic search in the dark, he concluded that they had been abducted by soldiers. The next morning Potts joined the men searching for those who had fled in the darkness. The baby had lost a booty, and after the tiny item was found, her crying led Potts to their hiding place. "Mama's feet were cut, bruised and so swollen she couldn't get her shoes on for several days, and the mosquitoes had bitten us so badly our eyes were nearly swollen shut and we were nothing but welts. Daddy said when he found us, that it was the happiest day of his life."

placed in the ambulance. Captain Guilfoyle sent a lieutenant back to camp to report these developments, and to assure Major Ilsley that he "had restored order and promised protection to the people." Major Ilsley hastily got off a dispatch to Colonel Biddle, regimental commander of the Ninth.[26]

The rest of the night was quiet, and at dawn Captain Guilfoyle marched his command back to Camp Bettens. Major Ilsley convened a Board of Inquiry, conducted by presiding officer Capt. John S. Loud, Captain Guilfoyle, and 1st Lt. Alfred B. Jackson, recorder. By the end of the day the Board had produced a six-page report, reviewing the events since Major Ilsley's command had marched into Suggs a few days earlier. The rustlers and racial insults were described, along with the inflammatory role of Phil DuFran. After detailing the incidents of June 16 and 17, the Board concluded that "primary" blame lay with "the Rustlers," but the fight on June 17 "was a retaliatory act" by some of the soldiers, with Private Champ and Smith as "ringleaders ... who are mainly responsible for the trouble."[27]

By the time this report was finalized, Private Johnson had been interred in a lonely grave near the camp. (He was joined later in the summer by another enlisted man, who apparently was killed accidentally on the firing range.) Marshal Jack Bell and several other citizens came out to Camp Bettens for "a pow-wow" with Major Ilsley, who offered strong assurances that soldiers under his command would cause no more trouble in Suggs. The delegation was shown that Major Ilsley "had all the men under arrest and a strong guard placed over them and a double line placed around the camp." Marshal Bell and the others returned to town, but a few days later another delegation made an effort to gain custody of the primary troublemakers.[28]

Early on Saturday, the morning after the fight, a report was dispatched by courier to Gillette, where it was telegraphed to Ilsley's superiors as well as to other points, including Buffalo. A rider pushed westward all day from Suggs to Sheridan, arriving at the county seat on Saturday evening with the electrifying story and an urgent request for the sheriff. The next morning Sheriff Willey and a deputy set out for Suggs. Colonel Biddle also decided to travel to Suggs, arriving from Fort Robinson at eight o'clock on Tuesday morning, June 21.[29]

By the time Colonel Biddle took command at Camp Bettens, Major Ilsley had conducted "a Summary Court for absent without leave" for thirty-four troopers. All thirty-four already had received AWOL punishment, but only Privates Emile Smith, Abraham Champ, and William Thompkins "were identified as participants in the disturbance." Colonel Biddle learned that these three men had been "arrested at once and are now under guard and general charges will be forwarded against them." Further charges were not pressed against the thirty-one other AWOL troopers, because there was "no testimony to connect them with the disturbance." The officers of the Ninth, who had seen their men taunted and insulted and discriminated against year after year, clearly had no inclination to expose them to serious charges. Colonel Biddle also found that Major Ilsley had "absolutely" halted all visits to town.[30]

About eleven o'clock on Tuesday morning, only three hours after Colonel Biddle reached Camp Bettens, he was visited by a delegation led by Sheriff Willey. Willey's deputy was there, along with Wild Charlie Taylor and four other citizens.[31]

"Gentlemen," greeted Colonel Biddle, "what can I do for you?"

"We have come down here to talk about the disturbance and the delivery of the men," replied Sheriff Willey.

Colonel Biddle had no intention of turning his men over to civil authorities. For one thing, he knew that any mob violence against black prisoners "would act in a most excitable manner on this command." The colonel emphasized to the sheriff that "we officers" are "servants of the people," and that he would "cheerfully" comply with whatever "the law would require of me of their delivery." But he tactfully pointed out the necessity "to confer with higher authority."

"You can place a deputy here in charge of these men till I hear," he offered.

Sheriff Willey said that he was "perfectly satisfied," adding that he felt "the men would be safer here than under his charge." Then he asked Colonel Biddle how long it would take to confer with superior officers. When the colonel replied "about three days," the delegation left.

"It was of the greatest importance to me to conciliate the feeling of these men," stated Colonel Biddle. He did not want to be served warrants on his men, "as under these circumstances I would have made myself liable to an interpretation of my action that I did not care to have to make." The colonel's tactics worked; there was no further effort to take custody of the soldiers. "The meeting between the citizens and myself was extremely amicable and agreeable."

Of course, Sheriff Willey may have been easy to convince. There was no place in Suggs where the despised prisoners would have been safe from a mob, and the sheriff certainly would not have wanted soldiers under his care to be lynched. Sheriff Willey had watched the violence and anarchy in adjacent Johnson County, and he surely wanted to avoid violent controversy in his county. If Colonel Biddle was pleased at keeping his men out of the hands of civil authorities, Sheriff Willey seemed just as pleased to return to town empty-handed. Sheridan County authorities were advised "to let the military deal with the soldiers concerned in the riot. It will cost the county from $5,000 to $8,000 to try them, and then they might not secure any convictions, when the government is sure to punish every one."[32]

Gen. John Brooke, departmental commander, dispatched Maj. John M. Bacon of the Seventh Cavalry as acting inspector general to conduct an official investigation at Camp Bettens. Arriving several days after Colonel Biddle, Major Bacon held hearings on June 28. Major Bacon took testimony from Colonel Biddle, Major Ilsley, Captain Guilfoyle, 1st Lt. G. S. Bingham, 2nd Lt. G. H. Preston, Pvt. Abraham Champ, Pvt. William H. Thompkins, and Mack Thompson, owner of the saloon where the trouble started on June 16. After recording twenty pages of testimony, Major Bacon concluded "that the riot was brought about by [Privates Smith and Champ] who had been insulted and maltreated in the town on the night of the 16th by a citizen, and that they induced a party of soldiers to return with them the next night to redress their wrongs." He stated that "Major Ilsley and his officers are in no way censurable," and commended them for the precautions they had taken and for their "prompt action in restoring order." Major Bacon also complimented Colonel Biddle for solving some "delicate problems" with diplomacy and wisdom. "I found the command in excellent discipline and condition,"

Disturbance at Suggs, Wyo., June 17th, 1892.

A Board of Officers was convened at Camp Bettens, Wyo., June 17th, ultimo, by order of Major IIsley to report upon all the circumstances connected with the disturbance at Suggs, Wyo., June 17.

The Board reports in substance as follows:-

The inhabitants of Suggs is made up of two elements-Town-people proper and a floating population, Rustlers.   First element peaceably disposed.   Second element not so.

Race predjudice and the presence in the 9th cavalry of one Philip DuFrand, who was an active agent of the cattlemen's party intensified the ill feeling on the part of the Rustlers.

The Rustlers followed officers and enlisted men when in town making necessary purchases and made insulting remarks

June 16- . Privates Smith and Champ visited town- the former mounted under orders, the latter dismounted without orders. Private Smith attempted to enter a house occupied by a prostitute. This was resented at point of revolver by her white lover, who in turn was covered by a revolver in the hands of Smith when Smith was covered by several revolvers in the hands of bystanders . Combatants separated.   Both sides left the building.   On return to camp privates Smith and Champ were fired upon, Smith receiving a bullet through his hat.

.Great excitement at camp.   Extra precautions taken to re-strain men and prevent trouble.

June 17.-Morning.- Everything quiet.   No apprehension of ...

One of the official military reports generated by the "Disturbance at Suggs."

192

closed Major Bacon, "and do not believe that further trouble between the citizens and soldiers will occur." It is not known that anything beyond company punishment was meted out to the offending troopers; apparently the army took care of its own in the wake of this controversial incident.[33]

Phil DuFran, of course, had played a key role in aggravating tensions. As a civilian employee, he had not had to answer roll call on the night of the riot, and there were rumors that he was in town blazing away on June 17. An outspoken troublemaker, DuFran's continued "presence was disquieting," according to Colonel Biddle. But General Brooke soon reported to the Adjutant General's Office in Washington: "I ordered him sent away, which had been done." Aware of the many threats on DuFran's life, Colonel Biddle sent a cavalry resort escort with the ex-scout, who was taken to the railroad at Gillette on June 24. In Gillette, with typical empty braggadocio, DuFran claimed that he "was going to headquarters to straighten himself, and also intimated that General Brooke would (more than likely) give him a commission."[34]

The Ninth Cavalry remained at Camp Bettens for several more months, but there was no more trouble. After the last soldiers packed up and left for Fort Robinson in November, Camp Bettens soon returned to sagebrush. The same fate awaited Suggs. The railroad never intended to place a permanent station at Suggs. A depot and section house were constructed across the river, and when the bridge was completed in September, the town of Arvada was platted on the west side of the Powder River.[35]

Today the only tangible remnant of the Battle of Suggs is a lonely grave beside the cottonwood tree at the site of old Camp Bettens.

Chapter 17

From Fort Russell to Laramie City

> **"In fact we are in the mud all over up to our eyes and in floundering to get out we seem to scatter the mud, darken the atmosphere, and—then sink deeper into the mire at each move."**
>
> SENATOR FRANCIS E. WARREN

A large crowd gathered on Sunday, April 24, to meet the train at the little frame depot at Fort D. A. Russell. Family members and friends of the ranchers, along with curious onlookers, came out for the arrival of the Invaders. The fort, located two miles northwest of Cheyenne, had grown steadily in the twenty-five years of its existence. Amenities on the post now included a bowling alley, which was being converted to house the forty-odd men who were expected to face legal action. The Invaders were about to become inmates of a famous frontier outpost.

Established in July 1867 as the Post on Crow Creek, the fort's initial mission was to protect Union Pacific construction crews approaching from the east. Within a few weeks the Post on Crow Creek was renamed to honor a Civil War hero, Brig. Gen. David A. Russell, who was killed at the Battle of Winchester in 1864. This installation was intended to be a regimental post, with permanent facilities for eight companies and with the capacity to supply wagon outposts to the north and west. Accordingly, an enormous diamond-shaped parade ground was laid out, 1040 feet from north to south and 800 feet east to west. Around the parade, frame structures began to be erected, including duplex officers' quarters, barracks, storehouses, a guardhouse, and a large hospital. Between Fort D. A. Russell and the new town of Cheyenne, a large supply depot was built. Hundreds of oxen and mules were stabled at Cheyenne Depot, which dispatched wagon trains laden with supplies, equipment, and clothing to army outposts, military units in the field, and Indian reservations.[1]

For the first dozen years of its existence, Fort D. A. Russell was a center of Indian war activity. A large garrison always was based at the fort, and the soldiers spent most of their payrolls in nearby Cheyenne. Local merchants enjoyed considerable trade with Cheyenne Depot. Citizens eagerly attended concerts staged by the regimental bands and dances held at the fort, while officers and their wives were welcome at social activities in town. Periodically, military and political luminaries stepped off a train at Fort D. A. Russell: Generals U.S. Grant, Phil Sheridan, and William T. Sherman; Presidents Grant, Rutherford B. Hayes, and Benjamin Harrison; along with a parade of other leaders of the day.

By the early 1880s, as Indians were confined to reservations, frontier outposts were closed across the West. But because of east-west and north-south railroad connections, Fort D. A. Russell was maintained and improved. The old frame buildings began to be replaced by brick structures, and a water system was installed throughout the post. By the time the Invaders arrived, Fort D. A. Russell was a substantial and handsome military community.

Several hundred people were waiting when the train chugged into Fort Russell from the north at fifteen minutes until four on Sunday afternoon. The regimental band was playing the customary Sunday concert on the parade ground, and the Invaders heard musical strains as they alighted from the train. Two lines of soldiers had formed as guards. The Texans bounded off the cars first. Their faces were blistered from the weather, and they were unshaven and unkempt, but they "swaggered along unconcernedly, looking somewhat wild." The stockmen followed, with Billy Irvine, limping from his foot wound, and Frank Wolcott bringing up the rear. [2]

The Invaders all pitched in to unload their baggage, equipment, and saddles, then piled everything into army wagons for the short trip to the bowling alley. The bowling alley was a frame building measuring 300 x 50 feet. (No "bowling alley" is identified on the fort plan, although there is an L-shaped "gym"; perhaps one of the "vacant barracks" offered by Major Egbert had been converted to a bowling alley.) Major Egbert ordered guards and a rope fence placed around the building, with written permission required for civilians to be admitted. Throughout the afternoon buckboards and carriages drove up, bringing well-wishers, as well as clothing, linen, and miscellaneous supplies. Visitors were not permitted into the bowling alley while the Invaders bathed, shaved, and changed clothes. In addition to setting up bathing facilities, soldiers carried cots into the building, lining them up between alleys rails and the long side walls. A sergeant and two privates were detailed to hang chandeliers from the rafters. The Texans tossed their warbags onto the cots toward the rear of the building, while the cattlemen established themselves at the front. [3]

During the afternoon E. W. Whitcomb enjoyed a "tearful reunion" with his family and "a levee" with his Cheyenne friends. That evening Frank Wolcott, natty in a tweed suit, welcomed a large crowd of visitors. Although Lafeyette Parker, manager of the Murphy Cattle Company, was ill and took to his bed, other prominent cattlemen accepted invitations to the homes of various officers. Gifts "of all kinds" were sent out to the Invaders, and congratulations were expressed. The Texans donned new clothing provided by their employers. But with no friends or family in Cheyenne, they played cards and kept to themselves. When they went outside for exercise, the hired gunmen were accompanied by a guard detail. [4]

THE INVADERS—Standing, left to right: Tom Smith, A. B. Clarke, J. N. Leslie, E. W. Whitcomb, D. Brooke (The Texas Kid), W. B. Wallace, Chas. Ford, A. R. Powers, A. D. Adamson, C. A. Campbell, Frank Laberteaux, Phil Dufran, Major Wolcott, W. E. Guthrie, W. C. Irvine, Bob Tisdale, Joe Elliott, John Tisdale, Scott Davis. Seated, rear, left to right: Fred Debillier, Ben Morrison, W. J. Clarke, L. H. Parker, Teschmacher, B. C. Schulze. Seated, second row, left to right: W. H. Tabor, J. A. Garrett, W. A. Wilson, J. Barlings, M. A. McNally, Mike Shonsey, Dick Allen, Fred Hesse, Frank Canton. Seated, front, left to right: Wm. Little, Jeff Mynett, Bob Barlings, S. Sutherland, Buck Garrett, G. R. Tucker, J. M. Benford, Will Armstrong.

The prisoners, clad in suits and ties, posed for a group photo. The label contained a few errors, most notably "D. Brooke (The Texas Kid)" in the top row, and "G. R. Tucker" seated on the ground. Dave Booker was at top, while young Starl Tucker was called "The Texas Kid." (Courtesy Wyoming State Museum)

In the ensuing days, Fred de Billier tried to keep the Texans busy by organizing baseball and football games. While baseball had been played in Texas since the 1860s, football as yet was little known in the Lone Star State. But de Billier, with his Ivy League and New York background, was familiar with both sports. He coached the Texans in "the fine points of baseball and football,"[5] and there were enough men for two teams. Balls and bats were available at every military post, since companies played each other, and any needed equipment could be purchased in Cheyenne.

A photographer was summoned from Cheyenne, and the cattlemen and their Texas gunmen gathered for a group photo. Forty-three men, dressed in suits and ties and a variety of hats, lined up in front of a building which might have been a warehouse or stable (perhaps it was the bowling alley). Eight Texans sat cross-legged in front, and another eight men sat behind them. Everyone else stood in the rear, with four men standing, on a bench perhaps, above everyone else. This famous photograph shows a proud, fine-looking group of men who seem little intimidated by their incarceration. The photographer shot another pose with all hats removed. But these men of the West required stronger diversions than posing for photographs and playing ballgames.

The Invaders were allowed to patronize the post canteen, an enlisted men's club which sold beer, wine, tobacco and sundries (the profits were utilized for the benefit of the soldiers). On Monday, May 9, Buck Garrett and Cliff Shultz were drinking at the canteen and began quarreling with Fred Fisher, a former trooper who had been dishonorably discharged. Buck, "a hell-diver with his fists," hurled a bottle or a brickbat or some other object at Fisher. The missile whizzed past Fisher and struck a guard in the

The photographer asked his subjects to remove their hats, a pose that is seldom seen. (Author's collection)

nose. With blood spurting from his nostrils, the guard dropped his rifle and collapsed to the floor. As a melee erupted, Fisher's brother, Charles, snatched up a rifle, which had a fixed bayonet, and charged. The bayonet ripped into the shoulder of Shultz, exerting a sobering effect on the brawlers.[6]

The Texans now were forbidden to enter the saloon area of the canteen, but this prohibition failed to dull their fighting instincts. One afternoon some of the Texans began playfully knocking the hats from one another's heads, and this roughhouse quickly accelerated into another brawl. One Texan went to the post hospital with two knife gashes in the neck, while the Texas Kid sported two black eyes. But the officers responded to the obvious combativeness of Starl Tucker—The Texas Kid. The officers began taking Starl along with them when they went into Cheyenne for a night on the town. "They evidently enjoyed his antics when he was drunk," remarked Starl's half-brother, George Tucker. George told of one such evening of drunken revelry when, "just to show off, Starl picked up a little dried-up fellow and threw him down a stairway." George reported that the man died of his injuries. Starl returned to the bowling alley that night "all proud of himself," awakening George to tell him about his wild evening with the officers. "He bragged about how funny the fellow looked going down those stairs."[7]

While the idle Texans restively tried to pass time, their employees conferred on legal strategy. The large legal team would be led by thirty-three-year-old Willis Van Devanter, a superb lawyer who had distinguished himself since arriving in Wyoming Territory in 1884. Establishing a practice in Cheyenne, Van Devanter became a prominent member of the Wyoming bar and held several public offices, including territorial chief justice in 1889-90. (His distinguished career was capped in 1910 by appointment as associate justice of the U.S. Supreme Court.) Judge Van Devanter became the trusted aide and confidant of Senator Francis E. Warren, and chief counsel for the Wyoming Stock Growers Association. Van Devanter had agreed to serve as state chairman of the Republican election campaign for 1892 when the Johnson County War rearranged his priorities. The plight of the cattlemen and their employees demanded immediate legal work, while the Republicans were expected to enjoy their usual election sweep. But the Republican Party in Wyoming was dominated by the cattlemen, and public outrage over the Johnson County invasion promised to generate considerable Democratic support in the November election. Despite political pressures, Van Devanter's most immediate duty was to devise a defense for the Invaders.[8]

On April 20 Van Devanter, who had corresponded with Senator Warren since early March about the worsening situation in Johnson County, wrote a long letter to Warren in Washington. He described the expedition as "poorly managed" and plagued with "grievous" errors in judgment—"none, however, so grievous as the error of going at all."[9]

Despite Van Devanter's stern disapproval of the Invasion, he was totally committed to the successful defense of his clients, the Invaders. Johnson County officials were clamoring to have the prisoners returned to Buffalo. Van Devanter reported to Senator Warren that Sheriff Red Angus was in Cheyenne trying to take the prisoners into custody. "Angus has been in a great state of drunkenness lately and said the other day that" the people of Buffalo would "make short work of them." Van Devanter and his law partner, John H. Lacey (the partners were brothers-in-law), were absolutely convinced "that it was certain death for these prisoners to return to Buffalo."[10] The lawyers determined to move the proceedings to a southern county, where a fair jury might be seated. Such a strategy should cause delays and open up other legal possibilities.

The cattlemen had arrived at Fort Russell supremely confident after being delivered safely from Johnson County. But the day after arriving they met at length with their lawyers, who offered sobering counsel about the virulent public opinion that was building in Wyoming. A blizzard of editorial criticism erupted from numerous Wyoming newspapers, especially those in the area near the path of the Invaders. On the evening of April 21 an "indignation meeting" was held in the Sheridan County community of Banner. A chairman and a secretary were elected, and a five-man Resolutions Committee formed. Several resolutions were composed condemning "the recent outrages committed in Johnson county," and addressed "To His Excellency, the President of the United States." On this same day, President Harrison responded to an appeal from Buffalo. "The governor of your state made a call upon me in conformity with the Constitution of the United States for aid in suppressing domestic violence and threatened bloodshed. I could know nothing of the situation except as it is stated by him, and could not refuse the aid of troops to preserve the peace. The prisoners will as soon as the state authorities are prepared to receive them, be turned over to the civil authorities." President Harrison, speaking "as your fellow citizen," offered soothing counsel to the people of Buffalo. Citizens of this isolated little town were impressed with a direct communication from the president of the United States: "The message was circulated among the people and is well received." There were numerous other petitions and appeals from various communities.[11]

Regardless of public criticism, the cattlemen's legal team and influential supporters maneuvered relentlessly on behalf of the prisoners. Of primary concern were Bill Jones and William Walker, the trappers who had been temporary captives of the Invaders at the

PETITION.

TO THE HONORABLE PRESIDENT OF THE UNITED STATES OF AMERICA,

WHEREAS: A BODY OF ARMED ASSASSINS HAVE VISITED THE COUNTRY IN THE VICINITY OF BUFFALO, JOHNSON COUNTY WYOMING, AND HAVE MURDERED SOME OF OUR CITIZENS UNDER A PRETENSE OF CORRECTING SOME WRONG DOINGS AMONG STOCKMEN'S PROPERTY ON THE PUBLIC DOMAIN, AND

WHEREAS, THE SHERIFF OF JOHNSON COUNTY WYOMING, IN THE DISCHARGE OF HIS OFFICIAL DUTIES, HAS CALLED UPON THE CITIZENS OF SHERIDAN COUNTY TO RENDER ASSISTANCE TO SAID SHEIFF AND CITIZENS OF JOHNSON COUNTY IN THE CAPTURE OF SAID MURDERING ASSASSINS, AND

WHEREAS, WE LEARN WITH ASTONISHMENT AND PROFOUND REGRET THAT YOUR HONOR, AS THE PRESIDENT OF THESE UNITED STATES AND COMMANDER IN CHIEF OF OUR ARMY AND NAVY, HAS ORDERED THAT THE MILITARY DEPARTMENT AT FORT MCKINNEY DO GIVE SAID MURDERING ASSASSINS A SAFE CONDUCT OUT OF OUR COUNTRY, AND THUS TAKE THEM AWAY FROM THE PROSCESS OF THE CIVIL LAW UNDER WHICH THEY SHOULD BE TRIED.

WE THEREFORE, AS CITIZENS OF SHERIDAN COUNTY WYOMING, FOR THE SAFETY OF THE CITIZENS OF THE GREAT NORTHWEST, HUMBLY PRAY AND PETITION YOUR EXCELLENCY AS THE PRESIDENT OF THE UNITED STATES TO RETURN THE SAID ASSASINS YOU HAVE TAKEN THAT THEY MAY HAVE A CIVIL TRIAL THAT, IF POSSIBLE, THE ENDS OF JUSTICE MAY BE SECURED.

AND WE FARTHER PRAY THAT YOU, AS THE PRESIDENT OF THIS GREAT NATION, WILL NOT SUFFER YOUR MIND TO BE INFLUENCED BY THE HONORABLE GOVERNOR OF WYOMING OR THE HONORABLE SENATORS FROM WYOMING, AS THEY HAVE PERSONAL INTERESTS IN THIS GREAT AND MOMENTOUS MATTER.

One of the protest petitions sent to President Harrison.

Owen Wister Again

On July 6, the day after the prisoners were transported to Laramie, Owen Wister boarded a train in Philadelphia. Earlier in the year he had arranged another hunting-camping trip. His faithful admirer, Dick West, was scheduled to work as guide. But since April, Wister had read about the troubles in Wyoming involving many of his ranching friends, and he had saved many newspaper clippings.

The violence, along with the incarceration of his friends, spoiled the upcoming expedition for Wister. Deciding against a western excursion for 1892, he nevertheless chose to announce his cancellation in person. Instead of simply sending a letter or telegram, he made a round trip of 5,000 miles to tell West in person. Perhaps revealing western attitudes he had absorbed, Wister explained that he wanted no one "to think that the reason for my giving this summer up is fear for my carcase." And, as an inveterate traveler, he allowed that "there is something modern and globe trotting in traveling 2,500 miles to say you're sorry you can't come."

Wister's Northern Pacific train pulled into tiny Cinnabar, between Billings and Custer in southern Montana, about half an hour past noon on Sunday, July 10. Dick West waited on the train platform; he even had brought Wister's saddle from previous trips. The two men walked beside the Yellowstone River, and West tried to talk Wister into staying, if not for the summer at least for one day. But Wister was adamant in his intention to return immediately. "Then we went back to Cinnabar and had some beer—very good—" before going to sit on the train. "The train left at six-fifteen, and West as it began to move jumped up from the seat and said, 'Well, by God Wister I guess you're gone!'—and I was—bringing my saddle with me." Cinnabar was 130 miles northwest of Buffalo, and as close as Wister came to Johnson County in 1892.

A regular visitor to Wyoming since 1885, Wister was detoured in 1892 by an unexpectedly hostile public reaction to the Johnson County invasion. But he remained captivated by Wyoming's ranching culture and by western violence, and soon Wister would produce a landmark literary interpretation of this compelling time and place.

KC ranch, and who could provide the most damaging testimony. Despite what Jones and Walker had witnessed at the KC, they had been treated with surprising benevolence by the cattlemen. Because their wagon had been burned while being used as an assault vehicle on the cabin, "Irvine paid what they said this loss was worth, gave his own hat to the younger man, who claimed to have lost his in the fire; gave them an order for grub on the foreman of Tisdale's ranch and told them to go south, to say nothing about what they had seen and heard, and keep marching." Marching south, as ordered, they arrived at the Tisdale ranch that night, where Dr. Charles Penrose, H. W. Davis, and Ed Towse had remained after the expedition had left to attack the KC. Dr. Penrose observed that Jones and Walker were visibly frightened "and anxious to get out of the country as fast as possible. I surmise that Wolcott and Irvine had impressed on them how important it would be for their welfare to say nothing and to disappear quickly."[12]

Penrose, Davis, and Towse soon left the Tisdale ranch, trying to escape the region, and so did the trappers. Continuing south, Jones and Walker "subsisted upon the country for several days and were driven into Casper by sheer starvation," reported the Cheyenne *Leader*. "Both were scared out of their boots," but when they sensed that the people of Casper were sympathetic, "they began to talk against the cattle men." Authorities recognized that Jones and Walker "were the only living witnesses who can testify positively against the regulators on a charge of murder," which probably meant that their lives were in danger. Subpoenas could not yet be issued, but Sheriff Red Angus suggested that these invaluable witnesses could be informally protected in Douglas. On Wednesday, April 27, Jones and Walker were delivered by Casper's city marshal to Douglas, where they "continued to talk," according to Dr. Penrose; "so that the friends of the cattle men thought it best to get rid of them."[13]

Sheriff Malcolm Campbell was in Washington, D.C., on business, leaving in charge Undersheriff E. H. Kimball, who also was editor of the Douglas *Graphic*. Although Jones and Walker could not be incarcerated, they were "placed under surveillance" in Douglas. For a week Jones and Walker "were allowed to run about town during the day and sleep in the office of the jail." On Wednesday, May 4, E. H. Kimball was summoned to Glen Rock, perhaps by a ruse to get him out of Douglas. That night the trappers arrived at the jail late and "apparently pretty drunk." When the deputy on duty in the office dozed off, Jones and Walker picked up a revolver apiece and walked out of the jail, intending to leave town. Apparently by prearrangement with Fred Harvey, a Douglas lawyer who was working as an agent for the cattlemen, Jones and Walker went to the livery stable of O. P. Witt, who had been engaged to ride with them to Nebraska. Jones and Walker were promised $2,700 apiece, to be delivered "at Grand Island when they got aboard the eastbound train." At Witt's livery stable, Jones and Walker "were met by eight well-known cattlemen who told them the plans were ready and for them to escape on two horses that were already saddled and waiting." The trappers obediently mounted up and followed Witt into the night. After riding about thirty miles, the party halted while Witt cut the telegraph lines. Later, when one of their mounts played out, Witt caught a ranch horse as a replacement. Ten miles past the Nebraska line, they reached tiny Harrison, where Fred Harvey was waiting at the depot. It was Thursday night when everyone boarded a train and steamed twenty-five miles to the east, stopping in Crawford.[14]

But Douglas officials had searched for Jones and Walker throughout the day, firing off telegrams "in all directions" and charging the trappers "with grand larceny for having stolen two revolvers from the Douglas jail." At the train station in Crawford, the city marshal alertly arrested Jones and Walker—"Two of the most thoroughly scared men in Nebraska," proclaimed newspaper reports. "Jones, especially, was terribly frightened and made no effort to conceal it." Harvey promptly engaged a Crawford attorney to help him obtain a writ of habeas corpus from a judge in Chadron, a larger town and the county seat, twenty-six miles to the northeast. When the city marshal refused to honor the writ, Harvey obtained a warrant for his arrest. At a cost of $65, Harvey arranged for a special train—an engine and a caboose—to come down from Chadron. Crawford's city marshal, defying the arrest warrant, appropriated Harvey's train and took his prisoners to jail in Chadron. Less than an hour after the special train steamed out of Crawford, a train from Wyoming arrived with officials from Douglas and Buffalo.[15]

On Friday the county judge announced a continuance of legal proceedings until Monday, and the trappers spent the weekend in jail surrounded by guards. In a crowded courtroom on Monday afternoon, May 9, O. P. Witt, through attorney Fred Harvey, "accused the trappers of selling United States horses and selling liquor to Indians." In addition to these trumped-up charges, papers also were filed regarding the theft of two revolvers. The presiding judge ruled that Jones and Walker should be released on the writs of habeas corpus. The moment the judge spoke the word "released," a deputy U.S. marshal from Omaha, who was seated near Jones and Walker, declared them under arrest. Local sheriff J. C. Dahlman also tried to arrest them, on the grand larceny charge from Douglas, which would have brought the trappers back to Wyoming. But Deputy Marshal Hepfinger immediately slapped handcuffs on Jones and Walker. "Great excitement prevailed in the court room when the rush was made by the officers to see who could get the men first," reported the Cheyenne *Leader*.[16]

A special train was waiting to whisk the "prisoners" to safety in Omaha (there were rumors that a train was en route from Wyoming, "loaded with rustlers who intended to hold the important witnesses at all hazard if they were found," said the *Leader*). Jones and Walker were hustled out of court by a side door, and Harvey and Witt came with them, as planned. On his way out of the courtroom, Witt handed a bill of sale for his Douglas livery stable to a deputy sheriff, remarking "that he had no more use for that country." Deputy Marshal Hepfinger rapidly escorted Jones, Walker, Harvey, and Witt to the railroad station. "The famous Wyoming trappers are now flying towards Omaha on a special train," announced a dispatch from Chadron, "and it is safe to predict that the only witnesses to the killing of Ray and Champion will never testify in a Wyoming court."[17]

This cynical prediction proved true. Following a rail journey across Nebraska, Deputy Marshal Hepfinger brought his prisoners to the federal building in Omaha about five-thirty Tuesday afternoon. Once inside the U.S. marshal's office, Jones and Walker finally had their handcuffs removed. Appearing immediately before a federal judge, Jones and Walker waived examination through their lawyers. The judge set bond at $200 each, then released them on personal recognizance. Cheyenne attorney Hugo Donzelman, who had been dispatched by the cattlemen to help complete the proceedings, promptly boarded a train for Kansas City with the men who were key witnesses against his employers. Decades later, Walker told Daisy F. Baber that he and Jones had been taken to Westerly, Rhode Island, and held there for nearly two years. According to Billy Irvine, Donzelman accompanied Jones and Walker to a location in New York State (Sheriff Malcolm Campbell said it was Massachusetts), where "they were kept for months," while legal proceedings against the cattlemen went on without them. Irvine wrote Dr. Penrose that the payoff checks which Donzelman gave the trappers were issued "on banks that never existed." Jones and Walker were never known to have visited Wyoming again, and Dr. Penrose was unable to learn anything else about them: "What was the end of the trappers I cannot find out."[18]

By the second week in May, therefore, one of the most crucial legal threats facing the Invaders was eliminated. The public again was forcefully reminded of the power and influence of the cattlemen. "Everybody is perfectly aware that these were frivolous charges," fumed the Cheyenne *Leader* about Jones and Walker supposedly selling liquor to Indians; "that their only purpose is to get the men out of Wyoming, have the charges dismissed, and then get them out of the country as quickly as the cars will carry them." The *Leader* went on to comment on "how fortunate it is that justice is 'blind.' If she were not blind, she might see some things transpiring ... which would give her a spasm."[19]

While Jones and Walker were being removed 2,000 miles away from Wyoming, the prisoners at Fort Russell learned of the murder of George Wellman in Johnson County. Then, a little later in May, Phil DuFran and Sam Sutherland were released from custody. Soon DuFran was employed to guide the Ninth Cavalry to Suggs. By that time, Major Wolcott also had been released from Fort Russell. Unlike DuFran and Sutherland, Wolcott was expected to return, but only after he attended to urgent business in Nebraska.

Wolcott was scheduled to visit in Omaha an old comrade in arms, Nebraska Senator Charles F. Manderson. A native of Philadelphia, Manderson became a lawyer and a prominent citizen of Canton, Ohio. Shortly after the outbreak of the Civil War, Manderson helped organize the Nineteenth Ohio Infantry, rising from captain to colonel of the regiment. Manderson was severely wounded in combat during Sherman's March to the Sea, and he was breveted to brigadier general of volunteers "for long gallant faithful and meritorious service during the war." For the remainder of his life General Manderson was active in the Grand Army of the Republic. In 1869 the thirty-two-year-old war hero moved to Omaha, continuing a legal career that would see him serve as president of the American Bar Association in 1900. General Manderson was elected to the U.S. Senate in 1883 as a Republican, then reelected in 1889.[20]

It was to this influential leader of a neighboring state that Wyoming cattlemen turned for additional help in Washington, D.C. General Manderson had known Major Wolcott during the Civil War, and in early May 1892, Senator Manderson wrote the secretary of war of behalf of his friend of "nearly 30 years." Senator Manderson praised the War Department and the president for acting "so promptly" to provide "proper protection to the lives and property of citizens where the State authorities seemed powerless to protect." Senator Manderson also offered a strong endorsement for Major Wolcott: "He is a high-toned, honorable and much respected gentleman and is that rare bird in that section of the country—a christian gentleman. He would do nothing mean or dishonorable and has all the courage and pluck needed to insist upon his personal and property rights."[21]

This gracious description of Wolcott may have been unrecognizable to a great many people in Johnson County, but Wyoming cattlemen intended to capitalize on Manderson as a staunch ally in the U.S. Senate. Several ranchers wrote a lengthy letter to Manderson presenting their version of the "war of honesty against thievery" in northern Wyoming. "We therefore respectfully ask you to co-operate with Messrs Carey and Warren, the United States Senators from Wyoming." Late in May, the supportive Major Egbert was persuaded to release Wolcott from Fort Russell so that he could pay a personal visit to Senator Manderson in another state. "What Maj. Wolcott is after now is to get all the cattle country placed under martial law," reported the Omaha *World-Herald*. The cattlemen were trying to apply enough pressure in Washington to persuade President Harrison to declare martial law in Wyoming. Arriving in Omaha on Saturday, May 28, Wolcott "took a flying trip with Senator Manderson" to Chicago. Then they returned to Omaha, where Wolcott spent a day "closeted with friends and talking business and rustlers." Manderson promised his old comrade only that he would present the cattlemen's case to higher authorities, which he already had done. "Faithful to his parole, Maj. Wolcott proceeded direct to Cheyenne and Russell, ... and is again in confinement with his brother cattle kings and their employees."[22]

One of Wolcott's "brother cattle kings" soon returned to Wyoming, following a long absence, and exerted his considerable abilities on behalf of his incarcerated friends. In his autobiography, John Clay stated that in July 1891 Frank Wolcott revealed to him plans to organize "a lynching bee." Clay said that he strongly advised Wolcott against this action, and "to count me out." Later in the year Clay left Wyoming for a long trip to Europe. A native of Scotland, Clay regularly returned to report to British cattle investors, but this time he traveled to continental Europe on an extended holiday. Finally sailing back to the United States in April 1892, he bought a newspaper during a stop at Queenstown, Ireland. Clay read "a lurid account of a fight between cowboys and owners of cattle in Wyoming. It was vivid and looked bad, as a number were killed on both sides." (Clay's biographer is convinced that he was kept informed of Wyoming events during this long European sojourn.) Clay stated regretfully that "if I had been actively at work on the range that winter the famous 'Johnson county invasion' would never have happened." Clay professed dismay that "I was accused of having planned and instigated the famous raid in to Johnson County, whereas I was innocent as an unborn babe."[23]

Despite Clay's protestations of innocence, the belief persisted that, as president of the WSGA, he was instrumental in planning and financing the Invasion. A well-educated man of broad experiences and sound business judgment, Clay may have been perceptive enough to distance himself from the planned assault, but he had no intention of abandoning his fellow cattlemen. By mid-June he was in Chicago, working at his land and livestock commission office at a noted office building on the loop, "The Rookery." After updating himself on the situation in Wyoming, Clay began aiding his friends "with every ounce of nerve in my body." There was a pressing need to raise money, for the daily upkeep of more than forty men and for the mounting legal expenses of a platoon of attorneys. After the Invaders "got into the hands of the lawyers," reflected Clay ruefully, "... betwixt them and the rustlers I have never quite made up my mind which was the lesser or greater of the evils." Although a fund had been collected to finance the expedition, "when Fort Russell was reached then the real financial music began." Numerous Wyoming ranchers contributed $1,000 apiece, but more fund-raising was necessary. According to Clay, "It cost the cattle-owners around $100,000."[24]

From Chicago, Clay launched a formidable correspondence, by letter and telegram, with a number of lawyers. After conferring with a Chicago law firm, he wrote Cheyenne attorney Henry Hay to develop a strategy of prolonging legal proceedings. The resulting growth of court costs would overwhelm the coffers of Johnson County, forcing them to break off legal action which no longer could be afforded. Clay emphasized that "the law of the State is very clear that no county can expend more than it has in hand any one year." A few days later Clay wrote Hay with the news that he was about to travel from Chicago to Omaha, before going "down into Texas for a little trip." Then he planned to return to Wyoming to devote personal attention to his ranching interests and to the legal machinations involving the Invaders.[25]

Senators Warren and Carey also maintained a steady correspondence with Willis Van Devanter, Henry Hay, and other attorneys for the Invaders. Warren agreed that "the sooner Johnson County begins to have the burden of guarding and maintaining the prisoners, the sooner things will come to a head." Discussing the overall situation with Henry Hay, Warren mentioned that "radically wrong and stupendous mistakes" were made by the Invaders. "By mistakes," he added revealingly, "I do not mean that to 'eradicate' the rustlers was a mistake, but the general plan and execution of it."[26]

Even though their attorneys and various officials were working to delay legal proceedings, the cattlemen were increasingly anxious to resume their lives. Fred de Billier and others showed signs of strain and some of the ranchers began criticizing those who were trying to help them. "The stockmen at Fort Russell are chafing in their imprisonment," reported the Cheyenne *Leader*. The Texans, after being confined at Fort Russell for more than two months, became dangerously restless. They "had several fierce quarrels among themselves, and talked a great deal about escaping." Rancher E.R.S. Broughton, an influential member of the WSGA, went out to the post to visit some of his fellow cattlemen. Broughton became alarmed that many of the most frustrated men were armed. Witnessing "a serious quarrel" between Billy Irvine and some of the Texans, Broughton returned to Cheyenne and told Willis Van Devanter. Soon the prisoners were relieved of all liquor, money, and weapons, "including pen knives," and the guard was doubled around the bowling alley. Henry Hay sent a report about the latest troubles at Fort Russell to Senator Warren, who had visited the prisoners during a recent trip to Cheyenne. "I am sorry to hear that they are undergoing another period of dissatisfaction and quarrelsomeness at the post ... ," replied Warren. "However, I must confess, I expected it and I think I said as much to you, and perhaps to them, when I was there."[27]

On June 25 Sheriff Red Angus "and his deputies" left for Cheyenne in yet another attempt to bring the prisoners back to Johnson County. But earlier Governor Barber had written the prosecuting attorney of Johnson County, "saying that the prisoners were held at Russell by the United States authorities," and that certain conditions must be met before they would be released to civil custody. "One thing he insisted upon ... was that the prisoners should not be taken back to Johnson county," because of the possibility of mob violence.[28]

Judge J. W. Blake already had informed Governor Barber that he did "not consider it necessary at this time to have these men taken to Johnson county." Blake was judge of Wyoming's Second Judicial District, which included Johnson and Albany counties and which headquartered in Laramie City, as it usually was called. Judge Blake emphasized to Governor Barber that while the prisoners were incarcerated at Fort Russell, they were "under absolute control of the War Department." He suggested that the prisoners might be brought to his court, where they would be "confined in the north wing of the penitentiary at Laramie, a portion of the building now unoccupied for any purpose, and where they will not under any circumstances come in contact with any of the convicts confined in another part of the building."[29]

On June 29 Judge Blake traveled by train across the Continental Divide to Cheyenne. He checked into the Inter Ocean Hotel and went to see Governor Barber and, presumably, various lawyers. Plans were laid finally to release the prisoners to civil custody, bringing them to Judge Blake's court for a change of venue hearing, moving the trial from Johnson County to some other location. "The prisoners will be turned over to civil authorities in a very few days," Judge Blake told a reporter, who also asked if the trial would soon begin.[30]

"Well, no," replied Judge Blake, "there are some other things which will have to be readjusted. One of those is the expenses of the trial. These everyone knows will be

The north wing, at right, of the old Wyoming Territorial Prison dates from 1872. The south wing and center portion were added in 1899. But in 1892 the rancher-prisoners had no intention of staying in a prison, and hired a hall downtown. (Photo by Karon O'Neal)

heavy. Now, if I should try the case, I shall not touch it until Johnson county makes good, money enough to carry on the trial." The reporter asked if the judge thought that Johnson County could provide enough funding. "Johnson county should and in fact must raise the money," emphasized Judge Blake. "I told the commissioners of that county just what I am telling you when they came over to see me some time ago."[31]

Within a few days preparations were made for the prisoners to leave Fort Russell, to the relief of military authorities, who had decided in May that we "don't want to keep them." (Gen. John Schofield, commander of the Army, received instructions not to receive the prisoners again without orders from the War Department.) But the cattlemen had no intention of staying in a vacant wing of a prison. Again financing their own up-keep, they arranged to stay in Hesse Hall, a two-story building near the depot in Laramie City. Mattresses were placed on the second floor, while the prisoners would "take their eatables on the first floor."[32]

At six o'clock Tuesday morning, July 5, a train pulled out of Cheyenne for the sixty-mile journey to Laramie City. There was no military escort for this trip, although the army was represented by an infantry captain from Fort Russell. The forty-three "prisoners" were accompanied by an honor guard led by Governor Barber, Wyoming Adjutant General Frank Stitzer, defense attorneys Willis Van Devanter and Hugo Donzelman, three attorneys for the prosecution, two deputy U.S. marshals, the city marshal of Cheyenne, the sheriff of Laramie County, the inspector general of the Wyoming militia, the District Court clerk, and Deputy Sheriff Howard Roles of Johnson County. Only a small crowd was on hand at the Laramie depot, "and no demonstration whatsoever was made." Deputy Roles took custody of the prisoners, who were marched to Hesse Hall. "All were in good spirits," reported the Cheyenne *Leader*.[33]

Judge Baker's courtroom was packed when the prisoners filed in a little after eleven o'clock. One by one, each prisoner "formally waived a preliminary hearing." The defense then requested a change of venue from Johnson County. The issue was argued by attorneys on both sides, and the defense produced twenty-seven witnesses "to prove that the prisoners can get a fair trial in Cheyenne." The prosecution expressed a preference for Laramie City, and there was sentiment for Rawlins and other communities. When the prisoners returned to Hesse Hall that afternoon, Deputy Roles had hired ten guards at $100 per month—more expense for Johnson County.[34]

On Wednesday the attorneys began questioning witnesses from different counties, attempting to determine the best location for the trial. "The same questions are asked each witness," reported the Cheyenne *Leader*. There were twenty witnesses each from Laramie and Albany counties, "and their examination is somewhat tedious, as well as uninteresting." Carbon and Uinta counties were allowed five witnesses each, and representatives from the prosecution and the defense were sent to examine these counties. Witnesses from Albany County began testifying that stockmen in and around Laramie had been overheard mouthing such expressions as, "They should all be hung." Furthermore, Judge Blake was told that Laramie City residents were angry that the prisoners were being held in Hesse Hall instead of the penitentiary.[35]

During the prisoners' second night in Laramie City, Fred de Billier leaped out of bed "and in an excited manner asked for protection from some imaginary foe." His

207

Second Street in Laramie City, ca. 1890. The "prisoners" were permitted to circulate downtown if accompanied by a guard. (Author's collection)

friends quieted him, "but he was suffering from the same hallucinations in the morning and was not able to go to court." Telegrams were sent to Henry Hay and Governor Barber, and they promptly entrained for Laramie City, arriving at noon Thursday. Barber, who was a physician, thought that de Billier had suffered a hernia in a recent baseball game at Fort Russell—until he saw him at Hesse Hall. "Do you hear that noise?" de Billier asked Barber. "There is someone up there going to poison us. Why don't they let me go into court? It's a scheme to do us up."[36]

De Billier continued to insist that someone was trying to kill him and Hubert Teschemacher. After examining de Billier, Dr. Barber concluded that "his mind was unbalanced," and he recommended "that he should be sent immediately to a lower altitude and placed in an institution where he can have the benefit of specialists." The problems of the past three months "have weighed heavily upon his mind, and being of an exceedingly sensitive nature he has allowed himself to become despondent." Popular among the ranchers, de Billier had worked to keep up the morale of the Texans, and his condition "had a depressing effect

Harvard-educated rancher Fred de Billier finally cracked under the strain of incarceration, and he was released to return home to New York. (Frank Leslie's Weekly, June 2, 1892)

NUMBER	SENT BY	REC'D BY	CHECK

Spaid

RECEIVED at *Cheïan 1006q July 7 1892*

Dated Laramie Wyo

To Henry J Hay

*Come at once bring
Barber Fred Nery ill
H. E. Teschemacher*

Telegram from Hubert Teschemacher regarding the breakdown of his friend Fred de Billier.

Sporting their best Victorian attire, witnesses from Johnson County pose for a group photo between court sessions. The bearded man standing seventh from the left appears to be Asa Mercer, who soon would write Banditti of the Plains. *The bearded man standing fourth from the right resembles Arapahoe Brown.*
(Courtesy Johnson County Jim Gatchell Memorial Museum)

upon his fellow prisoners." Prosecution attorneys expressed no objection to sending de Billier away, "and as soon as his friends decide upon a plan for his treatment an order will be secured from the judge allowing his removal." Senators Warren and Carey were notified and responded immediately. "Poor De Billier," wrote Warren, "I hope he will recover." Carey was "grieved," and he blamed "the intense strain" and "confinement."[37]

On Friday, July 8, the "deranged" Fred de Billier left for his family home in New York, accompanied by Henry Hay. In court Major Wolcott took careful notes as each witness testified. But most of the other cattlemen "looked weary and haggard." The Texans chewed tobacco and "lounged about" the courtroom, as each witness dealt with the question: "Do you think the prisoners can get a fair and impartial trial in your county?"[38]

Day after day the slow parade of witnesses continued in the courtroom. When not in court, the prisoners played cards or conversed at Hesse Hall, where the second-story porch overlooked the depot. If accompanied by a guard, prisoners could tend to business around town. Deputy Roles "speaks very highly of the conduct of the prisoners under his charge."[39]

Not until Tuesday, July 19, did Judge Blake finally arrive at a decision. At eleven o'clock he began reading his opinion, which "was listened to with the closest interest by both prisoners and audience." Judge Blake first stated that his position in the case was "a most embarrassing one, and one that had caused him more anxiety than any other matter which had ever come before him." He had concluded that "no county in the whole state was absolutely free from bias one way or another. It was agreed on all sides that this bias existed to such an extent in Johnson county that it was impossible to have the trial there."[40]

In addition to the matter of bias, another crucial point involved the fact that the large number of defendants made the number "of eligible jurors in any county a matter of vital importance in the selection of a place for a trial." Defendants were entitled to 516 peremptory challenges, while the prosecution had 258 challenges. Albany County, Wyoming's second-largest county, had 1,381 men and women eligible for jury duty, of whom 147 were exempt. Witnesses for the defense as well as for the prosecution had testified to hearing insulting remarks about the defendants in Laramie, while a group of 120 citizens had signed a set of resolutions which would prevent them from serving as jurors. About ten percent of eligible jurors "would naturally be unable to serve by reason of physical disability." Simple math made it clear to Judge Blake that it would be impossible to seat a jury in Albany County. Laramie County, with more than 2,600 potential jurors, was the only county in Wyoming in which twelve jurors might be found. Judge Blake "therefore ordered the change of venue from Johnson county to Laramie county."[41]

The trial thus would be held in Cheyenne, stronghold of Wyoming cattlemen. Although the defendants had displayed noticeable "anxiety" for the past couple of days, "their joy at the outcome was unconcealed." Judge Blake ordered that the prisoners would remain in the custody of Deputy Sheriff Roles, but when they returned to Hesse Hall "many of them made a rush for the telegraph office to send the news to their friends."[42]

Laramie City merchants and other citizens were upset that the trial would not be held in their community, and those who had testified to local prejudice against the defendants "are by no means very popular just at present." Conversely, Cheyenne businessmen were elated "that the trial is coming ... for it means the disbursement of quite a large amount of money." Not as elated was Laramie County Sheriff A. D. Kelly, because he would be responsible for a large number of controversial prisoners who wanted to come and go at will, and because he would have to summon "an immense number of jurors." Citizens in Johnson County and elsewhere were cynical about the placement of the trial. "When Cheyenne was decided upon," grumped Asa Mercer, who was a witness for the prosecution against holding the trial in Laramie County, "the opinion in many parts of the state was freely expressed that the cattlemen had won, and that the trial would be a howling farce." John Clay, a principal leader of the cattlemen, confirmed that movement of the trial to Cheyenne presaged victory. "This of course practically ended the case," Clay admitted in his autobiography, "but there was a lot of formality and legal matters to be complied with."[43]

Judge Blake had stated that it would be "over a week" before the defendants could be transferred to Cheyenne. Nearly two weeks passed while the prisoners grew bored and restless. Billy Irvine wrote a scathing latter to Senator Warren, complaining bitterly that martial law had not been imposed by the federal government, questioning Warren's friendship, and accusing him of everything from "double dealing" to "cowardice." As requested, Senator Warren passed the letter on to Senator Carey, who had just visited the president and attorney general on behalf of the cattlemen. Senator Carey mentioned the vicious letter to Henry Hay: "Irvine censures me because martial law was not declared. Why, Van Devanter understood before I left the State, that the United States would not under any circumstances go into a state and declare martial law."[44]

Senator Warren wrote a ten-page reply to Irvine. Graciously allowing for strain and confinement "and finally your transfer to the high altitude of Laramie City, I consider you must be in a morbid state of mind and hardly responsible for what you say." Among many other things, Senator Warren pointed out "that Wyoming is but one of 44 states ...; that it has 60,000 people out of the 60,000,000 in the United States; that we have only 1/100,000 of the population. ... We cannot ask and if we did ask, cannot get the President to ignore all other business matters at home and abroad to take up Wyoming alone. ... The President has burned the midnight oil on our account and so have other officers."[45]

Senator Warren could not resist a few counterpunches: "Billy, if you will permit me to suggest it, had there been a little more time used, perhaps maturer judgment and better reinforcements, etc., your expedition would have terminated differently." After all of his efforts, Senator Warren felt unjustly accused: "you have seen fit to take a position inimical to me, because of your groundless suspicions and semi-insane imaginations." Senators Warren and Carey had been roundly criticized by Wyoming newspapers, and now they were attacked by cattlemen. "Having both sides blaming my position is not pleasant," Warren complained. "Now, yourself and your friends do your worst with me," he closed. "I shall do the best I can for you all notwithstanding."[46]

Chapter 18

At the Holy City of the Cow

"Let no one mislead you by saying that we had the law on our side—we had the politics and the money, but not the law."

GEORGE TUCKER

In Laramie City on Monday, August 1, Judge J. W. Blake handed down his final orders in the cattlemen's case. Each side would pay the mileage and per diem of its respective witnesses. Johnson County would pay for the guards, as well as "the regulation price of 60 cents per day for the keep of the prisoners while at Laramie." Since their board cost five dollars per week each, the stockmen made up the difference—"80 cents a week each." Housing costs would be equally divided between Johnson County and the prisoners.[1]

The prisoners quickly packed their belongings and bedding, then boarded an eastbound train. The train pulled into the big depot at Cheyenne at four o'clock Monday afternoon. Johnson County Deputy Sheriff Howard Roles officially turned over the prisoners to Laramie City officers, who gave the men the run of the town. As the "prisoners" descended from the train, they enjoyed handshakes and subdued greetings from friends. "The prisoners straggled up town in small squads with acquaintances," reported the Cheyenne *Leader*. Baggage and bedding were taken to Keefe Hall, an opera house on the west side of the 300 block of Ferguson Street that had been hired for the prisoners, who were too numerous for the county jail. Indeed, during four months of incarceration, the cattlemen were never behind bars. Instead of the jail at Buffalo or Cheyenne, or the penitentiary at Laramie, they managed to arrange loose confinement at Fort McKinney, Fort Russell, Hesse Hall, and Keefe Hall.[2]

Sheriff A. D. Kelly employed four men at two dollars per day apiece to cook, wait tables, and wash dishes at Keefe Hall. Twenty-five to thirty-five dollars daily would be spent on meat, bread, milk, and other groceries. Soon after the inmates arrived, "a corps of barbers was summoned and the prisoners were trimmed up." A reporter from the Cheyenne *Leader*, which had not been sympathetic to the expedition, entered Keefe Hall. The reporter was greeted with profane taunts, including, "We know our friends and don't want any *Leader* ____ __ ____ in here." The prisoners advanced on the reporter, muttering "kick him out" and "fix him." But the *Leader* reporter wisely retreated from the building. Then a drunken citizen inadvertently wandered into Keefe Hall, only to be "jumped on by some of the Texans and unceremoniously bounced."[3]

Seventeen guards were hired at three dollars per day to work in three shifts at Keefe Hall. On the first evening, prisoners who had families in Cheyenne were permitted to spend the night at home, on condition that they "return to the bastile" at eight o'clock the following morning. An hour before midnight the Cheyenne *Leader* reporter bravely approached the deputy in charge at Keefe Hall. Seventeen prisoners were out for the night, but the deputy emphasized that on the second day "the rules will be more stringent, and those leaving the hall will be usually accompanied by a guard."[4]

But the promised new stringency did not develop. "The guards at the Keefe hall have a perfect sinecure," observed the Cheyenne *Leader* only two days after the prisoners arrived. "Just who and what they are guarding is seldom apparent to anybody, for all the prisoners roam about day and night at will and unattended by guards." Asa Mercer angrily noted that the cattlemen slept at their homes or hotels every night, "and the entire party took their meals where they chose, and had the run of the town day and night." On one evening at eight o'clock, no one could be found at Keefe Hall except three guards. And one morning as Mercer walked through a residential neighborhood to his downtown office, "he observed one of the imprisoned men come to the door in his night shirt, reach through a partial opening and get the morning paper lying on the door sill. A block farther down he saw another Invader taking his morning walk."[5]

The "prisoners" now enjoyed free run of bustling Cheyenne. Wyoming's largest city now boasted a population of 12,000. Among the most impressive buildings in "The Holy City of the Cow" were the state capitol and the massive Union Pacific depot and

Although this bird's-eye view of Cheyenne was produced a decade before the Johnson County War, most of the structures significant to 1892 already were in place. (Author's collection)

213

the three-story Inter Ocean Hotel. For the thousands of males in Cheyenne, numerous establishments offered drinking, gambling, and other varieties of entertainment—all of which were available to the men now "confined" at Keefe Hall in downtown Cheyenne.

The Wyoming cattlemen, of course, could afford any amusement the city offered, and they provided ample funding for their Texas employees. George Tucker testified that "the cattlemen . . . were not stingy with their money. They gave us the best that money could buy. And, besides, they gave each of us seven hundred dollars at one time." (This payoff was made when the Texans finally were free to return home.) Promised a wage of one hundred fifty dollars per month, with a fifty-dollar bonus apiece for each dead "rustler" (Nate Champion and Nick Ray), the Texans were in Wyoming for approximately four months. Seven hundred dollars would represent six hundred in wages plus one hundred in bonuses. "We drew extra money from time to time," explained Tucker. "The cattlemen paid all the transportation, equipment, living, and court expenses. Billy Irwin [sic] would buy us anything that we wanted. We could not have asked for nicer treatment in this respect than we got from them."[6]

"A bunch of our young fellows went to a whore house one night and smashed all the furniture in the place," related George Tucker. "It cost the cowmen three hundred dollars to repair the damage." During another night of revelry Frank Canton shot himself. "He got drunk," explained George Tucker. "He was out on the street flourishing his gun. He dropped it and it went off and the bullet went through the fleshy part of his leg. We carried him into the court house on a stretcher." The deputies in the courthouse were amused that yet another Texan had accidentally wounded himself, and Malcolm Campbell sarcastically remarked that "these invaders certainly had an unpleasant habit of shooting themselves." Frank Canton failed to mention this incident in his autobiography.[7]

One evening a group of cattlemen-prisoners took a train to Denver, more than one hundred miles to the south, to attend a Templar meeting. On another memorable night,

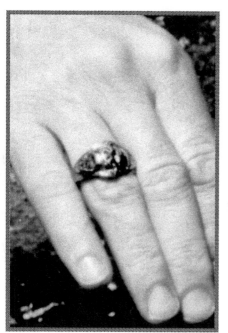

the cattlemen hosted a champagne dinner for the Texans. Each participating rancher brought two Texans to the dinner, and Governor Barber and Major Egbert were guests. As the champagne flowed freely, recalled Tucker, "Major Egbert got so far along that he fell out of his chair." Tucker had his own battle with the bubbly liquor, which he had never before consumed. "I started out taking the champagne at gulps. I expected a breathing spell, but every time I emptied my glass, some flunky would fill it up again. Pretty soon things began to go round."[8]

"Boys," announced Charley Campbell,

Reportedly a commemorative ring presented by Wyoming cattlemen to a Texas gunman. The ring is on the hand of a descendant from Paris, Texas, who did not wish to have his name or his deceased grandfather's published. (Courtesy of Bob Edwards)

214

"everything goes tonight except the top of the house." Campbell had brought George Tucker and Jeff Mynett to the banquet, and those two Texans hauled out revolvers with the intention of "going after the top of the house." The cattlemen hastily confiscated their guns, but it all was part of "the general hilarity of the occasion." Tucker warmly regarded the ranchers as "real sports" and "gentlemen in the grand manner."[9]

During the evening, Governor Barber approached Jeff Mynett and pinned a boutonniere on him. "Everybody there knew that the Governor was merely thanking Jeff for having killed Champion," observed Tucker. There may have been more gestures of thanks that evening. It has long been rumored that the Texans were given rings commemorating their Wyoming adventure. The dinner hosted by the cattlemen would have been an ideal occasion for the presentation of the rings. Perhaps it was on this evening that the cattlemen made a commemorative loving cup presentation among themselves. It is not known how many cups were made up, but one was given to Fred G. S. Hesse. A color photograph of this cup hangs on a wall at the TA Ranch, and purportedly this cup has long been stored in a Hesse family basement. The silver loving cup is ornately engraved:

Fred G. Hesse
In grateful remembrance of
untiring devotion on our behalf
during the trying time of the
Wyoming invasion of 1892

Below this inscription are three lines of names, but since they are on the bottom curve of the cup, these names are difficult to distinguish. In 1982 papers of Henry Hay pertaining to the Johnson County War were donated by his grandson to the American Heritage Center at the University of Wyoming. Part of this donation was a silver loving cup engraved to Hay with a similar inscription:

In grateful remembrance of
untiring devotion in our behalf
during the time of the
Wyoming Invasion of 1892

Campbell, D. R. Tisdale, L. H. Parker, W. J. Clarke
A. D. Adamson, A. B. Clarke
W. E. Guthrie, F. A. Laberteaux, J. N. Tisdale,
F. G. Wolcott, W. C. Irvine, R. M. Allen
R. Powers, E. W. Whitcomb, Scott Davis, F. M. Canton,
F.G.S. Hesse, H. E. Teschemacher

When the author was researching at the University of Wyoming in June 2001, this cup could not be produced. At some point during the previous two decades it seems to have been placed elsewhere. But since engraved loving cups were presented to Fred

Hesse and Henry Hay, how many other cups were exchanged by the cattlemen? Hesse's name was inscribed on the cup of Hays, suggesting that perhaps each of the eighteen signatories received loving cups. Participation in the invasion of 1892—the sieges at the KC and the TA, long horseback treks together, mutual incarceration, and courtroom battles—had created a bond. These men had been through combat alongside each other, and in the face of widespread criticism they bonded together over a period of four months. They celebrated that bond with banquets, rings, and loving cups.

While the prisoners enjoyed the night life in Cheyenne, during the day they spent considerable time in the district courtroom of Judge Richard H. Scott. "The big square room with its old-fashioned furniture, grim, dreary, uninteresting, a relic of frontier days, is not an inviting place." On Saturday, August 2, a large collection of papers was filed before Judge Scott. Forty-five men were charged with murdering Nathan D. Champion and Nick Ray. But Alex Lowther was dead, "Fred de Billier is at the Atlantic seaboard on sick leave," and "Capt. Tom Smith" was missing "under an alias." Smith was not present when the Invaders were arrested at the TA Ranch, and although he was present for the group photo, he since had vanished. Therefore, of the forty-five listed defendants, forty-two were present.[10]

These forty-two men made their first appearance before Judge Scott on Saturday, August 6. Their attorneys were Willis Van Devanter, Hugo Donzelman, M. C. Brown, and Walter Stoll, a bright young lawyer who a decade later would lead the prosecution against the notorious assassin Tom Horn. Judge Davidson and another attorney led the prosecution. A large crowd watched as each of the forty-two defendants answered "Not guilty" to

The Laramie County courthouse in Cheyenne stood across the street from Keefe Hall. The "prisoners" had a short walk from their quarters to the courtroom. (Courtesy Wyoming State Archives)

the charges of murdering Nate Champion, and then to the charges of murdering Nick Ray. "The reading of the informations consumed the greater part of the day," reported the Cheyenne *Leader*, and as they were identical ... the sitting was rather tiresome."[11]

Following this tedious process, Judge Davidson moved for the prosecution that only four of the defendants be tried first (if these four were exonerated, the other defendants could be tried by turns). Judge Scott denied this application, ruling that all defendants would be tried simultaneously for the murder of Champion, and setting the trial date for Monday, August 22. Then "the prosecution called the attention of the court to the fact that the defendants were permitted to go at large unattended by guards and to carry weapons concealed upon their persons, and asked that an order be issued that they be disarmed, kept out of saloons and retained in proper custody." Counsel for the prosecution then called the attention to defendant Frank Canton, "who was in court on a stretcher, as the result of an accidental discharge of a revolver carried by him." Judge Scott "directed the sheriff to disarm the prisoners and keep them in proper custody."[12]

At this late point in the day, counsel for the defense presented a petition from the sheriff of Laramie County. Because keeping the prisoners cost about one hundred dollars a day, and because Johnson County was unable to reimburse him for the expense, Sheriff Kelly asked "that the court grant the necessary relief to protect him from incurring loss." The prosecution "suggested" that if the defendants would apply for bail there would be no opposition. Defense counsel countered with a proposal for personal recognizance, but following a consultation with Billy Irvine, the defendants agreed to "remain in the custody of the sheriff until the time of the trial."[13]

Of course, exhausting the slender financial resources of Johnson County was a key to the defense strategy. "Johnson County has no funds to carry the thing to an end ... ," wrote John Clay to attorney Henry Hay. "We know that Johnson County is pretty sick already," added Clay, "and we must force the matter to an end with them." Clay, Hay, and former Governor George Baxter "held an informal meeting," and Clay "was deputized to call on Judge Scott." A key point was that prisoner meals, rent for Keefe Hall, even wages for the guards, was paid for by the incarcerated ranchers, "and other cattle-owners." Clay told Judge Scott "that we proposed to cut off the money supplies, and throw the prisoners into the actual charge of the sheriff. At the time I was talking to him the so-called prisoners could be found at any place but the hall they were supposed to be confined in. Three guards were there, but nobody else. The judge knew this as well as anybody else." As a result of these confidential conferences, Sheriff Kelly filed his petition of relief on August 6.[14]

That evening, Texans George Tucker and Jeff Mynett ignored the ban on saloons and "went down by the railroad track to a blind pig to get some beer." Tucker recalled staying "long enough to get about half-tight." Walking back toward Keefe Hall, they encountered Judge Davidson standing in the doorway of the Inter Ocean Hotel, "engaged in conversation with one of the rustlers' leaders." The prosecuting attorney invited the Texans to the bar, "and we all had drinks around several times." During their conservation, Judge Davidson "intimated to them that they were loosely guarded and could easily make their escape, and that if they made the attempt no effort, as far as the prosecution was concerned, would be made to recapture them."[15]

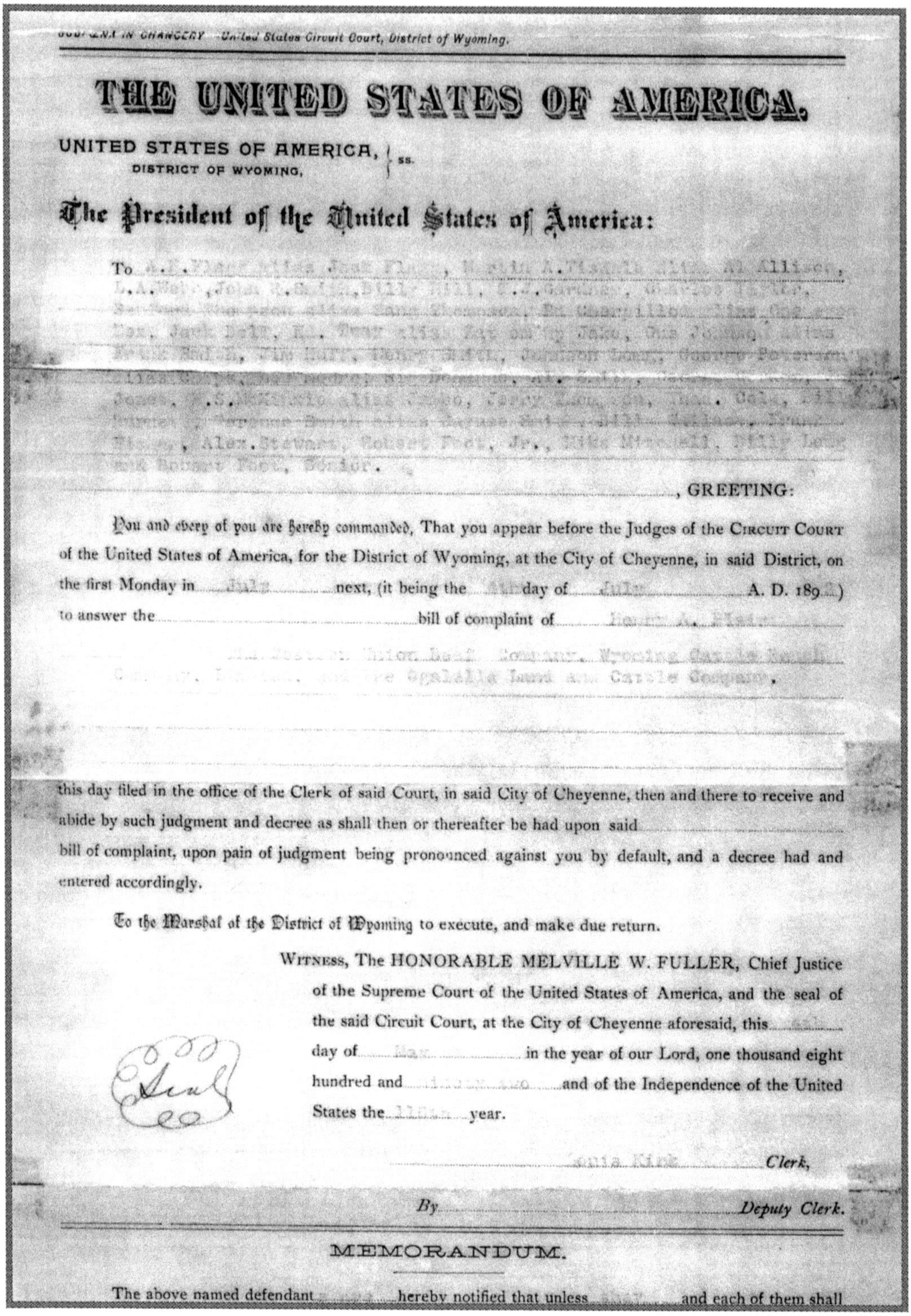

THE UNITED STATES OF AMERICA.

UNITED STATES OF AMERICA, } ss.
DISTRICT OF WYOMING,

The President of the United States of America:

To _____
_____
_____
_____
_____
_____
_____
_____
_____, GREETING:

You and every of you are hereby commanded, That you appear before the Judges of the CIRCUIT COURT of the United States of America, for the District of Wyoming, at the City of Cheyenne, in said District, on the first Monday in _____ next, (it being the _____ day of _____ A. D. 189__) to answer the _____ bill of complaint of _____ A. Blair

_____
_____

this day filed in the office of the Clerk of said Court, in said City of Cheyenne, then and there to receive and abide by such judgment and decree as shall then or thereafter be had upon said _____
bill of complaint, upon pain of judgment being pronounced against you by default, and a decree had and entered accordingly.

To the Marshal of the District of Wyoming to execute, and make due return.

WITNESS, The HONORABLE MELVILLE W. FULLER, Chief Justice of the Supreme Court of the United States of America, and the seal of the said Circuit Court, at the City of Cheyenne aforesaid, this _____ day of _____ May _____ in the year of our Lord, one thousand eight hundred and _____ and of the Independence of the United States the _____ year.

_____ Clerk,

By _____ Deputy Clerk.

MEMORANDUM.

The above named defendant _____ hereby notified that unless _____ and each of them shall

Part of the legal strategy in the summer of 1892 was counter-action by the cattlemen. In this case cattle baron Henry Blair secured restraining orders against Jack Flagg, Al Allison, Robert Foote, et al, but eventually all legal action was dismissed. (Courtesy Johnson County Jim Gatchell Memorial Museum)

Davidson seemed to harbor no ill feelings toward the defendants; indeed, as many people suspected, the prosecution may only have been going through the motions in a cause they saw as lost. Finding out about this incident, Willis Van Devanter informed Judge Scott "that Judge Davidson had acted thus far without due courtesy to the court, and very disrespectfully to the attorneys for the defence." Tucker and Mynett were summoned, and they confirmed the incident. Tucker reminisced that Judge Blake "stormed and swore that he would disqualify the attorney for what he had done." Meanwhile, Davidson had returned to Laramie City, and defense attorney Hugo Donzelman was dispatched to deliver an order for the prosecutor to appear in court. In Laramie City, Donzelman "found Judge Davidson intoxicated."[16]

On Wednesday morning, August 10, Judge Scott handed down his decision regarding Sheriff Kelly's relief petition. Although Johnson County "was practically bankrupt" and had refused to reimburse Albany County for legal expenses incurred at Laramie City, Judge Scott decided that he could not issue an order compelling Johnson County to pay Sheriff Kelly's more recent disbursements. Therefore, since he could not provide for the sheriff's expenses, and since the defense had declined bail, the only remaining alternative was to admit the prisoners to bail "on their own individual recognizances." Immediately, the prisoners entered into their own recognizances in two sums of $20,000 each, there being two indictments against each defendant. "The ranchers had no trouble in raising the money for our bonds," said George Tucker.[17]

The prisoners promptly were released from custody. Keefe Hall was quickly deserted, "and express wagons were kept busy carrying away the paraphernalia with which it had been littered." The bedding and cooking gear were removed, and the building was turned over to Mr. Keefe's representative. The Cheyenne *Leader* commented that many of the prisoners had "never slept in the hall at all, and the guards were an elegant superfluity except whenever it was necessary to preserve the peace among the Texans."[18]

The Texans departed for home before the end of the day. George Tucker, Jeff Mynett, and Dave Booker stayed in Cheyenne for a time, but the other Texans, "in exceedingly good spirits," headed for the train station. Most of them carried "a brand new gripsack, a Winchester rifle and a cartridge belt." A few of their fellow defendants beat them out of town, but most of the cattlemen, other friends, "and a number of spectators were gathered together to see the party off. There was a great deal of hand shaking and a number of congratulatory expressions." A few of the cattlemen also boarded the eastbound train. After a journey of five hundred miles to Omaha, the Texans were paid seven hundred dollars apiece, and placed on a train to Texas. "They were soldiers of fortune, who never should have been brought to the wind-swept plains of Wyoming," observed John Clay. "Tactically it was a mistake, for it put a false impression on the whole affair, more especially in the east."[19]

Like Clay, George Tucker in later years reflected on the role of the Texans: "We were in Wyoming as paid assassins of the big ranchers. We were brought there to murder men in violation of the law. Let no one mislead you by saying that we had the law on our side—we had the politics and the money, but not the law. We were not convicted of our crimes because we had the politics and the money with us." The longtime Texas law officer also had perceptive observations regarding the larger picture of the Johnson

County War: "The trouble as I saw it was a fight between the big ranchers and the small farmers. There undoubtedly were some rustlers among the latter group. But they could not have all been rustlers, for there would not have been enough cattle to go around."[20]

Less than two weeks after the prisoners were set free, they reassembled in Judge Scott's courtroom on Monday, August 22. Fred de Billier did not return to the site of his breakdown. Eleven Texans made the long trip back to Wyoming. Staying away were Tom Smith, George and Starl Tucker, Bob and Jerry Barling, Jeff Mynett, Will Armstrong, M. A. McNalley, and Bob Willey. Despite rumors that the absent Texans would arrive later in the day, prosecuting attorney Davidson "asked that their bonds be declared forfeited and that bench warrants be issued for their arrest." Judge Scott issued the order, but there was never any attempt to arrest the absent men. On his own motion, Judge Scott ordered continuance of Case No. 365 to the November term of the district court. Monday, January 2, 1893, was set as the trial date.[21]

During the five months preceding the trial, several pertinent events occurred. After the Texans left for home, and the Invaders-cattlemen dispersed to their various destinations, public excitement about the Johnson County War finally subsided. But interest was rekindled in October with the publication of a forty-four-page statement from hired gunman George Dunning.

Following the siege at the TA Ranch, Dunning had left his place of concealment and hiked into Buffalo, where he quietly was taken into the custody of Sheriff Red Angus. After trappers Bill Jones and Bill Walker were removed by the cattlemen to the East in May, George Dunning became the most valuable witness. He was taken secretly from Buffalo into hiding at a ranch, and for the most part George Dunning was forgotten.

On October 6, 1892, two months after the Invaders had been freed from custody pending trial, George Dunning emerged at the big brick courthouse in Buffalo. Dunning began to write "without solicitation, fear or threats from any party or parties whatsoever," as he swore in the presence of District Court Clerk T. P. Hill. Beginning with his recruitment by H. B. Ijams of the Wyoming Stock Growers Association, Dunning composed a detailed and revealing account of the expedition through the fight at the TA. A week later Cheyenne journalist Asa Mercer published Dunning's confession in his weekly newspaper, *The Northwestern Live Stock Journal*. But even if the confession reawakened public interest in the Invasion, there was no real effect upon the legal proceedings. Dunning had not been arrested at the TA and was not included on the list of defendants. By the time his confession was published, legal maneuvering was advancing to a conclusion, and Dunning did not play a part in the January proceedings which ended legalities.[22]

But the cattlemen were alarmed and incensed by the publication of the Dunning confession. In earlier years Mercer's *Live Stock Journal* had sold advertising to the WSGA, and in 1889 he vigorously endorsed in print the 1889 lynching of Cattle Kate and Jim Averell:

> There is but one remedy, and that is a freer use of the hanging noose. Cattle owners should organize and not disband until a hundred rustlers were left ornamenting the trees or telegraph poles of the territory. The hanging of two culprits

merely acts as a stimulus to the thieves. Hang a hundred and the balance will reform or quit the country. Let the good work go on and lose no time about it.[23]

By this time, however, the sagging fortunes of the cattlemen "dried up the sources of Mercer's percentage from the Stock Growers Association," according to a study by historian Lewis Gould. In 1890 Mercer had secured a place on the Wyoming state payroll by persuading Senator Francis Warren to appoint him alternate commissioner from Wyoming to the Chicago's World Fair of 1893. ("If you give me this place," Mercer had

written to Warren, "I will show up western stock interests in a way that will do us all good.") But Mercer turned hostile to his former ranching patrons in the summer of 1892, in an apparent effort to revive reader interest in his *Live Stock Journal*. He traveled to Laramie to testify before Judge Blake that the trial should not be held in Cheyenne, which was the top choice of the cattlemen and their attorneys. And in the *Live Stock Journal* Mercer penned virulent criticism of the cattlemen and their expedition, referring to the ranchers in August 1892 as "constitution breakers and murderers," and as "freebooters, land grabbers, and millionaires."[24]

Already under assault from numerous Wyoming newspapers, cattlemen were not pleased when Mercer, a former ally, added his journalistic voice to their opposition. Decades later, John Clay remained angry: "A gentleman called Mercer, editor of the *Stock Growers' Journal* [*sic*], a Cheyenne publication, that had existed on the cattleman's advertisements and other plunder that could be gathered from the cow business, had turned his back on his old friends."[25] In August 1892 Mercer lambasted Clay in the *Live Stock Journal:*

For years Asa Mercer depended on big cattlemen for advertising for his Northwestern Live Stock Journal. *But the Cheyenne-based journalist turned on his former benefactors during the Johnson County War.* (Courtesy Johnson County Jim Gatchell Memorial Museum)

Too great a coward himself to shoulder a musket and fight [Clay was in Europe], he sent one of his hired men [Charles Campbell], and contributed to the exterminators fund in cheap talk if not in shining shekels. Deliberately making a list of men to be killed and houses to be burned, this man and his co-workers plotted treason to the state with the powers and went forth to murder and burn. What cared he for the lives of his fellow man if by murder and arson more grass could be secured and greater returns made to his foreign shareholders?[26]

Charles Campbell, who was employed by Clay's commission company and who lived in Cheyenne, was free on bail when this article was published. Campbell "promptly went to the editor's office and took the change out of him with his fists. This was Campbell at a boiling point, goaded to violent action ... ," related an appreciative Clay, "not the gentle, lovable, sympathetic Charlie ... who made merry with his friends." Mercer, understandably, did not regard Campbell as "gentle, lovable, sympathetic." Writing in the third person, Mercer stated that Campbell and three other cattlemen "entered his office and made a personal attack upon him, undoubtedly with murder in their hearts."[27]

Soon after this pugilistic incident in his office, Mercer spent much of September on a speaking tour of Wyoming. In October he traveled to Chicago to attend a meeting of the National Commissioners of the 1893 World's Fair. (The Wyoming commissioner declined to attend, and Mercer was the alternate commissioner.) John Clay also was in Chicago, working at his office at the Rookery Building. On Saturday, October 22, Mercer, who "had not the slightest notion ... that he was going to be meddled with," was arrested for criminal libel, "based on his editorial attack on Mr. Clay." Two of his fellow commissioners immediately provided bail. But the following Tuesday afternoon, Clay filed an affidavit in superior court charging that Mercer had attacked him, through the *Northwestern Live Stock Journal*, "in a way which has damaged his character," and he asked for damages for $150,000. As Mercer left the afternoon session of the commissioners, he again was arrested. "He did not have time to take off his commissioner's badge," reported the Cheyenne *Leader*, "and was still wearing it when" he was escorted to "a chilly cell in the criminal court building." This time bail was not immediately forthcoming, and Mercer had to spend Tuesday night in his "chilly cell." Clay would never be able to collect $150,000 from Mercer, but having him thrown in jail, if only for one night, was a gratifying counterstroke to the harsh criticism in the *Live Stock Journal*. And for his part, Mercer soon would again wield a venomous pen against the cattlemen, this time in a highly controversial book.[28]

Part of Mercer's crusade against the cattlemen was campaigning for Democrats in the November election. Wyoming had been controlled by Republicans, the party supported by almost all of the big ranchers. But with so many citizens outraged by the cattlemen's murderous expedition into Johnson County, Democrats suddenly enjoyed swelling support. In a July letter, Senator Warren observed forlornly that "my political future, if I had one before, has been ruined by this northern cattle business."[29] Warren's senatorial seat was subject to the election of 1892 (state legislatures appointed U.S. senators until 1913, when the Seventeenth Amendment made the Senate subject to popular elections). Democrats swept elections throughout Wyoming in 1892, and the new Democratic legislature would appoint a senator from their party. The Democratic triumph of 1892 was another result of the Johnson County War.

By January 2, 1893, twenty-three of the defendants had gathered again in Cheyenne. None of the Texans returned—one already had been killed in a shootout—while cattlemen Fred de Billier and Hubert Teschemacher, whose brother recently had died in Switzerland, also were missing. By this time the public furor aroused the previous April had subsided to a considerable degree. "The thinking people began to wake up," reflected

John Clay. "They knew the men who had been actually in the raid, and the others who backed them as reputable citizens. They had spent endless money in the country."[30]

Willis Van Devanter and the rest of his legal team had been able to plan for five months for a successful conclusion to the trial. On Monday, January 2, two motions for a continuance were made on behalf of defendants Joe Elliott and A. D. Adamson. While Judge Scott listened to the lengthy arguments on both sides, the defendants wandered in and out of the courtroom. Judge Scott finally ordered all concerned to stay in the courtroom, whereupon a bored W. B. Wallace leaned back and took a nap. Postponing his decision until nine o'clock the next morning, Judge Scott on Wednesday refused the motion for continuance.[31]

The trial then proceeded with a protracted effort to seat a jury. Between the prosecution and the defense, a total of 414 peremptory challenges would be permitted. Many potential jurors did not want to serve, perhaps fearing consequences, and certain answers to examination created unacceptability for one side or the other. Because they exhibited bias, or because they did not believe in capital punishment, or because of "opinions gained from newspapers which could not be laid aside," one potential juror after another was asked to step down. Some were exempted because they were physically disqualified, and some because they were firemen. Eleven men were seated, but the twelfth could not be agreed upon. On Thursday, January 12, for example, sixty-five candidates were examined: fifty-five were excused for a cause, while the defense used ten peremptory challenges. On Friday, January 20, ninety were examined, with eighty-two excused for cause, and the other eight dismissed by peremptory challenge. By the noon recess on the next day, a total of 1,064 veniremen had been examined, but the jury still was incomplete.[32]

By now Johnson County was virtually bankrupt and unable to bear legal expenses. When the county attempted to pay with warrants, they were considered "scarcely worth the paper they were written on." Judge Davidson and other prosecuting attorneys, unable to work up much enthusiasm for a case in which they were paid in worthless warrants, took turns being absent from court. John Clay said that the trial became "a mere puppet show," and that another confidential meeting brought matters to a conclusion: "it was arranged after an afternoon and evening's talk that the Johnson authorities should dismiss the case."[33]

Following Saturday's noon recess, the sheriff of Laramie County informed Judge Scott that he had been told by Johnson County officials, including Prosecuting Attorney Alvin Bennett, that Johnson County was unable to reimburse him for maintaining the prisoners and for the expenses of securing jurors. Although directed to deliver fifty or more potential jurors, the sheriff said that he already had brought to court virtually every eligible juror in Cheyenne, as well as many in the countryside, and he no longer could afford the costs of sending deputies to the far reaches of the county. After Judge Scott turned to the prosecuting attorney with this matter, Bennett moved to dismiss the cases. But Willis Van Devanter contended that since the trial was being conducted in Laramie County, his clients still could be prosecuted in Johnson County, so he insisted that the case continue.

The defense lawyers then conferred with Bennett, while everyone in the courtroom strained to overhear them. After the lawyers returned to their tables, Bennett asked Judge Scott to continue empaneling the jury. The judge declared an open venire for the single remaining jury member. A deputy sheriff summoned a spectator, Adam Adamsky, who was approved by both sides without examination. Van Devanter insisted that the jury be sworn in with instructions to return a not guilty verdict. Bennett would not agree without consulting his fellow prosecutors, Davidson and Ballard, who were absent. Judge Scott granted a recess, but Bennett returned without having located either of his partners.

When court reconvened, Bennett entered a motion of *nolle prosquei*—formal notice that prosecution in the case now would end. Indictments of each defendant, including the absent Texans, were dismissed. A previous motion to forfeit bail bonds of the missing defendants was rescinded. After concluding formalities were finalized, the jury was dismissed and Judge Scott adjourned the proceedings. The case had not been tried, and the defendants had not been acquitted, but they could never again be arrested for the murder of Nate Champion and Nick Ray. Now free men, the ranchers shook hands and exchanged congratulations with each other and with a sudden swarm of friends.

William Walker

In Buffalo on June 18, 2005, the author had the pleasure of meeting two granddaughters of William "Bill" Walker, Oma Chapman and Lenora Redmond. Providing information about their grandfather, they stated that he was eighteen when he and fellow trapper Bill Jones stayed overnight at the KC Ranch cabin with Nate Champion and Nick Ray. Walker was a gifted fiddler, and provided entertainment that night even as the Johnson County Invaders closed in on the cabin. When his granddaughters knew him, long after the Johnson County War, Walker lived in Lyon, Colorado. They agreed that he was "always skittish." When he was seventy-two, Walker broke his hip and died in Casper in 1946. He was returned to Lyon for burial.

Chapter 19

Back to Texas

"[Tom] Smith died just as he caused many others to die."

KINGFISHER FREE PRESS

Tom Smith and Dave Booker were the first Johnson County War veterans to become embroiled in another shootout. As soon as they returned to Texas, Smith and Booker resumed working out of Paris as deputy U.S. marshals. Although it was known that they were subject to pending trial in Cheyenne, Smith and Booker were valued as tough officers who were unafraid of taking on the violent lawbreakers of Texas and Indian Territory.

On Friday night, November 4, 1892—while their Wyoming employers still were under loose custody in Cheyenne—Smith, Booker, and a third deputy marshal awaited a northbound train at Gainesville in North Texas, only a few miles below the Red River. Earlier in the evening at Fort Worth, the train had taken on an African-American passenger later thought to be a fugitive, "Commodore Miller." Miller recently had killed a Dallas policeman, then eluded a manhunt. Defying the segregation laws of Texas, the big African-American man seated himself in a white compartment. When the conductor ordered him to the "colored" compartment, he went reluctantly and unhappily.[1]

About eleven o'clock, with many passengers dozing, the train made a quick stop in Gainesville. The three officers, who were bound for Ardmore, Oklahoma, were among the new passengers who stepped aboard. One passenger was carrying whiskey, and as soon as the train crossed the Red River into Oklahoma, where liquor laws were very restrictive, Tom Smith moved forward to search the man for whiskey. Seeing the lawman approach, the suspect made his way into the colored compartment.

When Smith entered the compartment, Commodore Miller, apparently still seething from being ousted earlier, complained "in an offensive manner" about the presence of white men. "Deputy Smith replied that white men could ride where they pleased, and supplemented his remark with an oath."[2]

Miller angrily produced a revolver and shot Smith above the eye. As Smith collapsed in death, Miller fired again, striking the lawman in the hands. The other two officers bolted into the compartment, Booker leading the way with his revolver drawn. Miller squeezed off another round, grazing Booker's neck.

Booker's return shot caught his assailant in the abdomen. As Miller fell, Booker pumped three more slugs into his torso. Miller died within moments, his feet only inches from Tom Smith's head. The gun battle "caused the greatest excitement" among the passengers, who now were wide awake.[3]

When the train reached Ardmore, the two surviving officers debarked, along with the corpses. Deputy U.S. Marshal J. M. Chancellor, mentor to Buck Garrett, telegraphed Smith's widow in Taylor, Texas: "Tom Smith was killed tonight by a negro what shall we do with the body?" During the day it was arranged for Smith's remains to travel on a southbound train that would depart Ardmore at just before five on the morning of November 5, then arrive in Taylor that afternoon. Lodge members of the Knights of Pythias were scheduled to meet the train in Taylor, while W. H. Dickerson, a friend of Smith's from Paris, telegraphed Sallie Smith: "I will bring the body of Tom."[4]

After being killed in the line of duty, Deputy U.S. Marshal Tom Smith was buried in Taylor, Texas. (Photo by the author)

Perhaps recalling recent events in Wyoming, one newspaper rather unsympathetically remarked, "Smith died just as he had caused many others to die."[5] But Deputy Marshal Tom Smith was killed in the line of duty, and three of his five sons carried on the family tradition of law enforcement. Thomas C. Smith, Jr., served as a deputy sheriff, while Frank and Will Smith both worked for the Houston Police Department. Frank, the most active of the third generation of Smith lawmen, wore a badge for forty years. In 1915, as a member of the Dallas Police Department, Frank was wounded while making an arrest. He crowned his career with nine years as an FBI agent.[6]

Dave Booker's prompt action against the killer of Tom Smith doubtless was appreciated by other frontier peace officers, who understood all too well the constant danger of their work. During the next several years Booker arrested a succession of killers and thieves.[7] He was a member of the 1894 posse that tracked down bank robber Bill Dalton, although Deputy U.S. Marshal Loss Hart fired the rifle shot that killed the notorious fugitive.[8] Also in 1894, Booker led a posse that killed "several members" of a gang near Eagle Town in the Choctaw Nation.[9] During another 1894 gun battle, between Booker and another deputy and a killer named Will Ferguson, the outlaw squeezed off three shots before the officers shot him.[10]

Booker was transferred to the jurisdiction of Judge Isaac Parker on July 1, 1896.[11] Within the month, on July 30, Booker again demonstrated that he was an officer to be taken seriously. When he rode to the farm house of a man named Jack Wiggins to serve an arrest warrant, Wiggins met Booker at the gate, then became defiant when told that he was to be arrested. "I reasoned with him, but to no good purpose," explained Booker. "He started to the house, evidently to get his gun." When Wiggins reached the doorway, Booker fired a single pistol shot, inflicting a fatal wound. "By this time the women folks were after me and I had to do some smooth talking to keep one of them from using a gun on me."[12]

Headquartering in Ardmore, Booker worked for five more years as a deputy U.S. marshal, then accepted a position as chief of police. After leaving law enforcement, he acquired considerable real estate and was active in local politics. He married, for a second time, when he was forty-six, and raised a daughter and a stepdaughter. "He looked like a schoolteacher or a minister," observed Henry C. Somerville, who knew Booker well enough to disregard this mild appearance. "This soft-spoken, extremely well mannered old gentleman was one of the toughest gunfighters in Texas history. He killed a great many men, without fear or hesitation. He was good at law enforcement, but he would have been good at any business."[13] When he died in Ardmore of pneumonia, in 1927 at the age of seventy-six, Booker was widely praised as

The final resting place of Dave Booker is the Rose Hill Cemetery in Ardmore, Oklahoma, where he served as a peace officer after hiring his gun in the Johnson County War. (Photo by Karon O'Neal)

"one of the outstanding characters of the early days of Ardmore" and for his "reputation as a fearless officer."[14]

Like Tom Smith, Jerry Barling was shot to death soon after leaving Wyoming. Apparently still grieving over the loss of his young wife and baby in 1886, Jerry returned to Texas drinking freely. His brother Frank opened a new saloon in El Reno, twenty-five miles west of Oklahoma City. Fort Reno was a few miles to the west, but the town boomed with the famous Land Rush of 1889. In April 1893 Jerry went to El Reno to visit Frank and perhaps to help with the business. His principal activity, however, was consuming the saloon's product. One night, trying to return to Frank's home, he blundered to the wrong house.

After a stay of only four or five days, in the early morning hours of Tuesday, April 25, Jerry drunkenly collapsed on a back porch, again seeming to have missed Frank's house. The building was Smith's Restaurant, which contained living quarters in the rear for proprietor Delancey Smith and his family. Mrs. Smith was aware that someone was on the back porch, and she roused her husband at about four in the morning. Smith took his shotgun and ordered the unwanted visitor to leave. Mumbling a refusal and insisting that he was coming inside, Jerry grabbed the shotgun barrels and shoved Smith backward. After a brief scuffle the gun discharged, striking Jerry in the left leg. He collapsed and quickly bled to death, while Smith hastened to the police station. The local

A drunken Jerry Barling was killed in El Reno, Oklahoma, soon after returning from Wyoming. (Group photo, courtesy Wyoming State Museum)

newspaper observed that "Barling is said to have been drinking heavily all day yesterday and was under the influence of liquor at the time of the shooting and had a Colt .45 caliber six-shooter on his person."[15]

Buck Garrett returned to Ardmore, where he married Ida May Chancellor in 1893. Buck and Ida had one son, Raymond, born in 1896. Buck continued to ride as a posseman with his father-in-law, Deputy U.S. Marshal J. M. Chancellor. When helping to arrest a defiant Oscar Finley in 1894, the big posseman used his handcuffs to pound the horse thief into submission. In 1896 Buck was sworn in as a deputy marshal. Continuing to perform impressively, he was presented a silver-mounted, pearl-handled .38-caliber Colt revolver by an admirer in 1899.[16]

Buck left the federal force in 1902, but soon he became Ardmore's chief of police. In 1906, while attending a cattleman's convention in Oklahoma City, the genial Buck spent an evening with friends in Eva Ryan's "immoral resort." About three o'clock in the morning, with liquor flowing freely, an argument caused a man to assault Buck with a knife. Buck pulled a gun, but his first shot went wild, fatally wounding bystander Jim Peters. Peters was Buck's friend, and Garrett eventually was cleared of charges.[17]

In 1910 Buck won election as sheriff of Carter County (Ardmore was the county seat). Although intimidating to lawbreakers, Buck had an engaging personality and proved to be a natural politician. He joined the Woodmen of the World and the Benevolent Protective Order of the Elks, and he enjoyed a legion of friends. Sheriff Garrett won re-election five times, serving until 1922. In 1913 an oil field was developed in Carter County, and Ardmore became a boomtown. Backed by his lethal undersheriff, Bud Ballew, Garrett controlled his rowdy county with an able touch. Between 1915 and 1919, Ballew killed nine men in seven gunfights. During one of his three fatal shootouts in 1919, Deputy Ballew was assisted by Sheriff Garrett in gunning down two thieves during a robbery on the outskirts of Ardmore. (In 1922 the volatile Ballew was wounded during a wild shootout inside

Buck Garrett's ornate badge as police chief of Ardmore. He later was repeatedly elected county sheriff, although his tenure proved controversial. (Author's collection)

228

OFFICE OF

BUCK GARRETT
SHERIFF OF CARTER COUNTY
SAM HARRIS
UNDER SHERIFF

FIELD DEPUTIES:

FRED WILLIAMS, Ardmore
JAKE WILLIAMS, Ardmore
HORACE KENDALL, Ardmore
BILL BROOKS, Ardmore
FOOT DILLARD, Wilson

ARDMORE, OKLA.,

CARTER COUNTY COURT HOUSE

Letterhead of Sheriff Buck Garrett. (Author's collection)

Ardmore's courthouse, and a few weeks later he was shot dead during an angry encounter with the chief of police of Wichita Falls, Texas.)[18]

Sheriff Garrett eventually was accused of taking payoffs to allow prostitution, gambling, and violation of prohibition laws. Charges were filed late in 1921, and in 1922 the sheriff was removed from office. That same year he ran for sheriff again, and he continued to present himself—unsuccessfully—as a candidate every two years for the remainder of his life. Buck suffered a series of strokes, became estranged from his wife, and in 1925 was charged by the Internal Revenue Service with tax evasion in excess of $30,000. He was bedridden during his last campaign in 1928. But his wife returned to his side, and when he died in 1929, at the age of fifty-seven, he was widely lauded. More than one hundred honorary pallbearers were named for the funeral services of a pioneer lawman who "was covered with the glamour of the old days."[19]

Another Texan who had hired his guns in Wyoming—to the other side—also became a revered law enforcement figure in Oklahoma following the Johnson County War. Frank Canton, still a fugitive from Texas justice as Joe Horner, utilized influence from his prominent friends to obtain a full pardon from Governor James Hogg in 1894. Canton moved his family to Pawnee, Oklahoma, where he worked as county under-

sheriff and as a deputy U.S. marshal. In Pawnee in 1894, Canton shot suspected horse thief Lon McCool in the head and, in 1896, he killed fugitive Bill Dunn near the courthouse. The next year, answering the call of adventure while avoiding a potential controversy in the marshal's office, Canton journeyed to Alaska as a deputy U.S. marshal. In Alaska he was snowed in one winter, went prospecting

Frank and Annie Canton and their daughter, Ruby, about two years after the Johnson County War. (Courtesy Johnson County Jim Gatchell Memorial Museum)

229

on one occasion with Rex Beach, curtailed the lawless element in roaring Dawson, and otherwise enjoyed an exciting two years. In 1899 Canton went snow blind and returned to his wife and daughter, who had been staying with relatives in Buffalo.[20]

It was Canton's first visit to Buffalo since the Johnson County War, and hard feelings still existed. Now fifty years of age, Canton was badly pummeled during an altercation at the Occidental Saloon. Even so, the resilient Canton began working as a bounty hunter, before moving back to Oklahoma as a stock detective for the Texas Cattle Raisers Association. For several years Canton pursued rustlers with his old relentlessness, but without the murderous rumors that surrounded his tenure as a stock detective in Wyoming.

In 1907, through a fortunate political connection, Canton was appointed adjutant general when Oklahoma achieved statehood. General Canton commanded the Oklahoma National Guard for a decade and, resplendent in handsome uniforms, became a prominent figure at public events. Resigning when the Oklahoma Guard was about to be nationalized during the First World War, Canton went back to work for the Texas Cattle Raisers Association. He began writing article-length accounts of his adventures, and his autobiography was published three years after his death.

Canton died at seventy-eight in 1927. He lay in state in his general's uniform at the capitol in Oklahoma City, and his funeral featured Masonic rites and military honors.

A less renowned officer, Deputy U.S. Marshal Bill Little, returned to Texas and con-

Frank Canton (middle row, fourth from left) capped his career by serving as adjutant general of Oklahoma from 1907 to 1916. (Courtesy Western History Collections, University of Oklahoma Library)

tinued to work for years out of the Paris office. In October 1898 he led a posse to arrest "the celebrated Creek criminal John Watko, and his gang." The lawmen located the outlaws in a log cabin and advanced in force. The cornered gang opened fire with

Winchesters, but the range was too great. The posse, armed with more powerful rifles (Little had been given a lesson about superior firepower at the TA Ranch) took cover and began to blast the cabin with steel-jacketed bullets. One slug fatally wounded Watko. The gang tried to flee. Two of the outlaws were captured, while the other three managed to escape. Perhaps this latest firefight soured Little on law enforcement, or maybe he wanted another adventure in a faraway locale. By the next year he was threatening to turn in his badge "and go to South Africa to fight the Boers."[21]

After returning to Texas, Deputy U.S. Marshal Bill Little continued to work out of the Paris office. (Group photo, courtesy Wyoming State Museum)

Kinzie Pickard, among other Invaders, had all of the adventure he wanted in Wyoming. Nearly forty-two yeas old, Kinzie returned to Texas to live quietly with his family. Early in the twentieth century Kinzie and Lou Pickard moved to Jumbo in Pushmataha County, Oklahoma. Kinzie farmed and served as a precinct inspector for the remainder of his life. He died at the age of sixty-nine in 1931 and was buried in the Jumbo Cemetery. Lou lived until 1955, and their house was torn down in 1992.[22]

Like the other commissioned officers, George Tucker returned to his duties as soon as he reached Texas. He worked at least one case with Tom Smith before Tom was shot to death. For the next several years he rode frequently with his old friend and fellow deputy, Jeff Mynett. Most of their pursuits and arrests continued to take place in Indian Territory. In 1897 a new marshal took office in Paris, and Tucker, along with several other deputies, decided to transfer to Ardmore, where Buck Garrett was chief of police. Working out of Ardmore, in the fall of 1897 Tucker tracked Henry Mashore, involved in a recent train robbery at Chickasha. Tucker located Mashore at the home of Bob Terrell near Atlee. Mashore, spotting Tucker riding up, sprinted away with a Winchester in his hand. Tucker opened fire on Mashore, then was startled when Terrell triggered a Winchester round from less than twenty paces away. He missed, however, and Tucker shot him in the chest. Terrell collapsed and died without uttering a word. As had happened several times in the past, charges were filed against Tucker, but once again he won acquittal.[23]

When a new marshal took office in 1901, Tucker turned in his deputy's badge. "The general character of the work had changed completely since the old days," he explained. "One was now a process server, not a man hunter." For the next several years Tucker "drifted about," but in 1908 the fifty-three-year-old warhorse was selected chief of police of Waurika. After four years in office, Tucker returned to Ardmore to serve as assistant chief of police under an old friend, Chief Dave Booker. Three years later a stroke ended his long career as a lawman. Later he held commissions as a meat inspector and a game warden, "but that was puny work."[24]

In 1935, when he was eighty, Tucker produced reminiscences which totaled more than one hundred typed pages. Although apparently edited for publication, the manuscript was never published. In addition to the fifteen-page chapter on "The Wyoming Cattle War: 1892," much of the rest of the manuscript offers material on other Wyoming participants. Tucker's manuscript, on file at the Western History Collections of the University of Oklahoma, offers the most detailed and colorful recollection left by any of the Texas Invaders.

Chapter 20

Aftermath in Wyoming

"Hello, I understand that you are trying to kill me."

MIKE SHONSEY TO DUD CHAMPION

On Monday, April 3, 1893, the twenty-first annual meeting of the Wyoming Stock Growers Association convened in Cheyenne. Only a little more than two months had passed since the end of the trial, but several of the principals gathered in Cheyenne for the meeting. John Clay presided. Vice-President George Baxter and Secretary H. B. Ijams would continue to serve the WSGA for two more years, while Treasurer Henry Hay would remain in office until 1903.

In his keynote address, President Clay recounted "the so-called 'Invasion of Johnson County.'" Point by point he described the illegal forces which had inflamed the cattlemen, and he made it clear that he stood behind "the very flower of Wyoming's citizens, who had taken part in the expedition. . . . Gentlemen, I am not here to defend these parties," continued Clay. "Technically, legally, they did wrong, but I consider it no mean privilege to stand in this prominent position today and to say that I count everyone of them a friend. Notwithstanding their errors of judgment, we respect them for their manliness, for their supreme courage under the adverse fire of calumny, and the usual kicking a man when he gets down."[1]

Following Clay's remarks, Billy Irvine took the floor to offer an impromptu statement from a member of the expedition. "I tell you," he concluded, "I am tired of being kicked, cussed, cuffed and damned for what I believe to be the right thing." Irvine was generally respected and admired for his bold actions on behalf of Wyoming ranchers. In 1896, after John Clay stepped down following five years as WSGA president, Irvine was elected to succeed him. Irvine served until 1911, and his fifteen-year tenure was the longest in WSGA history.[2]

By 1895 the number of cattle in Wyoming had dropped to 300,000, perhaps one-third the total of a decade earlier, and sheep raisers drove large flocks onto Wyoming's grasslands. But most cattle ranchers and cowboys reflexively detested sheep and sheep-

Annual meetings of the WSGA were held in Cheyenne's Opera House. (Author's collection)

Pinkerton detective Tom Horn, using the alias "Thomas H. Hale," was in Johnson County by the spring of 1892 investigating the murder of George Wellman. There was suspicion that he was involved in other drygulchings of the Johnson County War. (Courtesy Arizona Historical Society Library)

herders. Despite their loss of preeminence and the widespread public criticism generated by the Johnson County invasion, Wyoming cattle ranchers met this new threat with violent resistance. In 1893 and 1894 there were several raids on sheep camps in Converse County by cattlemen enforcing "deadlines" they had announced. Wearing gunnysack masks, on different occasions these raiders shot and clubbed sheep, burned sheep wagons, and wounded or otherwise mistreated several sheepherders. No legal action was taken against the gunnysackers. In 1893 Wyoming cowboy Virgil Turner killed a sheepherder after initiating gunplay. In January 1894 more than 100 cattlemen and cowboys worked together to drive flocks from southwestern Wyoming, suffering no legal repercussions.[3]

During this period, Tom Horn began working for the interests of Wyoming cattlemen. A noted scout of the Apache wars, a Pinkerton detective, and a skilled cowboy and outdoorsman, Horn was in Wyoming by 1892, sent from Denver by the Pinkerton agency. (After Horn became famous as an assassin, suspicions grew that he was involved in the murder of John A. Tisdale and other Johnson County drygulchings, a view that is upheld by the distinguished western historian Robert K. DeArment and by Bob Edwards, a resourceful scholar of the Johnson County War.) In May 1892, using the alias "Thomas H. Hale," Horn was one of several men deputized by Marshal Joe Rankin to investigate the murder of George Wellman. "Hale was, and is, a Pinkerton man," Rankin later explained, "brought from Denver by the cattlemen, and appointed a deputy at their solicitation." Horn/Hale was selected by the cattlemen "because of his particular fitness for the work," noted Rankin. "When I was in Johnson County in September I questioned Mr. Hale as to why he had been unable to accomplish anything in the arrest of the six or seven men for whom we then had warrants, and rather complained to him because he had not done something in the matter. He said, 'I will be frank with you and state that I am instructed, through my office in Denver, to take no instructions from you whatever; that the cattlemen are our clients, and we are working for their best interests. My instructions from the Denver office were to try to drive the men out of the country and not arrest them. If they were arrested, and taken to Cheyenne and the evidence was not sufficient against them, they would be turned loose.'" In 1893 Horn was employed by the Swan Land and Cattle Company as a stock detective, and for the next several years his lethal skills were put to use by various Wyoming ranchers.[4]

In May 1893 a shooting in eastern Wyoming resulted in the death of Dudley Champion, brother of the martyred Nate, at the hands of Mike Shonsey. Sheriff

Malcolm Campbell reported that Dud Champion recently had been found "hiding in the brush near Billy Irvine's Ogallala ranch, and had been ordered away by Scott Davis." Champion angrily "threatened to kill various invaders on sight, Shonsey among them." Shonsey had been released from custody five

Mike Shonsey was heavily involved in the events of the Johnson County War, including the shooting death of Dud Champion. Shonsey prudently moved to Nebraska, where he raised a large family. The last surviving principal of the famous range war, he died in 1954 at eighty-seven. (Group photo, courtesy Wyoming State Museum)

months earlier with the other defendants and had returned to the 77 Ranch, just north of Manville. The 77 was part of George W. Baxter's Western Union Beef Company.[5]

Shonsey told his version of the story to a friend, Russell Thorp. On Monday afternoon, May 22, Shonsey rode out to check on a Texas trail herd being driven to the north. The trail driver arranged with Shonsey to pasture his remuda overnight. At that point Shonsey noticed an approaching rider, who twice pulled the brim of his hat low across his face. Sensing danger, Shonsey gripped his revolver. Finally recognizing Dud Champion, Shonsey called out, "Hello, I understand you are out to kill me."[6]

Although Champion growled that the accusation was "a damn lie," he reportedly reached for his pistol. But Shonsey whipped out his gun and triggered a shot. The bullet slammed into Champion's right side, knocking him out of the saddle. Champion fell on his back with his head toward Shonsey. Gripping his gun in both hands, he pointed the weapon above his head in the direction of Shonsey, who fired again.

With Champion dead, Shonsey asked the trail boss to ride into Lusk, about ten miles to the east, and inform the authorities. Shonsey then rode to his home at the 77 Ranch and changed clothes. Mounting a fresh horse, he rode through the night for nearly sixty miles to Douglas, where presumably he felt more secure under the jurisdiction of Sheriff Malcolm Campbell.[7]

The day after the killing, a posse rode out from Douglas to recover Champion's body. The coroner of Converse County impaneled three men as a coroner's jury, which inspected the site of the killing, four miles west of the 77 Ranch headquarters. The jury

Cabin of Arapahoe Brown. Nicknamed because of a relationship with an Arapahoe woman, he became a field commander during the siege of the TA, the high point of his life. (Courtesy Johnson County Jim Gatchell Memorial Museum)

236

determined that "the said Michal [sic] Shonsey was in danger of his own life from the hands of the said Dud Champion," and that Shonsey fired his pistol "in self defense of his own life" and "was justified by so doing." For the second time in 1893, the Wyoming legal system had cleared Mike Shonsey of any charges related to a killing. Prudently deciding not to press his luck, Shonsey moved to Nebraska, where he would raise a family and spend the rest of his long life.[8]

Among those who suspected ulterior motives in Champion's death was Asa Mercer, who asserted that Dud was killed because cattlemen felt that he would seek revenge for the murder of his brother. "A living Champion was looked upon as a constant menace—therefore, no Champions must be permitted to live." Mercer wrote that during a "pleasant conversation" around the campfire, Shonsey shot Champion dead without warning. The killer rode into Lusk, where a "preliminary hearing" ruled that "Shonsey fired in self-defense." Shonsey took the next train to Cheyenne, "settled up with George W. Baxter," then left Wyoming. According to Mercer, other witnesses soon appeared who "claimed that Champion had made no gun play and that his killing was unprovoked, cold-blooded murder on the part of Shonsey," but their arrival was too late to alter the coroner's inquest. (Of course, Mercer's depiction of these witnesses may have been as accurate as his version of the "preliminary hearing" in Lusk, which actually was conducted by officials from Douglas and which was filed there, not in Lusk.) Mercer wrote his account of the Johnson County War in *The Banditti of the Plains, or the Cattlemen's Invasion of Wyoming in 1892* [*The Crowning of the Ages*], completed in February 1894.[9]

In a brief Preface, Mercer proclaimed his book to be "an honest statement of the facts as they occurred. Personal acquaintance with the principal actors and accurate general knowledge of the country and its conditions, have given me unusual facilities for gathering reliable data.

Red Angus left the sheriff's office in 1893, but in later years he served as deputy county clerk and as county treasurer. Angus married in 1894, and he belonged to the Odd Fellows, the Masons, and the Grand Army of the Republic. He ran the Occidental Hotel for a few years, and Laurel Avenue—where he once had operated a dive—was renamed for him. Angus died at seventy-two in 1922 and was buried in Willow Grove Cemetery. (Photo by Karon O'Neal)

Every statement herein made is backed up by readily accessible proof."[10] Mercer included the George Dunning confession in an appendix. *Banditti of the Plains* was severely critical of the cattlemen, who certainly did not regard Mercer's book as "an honest statement of the facts."

Banditti of the Plains was printed at Mercer's expense in Denver in August 1894. Vague tales have been handed down that cattlemen obtained an injunction after filing a libel suit, that "the entire issue was impounded by a local court and ordered destroyed," and that Mercer suffered personal intimidation. But historian Lewis Gould learned that Mercer and his two sons traveled safely from town to town in northern Wyoming during September 1894, openly peddling copies of the book. "Further," stated Gould, "no evidence has been found to support the stories of book burning, injunctions, or personal threats against Mercer." An exhaustive study convinced Gould that: "The Mercer legend will not withstand critical examination. Acting from material motives, not disinterested concern for the oppressed, Mercer used the Johnson County invasion to further his own personal fortunes." But *Banditti* produced little improvement in Mercer's fortunes. His

Frances Warren, a Wellesley graduate and daughter of Sen. Francis Warren, married a dashing cavalry officer, John J. Pershing. The couple is pictured with their first two daughters and their son, Francis Warren Pershing. Another daughter soon joined the family. Tragically, Frances Pershing and her three daughters perished in a fire in 1915. (Courtesy Library of Congress)

job as state statistician ended in 1895, and he moved his family from Cheyenne to a homestead in the Big Horn Basin, near Hyattsville. Mercer penned a few more books, but none made any literary impact. He died in 1917 at the age of seventy-eight.[11]

Soon after the publication of *Banditti of the Plains,* Francis Warren and Willis Van Devanter engineered a Republican comeback in the November elections. In the wake of the Johnson County invasion, Democrats enjoyed victory in November 1892. John E. Osborne succeeded Amos Barber as Wyoming's first Democratic governor, and the Democrats won Warren's Senate seat. But leading Democrats battled among themselves for the Senate prize, and none could win the twenty-five votes necessary in the Legislature. In 1894 victorious Republicans returned Warren to the vacant Senate seat, which he retained until his death in 1929. An intelligent and highly respected politician, the Medal of Honor winner chaired the Senate Committee on Military Affairs and the Committee on Appropriations. As senator from the first equal-suffrage state, Warren worked diligently for the Eighteenth Amendment, and he was so persistent in efforts to reclaim arid lands that he was nicknamed the "Father of Reclamation." A fellow senator also called him "the greatest shepherd since Abraham," because the Warren Live Stock Company ran vast flocks of sheep along with cattle and horses. Francis Warren served as president of the National Wool Growers Association from 1901 to 1907, with no loss of political popularity.[12]

In 1905 Warren's daughter, Frances, married a dashing cavalry officer, Capt. John J. Pershing. The following year Captain Pershing was promoted over 862 senior officers, vaulting an unprecedented four ranks to brigadier general. Tragically, Frances Pershing and her three daughters died in a fire at the Presidio in San Francisco; only young Warren Pershing survived.

Senator Warren's first wife died in 1902, but he remarried nine years later. When Senator Warren died at the age of eighty-five, he was the last Union soldier to serve in Congress.

When Republicans regained Warren's Senate seat in 1894, they also recaptured the governor's office. The Johnson County War no longer exercised statewide political significance, and the deposed John Osborne would prove to be the only Democrat among Wyoming's first seven governors. Finally, in 1910, Joseph M. Carey returned to state politics, winning the governorship as a Democrat. Carey and Warren, of course, had entered the Senate at the same time, when Wyoming became a state. Warren's abbreviated term lasted only two years, but Carey served a full six

Senator Warren died in 1929 and was buried in Cheyenne. (Photo by Karon O'Neal)

years. In 1894 Senator Carey was responsible for the Carey Act, which authorized the Secretary of the Interior to patent up to one million acres of arid land to each of ten western states or territories, provided the lands were reclaimed or irrigated in small parcels to settlers. Wyoming was the first state to apply under the Carey Act, which remains in effect today.[13]

But Senator Carey's opposition of Free Silver cost him considerable support, and he became estranged from his longtime friend and political ally, Francis Warren. Carey was excluded from Wyoming's Republican inner circles and was not returned to the Senate in 1896. Carey concentrated on his livestock interests and the promotion of irrigation projects until 1910, when he announced his candidacy for governor. Unable to secure the Republican nomination, he accepted an offer from the Democrats and ultimately enjoyed an overwhelming victory to a four-year term. Governor Carey secured voting reforms that included the secret ballot, the direct primary, and ratification of the amendment for the direct election of senators. He established for Wyoming penal reform and a boys' industrial school. Living until his eightieth year, Carey saw his elder son, Robert, follow in his steps as WSGA president (1914-17) and as governor (1919-23).

Although statewide politics seemed little changed by the Johnson County War, the effects of the Invasion were deep and long lasting in and around Buffalo. Most Buffalo citizens, having been the subject of a warlike invasion, harbored an understandable bitterness against the Invaders and big cattlemen. This resentment was passed on to later generations until it became reflexive. While little boys in other communities played Cowboys and Indians, Buffalo children engaged in Cowboys and Rustlers. Adults considered it prudent not to discuss the subject. "I know more than one man in those days who took 'the last ride' just because he talked too much," claimed homesteader A. P. Dow. Dow, who had begun farming in the area in 1882, wanted no part of the hostilities: "I made up my mind, just as soon as I got a whiff of the trouble, that I would stand by and watch the show go on. And I did."[14]

Most people realized that Dow's noncommittal approach was wise, and it became habitual to be tight-lipped about the Johnson County War. During the 1930s, a WPA interviewer asked Charles Basch, eyewitness to the murder of John A. Tisdale, why "peo-

From Mercer's Belles to the Banditti

Asa Shinn Mercer was born in 1839 in Illinois. He completed college in 1861, then ventured west to visit his brother in Washington Territory, where he decided to settle. By 1864 Mercer had launched a scheme to bring marriageable women from the East to Washington. Mercer traveled to the East Coast, secured funds and transportation for forty-six single women, then journeyed with them to the Pacific Northwest. The arrival of the "Mercer's Belles" gained him a great deal of welcome publicity.

Mercer moved to Oregon for the next several years, continuing to publicize the Northwest until he finally relocated to Texas in 1876. In Texas he became a journalist, publishing a total of four newspapers over the next seven years. In 1883 he moved his family to Cheyenne, where he originated *The Northwestern Live Stock Journal*. Through his *Live Stock Journal*, Mercer became a journalistic champion of Wyoming cattlemen, who supported his newspaper with advertising. But after nearly a decade of being a ranchers' partisan, Mercer switched sides in a desperate attempt to save his failing newspaper. He criticized the cattlemen and their expedition, he printed George Dunning's confession, and he wrote *The Banditti of the Plains*, which gained him even more notoriety than "Mercer's Belles."

ple around Buffalo don't like to talk about the invasion." "Because it didn't pay to talk for years before or after the invasion," replied Basch, by now in his eighties. "You know Arapahoe Brown was killed and his body burned," insisted the old man, suggesting that another participant had been slain by Joe LeFors and Billy Irvine. "That's why people didn't talk in Johnson County."[15]

The fear of deadly retribution became ingrained throughout the area. During the second decade of the twentieth century, for example, a skeleton with its head bashed in was found in southern Montana. A homesteader speculated that the death was because of "the settling of some old grudge left over from the Johnson County War. We were not a great distance from the area where this trouble took place and it was then, and still is, a touchy subject."[16]

Robert Foote's store, where guns and ammunition had been dispensed to the besiegers of the TA, burned in 1895. Maj. Frank Wolcott wisely departed the region for Nebraska in 1894, working as a general agent at the Omaha stockyards, and later living in Grand Island and Lincoln. But certain prominent citizens of Buffalo who had supported big cattlemen ignored all pressure to leave their homes. Attorney Charles Burritt, for example, was sufficiently respected to win reelection as mayor until 1897. Banker Will Thom was elected to terms in each house of the Wyoming Legislature, where he was instrumental in the passage of a bill that partially reimbursed Johnson County for legal expenses.[17]

Former Invader Fred G. S. Hesse likewise refused to surrender the ranch he had built south of Buffalo. For a year following the Invasion, Hesse lived in Cheyenne, after sending his wife and children to the safety of relatives in Delaware. Then Hesse determined to resume family life at the ranch. He would overcome hard feelings by becoming a community leader. Ignoring lingering hostility, Hesse expanded his business interests into Buffalo. He presided over the Buffalo Manufacturing Company, and in 1898 Hesse and a partner bought the local electric plant. Hesse served as director of the First National Bank, and he and Will Thom organized the Wyoming Loan and Trust Company in 1906. That same year the Hesse family began running sheep on their land.

Hesse's son, Fred W., was elected first president of the Johnson County Wool Growers Association. Fred W. later became president of the Wyoming Loan and Trust Company, while also serving on the school board. All three of his daughters became Buffalo teachers. Fred W.'s sister, known to everyone as "Miss Vivienne," was a stalwart of the Episcopal Church and a beloved member of the community.[18]

Through long and productive service the Hesse family overcame enmities generated by the Johnson

Overcoming considerable local enmity, Fred G. S. Hesse remained in Buffalo to become one of its most successful citizens, as reflected by the prominent location of the family plot in Willow Grove Cemetery. (Photo by Karon O'Neal)

County War. When he was eighty years old, Fred W. Hesse reflected that "there is a degree of fraternal spirit between those of us that remain on both sides, because all have been subjected to uncalled for criticism, not so much from each other, but by rank outsiders. It was our fight," he added pointedly, "it was private, and should have been left that way."[19]

The "fraternal spirit" that Hesse observed ultimately reunited the citizens of Buffalo and Johnson County. Noted western novelist Elmer Kelton related to the author an encounter he had with a fellow soldier during World War II. The serviceman told young Kelton that he was from Buffalo, Wyoming. "Isn't that where they had the big cattle war?" asked Kelton. "Oh, yeah," replied the third-generation Buffalo resident. "I had a grandfather on both sides."[20]

So the old wounds healed in Johnson County. Homesteaders continued farming activities, and most ranches became relatively small operations. Increasingly, sheep replaced cattle on Johnson County ranges, but there was little of the violence between cattlemen and sheepherders that plagued other ranges in Wyoming.

Despite the quiet resolution of old wounds in Johnson County, generations of outsiders have remained fascinated by the spectacular events of 1892. Although Fred W. Hesse insisted that "our fight . . . was private, and should have been left that way," interest in the Johnson County War was so deep and widespread that it has commanded the steady efforts of novelists, historians, and filmmakers.

Chapter 21

"When You Call Me That, Smile!"

"County helps tell the world its story!"
BUFFALO *BULLETIN,* JUNE 14, 2001

The Johnson County War was a story worth telling, and the story began to be told almost immediately. Like other dramatic, violent events, the Johnson County War inspired the creative efforts of such chroniclers as novelists, balladeers, historians, and filmmakers. Owen Wister's novel, *The Virginian*, would exert a major impact on the popular culture of the Old West. Another classic novel inspired by the Johnson County War, *Shane*, was made into one of the greatest Westerns ever filmed. And one of the most spectacular flops ever filmed, *Heaven's Gate*, was an expensive but incoherent version of the famous range war. In 2002, one hundred and ten years after the Johnson County War, a new documentary and a fresh TV movie about the conflict appeared on the nation's small screens. For more than a century, then, the Wyoming range war has been reflected in folk ballads, novels, motion pictures, history books and articles, and television documentaries. Featuring cattle barons, cattle thieves, hired gunmen, vicious murders, heroic deeds, and a magnificent frontier setting, the Johnson County War always has radiated the power to grip the popular imagination.

Following the 1889 lynching of Ella Watson and Jim Averell, "the Ballad of Cattle Kate" began to be sung. Ten four-line verses told a sad story:

> *She was quickly hung by the neck*
> *From the limb of a scrub pine tree,*
> *Overpowered by strong men,*
> *Pushed off into eternity.*[1]

The murder by ambush of Ranger Jones and John A. Tisdale in 1891, on November 28 and December 1, respectively, inspired Patrick Burns, an Eighth Infantry musician stationed at Fort McKinney, to compose "The Murder of Tisdale and Jones." Burns sug-

243

gested that the ballad should be sung to the tune of "Poor Old Dad," and the twenty-four lines were sympathetic to the murdered men:

> *Pierced in the back by bullets while returning to their homes,*
> *They were shot out on the prairie and made the dust to bite,*
> *For afraid the cruel assassin was to meet them in a fight.*[2]

The murder of Nick Ray and the heroic stand of Nate Champion stimulated folk singers to fashion "The Ballad of Nate Champion," "The Invasion Song," and "Our Heroes' Grave." "The Ballad of Nate Champion" began: *"It was a little blood-stained book which a bullet had torn in twain/It told the fate of Nick and Nate, which is known to all of you."* "The Invasion Song" opens with the lines: *"Sad and dismal is the tale I now relate to you/'Tis all about the cattlemen, them and their murderous crew."* There is heartfelt praise for *"poor Nick and Nate, who gave their precious lives/To save the town of Buffalo. . . ."* "Our Heroes' Grave" also sings the praises of Nate Champion: *"His rifle he grasped and fought all day/ For many long hours he'd held them at bay."* Before the Texas gunmen were released from custody, before legal action against the cattlemen was halted in Cheyenne, ballads were being sung about the Johnson County War.[3]

In 1892 Jack Flagg furiously wrote his first-person account of the conflict. Before the end of 1893, Asa Mercer began composing the passionate history he entitled *The Banditti of the Plains.* Such nonfiction accounts would provide invaluable information

The cabin in Medicine Bow where Owen Wister stayed has been restored as a museum honoring the famous author. (Photo by Karon O'Neal)

244

and viewpoints. But the most important book to be influenced by the Johnson County War was a novel.

The Virginian was published a decade after the Johnson County War. Dedicated to his friend and Harvard classmate, President Theodore Roosevelt, Owen Wister's spectacularly successful book was released by the Macmillan Company on May 30, 1902. Within three months sales passed 100,000, then continued to soar as the public responded to Wister's tale of the Wyoming cattle country.[4] He already had introduced the Virginian in short stories; his first Western novel, *Lin McLean,* was published in 1898; and a collection of short Western fiction, *The Jimmyjohn Boss and Other Stories*, was published in 1900. But *The Virginian* was special, with its authentic background taken from Wister's journals, and a title character who would become the prototypical Western hero in countless novels, movies, short stories, and television shows. The Virginian was strong, brave, honest, and dangerous with guns or fists. But he was gentle and courtly with women, and despite his obvious leadership abilities, he was modest and quiet-spoken. And after being called a dirty name by the villainous Trampas, the Virginian uttered the most famous line in Western fiction: "When you call me that, smile!"[5] Until 1902 the cowboy story had been confined primarily to dime novels for juveniles, but *The Virginian* revealed the enormous appeal of tales of the cattle frontier for more mature audiences.

This landmark book is filled with individuals, anecdotes, and places that would have been recognizable to Johnson County War participants. The title character was based primarily on Wister's friend, George West, a Wyoming rancher who was not involved in the war. But ranch owner Judge Garth was modeled after Maj. Frank Wolcott. The rise of cattle stealing in Wyoming and the fictional attempts to combat rustlers in *The Virginian* were inspired by occurrences which led to the clash in Johnson County. The next-to-last paragraph in the book ended in a comment that reflected Wister's position: "Then, in 1892, came the cattle war, when, after putting their men in office, and coming to own some of the newspapers, the thieves brought ruin on themselves as well. For in a broken country there is nothing left to steal."

With the reading public captivated by *The Virginian*, widespread demand arose for a stage version. In 1903 Wister penned a four-act play based on his novel, and he composed musical introductions to the last three acts. *The Virginian* opened on Broadway at the Manhattan Theater on January 5, 1904. Tall, lean Dustin Farnum proved to be a striking embodiment of the strong, quietly courageous hero. Following a solid four-month run in New York, *The Virginian* went on the road. For more than a decade the show was a perennial favorite in theaters across the country.[6]

In this same period the American public developed a seemingly insatiable appetite for Western motion pictures. In 1903 *The Great Train Robbery,* a "Western" filmed in New Jersey, created a sensation as the first movie to tell a story. During the next few years the first movie star, Broncho Billy Anderson, offered filmgoers a sturdy Western hero in a new motion picture each week (*Broncho Billy and the Posse, The Escape of Broncho Billy, Broncho Billy's Mexican Wife,* etc.). In 1914 William S. Hart, an experienced stage actor who had played in *The Virginian,* began starring in Western films as a strong, tight-lipped hero along the lines of Wister's famous characters.

The first sound version of The Virginian *(1929) featured young Gary Cooper (left) telling Walter Huston (right, as Trampas), "When you call me that, smile."* (Author's collection)

Also in 1914 Paramount released the first film version of *The Virginian*. Directed by young Cecil B. DeMille, in his first solo assignment, the movie starred Dustin Farnum. Film superstar Douglas Fairbanks was captivated by *The Virginian*, and he paid $55,000 for movie rights. Reluctantly he decided that he was too short of stature to fulfill the image of a tall Western hero, so the second silent version of *The Virginian* was released in 1923 with Kenneth Harlan in the title role.[7]

The first sound version was produced in 1929 by Paramount, with lanky young Gary Cooper as the Virginian. Walter Huston was superb as Trampas, while an actor from Virginia, Randolph Scott, was hired for a bit part and as a dialect coach for Cooper. Paramount filmed *The Virginian* again in 1946, starring Joel McCrea who, like Cooper, was an expert horseman. The movie was shot in color. Pretty Barbara Britton played Molly and Sonny Tufts was excellent as the tragic Steve, but Brian Donlevy was miscast as Trampas. Two years earlier, a John Wayne movie, *Tall in the Saddle*, centered around the KC Ranch. In a scene reminiscent of the entrapment of Nate Champion and Nick Ray, the bad guys open fire on John Wayne and Gabby Hayes while they are holed up in a line shack.

When Westerns became popular on television, Wister's masterpiece was an in-

Like The Virginian, *the classic Western novel and movie* Shane *features a one-name hero involved in a Wyoming range war.* (Author's collection)

evitable series property. *The Virginian*, starring James Drury, debuted over NBC-TV in September 1962. The first weekly series to run for ninety minutes, *The Virginian* was a Wednesday night staple for nine seasons.[8] Drury made a cameo appearance in a 2000 TV movie, *The Virginian*. There were authentic costumes and sets, and lovely Diane Lane was fine as Molly, but Bill Pullman was weak in the title role.

Another Western classic, *Shane*, was strongly influenced by the Johnson County War. Jack Schaefer's novel, published in 1949, featured a strong, taciturn hero with one name who rides into the midst of a conflict between a cattle baron and homesteaders in a valley "nearly a full day's ride" from Sheridan (Buffalo is thirty-three miles from Sheridan).[9] The film, released by Paramount in 1953, starred Alan Ladd in the title role, while Jack Palance was nominated for an Academy Award for his sinister portrayal of a murderous gunfighter imported from Denver by the local cattle baron. In addition to his evil hired gun, the rancher's cowboys were arrogant bullies. And where Wister's hero helps the ranchers against the rustling element, Shane successfully fights for the homesteaders. Filmed by George Stevens in Wyoming's Grand Teton Mountains, *Shane* became one of the most famous Western movies of all time. Various sources point out that "the story of *Shane* is based on the Johnson County War, the archetypal cattlemen-versus-homesteaders conflict that serves as the background for *The Virginian* and *Heaven's Gate*."[10]

Heaven's Gate attempted to tell the story of the Johnson County War, but became one of the monumental disasters of film history. *Heaven's Gate* starred Kris Kristofferson as Harvard-educated Jim Averell—an odd combination, since there were Harvard men among the cattle barons, but the real-life Jim Averell was a homesteader who was lynched along-side Cattle Kate (Ella Watson) in 1889. In *Heaven's Gate,* Ella is shot to death in 1892 by Frank Canton, who is promptly slain by Averell! And the "cattle thieves and anarchists" of Johnson County in *Heaven's Gate* were socialistic Bulgarian immigrants. Director Michael Cimino produced visual magnificence, but the story line, mixing actual people and events with incongruously fictional insertions, proved confusing and unengaging. Furthermore, the handsome but lengthy film went dangerously over budget. Released in 1980 at a cost of $36 million, an incredible sum for the time, *Heaven's Gate* ran a confusing 219 minutes. It was immediately pulled from theaters for additional ed-iting. When re-released in 1981, *Heaven's Gate* still was an incomprehensible dud, and again it was pulled from theaters.[11]

In Heaven's Gate, *an expensive but confused movie about the Johnson County War, Kris Kristofferson plays Harvard-educated Jim Averell, who kills Frank Canton!* (Author's collection)

The most distorted version of the Johnson County War was presented in a 1955 episode of *Stories of the Century*, a weekly television series which claimed to tell true stories of the Old West. Each half-hour episode was said to be "Based on Official Newspaper Files and Records." The series star was Jim Davis, who played railroad detective Matt Clark. Introducing the episode on Nate Champion, Clark claimed that Champion, "a fugitive from most of the Southwestern states, moved on to Wyoming in 1892. He became one of the most feared, big-scale cattle rustlers in history, and struck a savage blow against Wyoming's struggle for survival."

The opening scene finds Champion being kicked out of Colorado by the local cattlemen's association. Champion is placed on a Wyoming-bound stagecoach, where his fellow passengers are Englishmen: Roger Benton and his ward, Joan Jamison. Benton has just purchased a ranch near Casper (the town of Buffalo is never mentioned), and since he does not "know a steer from a giraffe," he innocently employs Champion as his foreman. Champion hires a crew "of other desperate men" and steals so many cattle that the "Great Western Ranch" cancels a contract to supply beef to Wyoming's railroad construction crews. This crisis brings railroad detectives Matt Clark and Margaret Jones to the scene. Clark tells "Sheriff Smith" that he arrested Nate Champion two years earlier in Texas for stealing cattle from a stranded freight train. But Champion shot two guards and escaped custody.

Champion's chief henchman, Nick Ray, murders an old rancher named Riley, while Roger Benton is killed by his evil ward. The entire gang is attacked at the Benton Ranch by the detectives and Sheriff Smith and a posse. When Nate Champion and Nick Ray escape, they are pursued to Riley's KC Ranch by Matt Clark and Sheriff Smith. Champion and Ray open fire from the KC cabin, but Ray is fatally wounded by Clark. Another shot shatters a lantern and sets the cabin ablaze. Champion writes a note implicating Joan Jamison, then bolts outside firing his revolver.

"On the afternoon of April 7, 1892," narrates Clark, "Nate Champion found death as he ran from a flaming shack, a dangerous outlaw up until the final second of his life. His accomplice, Joan Jamison, was tried and convicted of Benton's murder."

Margaret Jones jokes to Matt Clark that if there is another epidemic of cattle theft, the railroad will have to "find a few thousand vegetarians" to lay track. This closing remark is about as plausible as the rest of the episode.

In the meantime, novelists continued to create reflections of the Johnson County War. Frederick Manfred published *Riders of Judgment* in 1957. Manfred's book offers a detailed portrayal of the Johnson County War, while changing the names of the individuals. The novel centers around Cain Hammett (who is the author's version of Nate Champion). Cain's brother Henry (Dudley Champion) is the leader of the Red Sash Gang. Another Hammett brother, Dale (Ranger Jones) is drygulched while bringing supplies and Christmas presents to his wife and children. Avery Jimson (Jim Averell) and Cattle Queen (Cattle Kate) are lynched in the same manner as their real-life counterparts. The ranks of the big cattle ranchers include titled Englishmen and Harvard graduates, along with a pompous, plump, former Union major, Wallace Tascott (Frank Wolcott), Irving Hornsby (Billy Irvine), and Jesse Jacklin (Fred Hesse), who, as manager of an Englishman's ranch, was rumored to have acquired 5,000 head of his employer's cattle. The cattle barons are supported by Governor Dexter Barb (Amos Barber) and Senator John Thorne (Francis Warren). The primary killer-stock detective is Hunt Lawton (Frank Canton), who had changed his name from Link Keeler (Joe Horner). But Hunt Lawton also displays many characteristics of Tom Horn, even announcing that, "Killin' is my specialty." [12] Therefore, Manfred's chief villain is a combination of Frank Canton and the enigmatic Tom Horn who, despite his fearsome reputation in Wyoming, played no apparent role in the Johnson County War.

Geographical features, such as the Crimson Wall (Hole-in-the-Wall), the Big Stonies (Big Horn Mountains), and the Bitterness River (Sweetwater River), are as easy to identify as the characters. Antelope (Buffalo) is the seat of Bighorn County (Johnson County). The big ranchers are organized into the powerful State Cattlemen's Association (WSGA), and in Cheyenne they enjoy the Cactus Club (Cheyenne Club, described in meticulous detail).

The storyline closely follows the events of 1891-92, climaxing with Cain Hammett

"Ridin' for the Brand"

The public reservoir of memories about the Johnson County War includes novels, films, songs, poems, history books—and a striking sculpture on the Main Street of Buffalo. Created by local artist Michael Thompson, the bronze grouping features a cowboy with a downed maverick lassoed to the saddle horn of his nearby horse. The cowboy is startled by the approach of a mounted stock detective. Armed with a Winchester, the detective bears a strong resemblance to Frank Canton.

Standing in a natural setting at the south end of Buffalo's commercial district, the bronze figures comprise a permanent interpretation of the town's most spectacular event. "Ridin' for the Brand" is handsome and evocative, one of the best pieces of cowboy-gunfighter art anywhere in the West.

The bronze sculpture group, "Ridin' for the Brand," was commissioned by Buffalo's First National Bank a century after the Johnson County War. (Photo by Karon O'Neal)

being besieged in his cabin by half a hundred ranchers and Texas gunmen. The siege is virtually identical to the fight at the KC cabin, except that before he is gunned down while sprinting toward the ravine, Cain kills five of his adversaries and wounds another dozen—a toll which Nate Champion would have envied. Because of the delay caused by Cain's heroic battle, the citizens of Antelope are able to sally forth and arrest the invaders. *Riders of Judgment* is a well-written and fascinating fictional account of the Johnson County War.

Another distinguished Western novelist, Oakley Hall, also utilized elements of the Johnson County War. *The Bad Lands,* published in 1978, centers on the story of Theodore Roosevelt and the Marquis de Mores around Medora, Dakota Territory, in the 1880s. Hall's classic novel, *Warlock,* published in 1958 with a movie version the next year, was a free interpretation of Tombstone, Wyatt Earp, Doc Holliday, and the shootout at the OK Corral. In *Warlock* as well as *The Bad Lands*, Hall changes the names of all characters and places, and he takes considerable artistic license with historic events. As *The Bad Lands* builds to a climax, Hall introduces a Johnson County-style invasion in Dakota Territory in 1884. "The Battalion," with fifty hired gunmen from Texas and Denver, is led by a "pigeon-chested"[13] Major Cutter. The Battalion besieges the Crowe brothers in a line shack, but soon find themselves pinned down by an army of citizens in the headquarters buildings of the CK Ranch. Major Cutter negotiates a truce, and the resulting trial proves to "be a farce."[14]

In 1976, two years before *The Bad Lands* was published, *Invasion of Johnson County* aired on television. The made-for-TV movie starred Bill Bixby in a modest retelling of the famous range war (Bixby had headlined such television comedies as *My Favorite Martian, The Courtship of Eddie's Father,* and *Goodnight, Beantown*). A one-hour *Real West* documentary, *The Johnson County War,* was aired in 1994. Narrated by country music star Kenny Rogers, the documentary has been rerun numerous times over The History Channel.

In June 2001 a California production crew filmed footage in Johnson County for a five-minute segment of a History Channel documentary about violence in the Old West. The production crew had the impression that the only reminder of the Johnson County War was "the remains of a falling down barn." But citizens of Buffalo enthusiastically introduced the producer to the Jim Gatchell Museum, the TA Ranch, the Occidental Hotel, and Tisdale Gulch. When the filmmakers began pondering the problems of assembling horses, wagons, weapons, costumes, and stunt men, local boosters began spreading the word. Within two days fifty "actors" had volunteered to fill the roles of cowboys, gunmen, and saloon girls. Costumes, horses, tack, wagons, and guns were donated for the project. "County helps tell the world its story," proclaimed a front-page headline of the Buffalo *Bulletin.* The newspaper was filled with color photos of citizens who, like their Buffalo predecessors who turned out to meet the Invaders of 1892, volunteered to recreate the proud and colorful heritage of their community.[15]

During the fall of 2002, The Hallmark Channel presented, in two parts, a four-hour TV movie, *The Johnson County War.* The title, suggesting a film version of the events involving Frank Canton, Nate Champion, Major Wolcott, Fred Hesse, *et al*, was misleading. *The Johnson County War* was based on Frederick Manfred's novel, *Riders of Judgment.*

Burt Reynolds starred as Hunt Lawton, the Frank Canton character, while Tom Berenger was cast as Cain Hammett, the fictional version of Nate Champion. Reynolds was chilling as the cold-blooded killer, and he bore a close resemblance to Frank Canton. Berenger was sturdy and courageous as the heroic opponent of the cattle barons and their gunmen, while television heartthrob Luke Perry portrayed his brother, Harry Hammett. Larry McMurtry contributed his talents as a screenwriter and executive producer.

The film features magnificent western vistas and, allowing for artistic license, scenes which bring the Johnson County War to cinematic life. The climactic scene is the assault upon Tom Berenger's cabin by nearly fifty ranchers and gunmen. Berenger's partner is shot down when he emerges from the cabin, but the fast-shooting Berenger drags him back inside. During the course of the siege, Berenger blasts five of his attackers with a shotgun, while drilling twelve more with a Winchester. His wounded partner accounts for two men before dying. Luke Perry, galloping past the cabin like Jack Flagg, shoots seven of the besiegers—with his sixgun. Burt Reynolds and two of his men ride in pursuit, but Perry kills all three. Meanwhile, two of the ranchers angrily shoot each other, making a total of thirty-one (out of fifty) casualties. A blazing "Go-Devil" flushes Berenger from his burning cabin, but moments after he is killed, Perry leads the citizens of Antelope onto the scene. The depleted force of attackers surrenders, expecting to be rescued by their powerful friends. But with more than half of their number killed by Tom Berenger and company, the cinematic Invaders receive harsher justice than their counterparts of 1892.

For more than a century novelists, historians, and filmmakers have depicted and interpreted the dramatic, violent story of this legendary range war. And in addition to books, articles, documentaries, and movie representations, there remain many tangible reminders of the Johnson County War. At the TA Ranch, Barb and Earl Madsen have worked resourcefully to preserve the rich heritage of their historic old spread. The TA now is a guest ranch, and it is possible to sleep beneath quilts in the sturdy log cabin that offered protection to the Invaders in 1892. Climbing into the loft of the most famous barn in the West, a modern visitor may peer out of the loopholes augured by Texas defenders. In 1999 the Madsens acquired Frank Canton's log cabin and later moved it to the TA, less than three miles from its original location at the Canton ranch.

Although ranch buildings no longer exist at the old KC headquarters, the site of Nate Champion's heroic defense is marked in the town of Kaycee, which also boasts the Hoofprints of the Past Museum. Another historical marker designates Tisdale Gulch, the murder site on the road from the TA into Buffalo.

In Buffalo the Jim Gatchell Memorial Museum exhibits a treasure trove of artifacts from the Johnson County War. Adjacent to the museum looms the 1884 courthouse, which still dominates Buffalo's main street. Just south of town, on a peaceful, shaded hill, is Willow Grove Cemetery, principal repository for Johnson County War veterans. Fittingly, Nate Champion and Nick Ray rest side by side. Ranger Jones is nearby, and so is fellow drygulch victim John A. Tisdale. Fred G. S. Hesse secured a prominent hillside location for himself and his family. Sheriff Red Angus was buried at Willow Grove, along with many of the men who followed him out of town to do battle with the Invaders.

Frank Canton's ranch cabin was moved in 1999 two miles from its original site to the TA Ranch. (Photo by Karon O'Neal)

The TA barn today includes an addition to the rear and west (left). But the loopholes augured by the 1891 defenders may be readily seen in the loft. (Photo by Karon O'Neal)

A couple of miles west of Buffalo, at the Wyoming Veterans' Home, offices are housed in a wing of Fort McKinney's old hospital, where wounded Texans Alex Lowther and Jim Dudley died. Although modern buildings were erected on the former parade ground, a long commissary warehouse and one or two other military structures still stand from 1892.

Fort Fetterman, a stopoff for the captive Invaders and their cavalry escort, is maintained as a Wyoming State Park. The Invaders also were scheduled to be held at the Wyoming Penitentiary outside Laramie. Although they found quarters elsewhere in Laramie, the venerable prison, handsomely restored, today is the centerpiece of Wyoming Territorial Park.

The Invaders were confined at length at Fort D. A. Russell, now F. E. Warren Air Force Base. The base museum is located beside the big parade ground of old Fort D. A. Russell, and a number of buildings from the 1892 era still are maintained. But the Invaders' "confinement" was rather loose, and they spent time in nearby Cheyenne, where they would have seen the State Capitol and the Union Pacific Depot and a number of commercial buildings and Victorian homes which continue to grace the city. Several elegant homes also would be recognized in Paris, Texas, by the Texas recruits.

In Paris and Cheyenne and Buffalo, at the TA Ranch and old Fort McKinney and Laramie, a modern visitor can view many of the sights and, perhaps, sense some of the ghosts of 1892.

Rest in Peace

1889	Ella "Cattle Kate" Watson, lynched, 27
	Jim Averell, lynched, 34
1890	Tom Waggoner, lynched
	Orley E. "Ranger" Jones, drygulched, 27
	John A. Tisdale, drygulched, 36
1891	Nick Ray, murdered, 27
	Nate Champion, murdered, 34
	Jim Dudley, accidentally shot
	Alex Lowther, accidentally shot
	Deputy U.S. Marshal George Wellman, drygulched, 33
	Deputy U.S. Marshal Tom Smith, shot on a train
1893	Jerry Barling, shot in El Reno, Ok., 30
	Dudley Champion, shot by Mike Shonsey, 34
1896	Ed Starr, shot in Montana
1901	President Benjamin Harrison, pneumonia, 67
1902	Tom Horn, hanged, 42
1907	John Durbin, 64
1909	Tom Sun, 68
1910	Maj. Frank Wolcott, 69
1919	George Dunning, 59
1921	Robert B. Conner, 72
1922	Sheriff Red Angus, 72
1923	Bob Barling, appendicitis, 57
1924	Senator Joseph M. Carey, 74
	William C. "Billy" Irvine, 72
1927	Frank Canton, 78
	David E. Booker, 76
1928	Albert Bothwell, 72
1929	Senator Francis E. Warren, 85
	Fred G. S. Hesse, 75
	Buck Garrett, stroke, 57
	Phil DuFran, 75
1931	Kinzie Pickard, 69
1932	Malcolm Campbell, 93
1933	Owen Wister, 78
1939	Robert Galbraith, 95
1954	Mike Shonsey, 87

Appendix

When a history book is published, renewed interest is stimulated in the subject and new information is often unearthed. Usually the author is frustrated because the new items cannot be included in the book. But with this Special Edition, released just one year after the initial publication of *The Johnson County War*, I enjoy the welcome luxury of providing readers with seven additional discoveries, ranging from unpublished photos to unearthed documents to fresh anecdotes. In addition to the four extras in this Appendix, there are three other extras on pages 113, 144, and 224.

I am grateful to Bob Edwards, of the Jim Gatchell Museum, and to Jim Headley, of the Buffalo *Bulletin*, for steering me to new information, as well as to Virginia Messer, of Eakin Press, for making this Special Edition available.

Previously unpublished photo of Nate Champion, standing at left. The strong brotherly resemblance indicates Dudley Champion, seated at right. Standing at right is a Wyoming cowboy known as "Pine Tree Pete" Watkins, while Lee Moore is seated at left. The man standing at center is unknown. The photo was taken in Chicago, probably in early 1891. (Courtesy Johnson County Jim Gatchell Memorial Museum)

Hall Cabin

During the winter of 1891-92, Nate Champion rented a homestead cabin from brothers Charlie and Bill Hall. The log cabin was sheltered by a bluff on Middle Creek in Hole-in-the-Wall country. A slumbering Champion and cowboy Ross Gilbertson were jumped at dawn on November 1, 1891, by several stock detectives, but Nate courageously routed his attackers.

Eventually the roof deteriorated and the cabin fell apart. But in 2004 the historic one-room structure was rebuilt on its original foundation stones, and in July a large crowd gathered to celebrate the event.

Reconstructed Hall Cabin on the day of its dedication.

Charging Documents of the
Johnson County Invaders

In May 2005, staff members of the clerk of the Johnson County District Court office were cleaning the records room in Buffalo's historic old courthouse. Also present was the editor of the Buffalo *Bulletin*, Jim Headley, who was conducting historical research. On May 18 thirteen folders were discovered, containing the original documents charging the Invaders of Johnson County with the murders of Nick Ray and Nate Champion.

The documents are in pristine condition, apparently never having left the Johnson County courthouse during the trial proceedings in Cheyenne and Laramie. Twelve of the four-page documents are identical, each one charging three or four of the Invaders with the murder of "Reuben N. Ray" (revealing for the first time that Nick Ray's first name was Reuben) and "a certain person" (Nate Champion, for some reason unnamed). The thirteenth document charged Dr. Charles Penrose, even though he was not present at the KC Ranch. Presumably Johnson County authorities hoped to connect Penrose with his friend and fellow physician, Acting Governor Amos Barber. Prominent cattlemen R. S. Van Tassell and Henry G. Hay provided Barber's bond.

Jim Headley was kind enough to telephone the author with news of this exciting discovery. The following month in June 2005 I traveled to Buffalo, and Jim provided me with copies of the documents. Now, of course, I wonder what future treasures will surface in Buffalo's court house or in the archives of the Jim Gatchell Museum.

(See photocopy of sample legal document, next page.)

STATE OF WYOMING,)
) ss.
County of Johnson.)

                                    In the District Court,
                                       For said County.

THE STATE OF WYOMING,   )
         ..... Plaintiff.)
         vs.   )
)
CHARLES B. PENROSE,   )
Otherwise called Dr. Penrose.
         .....Defendant.   )

                    MOTION FOR CONTINUANCE.

     Comes now said defendant and moves the court to con-

tinue the above entitled cause until the next term of court, for

the reason that the said defendant cannot attend the present term

of said court without greatly endangering his life, as will more

fully appear by the affidavits herewith filed.

                              Lacey VanDevanter
                              Attorneys for Defendant.

One of fifteen pages in the document folder charging Dr. Penrose.

Recently discovered photograph of "Fort Wolcott," the redoubt erected by the Defenders on a rise west of the TA barn. (Courtesy Johnson County Jim Gatchell Memorial Museum)

Endnotes

Chapter 1: A Visitor to Wyoming

1. Wister, 1885 Journal, Owen Wister Collection, American Heritage Center (Laramie, Wyoming), 3-5.

2. An authoritative biography of Wister was written by Darwin Payne, *Owen Wister.* Also see Fanny K. Wister, "Letters of Owen Wister," Pennsylvania *Magazine of History and Biography*, and Fred Erisman and Richard Etulain, eds., *Fifty Western Writers.*

3. Wister, 1885 Journal. 4.

4. John Clay, *My Life on the Range,* 143-44.

5. Wister, 1885 Journal, 5.

6. *Jack of Spades,* 13; Clay, *My Life on the Range,* 142; and Dan Thrapp, *Encyclopedia of Frontier Biography,* Vol. III, 1587.

7. Wister, 1885 Journal, 12.

Chapter 2: The Ranching World Changes

1. T. A. Larson, *History of Wyoming,* 114.

2. John W. Reps, *Cities of the American West,* 529.

3. *Ibid.,* 526, 529, 533-34.

4. Cited by Bickel in his article on Van Devanter in the *Dictionary of American Biography, Supplement III,* 788-89.

5. Moreton Frewen, *Melton Mowbray and Other Memories;* Woods, *Moreton Frewen's Western Adventures*; Woods, *British Gentlemen in the Wild West.*

6. Brisbin, *The Beef Bonanza,* 15.

7. For Clay's life and career, see John Clay, *My Life on the Range,* and Lawrence Woods, *John Clay, Jr.* Swan quote: William H. Forbis, *The Cowboys,* 64.

8. Clay, *My Life on the Range.*

9. *Ibid.,* 73, 242, 257, 265, 282; Margaret Hanson, *Powder River Country,* 256-57.

10. Clay, *My Life on the Range,* 152.

11. *Ibid.,* 176-77.

12. Hanson, *Powder River Country,* 241.

13. Clay, *My Life on the Range,* 144, 178-79; Hanson, *Powder River Country,* 242.

14. Clay, *My Life on the Range,* 180.

15. Larson, *Wyoming,* 128.

Chapter 3: The Wyoming Stock Growers Association

1. There are three institutional histories of the WSGA: Agnes Wright Spring, *Seventy Years: A Panoramic History of the Wyoming Stock Growers Association,* 1942; Maurice Frink, *Cow Country Cavalcade, Eighty Years of the Wyoming Stock Growers Association,* 1954; and John Rolfe Burroughs, *Guardian of the Grasslands, The First 100 Years of the Wyoming Stock Growers Association,* 1971. The WSGA's stock detective activities were explored in a 1948 master's thesis by Rebecca Bailey,

"Wyoming Stock Inspectors and Detectives, 1873-1890." Files of the WSGA are available at the American Heritage Center, University of Wyoming. John Clay, who joined the WSGA in 1883 and served as president from 1890 to 1895, discusses the association intimately and in meticulous detail in *My Life on the Range*. Also see W. Turrentine Jackson, "The Wyoming Stock Growers Association," *Agricultural History*, Vol. XXII, 1948.

2. Spring, *Seventy Years,* 73. John Clay stated that membership reached 400, while Maurice Frink said the total was 443.

3. Clay, *My Life on the Range,* 245.

4. *Ibid.,* 251.

5. Spring, *Seventy Years,* 74, 81.

6. *Ibid.,* 73-74, 84.

7. Joseph M. Carey biographical file, Wyoming State Historical Society, Cheyenne.

8. Francis E. Warren biographical file, Wyoming State Historical Society, Cheyenne.

9. Bailey, "Wyoming Stock Inspectors and Detectives, 1873-1890," 135, 137, 139.

10. *Ibid.,* 135.

11. Spring, *Seventy Years,* 93; Frink, *Cow Country Cavalcade,* 55; Charles Penrose, *The Rustler Business,* 8.

12. Clay, *My Life on the Range,* 269-70.

13. *Ibid.,* 268-69.

14. Frank M. Canton, *Frontier Trails,* 80.

15. *Ibid.,* 270.

16. Clay, *My Life on the Range,* 269-70.

17. *Ibid.,* 270.

18. Bailey, "Wyoming Stock Inspectors and Detectives, 1873-1890," 135, 149.

19. Correspondence cited in Bailey, "Wyoming Stock Inspectors and Detectives, 1873-1890," 151.

20. *Ibid.,* 150.

21. The definitive biography of Horner/Canton was written by Robert K. DeArment, *Alias Frank Canton.* Canton's autobiography, *Frontier Trails,* describes his early years, but makes no mention of his outlaw career.

22. Canton, *Frontier Trails,* 81.

23. Bailey, "Wyoming Stock Detectives and Inspectors," 69.

24. Canton, *Frontier Trails,* 80-82.

25. Chip Carlson, *Joe LeFors,* 69.

26. Frink, *Cow Country Cavalcade,* 90.

27. Canton, *Frontier Trails,* 91.

28. Correspondence cited in Bailey, "Wyoming Stock Inspectors and Detectives," 156.

29. *Ibid.,* 158.

30. Clay, *My Life on the Range,* 146.

Chapter 4: Johnson County: Future Battlefield

1. Fort McKinney is described in Robert Murray, *Military Posts in the Powder River Country of Wyoming,* 119-39, and Herbert Hart, *Old Forts of the Northwest,* 165-66.

2. For a thorough description of Buffalo and its citizens and happenings, see Buffalo's Centennial Book Committee, *Buffalo's First Century.*

3. Robert Murray, *Johnson County, 175 Years of History at the Foot of the Big Horn Mountains,* 72. This book offers a comprehensive and authoritative account of the county's institutions and events.

4. *Big Horn Sentinel,* February 20, 1886.

5. *Ibid.,* November 21, 1885.

6. Fanny Wister, ed., *Owen Wister Out West,* 116-17.

7. *Big Horn Sentinel,* November 1, 1884.

Chapter 5: Vigilante Background

1. An extensive history of the vigilante movement was presented by Richard Maxwell Brown in *Strain of Violence, Historical Studies of American Violence and Vigilantism* (New York: Oxford University Press, 1975.) Also see Frank Richard Prassel, *The Great American Outlaw, A Legacy of Fact and Fiction* (Norman: University of Oklahoma Press, 1993), W. Eugene Hollon, *Frontier Violence, Another Look* (New York: Oxford University Press, 1974), and Wayne Gard, *Frontier Justice* (Norman: University of Oklahoma Press, 1949).

2. Brown, *Strain of Violence*, 59-60.

3. *Ibid.*, 95, 113, 115.

4. *Ibid.*, 97, 105-06, 126-27, 163-67.

5. *Ibid.*, 109-10, 305-19.

6. Robert B. David, *Malcolm Campbell, Sheriff*, 18-21.

7. Granville Stuart, *Forty Years on the Frontier*, 195.

8. *Ibid.*, 196-197.

9. *Ibid.*, 196.

10. *Ibid.*, 197.

11. Barrows, *U-bet*, 204.

12. Stuart, *Forty Years on the Frontier*, 202-5.

13. *Ibid.*, 208.

14. Abbott, *We Pointed Them North*, 135.

15. Stuart, *Forty Years on the Frontier*, 209.

16. Abbott, *We Pointed Them North*, 135.

17. Roosevelt, *Ranch Life in the Far West*, 53.

18. Wallis Huidekoper, quoted in Brown and Felton, *Before Barbed Wire*, 119.

19. Abbott, *We Pointed Them North*, 134.

20. Stuart, *Forty Years on the Frontier*, 196, 209.

21. Robert K. DeArment to the author, March 7, 2002.

22. Brown, *Strain of Violence*, 101.

Chapter 6: The Killing Begins

1. Cheyenne *Daily Leader*, July 23, 1889.

2. John Clay, *My Life on the Range*, 272-73.

3. Charles Penrose, *The Rustler Business*, 17.

4. Lamar, ed., *Reader's Encyclopedia of the American West*, 182.

5. Helena H. Smith, *War on Powder River*, 122-23.

6. George Hufsmith, *The Wyoming Lynching of Cattle Kate*, 35-37.

7. *Ibid.*, 59-80.

8. *Ibid.*, 94-102, 131-39.

9. *Ibid.*, 139-52.

10. *Ibid.*, 42-44, 152, 211.

11. *Ibid.*, 113-20.

12. *Ibid.*, 108-13.

13. *Ibid.*, 103-07.

14. *Ibid.*, 120-26.

15. *Ibid.*, 126-29; Spring, *Seventy Years*, 252.

16. The lynching is described from all available sources by Hufsmith, *The Wyoming Lynching of Cattle Kate*, 179-200.

17. Cheyenne *Daily Sun*, July 25, 1889.

18. Hufsmith, *The Wyoming Lynching of Cattle Kate*, 238-46, 275-76, 282-83.

19. Penrose, *The Rustler Business*, 17.

20. A. S. Mercer, *Banditti of the Plains*, 19.

21. Hufsmith, *The Wyoming Lynching of Cattle Kate*, 285-89.

22. *Ibid.*, 286-87, 289-300; Spring, *Seventy Years,* 252-53, 258.

23. Clay, *My Life on the Range,* 271-74.

24. *Ibid.*, 273.

25. *Ibid.;* Wister Papers, June 25, 1891.

Chapter 7: The Troubles of 1891

1. Wister Papers, June-September 1892.

2. Roger Hawthorne, "Conflict and Conspiracy," *True West* (June 1984), 13-17.

3. *Ibid.*, 16.

4. *Ibid.*, 13-17.

5. Robert B. David, *Malcolm Campbell, Sheriff,* 142-43.

6. Charles Penrose, *The Rustler Business,* 17.

7. For a contemporary account of this event see the Buffalo *Bulletin,* June 25, 1891, which quotes the Newcastle *Journal.*

8. Hawthorne, "Conflict and Conspiracy," *True West,* 16-17.

9. Dunning confession in Mercer, *Banditti of the Plains,* 159.

10. *Ibid.*, 157.

11. Maurice Frink, *Cow Country Cavalcade,* 138; Frank M. Canton, *Frontier Trails,* 91.

12. David, *Malcolm Campbell, Sheriff,* 17; Penrose, *The Rustler Business,* 13-14.

13. Buffalo *Bulletin,* July 23, 1891.

14. John Clay, *My Life on the Range,* 276.

15. *Ibid.*

16. Margaret Hanson, ed., *Powder River Country,* 259-60; Dunning confession in Mercer, *Banditti of the Plains,* 172-73.

17. Champion's description of the incident was in the Buffalo *Bulletin,* December 17, 1891, and February 11, 1892. Champion also gave an account to William A. Martin, on page 15 of Martin's manuscript.

18. Carr related his story in 1935 to J. Elmer Brock. Hanson, ed., *Powder River Country,* 259-60.

19. Buffalo *Bulletin,* December 17, 1891.

20. Hanson, ed., *Powder River Country,* 269.

21. Dunning confession in Mercer, *Banditti of the Plains,* 157-58.

22. Buffalo *Bulletin,* May 14, 1891.

23. Letter from Fred G. S. Hesse, published in Buffalo *Bulletin,* July 2, 1959; Buffalo's Centennial Committee, *Buffalo's First Century,* 160-61; Fred G. S. Hesse, Biographical File, Johnson County Public Library; Lawrence Woods, *British Gentlemen in the Wild West,* 124; Buffalo *Bulletin,* June 2, 1892.

24. Letter from Hesse, Buffalo *Bulletin,* July 2, 1959.

25. Hanson, ed., *Powder River Country,* 201, 242. Jones usually is referred to as twenty-three, but the date of birth on his gravestone in Buffalo is October 7, 1864, which indicates that he was twenty-seven when he was killed.

26. Hanson, ed. *Powder River Country,* 261-62.

27. *Ibid.*

28. *Ibid.*; Buffalo *Bulletin,* December 10, 1891; Cheyenne *Daily Leader,* December 6, 1891.

29. Hanson, ed., *Powder River Country,* 267-68.

30. *Ibid.*, 267, 408-09; Penrose, *The Rustler Business,* 13.

31. Frink, *Cow Country Cavalcade,* 139.

32. Martin manuscript, 17.

33. Buffalo *Bulletin,* December 3 and 16, 1891.

34. The story of Tisdale's murder and aftermath is detailed in testimony reprinted in the Buffalo *Bulletin,* December 10, 1891, and in the Cheyenne *Daily Leader,* December 5, 1891.

35. *Ibid.*, and Hanson, ed., *Powder River Country,* 263-66.

36. Buffalo *Bulletin,* December 3, 1891.

37. *Ibid.,* December 5 and 10, 1891. The story of the lathered horses was told to the author by Col. Bob Edwards of Buffalo, who twice interviewed a grandson of one of the ladies.

38. Frank Canton, *Frontier Trails,* 84.

39. Buffalo *Bulletin,* December 10, 1891.

40. Hanson, ed., *Powder River Country,* 266.

41. Buffalo *Echo,* December 12, 1891.

42. Buffalo *Bulletin,* December 10, 1891.

43. Canton, *Frontier Trails,* 84.

44. Penrose, *The Rustler Business,* 17.

45. Mercer, *Banditti of the Plains,* 26.

46. Buffalo *Bulletin,* November 26 and December 24, 1891.

47. Cheyenne *Daily Sun,* December 25, 1891; Cheyenne *Daily Leader,* December 25, 1891.

48. Robert deArment, *Alias Frank Canton,* 113-14.

49. Cheyenne *Daily Leader,* December 27, 1891.

Chapter 8: Organizing the Expedition

1. Frank Canton, *Frontier Trails,* 87.

2. Buffalo *Bulletin,* February 11, 1892.

3. *Ibid.*

4. Charles Burritt to W. R. Stoll, May 6, 1892.

5. Quoted in Helena H. Smith, *The War on Powder River,* 159.

6. John Clay, *My Life on the Range,* 278-79; Charles Penrose, *The Rustler Business,* 18-19.

7. Penrose, *The Rustler Business,* 5, 19; Clay, *My Life on the Range,* 279.

8. Robert B. David, *Malcolm Campbell, Sheriff,* 151, 153.

9. Penrose, *The Rustler Business,* 22.

10. *Ibid.,* 20.

11. *Ibid.,* 19.

12. Sam T. Clover, *On Special Assignment,* 221-31.

13. David, *Malcolm Campbell, Sheriff,* 154-55; Penrose, *The Rustler Business,* 20.

14. Canton, *Frontier Trails,* 87; Robert deArment, *Alias Frank Canton,* 116-19.

15. Dunning confession, in A. S. Mercer, *Banditti of the Plains,* 171.

16. *Kingfisher Free Press,* November 10, 1892.

17. The Jaybird-Woodpecker Feud is described in C. L. Sonnichsen, *I'll Die Before I'll Run,* 232-81. Explanatory material also is on display at the Fort Bend County Museum in Richmond, Texas.

18. Harold Preece, *Lone Star Man,* 194-95.

19. *Kingfisher Free Press,* November 10, 1892.

20. Tucker manuscript, 47-50.

21. Dunning confession, in Mercer, *Banditti of the Plains,* 155-56, 159-60, 162.

22. *Ibid.,* 159-66.

23. *Ibid.,* 169-74.

24. *Ibid.,* 170.

25. Agnes Wright Spring, *Seventy Years,* 100.

26. Maurice Frink, *Cow Country Cavalcade,* 140; Dunning confession, in Mercer, *Banditti of the Plains,* 176.

27. Dunning confession, in Mercer, *Banditti of the Plains,* 174-75.

28. Penrose, *The Rustler Business,* 24.

Chapter 9: The Texas Gunmen

1. Statistics about the number, location, and chronology of gunfights have been compiled by Bill O'Neal, *Encyclopedia of Western Gunfighters,* 4-7, 10-14.

2. For a description of Paris and Lamar County, see A. W. Neville, *The History of Lamar County, Texas.*

3. The 1889 judicial expansion is described by Glenn Shirley, *West of Hell's Fringe,* 16, and by Judge Robert A. Burns, Paris, in a letter to James F. Barling (September 20, 1987). Also see George Tucker manuscript, 35.

4. Judge Robert A. Burns to James F. Barling (September 22, 1987).

5. Tucker manuscript, 72, and Dunning confession in A. S. Mercer, *Banditti of the Plains, 159.*

6. Information about the Barlings was provided to the author by Jim Barling, grandson of Robert G. Barling. Jim has collected family correspondence, obituaries, and geneaology information, including Dorothy Greenman Lee, *The Barling Family,* 206-220.

7. Frank R. Barling to R. C. Barling (August 22, 1891).

8. Deck, *Sheriffs of Carter County,* 9; obituary, McAlester *News-Capital* May 6, 1929); Riotte, "Buck Garrett, Man and Legend," *True West* (January-February 1970), 22-25, 44-45.

9. Helena H. Smith, *The War on Powder River,* 189, 211-12.

10. Information about Kinzie Pickard, including his full name, was provided to the author by genealogical researcher Kay Black of Antlers, Oklahoma.

11. Ardmore *Daily Press* (January 13, 1927); *Daily Ardmoreite* (January 13, 1927).

12. Tucker manuscript, 44, 65-70.

13. *Ibid.,* 1.

14. *Ibid.,* 3-9.

15. *Ibid.,* 10-11.

16. *Ibid.,* 11-12.

17. *Ibid.,* 12-14.

18. *Ibid.,* 14-17.

19. *Ibid.,* 15-17.

20. *Ibid.,* 18-19b.

21. *Ibid.,* 19b-20.

22. *Ibid.,* 20-22.

23. *Ibid.,* 23-26.

24. *Ibid.,* 26-28, 28b.

25. *Ibid.,* 35-36.

26. *Ibid.,* 35, 39-47.

27. *Ibid.,* 54-55.

28. *Ibid.,* 38-39, 59-60.

29. *Ibid.,* 45, 50-54, 56-59, 70-71.

30. *Ibid.,* 72.

31. *Ibid.,* 72-73.

32. *Ibid.,* 73, 83.

33. *Ibid.,* 73.

34. *Ibid.*

35. *Ibid.,* 74.

Chapter 10: Invasion: The First Four Days

1. George Tucker manuscript, 74.

2. *Ibid.,* and Charles Penrose, *The Rustler Business,* 24.

3. Frank Canton, *Frontier Trails,* 88-89; Dunning confession, in A. S. Mercer, *Banditti of the Plains,* 236; and Penrose, *The Rustler Business,* 23.

4. Penrose, *The Rustler Business,* 23.

5. *Ibid.,* 24. Ed David's son, Robert, would write *Malcolm Campbell, Sheriff,* published in 1932.

6. Penrose, *The Rustler Business,* 23-24.

7. Dunning confession, in Mercer, *Banditti of the Plains,* 178; Penrose, *The Rustler Business,* 24-25.

8. Todd interview, in Margaret Hanson, ed., *Powder River Country,* 293-94.

9. Dunning confession, in Mercer, *Banditti of the Plains* 178-79; William Martin manuscript, 37-39.

10. Penrose, *The Rustler Business,* 25; Tucker manuscript, 74.

11. Penrose, *The Rustler Business,* 25-26.

12. Dunning confession, in Mercer, *Banditti of the Plains,* 179; Penrose, *The Rustler Business,* 23-24. When Dr. Penrose decided to write his account of the Johnson County War, he corresponded with Billy Irvine, whose letters are quoted in *The Rustler Business.*

13. Sam T. Clover, *On Special Assignment,* 238-39; Canton, *Frontier Trails,* 89.

14. Penrose, *The Rustler Business,* 26; Dunning confession, in Mercer, *Banditti of the Plains,* 179.

15. George Dunning confessed that Shonsey said "there were 15 or 16 rustlers" (Mercer, *Banditti of the Plains,* 179). Dr. Penrose recalled that Shonsey "gave the information that fourteen rustlers had been the previous evening at the KC. ranch" (*The Rustler Business,* 26). Billie Martin remembered hearing that there were "several rustlers encamped at the neighboring ranch" (Martin m.s., 39). The Tisdale cowboys told the Texas gunmen "that there was a big dance over at the Kaycee ranch and that the rustlers were there" (Tucker manuscript, 75).

16. Clover to Blair (May 15, 1892), cited in Brayer, "New Light on the Johnson County War," *Westerners' Brand Book,* 1953; Penrose, *The Rustler Business,* 26.

17. Dunning confession, in Mercer, *Banditti of the Plains,* 180.

18. *Ibid.*; David, *Malcolm Campbell, Sheriff,* 179.

19. Tucker manuscript, 75; Clover, *On Special Assignment,* 241.

20. Penrose, *The Rustler Business,* 26; Clover, *On Special Assignment,* 240-41.

21. Dunning confession, in Mercer, *Banditti of the Plains,* 180-81. Dunning, who had only been around the Texans for three days, listed them as "Jack Jones, Elick Kinzie and one of the Bookers" (there was only one Booker).

22. David, *Malcolm Campbell, Sheriff,* 187. David wrote his book three decades after the Johnson County War, but with his close connections he heard details that are unavailable elsewhere.

Chapter 11: Last Stand at the KC

1. Dunning confession, in A. S. Mercer, *Banditti of the Plains,* 181.

2. Sam Clover said the main body rode away for the TTT at nine o'clock (*On Special Assignment,* 240); Dr. Penrose said it was at one o'clock (*The Rustler Business,* 26); George Tucker said it was "the middle of the night" (Tucker manuscript, 75).

3. Clover, *On Special Assignment,* 242.

4. *Ibid.,* 243; Irvine to Penrose, *The Rustler Business,* 27.

5. Clover, *On Special Assignment,* 243; Dunning confession, in Mercer, *Banditti of the Plains,* 182.

6. Dunning confession, in Mercer, *Banditti of the Plains,* 181-82; Irvine to Penrose, *The Rustler Business,* 27; William Martin manuscript, 42.

7. Frank Canton, *Frontier Trails,* 89.

8. Clover, *On Special Assignment,* 249.

9. David, *Malcolm Campbell, Sheriff,* 178-83.

10. Clover, *On Special Assignment,* 245-46; Martin manuscript, 42; Irvine to Penrose, *The Rustler Business,* 27; Dunning confession, in Mercer, *Banditti of the Plains,* 184-85.

11. Clover, *On Special Assignment,* 246-47.

12. Tucker manuscript, 75-76.

13. *Ibid.,* 76.

14. Dunning confession, in Mercer, *Banditti of the Plains,* 184; Clover, *On Special Assignment,* 248-49; Martin manuscript, 43.

15. Martin manuscript, 43.

16. Canton, *Frontier Trails,* 91; Martin manuscript, 44; David, *Malcolm Campbell, Sheriff,* 197-98, 209.

17. Champion's diary first was published by Sam Clover in the Cheyenne *Daily Leader* on April 14, 1892, and two days later in the Chicago *Herald*. This classic document has been reproduced many times. See, for example, Margaret Hanson, ed., *Powder River Country,* 301-02.

18. Clover, *On Special Assignment,* 250.

19. *Ibid.*

20. *Ibid.*

21. Canton, *Frontier Trails,* 91.

22. Buffalo *Bulletin*, June 30, 1892.

23. *Ibid.*; Tucker manuscript, 98-99; David, *Malcolm Campbell, Sheriff,* 200-01.

24. Irvine to Penrose, *The Rustler Business,* 26.

25. *Ibid.*; Canton, *Frontier Trails,* 92; Dunning confession, in Mercer, *Banditti of the Plains,* 186.

26. Irvine to Penrose, *The Rustler Business,* 28-29.

27. Tucker manuscript, 77.

28. Clover, *On Special Assignment,* 254-55.

29. *Ibid.*; Tucker manuscript, 77; Irvine to Penrose, *The Rustler Business,* 29; Canton, *Frontier Trails,* 92; David, *Malcolm Campbell, Sheriff,* 204.

30. Clover, *On Special Assignment,* 256-57; Irvine to Penrose, *The Rustler Business,* 29; Dunning confession, in Mercer, *Banditti of the Plains,* 187.

31. Canton, *Frontier Trails,* 92; Irvine to Penrose, *The Rustler Business,* 29; David, *Malcolm Campbell, Sheriff,* 209.

32. Tucker manuscript, 77.

Chapter 12: Siege at the TA

1. Buffalo *Bulletin,* June 30, 1892.

2. *Ibid.*; Frank Canton, *Frontier Trails,* 92; Clover, *On Special Assignment,* 262-64.

3. Canton, *Frontier Trails,* 92-93; Buffalo *Bulletin,* June 30, 1892.

4. Dunning confession, in A. S. Mercer, *Banditti of the Plains,* 187; Canton, *Frontier Trails,* 93.

5. Irvine to Penrose, *The Rustler Business,* 29; Dunning confession, in Mercer, *Banditti of the Plains,* 187-88.

6. Canton, *Frontier Trails,* 94; Irvine to Penrose, *The Rustler Business,* 30.

7. Canton, *Frontier Trails,* 93; Clover to Blair (May 15, 1892), in Brayer, "New Light on the Johnson County War," *Westerners' Brand Book* (February 1953), 1-2.

8. Irvine to Penrose, *The Rustler Business,* 30, 34; Clover, *On Special Assignment,* 266-68; David, *Malcolm Campbell, Sheriff,* 217.

9. Irvine to Penrose, *The Rustler Business,* 30; Marriage License and Certificate, Charles S. Ford and Nellie S. Sutherland, Johnson County, December 14, 1888.

10. Dunning confession, in Mercer, *Banditti of the Plains,* 189.

11. Canton, *Frontier Trails,* 45; Buffalo *Bulletin*, April 23, 1892.

12. Irvine to Penrose, *The Rustler Business,* 30-31; Dunning confession, in Mercer, *Banditti of the Plains,* 190-91.

13. Irvine to Penrose, *The Rustler Business,* 31; Canton, *Frontier Trails*, 95; George Tucker manuscript, 77.

14. Buffalo *Bulletin*, April 14, 1892; Cheyenne *Leader*, April 9, 1892.

15. Cheyenne *Leader*, April 4, 1892.

16. *Ibid.*, April 13, 1892.

17. *Ibid.*

18. *Ibid.*; Clover, *The Rustler Business,* 267-76.

19. Cheyenne *Leader*, April 13, 1892.

20. Buffalo *Bulletin*, April 14, 1892.

21. *Ibid.*

22. Irvine to Penrose, *The Rustler Business,* 31; Canton, *Frontier Trails,* 95-96; Dunning confession, in Mercer, *Banditti of the Plains,* 193; Tucker manuscript, 77.

23. Tucker manuscript, 77; Canton, *Frontier Trails,* 96; Irvine to Penrose, *The Rustler Business,* 31.

24. Buffalo *Bulletin,* April 14, 1892; Cheyenne *Leader,* April 13, 1892; Penrose, *The Rustler Business,* 39; David, *Malcolm Campbell, Sheriff,* 236.

25. Penrose, *The Rustler Business,* 37; Sheridan *Enterprise,* April 30, 1892; Buffalo *Bulletin,* April 14, 1892.

26. Cheyenne *Leader,* April 13, 1892; Omaha *World Herald,* April 13, 1892.

27. Canton, *Frontier Trails,* 97.

28. Tucker manuscript, 78; Canton, *Frontier Trails,* 96; David, *Malcolm Campbell, Sheriff,* 246-47.

29. Irvine to Penrose, *The Rustler Business,* 31.

30. Information provided by Barb Madsen, TA Ranch.

31. Tucker manuscript, 78.

32. Irvine to Penrose, *The Rustler Business,* 31; Cheyenne *Leader,* April 13, 1892.

33. Irvine to Penrose, *The Rustler Business,* 31-32.

34. Cheyenne *Leader,* April 13, 1892; Canton, *Frontier Trails,* 98.

35. Irvine to Penrose, *The Rustler Business,* 32.

36. Cheyenne *Leader,* April 13, 1892; David, *Malcolm Campbell, Sheriff,* 238.

37. Canton, *Frontier Trails,* 99; Capt. C. H. Parmalee to Governor Amos W. Barber, April 12, 1892.

38. Cheyenne *Leader,* April 13, 1892; Mercer, *Banditti of the Plains,* 69-70.

39. Mercer, *Banditti of the Plains,* 69.

40. Canton, *Frontier Trails,* 100.

41. *Ibid.,* 99-100; David, *Malcolm Campbell, Sheriff,* 246.

42. Irvine to Penrose, *The Rustler Business,* 36.

43. Canton, *Frontier Trails,* 100-101.

44. *Ibid.,* 99; Irvine to Penrose, *The Rustler Business,* 32.

45. Tucker manuscript, 78-79; Sheridan *Enterprise,* April 23, 1892.

46. Irvine to Penrose, *The Rustler Business,* 33.

47. *Ibid.;* Cheyenne *Leader,* April 13, 1892.

48. Cheyenne *Leader,* April 13, 1892; Buffalo *Bulletin,* April 14, 1892; Canton, *Frontier Trails,* 101-02.

49. Buffalo *Bulletin,* April 14, 1892; Cheyenne *Leader,* April 14, 1892; Col. Van Horn to General Brooks, April 13, 1892.

50. Tucker manuscript, 79.

Chapter 13: Surrender

1. Dunning confession, in A. S. Mercer, *Banditti of the Plains,* 160.

2. *Ibid.,* 189, 191, 192; George Tucker manuscript, 79.

3. Cheyenne *Leader,* April 13, 1892.

4. Ten telegrams of April 12 were reprinted the next day in the Cheyenne *Leader,* April 13, 1892.

5. Barber to Parmalee, April 11, 1892; Buffalo *Bulletin,* April 14, 1892.

6. Harrison to Barber, April 12, 1892; Brooks to Barber, April 12, 1892.

7. Buffalo *Bulletin,* April 14, 1892; Cheyenne *Leader,* April 14, 1892; Francis B. Heitman, ed., *Historical Register,* Vol. I, 982; Col. Van Horn to General Brooke, April 13, 1892.

8. Cheyenne *Leader,* April 13, 1892.

9. Tucker manuscript, 78.

10. *Ibid.,* 79.

11. Cheyenne *Leader,* April 13, 1892; Col. Van Horn to General Brooke, April 13, 1892.

12. *Ibid.*

13. Irvine to Penrose, *The Rustler Business,* 32.

14. *Ibid.*

15. Cheyenne *Leader,* April 14, 1892.

16. *Ibid.*; Buffalo *Bulletin,* April 14, 1892; Sam T. Clover, *On Special Assignment,* 282-83; Robert B. David, *Malcolm Campbell, Sheriff,* 272-73.

17. Cheyenne *Leader,* April 14, 1892.

18. *Ibid.*; Buffalo *Bulletin,* April 14, 1892; William Martin manuscript, 61; David, *Malcolm Campbell, Sheriff,* 273.

19. Cheyenne *Leader,* April 14, 1892; Irvine to Charles Penrose, *The Rustler Business,* 46.

20. Van Horn to Barber; Barber to Parmalee. These telegrams of April 13 were reprinted the following day in the Cheyenne *Leader.*

21. Angus to Barber; Barber to Angus. These telegrams were quoted in Penrose, T*he Rustler Business,* 44.

22. David, *Malcolm Campbell, Sheriff,* 276, 282, 288-89; Irvine to Penrose, *The Rustler Business,* 44-46.

23. Cheyenne *Leader,* April 11, 1892.

24. David, *Malcolm Campbell, Sheriff,* 274; Buffalo *Bulletin,* April 14 and May 19, 1892.

25. Cheyenne *Leader,* April 16, 1892; Buffalo *Bulletin,* April 13, 1892.

26. Cheyenne *Leader,* April 16, 1892.

27. *Ibid.*; Buffalo *Bulletin,* April 16, 1892.

28. Buffalo *Bulletin,* April 14, 1892.

29. Buffalo *Bulletin,* April 14, 1892; Penrose, *The Rustler Business,* 48; Clover, *On Special Assignment,* 284.

30. Dr. Penrose related his efforts to escape the troubled area in *The Rustler Business,* 36-42.

31. David, *Malcolm Campbell, Sheriff,* 254-56.

32. *Ibid.,* 276.

33. Dallas *Morning News,* April 17, 1892.

34. *Ibid.,* April 20, 1892.

35. *Ibid.,* April 21, 1892.

Chapter 14: Escape from Johnson County

1. George Tucker manuscript, 80; Angus to Barber, April 14, 1892; Barber to Angus, April 15, 1892; Barber to Van Horn, April 15, 1892; Barber to Angus, April 15, 1892; Brooke to Barber, April 15, 1892; See A. S. Mercer, *Banditti of the Plains,* 78-82

2. Van Devanter to Warren, April 20, 1892; Elkins to Barber, April 15, 1892.

3. Robert B. David, *Malcolm Campbell, Sheriff,* 296.

4. Irvine to Penrose, *The Rustler Business,* 46; General Brooke to War Department, April 18, 1892.

5. David, *Malcolm Campbell, Sheriff,* 296-98; Sam T. Clover, *On Special Assignment,* 284-86; Report of Major Fechet, May 2, 1892.

6. Clover, *On Special Assignment,* 285.

7. *Ibid.*; David, *Malcolm Campbell, Sheriff,* 299; Irvine to Penrose, *The Rustler Business,* 47; Francis B. Heitman, ed., *Historical Register,* Vol. I, 416, 916.

8. Clover, *On Special Assignment,* 286-88; Irvine to Penrose, *The Rustler Business,* 47.

9. Clover, *On Special Assignment,* 287.

10. Buffalo *Bulletin,* April 14, 1892; Sheridan *Enterprise,* April 23, 1892.

11. Irvine to Penrose, *The Rustler Business,* 47; David, *Malcolm Campbell, Sheriff,* 300-01.

12. *Ibid.*

13. Irvine to Penrose, *The Rustler Business,* 47.

14. Clover, *On Special Assignment,* 288.

15. David, *Malcolm Campbell, Sheriff,* 301.

16. General Brooke to General Schofield, April 21, 1892; Secretary of War Elkins to General Brooke, April 21, 1892.

17. *Ibid.*, 301-02; Irvine to Penrose, *The Rustler Business,* 47.

18. David, *Malcolm Campbell, Sheriff,* 302-06.

19. *Ibid.*, 305-07; Irvine to Penrose, *The Rustler Business,* 47.

20. David, *Malcolm Campbell, Sheriff,* 305-07.

21. *Ibid.*, 307.

22. *Ibid.*, 308-09.

Chapter 15: The Violence Continues

1. Robert B. David, *Malcolm Campbell, Sheriff,* 283-84; Burritt to H. A. Mann, May 8, 1892; Burritt to M. C. Brown, May 8, 1892; Burritt to W. R. Stoll, May 4, 1892.

2. Burritt to Henry A. Blair, May 14, 1892; Margaret Hanson, ed., *Powder River Country,* 381; Burritt to M. C. Brown, May 8, 1892; Burritt to W. R. Stoll, May 6 and May 7, 1892; S. M. Allen, May 1, 1892; David, *Malcolm Campbell, Sheriff,* 284-85.

3. Burritt to W. R. Stoll, May 8, 1892.

4. *Ibid.*; David, *Malcolm Campbell, Sheriff,* 285; Burritt to Henry A. Blair, May 14, 1892.

5. George Wellman's background is described in the newspaper accounts of his murder. Buffalo *Bulletin*, May 19, 1892. Also see David, *Malcolm Campbell, Sheriff,* 324-25.

6. Official report, U.S. Marshal Rankin to U.S. Attorney General William H. H. Miller, October 31, 1892.

7. David, *Malcolm Campbell, Sheriff,* 325-26; Burritt to Henry Blair, May 14, 1892.

8. Burritt to Henry Blair, May 14, 1892; Buffalo *Bulletin,* May 19, 1892.

9. Burritt to Henry Blair, May 14, 1892.

10. Buffalo *Bulletin*, May 19, 1892.

11. Burritt to Henry Blair, May 14, 1892.

12. *Ibid.*; Col. J. J. Van Horn to Assistant Adjutant General of the Army, May 12, 1892.

13. Burritt to Henry Blair, May 14, 1892.

14. *Ibid.*; Buffalo *Bulletin*, May 26, 1892.

15. Burritt to Henry Blair, May 14, 1892; Brayer, "The Murder Gun of Powder River," *Guns Magazine* (April 1955), 38; Floyd Bard to Buffalo *Bulletin* Editor Frank Hicks, November 16, 1960.

16. Buffalo *Bulletin*, May 26, 1892; Wister, June 26, 1891; David, *Malcolm Campbell, Sheriff,* 328; Floyd Bard to Buffalo *Bulletin* Editor Frank Hicks, November 16, 1960.

17. Buffalo *Bulletin*, August 18, 1955; Brayer, "The Murder Gun of Powder River."

18. Brayer, "The Murder Gun of Powder River"; Hanson, ed., *Powder River Country,* 351-53.

19. Hanson, ed., *Powder River Country,* 352-53.

20. *Ibid.*, 352, 472-75; Floyd Bard to Buffalo *Bulletin* Editor Frank Hicks, November 16, 1960; Marshal Joe Rankin to U.S. Attorney General William H. H. Miller, September 4, 1892.

21. Fowler to U.S. Attorney General William H. H. Miller, September 30, 1892.

22. Burritt to Henry Blair, May 14, 1892; Rankin to U.S. Attorney General Miller, September 4, 1892.

23. Robert A. Murray, *Military Posts in the Powder River Country*, 137; Buffalo *Bulletin*, May 19, 1892.

24. Murray, *Military Posts in the Powder River Country*, 137; Louis Kraft, *Gatewood & Geronimo*, 216; Buffalo *Bulletin*, May 19, 1892.

25. "Gatewood, Charles Baehr," in Dan L. Thrapp, *Encyclopedia of Frontier Biography*, Vol. II, 543-44; Kraft, *Gatewood & Geronimo,* 216-18.

26. Murray, *Military Posts in the Powder River Country,* 137; Hall, "Between the Lines," Cheyenne *Leader*, June 18, 1972.

Chapter 16: The Battle of Suggs

1. Investigation conducted by Maj. John M. Bacon, June 28, 1892, 15.

2. Buffalo *Bulletin*, June 9, 1892.

3. Wolcott, Hay, Baxter, Blair, Clay, and Van Devanter to Senator Carey, June 1, 1892; Senator Warren to Senator Carey, June 1, 1892.

4. Wolcott, Hay, Baxter, Blair, Clay and Van Devanter to Senator Carey, June 1, 1892, with note from Carey added to bottom of telegram; Senator Carey to Secretary of War Elkins, June 2, 1892; Sheridan *Post*, June 16, 1892.

5. General Brooke to General Schofield, June 3, 1892; General Schofield to General Brooke, June 4, 1892; Buffalo *Bulletin*, June 9, 1892.

6. "The Beginning and Ending of Suggs, Wyoming," in Arvada Historical Committee, *Wheel of Time*, 3-6.

7. Phil DuFran biographical file, Johnson County Library, Buffalo; newspaper clippings and legal documents from the files of Bob Edwards, Buffalo; *Eli P. DuFran vs. Christi DuFran*, divorce petition, May 31, 1888, District Court, Buffalo.

8. Sheridan *Enterprise*, May 21, 1892; General Brooke to Adjutant General's Office, July 22, 1892.

9. Bacon Investigation, 2.

10. *Ibid.*, 2-3, 11.

11. *Ibid.*, 14-15.

12. *Ibid.*, 2-3.

13. Board of Inquiry, June 18, 1892, 10-11.

14. Bacon Investigation, 2-3.

15. Board of Inquiry, 11-12.

16. *Ibid.*, 12.

17. Bacon Investigation, 3-4.

18. *Ibid.*, 4-5.

19. *Ibid.*, 5, 14; Buffalo *Bulletin*, June 23, 1892.

20. Buffalo *Bulletin*, June 23, 1892; Bacon Investigation, 5-6.

21. Buffalo *Bulletin*, June 23, 1892; Board of Inquiry, 10.

22. Buffalo *Bulletin*, June 23, 1892; Bacon Investigation, 17.

23. Sheridan *Enterprise*, June 25, 1892; Bacon Investigation, 9-10.

24. Buffalo *Bulletin*, June 23, 1892; Sadie Wagner, interview by Glenn Sweem, 1967.

25. Bacon Investigation, 5-6.

26. *Ibid.*, 6, 7, 10-11, 17, 19.

27. Board of Inquiry; Bacon Investigation, 7.

28. Buffalo *Bulletin*, June 23, 1892; Pat Walsh, in a letter to local historian Glenn Sweem (May 30, 1961), related the story of the trooper killed on the firing range. Walsh also stated that he and his little brother, *circa* 1903, "used to get all the lead we needed for reloading cartridges" from the old firing range. He sketched a diagram indicating the location of the graves, and he described the headboard.

29. Buffalo *Bulletin*, June 23, 1892; Sheridan *Post*, June 23, 1892; Sheridan *Enterprise*, June 25, 1892.

30. Bacon Investigation, 7-8.

31. Colonel Biddle related this visit and the ensuing conversation in his testimony to Major Bacon, 18-19.

32. Buffalo *Bulletin*, June 30, 1892.

33. Bacon Investigation. Bacon's conclusions are quoted from 21-22.

34. General Brooke to Adjutant General of the Army, July 22, 1892; Buffalo *Bulletin*, June 30, 1892.

35. Arvada Historical Committee, *Wheel of Time*, 3-6; Bob Edwards, "Black Men in Lonely Graves," *The Shootist* (January-February 2000), 21-24.

Chapter 17: From Fort Russell to Laramie City

1. A detailed history of Fort D. A. Russell has been written by Col. Gerald M. Adams, *The Post Near Cheyenne.* Also see Martha Fleishman and Carol Joy Justice, *Bugs to Blizzards, or An Army Wife at Fort D. A. Russell,* and Herbert Hart, *Old Forts of the Northwest,* 110-12.

2. Robert B. David, *Malcolm Campbell, Sheriff,* 309-11; Adams, *The Post Near Cheyenne,* 116.

3. David, *Malcolm Campbell, Sheriff,* 310-11; General Brooke to General Schofield, April 21, 1892.

4. David, *Malcolm Campbell, Sheriff,* 311-12.

5. *Ibid.,* 340.

6. George Tucker manuscript, 83-84; Adams, *The Post Near Cheyenne,* 97; David, *Malcolm Campbell, Sheriff,* 321-22; Dallas *Morning News* (May 11, 1892); Sheridan *Post,* July 14, 1892.

7. David, *Malcolm Campbell, Sheriff,* 322, and Tucker manuscript, 84.

8. Lewis Gould, "New Light on the Johnson County War," *Montana* (October 1967), 19-20.

9. Van Devanter to Warren (April 20, 1892), quoted in Gould, "New Light on the Johnson County War." *Montana,* 22-23.

10. Van Devanter to Warren (May 9, 1892), quoted in Gould, "New Light on the Johnson County War," 24.

11. Sheridan *Post,* April 28, 1892.

12. Charles Penrose, *The Rustler Business,* 37, 49.

13. *Ibid.,* 49; Cheyenne *Leader,* May 6 and 8, 1892; A. S. Mercer, *Banditti of the Plains,* 96-97.

14. Cheyenne *Leader,* May 6 and 8, 1892; David, *Malcolm Campbell, Sheriff,* 315.

15. Cheyenne *Leader,* May 6, 8 and 10, 1892; David, *Malcolm Campbell, Sheriff,* 317-18.

16. Cheyenne *Leader,* May 10, 1892.

17. *Ibid.*

18. Penrose, *The Rustler Business,* 49-50; David, *Malcolm Campbell, Sheriff,* 320.

19. Cheyenne *Leader,* May 10, 1892.

20. Francis B. Heitman, *Historical Register,* I, 367.

21. Manderson to Elkins, May 4, 1892.

22. Paxton, *et al,* to Manderson, April 23, 1892; dispatch from the Omaha *World-Herald* in the Cheyenne *Leader,* May 31, 1892.

23. John Clay, *My Life on the Range,* 276, 279-80; Lawrence M. Woods, *John Clay, Jr.,* 122-26.

24. Clay to Hay, June 18 and 22, 1892; Clay, *My Life on the Range,* 285.

25. Clay to Hay, June 25, 1892.

26. Warren to Hay, June 28 and July 1, 1892.

27. Cheyenne *Leader,* June 14, 1892; Van Devanter to Senator Carey, June 27, 1892, quoted in Gould, "New Light on the Johnson County War," 22; Warren to Hay, June 28, 1892.

28. Cheyenne *Leader,* June 26, 1892.

29. Blake to Barber, quoted in Mercer, *Banditti of the Plains,* 122-23.

30. Cheyenne *Leader,* June 30, 1892.

31. *Ibid.*

32. Van Devanter to Warren, May 9, 1892, quoted in Gould, "New Light on the Johnson County War," 24; Murray, *The Army on the Powder River,* 45-46; Cheyenne *Leader,* July 6 and 7, 1892.

33. Cheyenne *Leader,* July 6, 1892.

34. *Ibid.*

35. *Ibid.,* July 8, 1892.

36. *Ibid.*; Warren to Hay, July 15, 1892; Carey to Hay, July 15, 1892.

37. Cheyenne *Leader,* July 9, 1892.

38. *Ibid.*

39. *Ibid.,* July 8, 1892.

40. *Ibid.,* July 20, 1892.

41. *Ibid.*

42. *Ibid.*
43. *Ibid.*; Mercer, *Banditti of the Plains,* 124-25; Clay, *My Life on the Range,* 280.
44. Warren to Irvine, July 23, 1892; Carey to Hay, July 22, 1892.
45. Warren to Irvine, July 23, 1892.
46. *Ibid.*

Chapter 18: At the Holy City of the Cow

1. Cheyenne *Leader*, August 2, 1892.
2. *Ibid.*
3. *Ibid.*; Robert B. David, *Malcolm Campbell, Sheriff,* 341.
4. Cheyenne *Leader*, August 2, 1892.
5. *Ibid.*, August 3, 1892; A. S. Mercer, *Banditti of the Plains,* 125-26.
6. George Tucker manuscript, 86.
7. *Ibid.*, 80, 85-86; David, *Malcolm Campbell, Sheriff,* 346.
8. Tucker manuscript, 82.
9. *Ibid.*
10. John Clay, *My Life on the Range,* 282; Cheyenne *Leader*, August 3, 1892.
11. Cheyenne *Leader*, August 7, 1892.
12. *Ibid.*
13. *Ibid.*
14. Clay to Hay, July 21, 1892; Clay, *My Life on the Range,* 280-81.
15. Tucker manuscript, 81; Cheyenne *Leader*, August 11, 1892.
16. Cheyenne *Leader*, August 11, 1892.
17. *Ibid.*; Tucker manuscript, 81.
18. Cheyenne *Leader*, August 11, 1892.
19. *Ibid.*; Clay, *My Life on the Range*, 282.
20. Tucker manuscript, 85.
21. Cheyenne *Leader*, August 11, 1892.
22. The Dunning confession is reprinted in Mercer, *Banditti of the Plains,* 151-95.
23. August 1889 issue of *Northwestern Live Stock Journal,* quoted in Lewis Gould, "A. S. Mercer," *Arizona and the West* (Spring 1965), 8.
24. Gould, "A. S. Mercer," *Arizona and the West,* 8, 13.
25. Clay, *My Life on the Range,* 76.
26. *Northwestern Live Stock Journal,* August 23, 1892, quoted in Cheyenne *Leader.* October 29, 1892.
27. Clay, *My Life on the Range,* 76; Mercer, *Banditti of the Plains,* 121.
28. Cheyenne *Leader*, October 29, 1892.
29. Warren to Irvine, July 23, 1892.
30. Clay, *My Life on the Range,* 283.
31. David, *Malcolm Campbell, Sheriff,* 346.
32. *Ibid.*, 346-48.
33. Clay, *My Life on the Range,* 284. See the Cheyenne *Leader*, January 3-22, 1893, for a day-by-day account of the trial.

Chapter 19: Back to Texas

1. This bloody incident is described in: Kingfisher *Free Press* (November 10, 1892); Muskogee *Phoenix* (November 16, 1892); Oklahoma City *Evening Gazette* (November 4, 1892); Louisville Courier *Journal* (Kentucky, November 5, 1892); Lexington *Leader* Kentucky, November 12, 1892.
2. Louisville *Courier Journal* (November 5, 1892).
3. *Ibid.*
4. Western Union telegraphs: J. M. Chancellor to Mrs. T. C. Smith (November 4, 1892); J.

M. Chancellor to (illegible, November 4, 1892); W. H. Dickerson to Mrs. T. C. Smith (November 4, 1892).

5. Kingfisher *Free Press* (November 10, 1892).

6. Dee Cordry, "The Incredible Story of Tom and Frank Smith," http://209.35.75.65/smith.htm, 3-8.

7. See, for example: Oklahoma City *State Capital* (March 3 1894); *Daily Ardmoreite* (May 9, 1894; January 15, 1896; April 7, 1896; September 17, 1896; October 2, 1896; October 22, 1896; December 3, 1896; December 9, 1896; April 19, 1899).

8. Glenn Shirley, *West of Hell's Fringes,* 198-99.

9. *Daily Ardmoreite* (April 7, 1896).

10. Chickasaw *Express* (June 27, 1894).

11. Annual Report of the Attorney General for 1896; *Daily Ardmoreite* (October 14, 1896).

12. *Daily Ardmoreite* (July 31, 1896, and August 2, 1896); *Daily Oklahoman* (August 2, 1896).

13. Somerville, "Five Months Term in the Piney Woods," *Frontier Times* (June-July 1967), 31.

14. Ardmore *Statesman* and *Daily Ardmoreite* (January 13, 1927); Ardmore *Daily Press* (January 13, 1927, and January 14, 1927); *Daily Ardmoreite* (October 26, 1930); Probate of D. E. Booker (January 15, 1930); Probate of Bettie B. Booker (January 27, 1932).

15. El Reno *Daily Herald* (April 25, 1893); Dorothy Greenman Lee, *The Barling Family,* 210-11.

16. *Daily Ardmoreite* (February 10, 1894, and February 12, 1899); Gilday and Salt, eds., *Oklahoma History South of the Canadian,* Vol. II, 933-34; McAlester *News-Capital* (May 6, 1929).

17. Shawnee *Herald* (June 30, 1902); *Oklahoma Times-Herald* (Oklahoma City, March 15, 1906); *Daily Ardmoreite* (March 16, 1906); Paul's Valley *Enterprise* (March 22, 1906); Paul's Valley *Sentinel* (March 22, 1906); Oklahoma *Post* (Oklahoma City, March 24, 1906); Beaver *Journal* (March 29, 1906); Muskogee *Times-Democrat* (February 14, 1908).

18. McInnes, "Bud Ballew: The Legend of Carter County." *NOLA Quarterly* (January-March 2002), 3-9.

19. Gilday and Salt, eds., *Oklahoma History South of the Canadian,* Vol. II, 933-34; *Daily Oklahoman* (Oklahoma City, August 16, December 24, and December 25, 1920; November 22, 1921; January 5, 1922; January 23, 1925; November 7, 1928; May 7, 1929); Oklahoma City *Times* (December 20, 1921); *Daily Ardoreite* (February 10 and 17, 1922); Oklahoma *News* (Oklahoma City, February 17, 1922); Blackwell *Morning Tribune* (July 15, 1925); McAlester *News-Capital* (May 6, 1929).

20. For Canton's life after the Johnson County War see his autobiography, *Frontier Trails,* and Robert K. DeArment, *Alias Frank Canton.*

21. *Daily Ardoreite* (June 17, 1896); Kingfisher *Free Press* (November 3, 1898, and November 30, 1899).

22. Information provided by Kay Brown Black of Antlers, Oklahoma.

23. Tucker manuscript, 87-100.

24. *Ibid.,* 101-02.

Chapter 20: Aftermath in Wyoming

1. John Rolfe Burroughs, *Guardian of the Grasslands,* 167.

2. *Ibid.*

3. Walter, "Economic History and Settlement of Converse County, Wyoming," *Annals of Wyoming,* 295-96; Bryant B. Brooks, *Memoirs of Bryant B. Brooks,* 160; George W. Rollins wrote authoritatively about the 1894 range war in southwestern Wyoming in his doctoral dissertation, 255-68.

4. Carlson, *Tom Horn, Blood on the Moon,* 44-52; Rankin to U.S. Attorney General, October 31, 1892; Robert K. DeArment, *Alias Frank Canton,* 141-44; Edwards, personal correspondence and conversations with the author.

5. Robert B. David, *Malcolm Campbell, Sheriff,* 358-59.

6. Margaret Hanson, ed., *Powder River Country,* 476-77.

7. *Ibid.,* 477.

8. Coroner's Inquest, May 24, 1893.

9. A. S. Mercer, *Banditti of the Plains,* 140-41.

10. *Ibid.,* 3.

11. Adams, *Six-Guns and Saddle Leather,* 485-86; Lewis Gould, "A. S. Mercer and the Johnson County War, A Reapprisal," *Arizona and the West* (Spring 1965), 19-20.

12. Warren's life is described in his entry in the *Dictionary of American Biography* and T. A. Larson's *History of Wyoming.*

13. For an outline of Carey's life see Howard R. Lamar, *Reader's Encyclopedia of the American West,* 162-64.

14. A. P. Dow, WPA interview.

15. Charles Basch, WPA interview.

16. Percy Wollaston, *Homesteading,* 53.

17. *Buffalo's First Century,* 5, 7, 39; Dan L. Thrapp, *Encyclopedia of Frontier Biography,* III, 1587.

18. *Buffalo's First Century,* 133, 159-61.

19. Jack Gage, *The Johnson County War,* vi.

20. Elmer Kelton interview. Kelton apparently talked to a young soldier whose parents were the son and daughter, respectively, of cattleman W. C. Irvine and "rustler" Lee Moore.

Chapter 21: "When You Call Me That, Smile!"

1. "The Ballad of Cattle Kate" is reproduced in Olive W. Burt, "We Sing of Murder," 3-4.

2. "The Murder of Tisdale and Jones" may be found on a typescript on file at the Johnson County Public Library in Buffalo.

3. "The Ballad of Nate Champion," "The Invasion Song," and "Our Heroes' Grave" are reproduced in Ariel A. Downing, "Music as Artifact: The Johnson County War Ballads," *American Music Research Center Journal* (1998/99), 35-53.

4. Darwin Payne, *Owen Wister,* 198-201, 208, 214.

5. Owen Wister, *The Virginian,* 21.

6. Payne, *Owen Wister,* 213, 216-26.

7. Payne, *Owen Wister,* 283-84, 300, 313-14; Brian Garfield, *Western Films,* 338-39; Parish and Pitts, *The Great Western Pictures,* 382-86.

8. Richard West, *Television Westerns,* 101-02.

9. Jack Schaefer, *Shane,* 45.

10. Jay Hyams, *The Life and Times of the Western Movie,* 115. Western film expert Brian Garfield, in *Western Films,* 290, states that *Shane*'s "range tyrants and homesteaders story is based loosely on the historical Johnson County War."

11. Garfield, *Western Films,* 188-89; Hyams, *The Life and Times of the Western Movie,* 226.

12. Frederick Manfred, *Riders of Judgment,* 283.

13. Oakley Hall, *The Bad Lands,* 298.

14. *Ibid.,* 361.

15. Buffalo *Bulletin* (June 14, 2001).

Bibliography

Documents and Court Records

Wyoming Stock Growers Association Papers. American Heritage Center, Laramie, Wyoming.

Board of Inquiry at Camp Bettens, Wyoming, June 18, 1892.

Champion, Dud. Coroner's Inquisition. Converse County, Wyoming, May 23, 1893.

Crosthwaite, Frank B., Examiner. Report to United States Department of Justice regarding conduct of U.S. Marshal Joseph Rankin. November 2, 1892.

DuFran, Eli P., vs. Christie DuFran. Johnson County District Court, May 31, 1888.

Ford, Charles S., and Nellie Sutherland. Marriage License, December 14, 1888. Johnson County Courthouse, Buffalo, Wyoming.

Hill, T. P., District Court Clerk for Johnson County, Wyoming. "George Dunning's Confession." October 29, 1892.

Investigation of Disturbance at Suggs. Conducted by Maj. John M. Bacon, Acting Inspector General, at Camp Bettens, Wyoming. June 28, 1892.

Investigation by Maj. John M. Bacon, Acting Inspector General, at Camp Bettens, Wyoming. June 28, 1892.

Johnson County, Wyoming, Commissioners Court Minutes, 1892-93. Vol. 5B.

Justice Department file no. 6319/92. Wyoming Room, Sheridan County Fulmer Public Library, Sheridan, Wyoming.

"New Land District in Wyoming." Forty-ninth Congress, First Session, House of Representatives. Report No. 538, February 16, 1886.

Rankin, J. P., United States Marshal. Correspondence from the National Archives, on file at the Johnson County Public Library, Buffalo.

Sheriff's Day Book, Vol. B. Johnson County, Wyoming.

Use of U.S. Troops in Cattle Troubles in the State of Wyoming and the Use of U.S. Troops in Suppressing Insurrection in That State. United States Adjutant General's Office, National Archives and Records Service, General Services Administration. Microfilm, 39641147. Contains reports, telegram, and official correspondence.

Collections

J. Elmer Brock Papers. American Heritage Center, Laramie, Wyoming.

Charles H. Burritt Letters. American Heritage Center, Laramie, Wyoming.

Joseph M. Carey Papers. Wyoming State Archives, Cheyenne.

Hay Family Papers. American Heritage Center, Laramie, Wyoming.

Fred G. S. Hesse Collection. American Heritage Center, Laramie, Wyoming.

Burton S. Hill Collection. American Heritage Center, Laramie, Wyoming.

Francis E. Warren Papers. American Heritage Center, Laramie, Wyoming.

Owen Wister Collection. American Heritage Center, Laramie, Wyoming.

Wyoming Stock Growers Association Collection. American Heritage Center, Laramie, Wyoming.

Manuscripts

Anspaugh, Alice. "A Summary of the Activities of Rev. Marvin Radar during The Johnson County War." Typescript on file at Johnson County Public Library, Buffalo.

Barnum, Zoe C. "The History of Johnson County." Typescript, 1923. Wyoming Room, Sheridan County Fulmer Public Library, Sheridan, Wyoming.

Evans, Ralph. Reminiscences, typescript on file in local history section, Ardmore Public Library, Ardmore, Oklahoma.

Gatchell, T. J. "The Life of W. G. Angus." Biographical file, Johnson County Library, Buffalo.

Lindsey, Seldon T. "The Story of My Life." Unpublished manuscript.

Martin, William A. "Negus in Johnson County, A History of the Johnson County Stock War." Manuscript in the Johnson County Public Library, Buffalo.

Rietz, Minnie A. "Johnson County." Typescript. Wyoming Room, Sheridan County Fulmer Public Library, Sheridan, Wyoming.

Thom, W. J. "Early Business Men of Buffalo, Wyoming." Typescript. American Heritage Center, Laramie, Wyoming Room, Sheridan County Fulmer Public Library, Sheridan, Wyoming.

Tucker, George R. Autobiographical manuscript. John Alley Collection, Western History Collections, University of Oklahoma, Norman.

Letters and Telegrams

Angus, W. G., to Sheriff M. B. Campbell, telegram (April 15, 1892).

Bard, Floyd C., Letter to the Editor. *True West* (July–August 1957), 3.

Barling, Jim, to Bill O'Neal (June 2 and June 15, 2000).

Barling, R. C., to F. R. Barling (August 22, 1891).

Black, Kay Brown, to Bill O'Neal (June 25, 2001).

Burns, Judge Robert A., to James F. Barling (September 22, 1987).

Burritt, Charles H. Letters, 1892, published in Buffalo *Bulletin* (January 1961).

Chancelor, Deputy Marshal J. M., to Mrs. T. C. Smith, telegram (November 4, 1892).

DeArment, Robert K. Letter to author, March 7, 2002.

Edwards, Bob, to Bill O'Neal (November 15, 2002).

Field, Sharon Lass, to Glenn Sweem (February 15, 1984).

Lonnie to Ma (April 15, 1892). Johnson County Jim Gatchell Memorial Museum, Buffalo.

Manderson, Senator Charles F., to Secretary of War Stephen B. Elkins (May 4, 1892).

McCullough, Harrell, to Pat Wagner, editor, *True West,* n.d. On file in local history section, Ardmore Public Library, Ardmore, Oklahoma.

Roff, Charles L., Letter to the Editor. *True West* (May-June 1970).

Smith, Mrs. Sallie, to Gray Harris, telegram (November 4, 1892).

Walsh, P. J., to Glenn Sweem (May 30, 1961 and June 12, 1967).

Warren, Francis E., to W. C. Irvine. July 23, 1892.

Interviews

Dow, A. P. WPA interview, n.d.

Hayden, Charles Emery. WPA interview, December 28, 1938.

Kelton, Elmer. Interview by author, September 5, 2002, Lubbock, Texas.

Robey, Daisy D. WPA interview, March 27, 1939.

Wagner, Sadie. Interview by Glenn Sweem, 1967.

NOTE: These interviews are on file at the Johnson County Public Library in Buffalo.

Miscellaneous

Appeal to United States Senator C. F. Manderson from numerous cattlemen. April 23, 1892.

Bailey, Rebecca Williamson Carter. "Wyoming Stock Inspectors and Detectives, 1873-1890." Master's thesis. Laramie: University of Wyoming, 1948.

Barling family information, provided to the author by James F. Barling.

Burt, Olive W. "We Sing of Murder." On file at Johnson County Public Library, Buffalo.

"Cheyenne Historic Downtown Walking Tour." Cheyenne: Downtown Development Authority, 1998. Pamphlet.

Harvey, Mark E. "A Civil War in Wyoming: A Centennial Commemoration of the Johnson County War." Master's thesis. Laramie: University of Wyoming, 1992.

"Historic Main Street Walking Tour, Buffalo, Wyoming." Brochure published by the Buffalo Chamber of Commerce.

Hollister, Charles A. "The Organization and Administration of the Sheriff's Office in Arizona." Master's thesis. University of Arizona, 1946.

Major Frank Wolcott, Alias The Jack of Spades. Pamphlet, reprinted in Cheyenne: Powder River Press, 1971.

Madden, Terry Jo. "They Had a Little List: The Johnson County War and Its Aftermath, Wyoming, 1892." Master's thesis. Portland: University of Portland, 1977.

Petition to President Benjamin H. Harrison, from citizens of Johnson County, Wyoming. N.D.

Rollins, George W. "The Struggle of Cattleman, Sheepman and Settler for Control of Lands in Wyoming, 1867-1910." Doctoral dissertation, University of Utah, Salt Lake City, 1951.

Van Valkenburgh, Lois. "The Johnson County War: The Papers of Charles Bingham Penrose in the Library of the University of Wyoming, with Introduction and Notes." Master's thesis. Laramie: University of Wyoming, 1939.

Newspapers

Beaver (Oklahoma) *Journal*
Big Horn Sentinel (Buffalo)
Blackwell (Oklahoma) *Morning Tribune*
Buffalo *Bulletin*
Buffalo *Echo*
Casper *Star-Tribune*
Cheyenne *Daily Leader*
Cheyenne *Daily Sun*
The Daily Ardmoreite
Daily Oklahoman (Ardmore)
Dallas *Morning News*
Denver *Post*
Douglas *Graphic*
Guthrie *Leader*
Kingfisher *Free Press*
McAlester *News-Capital*
Muskogee *Times-Democrat*
Oklahoma City *Times-Journal*
Oklahoma Post (Oklahoma City)
Omaha *World Herald*
Paul's Valley (Oklahoma) *Enterprise*
Paul's Valley *Sentinel*
Shawnee *Herald*
Sheridan *Enterprise*
Sheridan *Post*

Books

Abbott, E. C., and Helena Huntington Smith. *We Pointed Them North.* Norman: University of Oklahoma Press, 1955.

Adams, Col. Gerald M. *The Post Near Cheyenne, A History of Fort D. A. Russell, 1867-1930.* Cheyenne: High Flyer Publications, 1997.

Adams, Ramon F. *Six-Guns and Saddle Leather.* Norman: University of Oklahoma Press, 1969.

Arvada Historical Committee. *Wheel of Time, 1800's-1984.* Privately printed.

Atherton, Lewis. *The Cattle Kings.* Bloomington: Indiana University Press, 1961.

Babor, D. F. *The Longest Rope.* Caldwell, Idaho: Caxton Printers, 1947.

Bakken, Gordon Morris, ed. *Law in the Western United States.* Norman: University of Oklahoma Press, 2000.

Barrows, John R. *U-bet.* Caldwell, Idaho: The Caxton Printers, Ltd., 1934.

Beery, Gladys B. *The Front Streets of Laramie City.* Laramie, Wyoming: Albany Seniors, Inc., 1990.

Brayer, Herbert O. *Range Murder: How the Red Sash Gang Dry-Gulched Deputy United States Marshal George Wellman.* Evanston, Illinois: Branding Iron Press, 1955.

Brisbin, Gen. James S. *The Beef Bonanza; or, How to Get Rich on the Plains.* Norman: University of Oklahoma Press, 1959.

Brooks, Bryant B. *Memoirs of Bryant B. Brooks.* Glendale, California: The Arthur H. Clark Company, 1939.

Brothers, Ron. *The Death and Cemetery Records of Lamar County, Texas, 1831-1998,* 3 Vols. Paris, Texas: Ron Brothers, 1999.

Brown, Mark H., and William R. Felton. *Before Barbed Wire.* New York: Bramhall House, 1956.

Brown, Richard Maxwell. *Strain of Violence, Historical Studies of American Violence and Vigilantism.* New York: Oxford University Press, 1975.

Browning, James A. *Violence Was No Stranger.* Stillwater, Oklahoma: Barbed Wire Press, 1993.

Buffalo's Centennial Book Committee. *Buffalo's First Century.* Buffalo, Wyoming: Buffalo Bulletin, Inc., 1984.

Burns, Robert Homer, Andrew Springs Gillespie, and Willing Gay Richardson. *Wyoming's Pioneer Ranches.* Laramie, Wyoming: Top-of-the-World Press, 1955.

Burroughs, John Rolfe. *Guardian of the Grasslands, The First 100 Years of the Wyoming Stock Growers Association.* Cheyenne: Pioneer Printing and Stationary Co., 1971.

Burt, Struthers. *Powder River, Let 'Er Buck.* New York: Farrar and Rinehart, 1938.

Canton, Frank M. *Frontier Trails, The Autobiography of Frank M. Canton.* Norman: University of Oklahoma Press, 1966.

Carlson, Chip. *Joe LeFors, "I Slickered Tom Horn."* Cheyenne: Beartooth Corral, LLC, 1995.

———. *Tom Horn, Blood on the Moon.* Cheyenne: High Plains Press, 2001.

Carroll, John M., ed. *The Black Military Experience in the American West.* New York: Liveright Publishing Corporation, 1971.

The Cattle Barons' Rebellion Against Law and Order, First Eyewitness Accounts of the Johnson County War in Wyoming, 1892. Evanston, Illinois: The Branding Iron Press, 1955.

Chatterton, Fenimore. *Yesterday's Wyoming.* Aurora, Wyoming: Powder River Publishers and Booksellers, 1957.

Clay, John. *My Life on the Range.* Norman: University of Oklahoma Press, 1962.

Clover, Sam T. *On Special Assignment.* Boston: Lothrop Publishing Company, 1903.

David, Robert B. *Malcolm Campbell, Sheriff.* Casper, Wyoming: Wyomingana, 1932.

DeArment, Robert K. *Alias Frank Canton.* Norman: University of Oklahoma Press, 1996.

Deck, Jean. *Sheriffs of Carter County.* Ardmore, Oklahoma: n.p., 1990.

Drago, Harry Sinclair. *The Great Range Wars, Violence on the Grasslands.* Lincoln: University of Nebraska Press, 1970.

Erisman, Fred, and Richard W. Etulain, eds. *Fifty Western Writers.* Westport, Connecticut: Greenwood Press, 1982.

Flagg, Oscar H. *A Review of the Cattle Business in Johnson County, Wyoming, since 1882, and the Causes That Led to the Recent Invasion.* New York: Arno Press and the New York *Times,* 1969.

Fleishman, Martha, and Carol Joy Justice. *Bugs to Blizzards, or An Army Wife at Fort D. A. Russell.* Cheyenne: Pioneer Printing and Stationery Co., 1974.

Forbis, William H. *The Cowboys.* New York: Time-Life Books, 1973.

Frewen, Moreton. *Melton Mowbray and Other Memories.* London: H. Jenkins, Ltd., 1924.

Frink, Maurice. *Cow Country Cavalcade, Eighty Years of the Wyoming Stock Growers Association.* Denver, Colorado: The Old West Publishing Co., 1954.

Frye, Elnora L. *Atlas of Wyoming Outlaws at the Territorial Penitentiary.* Cheyenne: Pioneer Printing and Stationery, 1990.

Gage, Jack R. *The Johnson County War: Is a Pack of Lies/Ain't a Pack of Lies.* Cheyenne, Wyoming: Flintlock Publishing Co., 1967.

Gard, Wayne. *Frontier Justice.* Norman: University of Oklahoma Press, 1949.

Garfield, Brian. *Western Films, A Complete Guide.* New York: Rawson Associates, 1982.

Gilday, John P., and Mark H. Salt, eds. *Oklahoma History South of the Canadian.* Vol. II, N.p. n.d.

Hanson, Margaret Brock, ed. *Powder River Country, The Papers of J. Elmer Brock.* Cheyenne, Wyoming: Frontier Printing, Inc., 1981.

Hardy, Phil. *The Western.* New York: William Morrow and Company, Inc., 1983.

Hart, Herbert M. *Old Forts of the Northwest.* Seattle: Superior Publishing Company, 1963.

Heitman, Francis B., comp. *Historical Register and Dictionary of the United States Army.* 2 vols. Washington, D.C.: Government Printing Office, 1903.

Hollon, W. Eugene. *Frontier Violence, Another Look.* New York: Oxford University Press, 1974.

Hufsmith, George W. *The Wyoming Lynching of Cattle Kate, 1889.* Glendo, Wyoming: High Plains Press, 1993.

Hyams, Jay. *The Life and Times of the Western Movie.* New York: Gallery Books, 1983.

Kraft, Louis. *Gatewood & Geronimo.* Albuquerque: The University of New Mexico Press, 2000.

Lamar, Howard R., ed. *The Reader's Encyclopedia of the American West.* New York: Thomas Y. Crowell Co., 1977.

Larson, T. A. *History of Wyoming.* Lincoln: University of Nebraska Press, 1978.

Leckie, William H. *The Buffalo Soldiers.* Norman: University of Oklahoma Press, 1967.

Lee, Dorothy Greenman. *The Barling Family.* Privately published, 1986.

Linn, James Weber. *James Keeley, Newspaperman.* New York: The Bobbs-Merrill Company, 1937.

Mercer, A. S. *The Banditti of the Plains, or The Cattlemen's Invasion of Wyoming in 1892.* Norman: University of Oklahoma Press, 1954.

Mokler, Alfred James. *History of Natrona County, Wyoming, 1888-1922.* Chicago: The Lakeside Press, 1923.

Murray, Robert A. *The Army on the Powder River.* Bellevue, Nebraska: The Old Army Press, 1966.

———. *Johnson County, 175 Years of History at the Foot of the Big Horn Mountains.* Buffalo, Wyoming: Buffalo Chamber of Commerce, 1981.

———. *Military Posts in the Powder River Country of Wyoming, 1865-1894.* Buffalo, Wyoming: The Office, 1990.

Neville, A. W. *The History of Lamar County.* Paris, Texas: The North Texas Publishing Co., 1937.

———. *The Red River Valley, Then and Now.* Paris, Texas: The North Texas Publishing Co., 1948.

Norton, Patty Virginia, and Dr. Layton R. Sutton, compilers and eds. *Indian Territory and Carter County, Oklahoma, Pioneers,* Vol. I. Dallas, Texas: Taylor Publishing Co., 1983.

O'Neal, Bill. *Encyclopedia of Western Gunfighters.* Norman: University of Oklahoma Press, 1979.

Parish, James Robert, and Michael R. Pitts. *The Great Western Pictures.* Metuchen, New Jersey: The Scarecrow Press, Inc., 1976.

Payne, Darwin. *Owen Wister.* Dallas: Southern Methodist University Press, 1985.

Penrose, Charles Bingham. *The Rustler Business.* Douglas, Wyoming: Douglas Budget, 1959.

Powder River Heritage Committee. *Our Powder River Heritage.* Cheyenne: Frontier Printing, Inc., 1982.

Prassel, Frank Richard. *The Great American Outlaw, A Legacy of Fact and Fiction.* Norman: University of Oklahoma Press, 1993.

Preece, Harold. *Lone Star Man: Ira Aten, Last of the Old Texas Rangers.* New York: Hastings House, Publishers, 1960.

Reps, John W. *Cities of the American West, A History of Frontier Urban Planning.* Princeton, New Jersey: Princeton University Press, 1979.

Roosevelt, Theodore. *Ranch Life in the Far West.* Flagstaff, Arizona: Northland Press, 1985 [1888].

Rush, N. Orwin. *Mercer's Banditti of the Plains.* Tallahassee: The Florida State University Library, 1961.

Sandoz, Mari. *The Cattlemen.* Lincoln: University of Nebraska Press, 1958.

Shirley, Glenn. *West of Hell's Fringe: Crime, Criminals, and the Federal Peace Officers in Oklahoma Territory, 1889-1907.* Norman: University of Oklahoma Press, 1978.

Sievers, Harry J. *Benjamin Harrison, Hoosier President.* Newton, Connecticut: American Political Biography Press, 1996.

Smith, Helena Huntington. *The War on Powder River.* Lincoln: University of Nebraska Press, 1966.

Sonnichsen, C. L. *I'll Die Before I'll Run.* New York: The Devin-Adair Company, 1962.

Spring, Agnes Wright. *Seventy Years: A Panoramic History of the Wyoming Stock Growers Association.* Cheyenne: Wyoming Stock Growers Association, 1942.

Stuart, Granville. *Forty Years on the Frontier.* Cleveland: The Arthur H. Clark Company, 1925.

Thrapp, Dan L. *Encyclopedia of Frontier Biography.* 3 vols. Glendale, California: Arthur H. Clark Co., 1988.

Walker, Tacetta B. *Stories of Early Days in Wyoming: Big Horn Basin.* Casper, Wyoming: Prairie Publishing Co., 1936.

Watson, John. *The Real Virginian.* Tucson: Westernlore Press, 1989.

West, Richard. *Television Westerns, Major and Minor Series, 1946-1978.* Jefferson, North Carolina: McFarland & Company, Inc., 1987.

Wister, Fanny Kemble, ed. *Owen Wister Out West: His Journals and Letters.* Chicago: University of Chicago Press, 1958.

Wollaston, Percy. *Homesteading.* New York: The Lyons Press, 1997.

Woods, Lawrence M. *British Gentlemen in the Wild West.* New York: The Free Press, 1989.

———. *John Clay, Jr.: Commission Man, Banker and Rancher.* Spokane: Arthur H. Clark, 2001.

Writers' Program of the Works Progress Administration. *Wyoming, A Guide to Its History, Highways, and People.* New York: Oxford University Press, 1941.

Novels

Hall, Oakley. *The Bad Lands.* New York: Atheneum, 1978.

Manfred, Frederick. *Riders of Judgment.* New York: Random House, 1957.

Schaefer, Jack. *Shane.* New York: Houghton Mifflin Company, 1949.

Wister, Owen. *The Virginian.* New York: The Macmillan Publishing Company, Inc., 1902.

Films

Heaven's Gate (1980)

Invasion of Johnson County (1976)

"Johnson County Cattle War," *Vendettas* (2001)

The Johnson County War (2002)

"The Johnson County War," *Real West* (2004)

"Nate Champion," *Stories of the Century* (1955)

Shane (1953)

Tall in the Saddle (1944)

The Virginian (1929)

The Virginian (1946)

The Virginian (2000)

Articles

Baker, E. D. "A Rustler's Account of the Johnson County War," *Westerners' Brand Book, 1945-46, Chicago Posse.*

"Bill Dalton Dead." *The Daily Ardmoreite* (June 9, 1894).

Black, Kay Brown. "Was Your Ancestor a Mercenary in the Johnson County, Wyoming, War?" *Northwest Texas Genealogy and History Bulletin,* vol. 10, no. 2 (August 1992).

Brayer, Herbert O. "The Murder Gun of Powder River." *Guns Magazine* (April 1955).

———. "New Light on the Johnson County War." *Westerners' Brand Book, Chicago Corral,* 9, no. 12 (February 1953).

Brock, J. Elmer. "A Timely Arrival." *Annals of Wyoming* (January 1943).

———. "Who Dry-Gulched the Hoe Ranch Foreman?" *The Denver Westerners' Brand Book,* IX (1953).

"Buck Garrett Admired by Early Day Outlaws as 'Man's Man'." *The Daily Ardmoreite* (February 9, 1970).

Canton, F. M. "The Wyoming Cattle War." *Cattleman* (March 1919).

Cordry, Dee. "The Incredible Story of Tom and Frank Smith, Lawmen of Texas and Oklahoma." http://209.35.75.65/smith.htm

DeArment, R. K. "A Tale of Two Franks and a Pistol." *True West* (April 1999).

Downing, Ariel A. "Music as Artifact: The Johnson County War Ballads." *American Music Research Center Journal,* vol. 8/9 (1998-99).

Edwards, Bob. "Black Men and Lonely Graves." *The Shootist* (January-February 2000).

———. "Shootout at the T. A. Ranch." *Trail's End Magazine* (October-November 1999).

———. "Siege at the TA Ranch." *Trail's End Magazine* (October-November 1999).

———. "W. G. 'Red' Angus." *The Sentry,* vol. II, no. 4 (October 2002).

Ellis, Olive Herman. "Robert Foote." *Annals of Wyoming* (January 1943).

Fenwick, Robert W. "Few Scars Left From Cattle War." Denver *Post* (June 25, 1967).

Gould, Lewis. "A. S. Mercer and the Johnson County War: A Reappraisal." *Arizona and the West* (Spring 1965).

Gould, Lewis. "New Light on the Johnson County War." *Montana, the Magazine of Western History,* vol. XVII, no. 4 (October 1967).

Hall, Oakley. "Powder River Country." *American Heritage* (April 1989).

Hall, Pat. "Between the Lines." Cheyenne *Leader* (June 18, 1972).

Hawthorne, Roger. "Conflict and Conspiracy." *True West* (June 1984).

Henderson, Sam. "The Many Careers of Sheriff Buck Garrett." *The West* (July 1968).

Hill, Burton S. "Buffalo: Ancient Cow Town." *Annals of Wyoming,* 35, no. 2 (October 1963).

Hope, B. W. "Joe Elliott's Story." *Annals of Wyoming,* vol. 45, no. 2 (Fall 1973).

Hutchins, John M. "The Jekyll-Hyde Gunman of the Johnson County War of 1892." *Denver Westerners Roundup,* Vol. 48, no. 2 (March-April 1992).

Jackson, W. Turrentine. "The Wyoming Stock Growers' Association: Political Power in Wyoming Territory, 1873-90." *Agricultural History,* vol. XXII, 1948.

Kittredge, William, and Steven M. Krauzer. "'Mr. Montana' Revised." *Montana, The Magazine of Western History,* vol. XXVI, no. 4 (Autumn 1986).

Lingle, C. M., ed. "The Cattle Barons' Rebellion against Law and Order." Buffalo *Bulletin* (April 24, 1892).

Lott, Howard B. "The Old Occidental." *Annals of Wyoming* (April 1955).

MacMillan, D. "The Gilded Age and Montana's DHS Ranch." *Montana, The Magazine of Western History,* vol. XX, no. 2 (Spring 1970).

McDermott, John D. "Writers in Judgment: Historiography of the Johnson County War." *Wyoming Annals* (Winter 1993-94).

McInnes, Elmer D. "Bud Ballew: The Legend of Carter County." *Quarterly of the National Association for Outlaw and Lawman History,* vol. XXVI, no. 1 (January-March 2002).

McLaird, James D. "Ranching in the Big Horns: George T. Beck, 1856-94." *Annals of Wyoming,* Vol. 39, No. 2 (October 1957).

Metzger, S. S. "The Wyoming 'Rustlers' War.'" *The Pacific Monthly,* vol. 25, no. 4 (April 1911).

Morriss, Andrew P. "Decius S., Wade's Necessity for Codification." *Montana Law Review,* vol. 61, no. 2 (Summer 2000).

————. "Miners, Vigilantes & Cattlemen: Overcoming Free Rider Problems in the Private Provision of Law." *Land and Water Law Review, University of Wyoming College of Law,* vol. XXIII, number 2 (1998).

————. "Private Actors & Structural Balance: Militia & the Free Rider Problem in Private Provision of Law." *Montana Law Review,* vol. 58, no. 1 (Winter 1997).

————. "'This State Will Soon Have Plenty of Laws'—Lessons From One Hundred Years of Codification in Montana." *Montana Law Review,* vol. 56, no. 2 (Summer 1995).

Morriss, Andrew P., Scott J. Burnham, Hon. James C. Nelson. "Debating the Field Code 105 Years Late." *Montana Law Review,* vol. 61, no. 2 (Summer 2000).

Murray, Robert A. "Guns of Wyoming's Cattle War." *Shooting Times* (July 1967).

————. "The United States Army in the Aftermath of the Johnson County Invasion." *Annals of Wyoming,* vol. 38, no. 1 (April 1966).

Myers, Sue. "George Campbell's Memories of the Battle at the TA Ranch." *The Sentry* (August 2001).

————. "The Johnson County War: Suggs—The final chapter." *The Sentry* (April 1992).

Reese, William S. "Granville Stuart of the DHS Ranch, 1879-1887." *Montana, The Magazine of Western History,* vol. XXI.

Repanshek, Kurt J. "Was Nate Champion really a hero, or just another bit player?" Cheyenne *Daily Leader* (June 28, 1988).

Richards, Colin. "The Old West Speaks: Nate Champion Tells about the Wyoming Range War." *Real West* (March 1970.

Riotte, Louise. "Buck Garrett, Man and Legend." *True West* (January-February 1970).

————. "Bloody Caddo." *True West* (May-June 1970).

Rush, N. Orwin. "Asa Mercer's Little Black Book." *Persimmon Hill,* vol. 9.

Ryland, Lee. "Deep Ran the Blood in Buffalo." *True West* (January-February 1964).

Samuelson, Nancy B. "Westerly, Rhode Island and the Johnson County War." *Quarterly of the National Association for Outlaw and Lawman History,* vol. XXIV, no. 4 (October-December 2000).

Scahafer, A. L. "Joe Rankin's Ride." *True West* (September-October 1966).

Schubert, Frank N. "The Suggs Affray: the Black Cavalry in the Johnson County War." *The Western Historical Quarterly,* IV, no.1 (January 1973).

Smith, Brad. "The Gunfight That Killed a Town." *South Dakota Magazine* (September-October 1991).

Smith, Helena Huntington. "George Dunning: Mystery Man of the Johnson County Invasion." *Montana Magazine* (Autumn 1963).

Stegner, Wallace. "Owen Wister: Creator of the Cowboy Myth." *American West,* vol. XXI, no. 1 (January-February 1984).

Trenholm, Virginia Cole. "Last of the Invaders." *True West* (January-February 1962).

Watkins, George T., III. "Johnson County War." *The Pacific Northwesterner,* vol. 5, no. 2 (Spring 1961).

Will, George F. "The Barefoot Billionaire." *Newsweek* (June 1, 1992).

Williams, Gary. "Dunning's Strange Confession: $5 a day to Ride, $50 to Kill!!!" *The West* (July 1964).

Index

Oelrichs, C. M., 9
Ogallala Land and Cattle Company, 14
Ogallala Ranch, 112, 158, 164, 165
Oklahoma National Guard, 230
Olive, Print, 183
Omaha *World Herald*, 136
Omaha, Nebraska, 146, 203
On Special Assignment, 89
101 Ranch, 70, 71
open-range ranching, 6, 10, 13, 14-15, 16, 23, 47-48
Opera House, 234
Oregon Trail, 56, 59
Orin Junction, 107, 159, 165
Osborne, John E., 44, 47, 238, 239
"Our Heroes' Grave," 244
Owen, Red, 49

P

Palance, Jack, 247
Palestine, Texas, 100
Paris, Texas, 94, 97-98, 99, 103, 133, 159-160, 225, 254
Parker, Judge Isaac, 98, 102
Parker, J. Brown, 115
Parker, L. H., 89, 91, 108, 150, 153, 195, 215
Parmalee, C. H., 144, 146, 148, 149, 152
Parmalee, Judge Carroll, 83
Parrott, George "Big Nose," 47, 56
Pawnee, Oklahoma, 229
"pea pickers," 14
"Peg Leg," 103
Penrose, Dr. Charles B., 52, 53, 62, 67, 70, 72, 84, 86, 87, 89, 90, 91, 96, 106, 107, 110, 111, 112, 125, 136, 143, 145, 149, 157-159, 201, 203
Perry, Luke, 252
Pershing, Frances, 239
Pershing, Francis Warren, 238
Pershing, John J., 23, 169, 238, 239
Pershing, Warren, 239
Peters, Jim, 228
Peterson, George, 115
Pickard, Kinzie A., 100, 101, 112, 150, 231, 255
Pickard, Lou, 231
Pickard, Lucille, 100

Pickell, Bill, 55
Pierce, John, 127
Pinhook, Texas, 97
Pinkerton Detective Agency, 23, 46, 65, 235
Platte River, 158
Platte River Canyon, 168, 169
Plummer, Henry, 44
Plunkett, Horace, 183
Poison Creek, 126
Post on Crow Creek, 194
Potts family, 189
Potts, Jim, 177-178
Potts, Joe, 177
Potts, Sadie, 189
Powder River, 39, 115, 117, 120, 171, 183
Powder River Cattle Company, 12, 39
Powder River Crossing, 163
Powder River Valley, 10
Powder-Wilder Cattle Company, 89
Powers, A. R., 89, 91, 109, 150
Powers, Kate, 78
Powers, R., 215
Pratt, Col., 88
Preston, Lt. G. H., 181, 184, 191
Pullman, Bill, 247
Pullman strike, 46
"pumpkin pilers," 14
Pushmataha County, Oklahoma, 231

R

Rader, Rev. Marvin, 143, 156, 157
Rankin, Jim, 55
Rankin, Joe, 55, 145, 159, 172, 173, 178-179, 180, 235
Rankin, Robert, 55
Rawlins, Wyoming, 55, 62
Ray, Nick, 74, 76, 110, 112, 115-125, 134, 155, 156, 157, 214, 216, 217, 224, 244, 246, 249, 252, 255
Reader's Encyclopedia of the American West, 53
Red Fork Ranch, 120
Red Mike, 49
Red Sash Gang, 175-176, 249
Reed, Austin, 178
Reel, A. H., 27, 29
Regulators, 43
"Rendezvous," 5

Republican Party in Wyoming, 198, 222, 238, 239
Reynolds, ———, 105
Reynolds, Burt, 252
Richards, Col. DeForrest, 87, 159, 158
Richmond, Texas, 92, 93-94, 104
Riders of Judgment, 249, 251
"Ridin' for the Brand," 250
Robinson, Nebraska, 182
Rock Creek, 38
Rock Creek Station, 11
Rogers, Kenny, 251
Roles, Howard, 82, 207, 210, 212
"Rookery, The," 204
Roosevelt, Theodore, 1, 19, 44, 48, 50, 78, 245, 251
Rose Hill Cemetery, 227
Ross, Sul, 94
Rothwell, Sophia, 83
Round Rock, Texas, 71, 78
roundup, 20, 26, 27, 86, 172
roundups, 18, 19, 20, 25, 26, 27, 30, 72, 76, 86, 172
Russell, David A., 194
Russell, Majors & Waddell, 89
Ryan, Eva, 228

S

San Angelo, Texas, 187
San Francisco's Committee of Vigilance, 44
Sanders, Wilbur Fisk, 44
Schaefer, Jack, 247
Schmerer, Jake, 42
Schofield, Gen. J. M., 165, 182, 183, 207
Schultz, Cliff, 101, 105, 150
Scott, Captain, 163
Scott, Judge Richard H., 216, 217, 219, 220, 223-224
Scott, Randolph, 246
Searight, G. A., 29
76 Ranch, 11, 76
77 Ranch, 236
Seventeen Mile Ranch, 164
Seventeenth Infantry, 165, 168
Seventh Cavalry, 191
Seventy-One Quarter Circle Ranch, 65
Shane (film), 247
Shane (novel), 243, 247
sheepraising, 23, 233, 235, 239, 241, 242

About the Author

Bill O'Neal is the author of more than twenty books on frontier history and Western films. He has appeared on television documentaries for The History Channel, TBS, The Learning Channel, TNN, and The A&E Channel. Bill is a member of the Western Writers of America and of numerous histor-ical organizations, and he taught history for more than three decades at Panola College in Carthage, Texas. His wife, Karon, is chair of Panola's math depart-ment, and assists with research and manuscript preparation for each of his books.

Printed in the USA
CPSIA information can be obtained
at www.ICGtesting.com
LVHW080141270923
759135LV00049B/589